JOHN MASEFIELD'S GREAT WAR:

Collected Works

JOHN MASEFIELD'S GREAT WAR:

COLLECTED WORKS

Edited with an introduction by

Philip W. Errington

Pen & Sword
MILITARY

First published in Great Britain in 2007 by
Pen & Sword Military Classics
an imprint of
Pen & Sword Books Ltd
47 Church Street
Barnsley
South Yorkshire
S70 2AS

ISBN 978-1-84415-650-4

A CIP catalogue record for this book is
available from the British Library.

Typeset in Sabon by
Phoenix Typesetting, Auldgirth, Dumfriesshire

Printed and bound in England by
Biddles Ltd, Kings Lynn

Pen & Sword Books Ltd incorporates the Imprints of Pen & Sword
Aviation, Pen & Sword Maritime, Pen & Sword Military, Wharncliffe
Local History, Pen & Sword Select, Pen & Sword Military Classics and
Leo Cooper.

For a complete list of Pen & Sword titles please contact
PEN & SWORD BOOKS LIMITED
47 Church Street, Barnsley, South Yorkshire, S70 2AS, England
E-mail: enquiries@pen-and-sword.co.uk
Website: www.pen-and-sword.co.uk

I dedicate my share
of this book to my wife.

Contents

Introduction

. . . no writing can give any effect of it and no historian know (let alone tell) the truth of it. So much of it all is noise and smell and motion, and shocks to mind and sense, that it cannot go into words . . . [1]

On 4 August 1914, the date on which Great Britain declared war on Germany, Siegfried Sassoon was aged twenty-seven, Rupert Brooke had just turned twenty-seven, Wilfred Owen was twenty-one and John Masefield was thirty-six. The future Poet Laureate was not to fight in the trenches or to be counted among the Great War Poets. He was a generation apart and that period of time had allowed him experience – as homeless vagrant, unskilled labourer, bar-hand and factory-worker – of America. Masefield's war commenced with work as a hospital orderly in France and then as commander of an ambulance boat at Gallipoli, but it was in 1916 when he undertook a lecture tour of the United States that his unique gifts began to be used. He reported back to the British Government and, aware of the need to counteract German lies about Gallipoli, wrote a book described by Edward Marsh as 'supreme' and Neville Lytton as 'a masterpiece'.[2] *Gallipoli* led to a request from Douglas Haig for Masefield to chronicle the Battle of the Somme. If Masefield failed to contribute to the literary landscape of the Great War, his historical writing, propagandist journalism and lectures demonstrate a writer contributing to the immediate needs of his country at war. Masefield was the historian of the moment and it is through collecting together all his Great War work, published across three continents, that he emerges as a major figure: as historian, propagandist, journalist and best-selling writer. For the modern historian Masefield provides an eye-witness account which helped influence the reactions of a contemporary English and American audience to the Great War.

Masefield was born on 1 June 1878 in Ledbury, Herefordshire. Orphaned at an early age, he was educated aboard the Mersey school-ship *Conway* as training for service within the merchant marine. Life at sea proved a disaster, however, and Masefield deserted ship in New York in 1895 turning, instead, to homeless vagrancy. The opening poem in Masefield's first volume of poetry comprises 'A Consecration' in which the author states he will write of the under-dog. It was a sympathy resulting from personal experience. Eventually gaining employment in a

New York saloon bar, and then a carpet factory, Masefield learnt of 'the dirt and the dross, the dust and scum of the earth' at first-hand.[3] He returned to England in 1897 and although plagued by ill-health, the would-be poet achieved success in 1899 with the publication of his first poem in a periodical. His first volume of verse, *Salt-Water Ballads*, was published in 1902 and a second volume, *Ballads*, followed in 1903. These collections include 'Sea-Fever' and 'Cargoes' respectively.

In 1903, Masefield married Constance de la Cherois Crommelin (1867–1960), a woman eleven and a half years his senior. The couple were to have one daughter, Judith (1904–1988) and one son, Lewis (1910–1942).

The early work of Masefield included poetry, short stories, historical works (*Sea Life in Nelson's Time*, for example), novels, plays, children's books and journalism. It was a time of literary apprenticeship for the writer but Masefield later wrote that his work 'was not what I had hoped'.[4] This changed in 1911 with publication of *The Everlasting Mercy* when Masefield arrived on the literary scene with a new and shocking voice. This long narrative poem concerning the spiritual enlightenment of a drunken poacher caused a sensation. Lord Alfred Douglas stated the work was 'nine-tenths sheer filth' while Masefield was awarded the Edmond de Polignac prize by The Royal Society of Literature and J.M. Barrie called the poem 'incomparably the finest literature of the year'.[5] Masefield continued writing long narrative poetry in 1912 with *The Widow in the Bye Street* and *Dauber* in 1914.

Masefield was therefore a major literary figure when war was declared. He had upset poetic diction (*The English Review*'s publication of *The Everlasting Mercy* had printed blank spaces rather than offend the public with the word 'bloody'); he had published 'Sea-Fever' and 'Cargoes' (which John Betjeman later stated would be 'remembered as long as the language lasts');[6] he had enjoyed some success on the London stage; his novels had achieved cheap reprint status and his friends included Rupert Brooke, John Drinkwater, John Galsworthy, Harley Granville-Barker, Lady Gregory, Thomas Hardy, Gilbert Murray, Arthur Ransome, Charles Ricketts, Bernard Shaw, Jack B. Yeats and W.B. Yeats.

During the first part of 1914 John and Constance Masefield, whilst retaining their London home in Hampstead, moved their 'country retreat' from Rectory Farm, Great Hampden, near Great Missenden in Buckinghamshire to Lollingdon Farm on the Berkshire Downs. It was here that the Masefields entertained Rupert Brooke in July 1914. Masefield later wrote:

In the first week of July, 1914, I was in an old house in Berkshire, a house built eight centuries before by the monks, as a place of rest and contemplation and beauty. I had never seen England so beautiful as then, and a little company of lovely friends was there. Rupert Brooke was one of them, and we read poems in that old haunt of beauty, and wandered on the Downs. I remember saying that the Austro-Serbian business might cause a European war, in which we might be involved, but the others did not think this likely; they laughed.[7]

The events of August 1914 prompted Masefield's first poem of the Great War. 'August, 1914' appeared in *The English Review* one month later. Masefield was conscious, as ever, of the past. The beauty of the English countryside had been loved by 'unknown generations'. Into this setting the threat of 'war at hand and danger pressing nigh' entered and the men of the past 'brooded by the fire with heavy mind' before resolving to join the conflict. Masefield found continuity and companionship with the past and suggests 'above these fields a spirit broods'. As early as July 1916 Masefield forbade the inclusion of the poem in an anthology stating '. . . it is a special poem, about which I have a special feeling'.[8] Whilst reciting the poem at Yale University in 1916 he apparently broke down when he reached the line 'And died (uncouthly most) in foreign land'. Masefield stood silent, unable to continue, before asking to be excused for not finishing the poem.

But what of Masefield's own 'heavy mind'?

It seems that at the end of 1914 the Masefields stayed in London rather than move to Lollingdon. Masefield was not confident of a short military campaign and, hearing that his friend and journalist H.W. Nevinson was to go to France (probably for the *Daily News*), he wrote:

> We are glad you are going out; that will give us the truth of the matter. We hope you'll be able to see a lot and get it through . . . Come and see us as soon as you get back; though I suppose that won't be till Christmas next year. As was said under Augustus: 'O my German people, in what slow jaws you will be chewed.' We hope you will see all the big bites . . .[9]

By December 1914 Masefield himself was a corporal, probably in the RAMC. Masefield's biographer stated he was 'too old for the army'.[10] This is incorrect: Masefield noted in a letter, from 1916, that he 'was medically rejected, then accepted for the reserve of officers'.[11] Writing to Russell Loines in December 1914, Rupert Brooke stated:

> . . . it's astonishing to see how the 'intellectuals' have taken on new jobs. No, not astonishing: but impressive. Masefield drills hard in Hampstead and told me with some pride, a month ago, that he was a Corporal and *thought* he was going to be promoted to Sergeant soon . . . [12]

For Constance Masefield, the outbreak of war brought the end of the school she had run with her close friend, Isabel Fry. It appears that Fry eagerly wanted to identify herself with essential national work and that early in the war she volunteered as a trainee farm labourer. With little to keep the Masefields in London their country retreat in Lollingdon beckoned. Presumably Masefield gave up his Hampstead drilling.

By the second week of January 1915 Constance Masefield had started writing a journal. In this she records that she and her husband (known to family and friends as 'Jan') left Hampstead for Lollingdon intending to live a 'quiet life'. On 21 January Constance noted:

> Jan is awfully depressed over the war. So much that he loves of fine thought, and leisure and fineness of life will be destroyed by it. He is uncertain whether he ought to take some more active part. He has declared himself ready if he is wanted and that I think is his right course.[13]

The circumstances of Masefield's early war work are not clear. On 16 February 1915 Constance confided, however, in her diary:

> . . . now that Jan feels he must go out to the French Red Cross I don't know *how* I shall get along. I don't believe *any* wife will miss her husband so much, but if he is needed it must be done. The sacrifice is terrible. Each day that we live together seems more wonderful.[14]

and two days later, Masefield was resolved, for Constance wrote:

> . . . it is decided that Jan is to go out under the Red Cross. He was up in town all yesterday, saw the Secretary, accepted the work, tried on khaki tunics, breeches and caps, found his size, was inoculated and got back to dinner at 8. Oh dear. The pain is very acute. . . . Jan is very quiet and resolute. Of course I am glad to think he will have been of use.[15]

Masefield left on 1 March 1915 for what would become a stay in France of around six weeks. Writing to his wife, Masefield tried to be positive and noted '. . . the only pleasure is it has begun now and is therefore coming to an end'.[16] Constance, however, took a different view and wrote two days later in her diary:

> Jan has gone. He left two days ago and I can't yet realise it. I forgot to write to him tonight feeling somehow that he was only gone quite temporarily, and then with a stab of pain I realised the miles and miles of country that lay between, and the sea and the sky and all the misery. Oh dear life is very bitter now. I can't dwell on the pain or I shouldn't get along at all. There is no pain like this lonely sense of separateness.[17]

From London Masefield went to Folkestone and then Dieppe for Paris. By 3 March he had arrived at the château of Arc-en-Barrois, Haute Marne (to the south-west of Chaumont). As soon as Masefield arrived he was asked 'to help in taking off a man's arm at the shoulder'.[18] He reported to Constance that:

> . . . I did my part all right, and got a compliment from the chief. I felt too great pity and interest to feel queer. The man is doing well, such a nice fellow . . .[19]

The château itself was 'a well built foursquare place, very big and roomy, but badly built for our work, as the stairs wind, the kitchens are underground and there are no lifts'.[20] It had been originally built in the thirteenth century but during the French Revolution the walls were razed to the ground and the property confiscated. By 1814 the ruin had been returned to the owner's daughter, Princess Adelaide of Orléans, and she rebuilt it for her brother, Louis Philippe, who used it as a hunting lodge. Set among pine forests with a lake at the back and nestling in 'a sort of crater', Masefield described it as 'solid, but not beautiful'.[21]

Masefield's role was that of orderly and he described his work as 'hard and continuous but it simply has to be done . . .'[22] The British Red Cross knew of the hospital and inspected it, but it was partly financed by private funds – by 'Miss Kemp of the Nurse Missionary League' – and it was not strictly a Red Cross responsibility.[23] Masefield probably went to Arc-en-Barrois due to a personal friendship with R.C. Phillimore (1871–1919) of Kendals Hall in Radlett. Masefield's letters to Constance frequently refer to 'Bobby' and Masefield had enjoyed the friendship of this politician and poet for several years. In 1913 Masefield contributed an introduction to Phillimore's only volume of poetry and, according to Phillimore's obituary in *The Times*, 'when the war broke out he went to work in an English hospital for French soliders'.[24] Certainly Bobby Phillimore was at Arc-en-Barrois before Masefield and met the new volunteer off his train at Chaumont. Phillimore himself overstrained a weak heart at Arc-en-Barrois and suffered four years of illness before an early death at the age of 48. Others already at Arc-en-Barrois included Henry Tonks (1862–1937) the artist and teacher from the Slade School who had some medical training and the Impressionist British-American painter, Wilfrid de Glehn (1870–1951) and his wife Jane de Glehn (1873–1961). Masefield soon settled into this group and identified that one problem with the hospital was staffing with 'the untrained amateur female "helper" . . .'[25] who failed to do hard work and became a nuisance.

For Masefield his routine included serving dinner, carrying the wounded, attending operations, collecting patients from the supply trains, carpentry, and masterminding a fire brigade (the hospital was, owing to inadequate fire precautions, 'about the vilest old death trap God ever permitted'.)[26] It was highly physical and dirty work. Masefield wrote to Constance:

> Don't worry about my being over worked, I'm broken in to it now; at first it was very hard. It's funny: I'm slight and slack-looking and not physically strong, but I can do the stretcher work better than any of the orderlies; perhaps I am younger, or perhaps it is that I learned to use my working muscles while they were strengthening their playing muscles.[27]

and later confided

> I'm probably soaked and drenched with dangerous germs from septic wounds . . . my uniform is in a mess; it gets soaked with pus and blood and wine, men's dinner, water, sawdust, filth of all sorts, grease, sago, soup, jam, and worse things almost daily. Probably we all smell rather gamey, but then the crowning stink of the château rather saves me. On south westerly days like this we waft abroad half across the village.[28]

Masefield's letters to his wife reveal a solid volunteer, able and willing to work with a growing understanding of the horror of modern warfare. He longed to be home but sought fortitude by contemplating a wider picture. After only a few days at the hospital he wrote:

> The main thing here is not the war but our own share in it. We have our own part of it to take by the throat each day and I think every soul in the hospital staff is sopped with sweat in doing so day in day out. The work is hard all through and four times a day excessively hard, carrying wounded in and out and carrying meals up and down, but I'm very well, and whenever I look at these poor fellows my soul boils. Nothing else in the world matters but to stop this atrocious thing. Blood and intellect and life are simply nothing. Let them go like water to end this crime. You've no idea of it, you can't even guess the stink of it, from the bloody old reeking stretchers to the fragments hopping on crutches, and half heads, and a leg gone at the thigh, and young boys blinded and grey headed old men with their backs broken. I never knew I loved men so much. They are a fine lot, a noble lot, I love them all . . . [29]

Collecting the wounded from trains, loading them into cars and carrying them to the hospital was a harrowing experience:

> One had been lying out for four days on the battlefield, without tending or food, one had a leg smashed to pieces, and another had been blown by a shell and had bits of rope in his face and no eyes

and no nose, and his knee broken and his wrist, and another had been blown by a shell and then blown by a bomb and another had septic diarrhoea and is dying now . . .[30]

Against this distress Masefield identified death as a release and freedom from pain:

. . . we've had another death, and another, if not two more, are pretty sure to die. I have hated today here, not for the work, nor for the death, for when one sees it here, death does not seem so evil as what precedes it, but because of all the fearful pain I've watched and been unable to help.[31]

Masefield's reaction to helplessness was to commit to physical work within the hospital, not written work. He confided to Constance, on 17 March:

. . . one must not say 'O, it is waste, your doing such work, you ought to write'; it is not waste; the real waste is war and spilt life and poor beautiful men bled dead for want of a man to hold them. I could not write, thinking of what goes on in those long slow filthy trains, full of mad-eyed whimpering men . . .[32]

and later, on 28 March:

. . . We literary men have been very evil, writing about war. To fight is bad enough, but it has its manly side, but to let the mind dwell on it and peck its carrion and write of it is a devilish, unmanly thing, and that's what we've been doing, ever since we had leisure, circa 1850.[33]

Masefield's former editor at the *Manchester Guardian*, C.P. Scott, contacted Masefield in France at the beginning of April 1915 and invited a contribution to the newspaper. Masefield responded:

Thank you for asking me to write my own impressions – at present it is all much too near for that . . . [34]

The poet who had shocked Edwardian England with a drunken poacher's brawl in *The Everlasting Mercy* could not express himself in print. The only poem Masefield published concerning these experiences would come two and a half decades later. *The Queen's Book of the Red Cross*, published in 1939 with contributions from fifty British authors and artists, included one poem by Masefield. It is simply entitled 'Red Cross'.

Just over a fortnight into his time at Arc-en-Barrois Masefield had started to formulate a plan with several like-minded colleagues. The intention was to create an open-air hospital close to the front in the area around Vosges. With the arrival of spring weather Arc-en-Barrois was susceptible to widespread infection although there were also fewer wounded arriving. By the second week of April Masefield started the journey home to develop his plans further.

Back at Lollingdon, however, devastating news reached Masefield: Rupert Brooke had died of blood poisoning on the way to Gallipoli. Masefield responded to a letter from Violet Bonham-Carter and wrote:

> He was the best of the young men growing up in England, and the gentlest, and the wisest. His death is like a putting back of the time. He would not have lived long, his hold on life never seemed sure, but a nature so beautiful ought to have had everything before being ended like this ... ... He will never be dead to any who ever knew him.[35]

and writing to Edward Marsh on the same day Constance Masefield eulogised:

> It is impossible to believe that Rupert is dead. We cared for him very much, and each time we met we seemed drawn nearer to him. Something most beautiful has come out of life ... [36]

Three months later Brooke's mother sent Masefield a keepsake. A copy of W.B. Yeats' *The King's Threshold: and On Baile's Strand* (published by A.H. Bullen in 1904) with Brooke's bookplate and his initials on the inside front cover was cherished by Masefield until own death over half a century later.[37]

By the end of April 1915 Masefield had started raising funds for his new medical scheme. For about a month he wrote lengthy private letters to friends, relations and acquaintances asking for money. One of the earliest was to C.P. Scott:

> While I was in the French Hospital attached to the Army of the Argonne I was terribly impressed by the condition in which many of the wounded reached us. Most of the wounds of this war are torn, smashed, burnt and dirty, but it often happened that the journey from the outer trenches to the hospital took two, or even three days. This delay caused many deaths and untold suffering.
>
> I and some of my fellow workers want to prevent some of this death and pain by establishing (to begin with) a travelling Field Hospital, in tents and huts, close to the front, behind the Army of the Argonne, in which fifty men may be treated at one time within, at most, a few hours of their being wounded. This Hospital would be managed by English men and women under the French Military

Service de Sauté. We feel that such a Hospital could be fully equipped for £3500.

I am trying to get conditional promises of money towards this sum so that I may prove that I have support when I ask M. Millerand for his sanction to the scheme. Will you promise to help with a gift of money? We have been promised a fine motor ambulance, and we have the nucleus of a strong experienced volunteer staff of workers . . . [38]

The intention was to raise the money, gain the support of the French Minister of War and then launch a public appeal. Recipients of letters included Max Beerbohm, Edward Carpenter, Edward Clodd, Sydney Cockerell, Austin Dobson, Edmund Gosse, E.V. Lucas, Lady Ottoline Morrell, Gilbert Murray, Sir William Ramsay, Charles Ricketts, Lady Anne Ritchie and William Rothenstein. Later letters noted the anticipated cost as £4000. By the end of May, Masefield was beginning to get frustrated. He confided in his sister, Ethel, his irritation in 'having to be in England with only one pair of hands, and having to get one's news from the despicable English press'.[39]

At the beginning of the second week of June, Masefield could report to his brother, Harry, that:

We have raised about £3000 from private friends and are now waiting for the French to sanction us. We may be asked to go to the Dardanelles, instead of to the Argonne, as the need may be greater there . . . [40]

Masefield kept the potential new theatre of war quiet. Writing to *The New York Times* he offered to 'sell manuscripts, typescripts and autograph copies of my books and poems to any of my American readers who may wish to buy them' to raise funds for his mobile hospital. A letter to Mary Cabot Wheelwright (1878–1958), dated 27 July 1915, reveals that Masefield parted with 'my autograph of the Wanderer' in exchange for a gift to the fund.[41]

By the middle of July, Masefield was requested to visit the West and South of France to assess military hospitals. His trip lasted about a fortnight and was chiefly in the Tours area. He wrote to Constance of the horrors:

Today, I drove out and saw over one huge hospital and called on two others before 10 a.m. The big place was filled mainly with cases of lunacy and idiocy, dumbness, deafness etc, men whose minds had given way in the trenches, and who are now being taught ABC and begin at the beginning again. Most of the cases were down doing mecano-therapy in the city, so I did not see them, but I saw one huge dark crowded ward, with the beds all jammed together and many

9

men in them, and wondered rather that they should be kept so, and on asking, was told that it was the cell of the malingerers, who pretended to be mad, so as not to go again to the trenches, and were fed on bread and milk, only twice a day and were kept in complete boredom till they had had enough . . . [42]

and one day later he wrote that

I know what the French want and do not want now . . . It has been hateful stopping so long here . . . I have hated this job more than words can say; still, I have seen a little, and drawn a few conclusions.[43]

It was an abortive trip for, eventually, the French decided not to accept any additional foreign units and Masefield was asked to divert his attentions to Gallipoli.

The planning for Gallipoli had apparently failed to anticipate adequate medical facilities. John North in *Gallipoli – The Fading Vision* reveals that, according to the Australian official historian:

. . . less than two days before the troops were to start for the Peninsula the medical arrangements were 'entirely in the air', and after the first landings, 'dirty, verminous transports', without doctors or stores, carried their cargoes of the dying and the dead from ship to ship in an effort to find accommodation. At the Anzac landing only one hospital ship was ready to receive the wounded, and within three hours it had left for Alexandria. There followed a breakdown of all medical arrangements . . . [44]

Masefield was asked to apply his funds to organising a motorboat ambulance service and started writing to all his contributors telling of the change in plan. So it is that Masefield's service card for The British Red Cross Society shows July 1915 as the date of engagement and notes he was in charge of a motor launch at Mudros. On 13 August he left for Gallipoli writing to Harry Masefield, that 'of all the damnable blind stupid follies in God's earth war is about the worst and the most criminal'.[45] He arrived around the second week of September 1915.

The Times reported that Masefield 'found the money for the picket and also for a barge' causing Constance to write to the editor. She corrected the record and stated that 'the money has been most generously given by some 40 of our personal friends . . .'[46]

The launches took casualties from base hospitals in Gallipoli to Mudros, the hospital being on the harbour of the island of Lemnos. (From there, wounded were taken by hospital ship to Malta or Alexandria if necessary.) The names of the launches were *Doreen*,

10

Griffin, *Miaou*, *Lytham* and the *Agnes*. Masefield was in charge of the latter. A barge was named the *John and Ada* and it is possible Masefield had some role in naming a launch after his wife's friend's sister, Agnes Fry, and a barge after the Galsworthys.

On the journey to Gallipoli, Masefield passed Skyros, the burial place of Brooke. As the day faded 'a freak of light shewed us Skyros, very far away, just before dark, against a pink stretch of sky'.[47] Then 'at midnight, as we passed it, I saw it as a black bulk with a light on it'.[48] In February 1916 Masefield published two sonnets associated with Brooke within *Good Friday and other poems*, both untitled. The second sonnet had been first written in a letter to Edward Marsh. It claimed 'From one grave that island talked to me' and was originally entitled 'Skyros'.[49]

Describing his experiences to Harry, Masefield noted:

Gallipoli was a crowded and disappointing time, and I got dysentery there, which lost me about a stone . . . I was at Anzac with the Australians, and had in a brief time a full experience of war; lice, fleas, dysentery, shells, bombs, shrapnel, sniping and a chase by a submarine . . . [50]

and to Florence Lamont he later recalled:

I was under very heavy fire (as we called it) in Gallipoli, but there there was the sea and one could not run away.[51]

By mid October, Masefield was back in England and, after writing to his subscribers about the 'motor-boat and lighter for use in the Dardanelles in Red Cross work',[52] considered his next contribution to the war effort.

Gilbert Parker (1862–1932), one of the leading figures at the secret propaganda and intelligence department known as 'Wellington House', had American publicity in his charge for over two and a half years after war was declared. For Parker it was crucial to assess attitudes in the United States and counteract German propaganda. Masefield had been invited as early as May 1915 by the J.B. Pond Lyceum Bureau to present a lecture series and Parker saw this as an opportunity. By November 1915 the Bureau had announced the 'first American tour of John Masefield, the Sailor Poet, in Lectures of Literary Interest'.[53] Masefield later admitted to the American press that 'he was, in a way, a sort of official detective'.[54] Parker had found his latest recruit to the cause. On 1 January 1916 Masefield wrote to Edmund Gosse 'I am just off to America, on a mission . . .'[55]

Pond advertised four subjects upon which Masefield would lecture: 'William Shakespeare', 'English Tragedy', 'English Poetry' and 'Chaucer' although his prospectus also notes 'Where specially desired, Mr. Masefield may be willing to talk on his recent experiences in France and at the Dardanelles while engaged in Red Cross work'.[56] Masefield was in the United States for three months between 12 January and 18 March 1916 visiting over thirty towns or cities on the East Coast, the Mid-West and the South.

The New York Times reported, on 13 January 1916 that Masefield 'said that this was his first visit to New York for twenty years, and judging from the glimpses he obtained coming up the harbor it was a very different city to the New York he saw in 1896 . . .'[57] With tales of Masefield's work as a bartender and in a carpet factory the press were apparently keen to portray Masefield as a distinguished visitor who had experienced American life and was able to identify significant progress made over an absence of twenty years. In 1908, before publication of his first novel, Masefield had asked his publisher

> . . . not to mention my unhappy past, in America and elsewhere to people connected with the Press. Those squalid hours, and my early work based upon them, have given me a picaresque reputation which is in the way of the serious reputation I now seek . . . [58]

Now the squalid hours might win friends and the press reported them with gusto. Asked about his experiences of war Masefield stated that 'When you have served some time in the ambulance corps your feeling for the wounded becomes so intense that you would sooner lose your right arm than drop the stretcher.'[59]

New York and the East Coast were 'very generally pro-Ally'[60] and Masefield apparently enjoyed Boston, Bridgeport, Stamford, Philadelphia and New York itself. Upon arrival in New York he noted:

> There is a rather angry feeling that the solid, well-organised German element should have such power here and a still angrier feeling that it should have taken American citizenship and yet talk of a Fatherland. This no doubt will lead to a good deal of talk and legislation in the future. As a whole, the place is strongly pro-Ally, and I notice in all sorts of ways among the nicer people a fear that Europe (the Allied Europe) despises America, for not having done something for Belgium, humanity, or even for herself. There is a fear too, that America has lost spiritually, and will miss the great spiritual awakening which perhaps all people expect from the Allied nations after the Victory.[61]

In the South Masefield included Memphis and Nashville in his itinerary and reported to Gilbert Parker that the region was 'more generally pro-Ally, the people being more impulsive, more kindly towards English ideals'.[62] However, experiences in Chicago, Pittsburgh, Cincinnati, Milwaukee, Minneapolis and St Louis suggested to Masefield that 'German influence dominates and cowes the Middle West'.[63] He particularly loathed Chicago:

It is a terrible city . . . Truly for dingy grubby dirty don't care ruination this town would take some beating. I never saw any place so truly stamped with the legend 'This is what you come to if you sell your soul to the devil' . . . [64]

'Four slimy female reporters' who approached him at Grand Rapids were 'all dirty and evil looking, like retired whores . . .'[65] The Germans were ostracised, wrote Masefield, 'since the swine sank the *Lusitania*'[66] but were skilfully manipulating the Mid-West press and infiltrating the universities. By the middle of February Masefield had begun to despair:

Of course the German organisation cannot fail to succeed in a nation so . . . apathetic and prone to believe what it is told. The Bosche have their task made easy for them here, it is handed to them, as they say here, with parsley round it.[67]

But what of the Americans on Masefield? One reporter rather savaged his lecturing style but then concluded:

. . . one could have wept aloud with gratitude that in this day of shallowness and pose there could be anything so honest and genuine – and a great poet, too – as John Masefield. One adored him![68]

On 28 February 1916 Masefield delivered his lecture on 'The Tragic Drama' and met, for the first time, Florence Lamont, wife of the well-known banker Thomas W. Lamont. The Lamonts were, according to their son, 'in the forefront of notable Americans supporting the Allied cause'.[69] The friendship between the Masefield and Lamont families would last until the death of the Masefields' daughter, Judith, in 1988, and Masefield had found an influential American ally. He wrote to Florence Lamont as he returned to England that '. . . we must set to work, we two, to make England and America tremendous friends . . .'[70]

Upon Masefield's return to England – he was home by the end of March 1916 – his report and recommendations to Gilbert Parker were printed for the use of the Foreign Office as 'an official paper' and Parker noted that 'your brief reports have been the joy of us all'.[71] It is significant that Masefield urged the use of writers to counter German lies, publishing, for example, 'in the big American monthlies'. He also noted that 'the failure in the Dardanelles has damaged us in America in many ways' and suggested that, given his experiences in Gallipoli and America he might 'be allowed to prepare an article upon the venture, for publication in America'.[72] Masefield's *Gallipoli* became a book, published in both England and America but it is now obvious that Masefield was not intending to write a well-balanced historical analysis. Masefield's pen had been turned to war propaganda.

Masefield started writing *Gallipoli* in April 1916. Commenting later to *The New York Times*, he noted:

> The Government put me on the job, inasmuch as I had been through part of the campaign, and placed before me all the official records. The book had to be written quickly . . . [73]

The text was completed on 19 June, with the English and American publishing contracts signed on 20 July and 4 August respectively. The book was an immediate success: the first English edition of 10,000 copies was published in September 1916 and exhausted within a month of publication – new impressions were required for the next four consecutive months and the book remained in print until the mid 1930s. Before the end of September the publishers, Heinemann, advertised the book with a review from the *Daily Telegraph*:

> . . . told in noble and powerful prose, it grips the mind of the reader with an intensity and an enthusiasm which no other war book has achieved . . . Mr. Masefield has written a masterpiece. [74]

Heinemann advertisements noted 'In Enormous Demand' during October 1916 and proudly stated that the edition had reached its '50th Thousand' by March 1917. [75]

Throughout Masefield's literary career his fictional heroes were invariably defeated. Concluding his poem 'The *Wanderer*' in 1914 Masefield wrote:

> Life's battle is a conquest for the strong;
> The meaning shows in the defeated thing. [76]

and, consequently, he was a writer perfectly suited to writing of Gallipoli. The theme of glory in defeat touched a national consciousness and Masefield convinced his audience to view the campaign as a celebration of the common soldier. His prose conveys a sense of drama, physicality and movement. He provides detailed descriptions with insight. Above all, with prefatory quotations translated from the eleventh or twelfth century *Song of Roland*, based on the slaughter of the Franks by the Basques in 778, Masefield provided a sense of epic. In his study of Masefield, published in 1977, Sanford Sternlicht stated:

> No lover of English language and literature should ignore this book, for *Gallipoli* is the masterpiece of its own sub-genre: battle history. As Erich Maria Remarque's *All Quiet on the Western Front* is the great work of fiction of World War I and as Robert Graves' *Goodbye to All That* is the finest biography of a solider in that war, so *Gallipoli* is the best battle history that emerged from the holocaust of 1914–1918. [77]

Contemporary applause included that of H.W. Nevinson who described the work as an 'accurate, brilliant and poetic sketch'.[78] Yet for a new edition in 1923 Masefield wrote of the difficulties the book presented: it needed to counteract enemy criticism and was hampered by inadequate research opportunities and censorship. Ian Hamilton had been consulted by the author (and provided useful statements such as 'The fact is we shan't know the real truth about it until the Turks tell their own story at the end of the war'.)[79] Masefield wrote to William Rothenstein in November 1916 to state:

> I am very glad indeed to think that you like *Gallipoli*. Some day, perhaps fairly soon, the truth about that affair will be known, and then some measure of justice will be done perhaps.[80]

and to Harry Masefield he noted:

> . . . Getting things through to France is probably a lot easier than getting them through to Gallipoli, where there was always much trans-shipment and more theft than you would believe. I never got any of my own things, and only about half my letters, and I met one poor Colonel who had been out there five months and had only received one tin of boot polish and said he would never have had that but that it leaked, and shewed the thieves what it was. All his other things had been bagged. I met a General, too, who had had his case of whiskey opened, and all the bottles taken, and stones substituted. Still, somebody, I suppose, profited, though it was cruel enough at the time on that god-forgotten peninsula.
>
> I've written a little tale of the campaign and it should be out fairly soon, both here and in America. I discreetly pass over all these little things in what I say, and over a lot more big things, which will some day be known and will rouse a pretty fury.[81]

Wellington House was presumably satisfied and, before publication of *Gallipoli*, devised a new use for Masefield. On 18 August 1916 C.F.G. Masterman (1874–1927), then in charge of operations, wrote to M.W. Lampson (presumably Miles Lampson, 1880–1964, later minister to Peking and high commissioner for Egypt and the Sudan). The letter noted:

> . . . You know probably about his mission. He is going into the American Red Cross hospitals deliberately as an orderly in the humblest position in order to write his experiences for the American press. Although a poet, he is first class, and I think we should do everything for him we can . . . [82]

A septic arm delayed departure, but by the end of August Masefield had left for France. Constance Masefield, having lapsed once again in writing

15

her diary, provided a succinct summary in December 1916 of important events:

> In August Jan having finished *Gallipoli* went out to France in order to inspect American hospitals and ambulance work. For a fortnight he worked in a motor ambulance in the Verdun district. Then he went back to Paris and besides inspecting hospitals was sent for by Sir Douglas Haig to British Head Quarters. A plan was suggested by Lord Esher of his going out to write the history of the Somme battle, and since his return in November that plan has been gradually developed though even now he only knows that he has been given the rank of Hon. Sec. Lieut. and is to go out sans pay to do what he can.[83]

Lord Esher (Reginald Baliol Brett, 1852–1930) was, at the time, head of British Military Intelligence in France. As a supporter of Ian Hamilton, *Gallipoli* would not have escaped his attention and there is also a suggestion that Esher was acting for Douglas Haig in a public relations role. Masefield had lunch with Haig around 20 October:

> My second day began with the terror of an invitation (or royal command) to lunch with Sir Douglas.
> I polished myself till I shone and . . . going on to GHQ we stuck in the mud, and had to get soldiers to pull us out, so that we arrived 40 mins late and covered with filth. Owing to this, I barely saw Sir Douglas, but he was like Ian and Lord Methuen and these other wonderful men, rolled into one. No enemy could stand against such a man. He took away my breath.
> I don't know what it is in such men. It is partly a very fine delicate gentleness and generosity, and then partly a pervading power and partly a height of resolve . . . He is a rather tall man, with grey hair, a moustache, and a delicate fine resolved face, and a manner at once gentle and eager. I don't think anybody could have been nicer . . . [84]

In another letter to his wife Masefield reported:

> Sir D.H. says that I may go to the front, stay there as long as I like and do the story of the battle.
> One of his staff says that I may have a car and a guide, whenever one of each kind may be to spare . . .
> Lord Esher kindly says that he will represent these things to those in power and will try to get me given a commission . . . [85]

The new project filled Masefield with enthusiasm, especially since his work for Wellington House was not going well. Although he had seen American skill with facial surgery at Neuilly and accompanied different sections of the Field Service at Verdun he lamented 'I do not find the Americans as helpful as I could wish. They seem not centrally organised, but working in independent, unrelated groups'.[86] Gilbert Parker apparently expected Masefield to visit as many American hospitals as possible but information was unreliable. The number of places to visit kept increasing and Masefield's frustration is apparent in a letter from 9 October:

> I've had a dreadful marching to and fro in Paris getting information. I've walked at least 11 miles and had little to shew for it. This is the sort of thing.
> Responsible A[merican]s give me a list of American Paris hospitals in the nearer suburbs. I go to one, say at Swiss Cottage, and find it closed. I go to the next, say at Clapham, and find that it is not American, but a French military establishment in a house left by an American, a very different thing. I go to a third, say at Greenwich, and find it closed 18 months ago. I go to a fourth, say at Lewisham, and find that it is not a hospital at all, but a big office of the French Government in which the accounts of all Foreign hospitals are kept and audited . . . [87]

As at Arc-en-Barrois Masefield was subjected to the harrowing nature of Great War injuries. On 12 October he wrote to his wife:

> As you know, I've seen pretty nearly every kind of wound, including some which took a stout heart to look at, but the burns easily surpassed anything I've ever seen. There were people with the tops of their heads burnt off and stinking like frizzled meat, and the top all red and dripping with pus, and their faces all gone, and their arms just covered with a kind of gauntlet of raw meat, and perhaps their whole bodies, from their knees to their shoulders, without any semblance of skin. One can't describe such wounds . . . [88]

And, presumably, Constance started to wish her husband would stop trying. Masefield's experiences were, it seems, beginning to change his pro-American stance. At the beginning of October he wrote:

> I am beginning to open my eyes, and to say to myself, that America, as a nation, has done Nothing, and that all that is being done is done by people who live and make their living in France, and by a few generous young men in search of adventure.
> The enemy fire a good many duds, or shells that don't burst, and these the soldiers call 'Yanks' (or too proud to fight) . . . [89]

A few weeks later Masefield decided that he would find it difficult to write pieces for Gilbert Parker and Wellington House praising the Americans:

My general impression of the A[merican]s now is, that by all means they want to keep out of the war, that they will keep neutral by making money out of either party and by being always ready to betray either, and by criticising both. Some little sop of conscience money they will dribble out here and there; and for the rest, they want to spare themselves a little unpleasantness and so yield to any pressure applied. I really have very little enthusiasm left for them, and the thought that I am to praise them and to let their dirty vanity be swelled by what I say is exceedingly repugnant. I can praise the young men and (to a less extent) the big hospital and a little of the individual effort, but glorify them I will not, and so I shall tell G[ilbert] P[arker] . . . [90]

Parker did eventually receive two articles on the American Ambulance Service: 'The Harvest of the Night' and 'In the Vosges'. Both are included in this present collection more for the sake of completeness than for any great insight they provide. The writing is at times remarkably bad and one gets a sense that the writer was producing work to fulfil an obligation. Masefield's attentions had anyway been turned, at the invitation of the British Commander in Chief in France, to other matters.

Masefield first saw the Somme battlefield towards the end of October 1916. After a brief description of the Virgin and child precariously hanging over the town of Albert, Masefield once again attempted the indescribable for his wife:

To say that the ground is 'ploughed up' with shells is to talk like a child. It is gouged and blasted and bedevilled with pox of war, and at every step you are on the wreck of war, and up at the top of the ridge there is no ground, there is nothing but a waste of big grass-less holes ten feet deep and ten feet broad, with defilement and corpses and hands and feet and old burnt uniforms and tattered leather all flung about and dug in and dug out again, like nothing on God's earth . . . [91]

The following day Masefield turned to the mud:

It rained very hard one day, and the mud was worth a visit for itself alone . . . To call it mud would be misleading. It was not like any mud I've ever seen. It was a kind of stagnant river, too thick to flow, yet too wet to stand, and it had a kind of a glisten or shine on it like reddish cheese, and it looked as solid as cheese, but it was not solid at all and you left no tracks on it, they all closed over, and you went in over your boots at every step and sometimes up to your calves. Down below it there was a solid footing, and as you went slopping along the army went slopping along by your side, and splashed you from head to foot . . . [92]

After a few months at home from November 1916 to February 1917 (during which Masefield wrote to J.B. Pond to suggest another American tour and to the *Daily Chronicle* about America's role in the war), he returned to France to start his research.

Masefield arrived in France by 26 February. His research would form two parts. He was, firstly, to visit the battlefields and become familiar with the geography of the land. He would then return to London via Paris where he hoped to gain access to written archives. The promised car and guide did not, it seems, materialise and Masefield was at first rather lost. It appears that Neville Lytton (1879–1951), then a press liaison and press officer, came to his assistance. Writing in his *The Press and the General Staff*, Lytton noted:

> . . . I found [Masefield] wandering about . . . like a soul in distress; no one seemed to be looking after him and his opportunities of getting into touch with the war appeared to me to be nil. The ignorance and irreverence that professional soldiers have in regard to the great men of other professions is astounding. Directly I found out Masefield's identity, I applied to have him attached to my mission and my request was granted . . . [93]

Masefield appreciated Lytton's efforts – and presented to him a copy of his *Sonnets and Poems*.[94] Writing to his wife, Masefield noted:

> I cannot tell you what a charming person NL is. It is wonderful to be in this accursed kind of life with one of one's own kind. He is a most winning attractive person, and if you can, without trouble, send me a *Sonnets*, I should like to give it to him.[95]

When published in 1917, Masefield dedicated *The Old Front Line* not to Douglas Haig but to Lytton, whom he described to Constance as 'extraordinarily helpful and nice'.[96]

Masefield's days were, it appears, spent walking across the battlefield. In a letter to Constance, dated 3 March, Masefield wrote:

> The work is very interesting, but hard, for I am walking all day long from directly after breakfast until tea. Today, my second day of full walking, I went 15 miles . . . [97]

and in a letter dated 20 March he wrote:

> . . . I had a gruelling day yesterday, walking from Le Sars to Le Barque, from there to Bois de Delville, across the battlefield, and from the Bois to Albert, some 25 or 30 Kiloms all told, with the necessary divagations; for there is no walking direct . . . [98]

These are typical of Masefield's routine, for his letters home record the places he visited and the distance walked. On 23 March he noted that 'I get from these walks a far more vivid sense of what the Boche fortifications were'[99] although by the end of the month he started to despair:

> . . . The field is really a vast one, and very very confusing, being, in a way, so like, now that it has been so devastated . . . [100]

A fortnight later familiarity with the battlefield was merely one factor in Masefield's sense of understanding:

> I don't believe that anyone can have a clear idea of what the Somme fighting really was. I am beginning to grasp the ground now, and to see clearly the enemy's theories, and the depth of our own supineness and stupidity before the war, and the inadequacy of our thought . . . [101]

The work was beginning to become protracted and Masefield slowly realised that he could not rely on the type of assistance he had received when writing *Gallipoli*. On 18 April he wrote to Constance:

> . . . If I only had a car, or a billet in Albert again, I could finish this month; but I can't possibly as things are. Getting to and from takes such ages, and then the mud is so fearful it is impossible to walk a mile on the field in less than an hour, and the actual field is about 20 miles by 6 miles . . . and the roads are foul and the land is shell holes. I go out every day and try to get done, but I have still a whole heap of places to try to get the hang of. You see, in G[allipoli] I had Ian, and could go ahead, but here I am not going to have anybody, and must depend solely on what I can pick up here by myself. It is the devil, and damnably costly, and my boots have gone in the mud . . . [102]

Time spent with soldiers helped to confirm Masefield's opinions. 'Our soldiers are wonderfully kind gentle men'[103] he wrote and he had an especially high regard for Australians who were

> . . . jolly good fellows; though I fear they all think that we let them down at Suvla. The truth is, I'm afraid we did. It is heartbreaking to say it, but we did. We sold them a pup as they put it, that is, did not deliver a full sized dog.[104]

and, as this suggests, Masefield was starting to be highly critical. Writing about machine guns on 29 April he stated:

> One gun has as big a fire as 500 men; as I should think was plain to anybody, not a professional soldier. Yet at the beginning of the

war, when Wells wrote on this point, a professional soldier replied, that Wells should write about things of which he really knew, and leave the use of machine guns to soldiers, who knew their limitations, etc. I don't know why; but that kind of a critical ass has more power in England than in other countries.[105]

Masefield increasingly felt the British to be unimaginative and backward in employing the potential advantages that modern technology allowed. He confided to Constance that 'it is terrible to see that the world has gone on 100 years without the soldier noticing'.[106] Only the tank, Masefield conceded, showed imagination but was flawed in the execution:

... It is true, we tried the tank, but it seems to me that we tried it much too much as an experiment, and too little as a weapon certain to have some success.[107]

On 12 May Masefield stated 'the battlefield is fairly clear in my head now'[108] and contemplated the next phase of his research:

I don't look forward to foul London and the record office after so much out of door life. To be out of doors from 8 till 6 and not to read or write at all is pleasanter than to sit in foul air, stewing over papers.
   I probably know more of the Somme field than any of the soldiers who fought there. Parts of it do not attract me, parts repel me, some of it is romantic, some strange, some unearthly, some savage . . . [109]

The American publishing contracts for *The Old Front Line* hint at the problems Masefield was to encounter in writing of the Somme. The first contract, signed before Masefield had left for France, is dated 19 January 1917 and refers to 'a work the subject of which is an account of the Battle of the Somme'. A later contract is dated 15 June 1917 and refers to 'a work the subject or title of which is The Story of the Battle of the Somme'.[110] The contract has become less precise: 'the subject . . . is an account' becomes 'the subject or title . . . is The Story of . . .' Masefield's expected great sequel to *Gallipoli* became two truncated volumes: *The Old Front Line* (published in 1917) and *The Battle of the Somme* (published in 1919). In his foreword to the latter, Masefield explained:

In June, 1917, when I felt that I knew the ground so intimately well, from every point of view, that I could follow any written record or report of the fighting, I returned to England, hoping to be permitted to consult the Brigade and Battalion diaries, as in 1916, when I wrote a history of the campaign in Gallipoli. It was not possible for me to obtain access to these documents, and as only four others, of any worth, existed, my plan for the book had to be abandoned.

21

Feeling that perhaps some who had lost friends in the battle might care to know something of the landscape in which the battle was fought, I wrote a little study of the position of the lines, as they stood on July 1, 1916. This study, under the title *The Old Front Line*, was published at the end of 1917. I then attempted to write an account of the battle from what I had seen and heard, and had written as much as is here printed, when I was turned to other work, of another kind, many miles from Europe and the war.[111]

Neville Lytton later wrote:

I had . . . read his book on Gallipoli and it had made a profound impression on me . . . here at last I thought was a second Homer . . . It is incredible that, after producing such a masterpiece as Gallipoli, his unique gifts should have been wasted . . . [112]

Masefield had intended to complete his research one day, as a letter to Annie Horniman reveals:

I must apologize for the book's shortness. It was, simply, the preface to my book on the Somme fighting, which has been laid aside while I speak about the war here. I hope to finish the book someday, and then it will not be such short measure.[113]

And where was Masefield speaking about the war? Once again he was in America on a lecture tour.

As noted, Masefield had written to J.B. Pond during November 1916 to propose 'another lecture tour for the winter of 1918'.[114] Although the seven month tour commenced on a commercial basis it concluded as a tour of the training camps for soldiers and sailors under the auspices of the Y.M.C.A. This time, of course, Masefield was speaking to Allies. He had written to Florence Lamont in April 1917:

So we are now Allies. It must seem strange to Americans to be allied with us in a war. I hope that it may be a real alliance . . . [115]

and the desire to speak directly to troops came from Masefield's sense of a spirit of co-operation. A further contrast to the earlier tour was the inclusion of the West Coast and South-West in a gruelling itinerary, described by J.B. Pond as a 'fully booked' tour.[116] At the beginning of 1918 Masefield had been invited by *The New York Times* to contribute a statement on America's part in the war (see 'America's Part to Bring Victory and a Real Peace') and before the end of January Masefield was in New York himself having had 'a dismal journey across'[117]. On this trip Masefield discovered train-sickness to add to his predilection for sea-

22

sickness. 'Still', he wrote to Florence Lamont, 'who would not be sick for England?'[118]

At the beginning of February, Masefield wrote to Margaret Bridges, daughter of the Poet Laureate and a great friend, that:

... it has been a crowded and feverish time, with speaking once a day, sometimes twice, and many interviewers and reporters, and beastly lunches and teas where I have to say a few words, and then off to a hot train for 3 or 400 miles to repeat the process.[119]

and, a few days later, despaired of journalists in Chicago:

I am still here, speaking to city audiences of varying sizes, and being mis-reported by journalists who do not know their job. I've been described as a red revolutionary, and as a believer in brute force, and as a pacifist, and I have now grown weary of denying, but let them say what they will.[120]

In general, however, Masefield was receiving a great deal of press coverage. On 27 January *The New York Times* had included an article by Montrose J. Moses under the title 'Prospect of Labor's Ruling British Parliament' which was sub-titled 'Official Historian of Haig's Army, John Masefield, talks about politics, battle scenes, German unrest, peace outlook, and after-the-war problems'. Much of the article directly quoted Masefield and these extracts are included in the present collection. As ever, Masefield's humour broke through and this enabled the article to end on a note of black comedy:

As Mr. Masefield talked he fingered the identification tag on his wrist. He fondled it as if there were running through his mind the idea that, though the bosche may deprive him of his life, he cannot take from him the record which shows that he is entitled to the burial service of the Church of England. As he fingered it, a sad flicker of a smile crossed his face. 'You know,' he said, 'I ought to have four of these identification tags – one on the other wrist and one on each ankle. We cannot take one chance with the bosche'.[121]

As the months wore on, Masefield grew increasingly homesick and anxious to promote England's role in the war. At the beginning of March, he wrote to Florence Lamont:

I am trying to fix a lecture for Aeolian Hall, on April 23rd, and think of speaking *solely* of England's share in this war. Do you think that this would be wise, as well as acceptable? You see, it is St. George's Day, which gives an excuse; but I don't want to do an unwise thing. Will you consider this?[122]

And a few days later repeated his request with one of the few occasions he used the word 'propaganda' within private wartime correspondence:

> . . . I want your advice very much on this matter of my talk, and of propaganda generally . . . [123]

The lecture was advertised by J.B. Pond as the 'Farewell Appearance of John Masefield England's Soldier Poet' where for $15 a box, and seats from 50c to $2 the public could hear the lecture 'England and the War'.[124] In August 1918 Macmillan published in America two of Masefield's lectures as *The War and the Future*. The St. George's Day speech was included as 'St. George and the Dragon'. English publication would occur in 1919 by Heinemann when the volume was entitled *St. George and the Dragon*. The texts have been included in the present volume chronologically by their date of delivery rather than publication.

During his time in America Masefield wrote to Florence Lamont about his desire to return to France:

> . . . I long to be back in France; in the trenches if they will take me; for I don't feel that I have done any good here, talking to special audiences, instead of to colleges and all comers, free of charge, and if I'm to be wasted I'd like to be wasted properly . . . [125]

This led to Masefield's plan to speak to military camps:

> Do you think it would be acceptable if I were to go to the camps here, in the east and middlewest, to speak on England's achievement in the war, free, to the men, and everyone who cared to come? I daresay they would wish me at the devil, me and my England, tho I would try to make it a pleasant talk.[126]

and the announcement was made on 1 June – Masefield's fortieth birthday – that he would tour the camps with the support of the Y.M.C.A. *The New York Times* reported that:

> . . . speaking of the work of the Y.M.C.A. during the war, Mr. Masefield said that he considered the wartime Y.M.C.A. one of the greatest products of the war, and the Secretaries of the Y.M.C.A. at the front are invaluable in making the life of the soldiers in the trenches agreeable and sustaining their spirits and morale.
>
> 'Morale is as important to armies as heavy artillery,' Mr. Masefield said, 'and I feel proud to be able to work with the Y.M.C.A. in the great work it is doing to keep up the morale and contentment of the American troops abroad'.[127]

Masefield reported to Margaret Bridges that:

. . . the camps are amazing places, with hotels for the soldiers' lady friends to stay at, and theatres, and movie-theatres, and rifle-ranges, where you can hit clay pigeons at a cent a go, and the most excellent huts and lecture halls, and generally a music hall as well, besides billiard rooms with fifty tables. They give the men a jolly good time here, and the men are splendid. It is a treat to talk to them.[128]

and later that:

. . . all this army and navy are superb . . . splendid, alert, full of what is here called 'pep', and also full of initiative and invention. It is wonderful to think that this fresh and magnificent army is really entering France on our side.[129]

Whilst in America, Masefield was invited by the *Manchester Guardian* to contribute to a special issue on the first Russian Revolution of March 1917 (February in the Russian calendar). Masefield was enthusiastic and called it 'the profoundest and most living event of our time'.[130] He was apparently silent on the second revolution of November (October) although he later recalled seeing Lenin in the British Museum Reading Room around 1908 and, on one occasion, holding the door open for him.[131]

In June, Masefield received honorary degrees from Harvard and Yale (see 'The Common Task' for his acceptance speech at Yale) and in early August he concluded his tour. To Florence Lamont he confided that it had been a 'cushy job' and hoped he would return to France:

Joy, joy, joy, to be going back to the front
To lie inside a hole and try to see a stunt
With a gasmask on your face and a helmet on your head
Above you, stinks of shells, beneath you, stinks of dead,
Around you howls and bangs and little flitting rats
And clods and flying shards to hit you heavy bats,
And roars and dust and glimmers and curses loud and deep,
And little tickling things which keep you from your sleep.[132]

By the time Masefield was back in England the war had but another three months to last. Masefield had a new home in Oxford to discover and busied himself in writing: to A.G. Gardiner of the *Daily News* he stated:

. . . I am rather snowed up with official work . . . travelling continuously eats into my time and I've had a lot to do lately . . . [133]

Despite a lack of time, Masefield did make himself available to a young writer, lately returned to England. Writing to Siegfried Sassoon, Masefield noted:

25

. . . It will be a great pleasure to me to see you. My movements are uncertain, but I shall probably be here for week-ends for some time to come, and I hope that we may meet when you are near Oxford.

I have followed your work for some time with great interest and admiration. You have done some splendid work, and I have much admired the way you have stood up for the *Cambridge Magazine*. I would have written to you long ago, but had a natural shyness, lest I should be . . . one of the old anti-Christs to be bowled out of the way . . . [134]

Sassoon visited Masefield on 9 November 1918 (as recorded in Sassoon's diaries) and he left with a photograph of Masefield in uniform inscribed 'for Siegfried Sassoon from John Masefield Nov 9. 1918'.[135] Although Sassoon was not uncritical of Masefield the two writers enjoyed a number of meetings and an occasional correspondence until Masefield's death four months before that of Sassoon in 1967.

By the beginning of October, Masefield was working for the 'Department of Hospitality to American Forces' under the Ministry of Information based in requisitioned accommodation in Horrex's Hotel just off the Strand. The department was formed, under the directorship of Lieutenant-Colonel R. McCalmont, from 'The British Committee for Entertaining American Forces' and the new name was implemented at the end of September 1918. Masefield set about recruiting potential speakers and wrote to numerous friends:

Part of the work of this Department is to supply Lecturers and Public Speakers to the Rest Camp and Permanent Stations of American Soldiers and Sailors now in this Kingdom.

Lectures and speeches about particular events and aspects of the war, about this country's many shares in it and contributions to it, and about English life, history, achievements, ideals, hopes and institutions, are much liked by these men, who come here knowing nothing of our share in this struggle and little of our aims and past . . . [136]

Recipients included E.P. Bell, Cecil Roberts, Ronald Ross and Walter de la Mare.

When the Armistice was signed, Masefield was in London. He wrote two days later to Florence Lamont:

It is over now . . . so now we have peace, and some prospect of unwinding the accursed chain to some purpose. The day of peace was dark, with a lowering sky and rain, so much rain, that the tumults were kept within bounds. Flags, yells, a little gunfire and a little drunkenness saw the day through. Yesterday, being fine, they went further and burnt a bonfire in Piccadilly Circus. Tonight, being fine, and the streets lighter, I expect something rowdier and more drunken. But it has been a happy time of deliverance, a setting free from death, a loosing of bonds . . . may this great, kind, generous and truly noble people find its reward in beauty and happiness after all these years of death and hell.[137]

Ever diligent, Masefield continued to speak for the Department of Hospitality to American Forces. He was, consequently, unable to review H.W. Nevinson's *The Dardanelles Campaign* on the day of publication for the *Manchester Guardian* (see 'The Most Heroic Effort'). Masefield apologised to his friend:

> . . . I had to go up to the north to speak, and was away for the best part of a week. This delayed matters, and then, at the best, I'm a very bad reviewer. Either a man speaks, like yourself, with the tongue of men and angels, or he is just sounding brass to me, and belongs with Alexander the coppersmith . . . [138]

At the beginning of December 1918 Masefield was in Manchester 'to speak, as usual, on Anglo-American friendship'.[139] However, the Department was formally closed down on 31 December 1918.

The periodical *Answers* ran a feature before the end of the year. They noted that

> . . . the new era which is heralded by the dawning of peace is full of grave problems, and the termination of hostilities does not mean that our energies can be relaxed. On this page will be found a collection of views which have been expressed, on our invitation, suggesting the most vital matters which should engage our attention after the war.[140]

Masefield's views had, it seems, become important to the press. It seems appropriate also to include in this collection a short article entitled '1919–1920: Signs of the Times' in which Masefield, at the invitation of the *Manchester Guardian* wrote about 'the significance of the past year'.

On 20 December 1918, Masefield was at home in Oxford. In a small canvas-bound notebook he started writing his first long narrative poem since 1913. *Reynard the Fox* was published in 1919 just after *The Battle of the Somme* had been issued in a small limited edition. Haig and Esher never got their official history of the Somme and yet even Neville Lytton was wrong about Masefield's writing. Masefield the poet had not been wasted during the war. *Reynard the Fox* is not simply 'the tale of the hunting of a fox'.[141] In 1946, for a new edition, Masefield finally admitted:

It is . . . a symbol of the free soul of humanity, then just escaped
from extinction by the thoughtless, the debased and the determined
leagued against it for four years of war.[142]

Although excluded from the present collection, Masefield had eventually
written his epic poem of the Great War.

Dr Philip W. Errington
Deputy Director,
Department of Printed Books and Manuscripts, Sotheby's
Honorary Research Fellow,
Department of English, University College London

Notes

1. John Masefield (JM), letter to Florence Lamont (FL), 19 May 1917 (*ed.*
   Corliss Lamont and Lansing Lamont, *Letters of John Masefield to Florence
   Lamont*, London: Macmillan, 1979 (*LtoFL*), p.43)
2. Marsh was quoted by Constance Masefield (CM) in a letter to JM, 3 Oct
   1916 (Constance Babington Smith, *John Masefield – A Life*, Oxford:
   University Press, 1978, (CBS), p.159). Neville Lytton, *The Press and the
   General Staff*, London: Collins, 1920, (Lytton) p.81
3. See 'A Consecration', *Salt-Water Ballads*, London: Richards, 1902, pp.1–2
4. JM, *So Long to Learn*, London: Heinemann, 1952, p.185
5. See Muriel Spark, *John Masefield*, London: Nevill, 1953, p.5 for Lord Alfred
   Douglas' comment. Barrie's words were delivered while awarding a Royal
   Society of Literature prize in 1912. (See *The Times*, 29 Nov 1912, p.6)
6. John Betjeman, 'Preface' to JM, *Selected Poems*, London: Heinemann,
   1978, p.vii
7. JM, 'St. George and the Dragon', *St. George and the Dragon*, London:
   Heinemann, 1919, p.13
8. JM, letter to Mr Marsh (?of Yale – not Edward Marsh), 7 Jul 1916 (Beinecke
   Rare Book and Manuscript Library, Yale University)
9. JM, letter to H.W. Nevinson (HWN), 11 Aug 1914 (Bodleian)
10. CBS, p.119
11. JM, letter to FL, 7 Sep 1916 (*LtoFL*, p.18)
12. Rupert Brooke, letter to Russell Loines, [Dec 1914], (*ed.* Geoffrey Keynes,
    The Letters of Rupert Brooke, London: Faber and Faber, 1968, p.644)
13. Constance Masefield (CM), Diaries, [TS copy within Constance Babington
    Smith Archives (The John Masefield Society Archives) (CBSA)]
14. Ibid.
15. Ibid.
16. JM, letter to CM, 1 Mar 1915 (*ed.* Peter Vansittart, *John Masefield's Letters
    from the Front 1915–1917*, London: Constable, 1984 (*LftF*), p.48)
17. See note 13
18. JM, letter to CM, 4 Mar 1915 (*LftF*, p.53)
19. Ibid.
20. Ibid.
21. JM, postcard to CM, 22 Mar 1915 (HRC, University of Texas)
22. JM, letter to CM, 4 Mar 1915 (see *LftF*, p.53)

23. Joy Fawcett (Archivist, The British Red Cross Society), letter to Constance Babington Smith, 4 May 1977 (CBSA)

24. *The Times*, 15 Sep 1919, p.13

25. JM, letter to CM, 17 Mar 1915 (*LftF*, p.69)

26. JM, letter to CM, 5 Mar 1915 (*LftF*, p.54)

27. JM, letter to CM, 12 Mar 1915 (*LftF*, p.64)

28. JM, letter to CM, 6 Apr 1915 (*LftF*, p.90)

29. JM, letter to CM, 5 Mar 1915 (*LftF*, p.54) Vansittart transcribes the text as 'doing some day in day out'.

30. JM, letter to CM, 10 Mar 1915 (*LftF*, p.63)

31. JM, letter to CM, 23 Mar 1915 (*LftF*, p.73)

32. JM, letter to CM, 17 Mar 1915 (*LftF*, p.69)

33. JM, letter to CM, 28 Mar 1915 (*LftF*, p.79)

34. JM, letter to C.P. Scott (CPS), 12 Apr 1915 (John Rylands University Library of Manchester)

35. JM, letter to Violet Bonham-Carter, 27 Apr 1915 (Berg Collection, New York Public Library)

36. CM, letter to Edward Marsh (EHM), 27 Apr 1915 (Berg Collection, New York Public Library)

37. The volume formed part of Masefield's library at his death (see Blackwell's Catalogue No. 896 *Catalogue of Presentation and Association Copies . . .* (1970) Item 434; Blackwell's Catalogue No. A1040 *Autograph Letters . . .* (1975) Item 328; and Blackwell's Catalogue No. A1092 *Private Press Books* (1977) Item 505)

38. JM, letter to CPS, 29 Apr 1915 (John Rylands University Library of Manchester)

39. JM, letter to Ethel Ross, 31 May 1915 (formerly in the collection of Mrs. Rosemary Magnus (RVAM))

40. JM, letter to Harry Masefield (HM), 8 Jun 1915 (RVAM)

41. JM, letter to Mary Cabot Wheelwright, 27 Jul 1915 (Pierpont Morgan Library)

42. JM, letter to CM, 17 Jul 1915 (Bodleian)

43. JM, letter to CM, 18 Jul 1915 (Bodleian)

44. John North, *Gallipoli – The Fading Vision*, London: Faber and Faber, 1936, pp.73–74. North comments, incidentally, on Masefield's *Gallipoli* that 'the strength and the felicity of its diction lulls the spirit; and it has been largely responsible for the poetical growth of the Gallipoli legend' (p.20)

45. JM, letter to HM, 13 Aug [1915], (RVAM)

46. *The Times*, 20 Aug 1915, p.3 and 27 Aug 1915, p.9

47. JM, letter to EHM, 11 and 12 Sep 1915 (Berg Collection, New York Public Library)

48. JM, letter to EHM, 14 Oct 1915 (Berg Collection, New York Public Library)

49. JM, letter to EHM, 16 Oct [1915] (Berg Collection, New York Public Library). First published, untitled, within *Good Friday and other poems*, New York: Macmillan, 1916. The sonnet was first published in England, as sonnet XXIII, within *Sonnets and Poems*, Letchworth: Garden City Press, 1916. The title 'Skyros' was first printed in *ed.* Philip W. Errington, *Sea-Fever: Selected Poems of John Masefield*, Manchester: Carcanet, 2005

50. JM, letter to HM, 13 Jun 1916 (RVAM)

51. JM, letter to FL, 21 Oct 1916 (TS copy within CBSA)

52. JM, printed letter, Oct 1915 (a copy addressed to Edward Marsh is present within the Berg Collection, New York Public Library)
53. [J.B. Pond Lyceum Bureau], *John Masefield . . . in Lectures of Literary Interest*, New York: J.B. Pond Lyceum Bureau, [1915] (Hamilton College)
54. *The New York Times Magazine*, 27 Jan 1918, p.11
55. JM, letter to Edmund Gosse, 1 Jan 1916 (Brotherton Library, University of Leeds)
56. See note 53
57. *The New York Times*, 13 Jan 1916, p.12
58. JM, letter to Grant Richards, 21 Apr 1908 (Fales Library, New York University)
59. *The New York Times*, 13 January 1916, p.12
60. 'A Report on American Opinion and some Suggestions', *A Supplement to the American Press Résumé (April 7, 1916)* (National Archives)
61. JM, letter to CM, undated within *LftF*, p.105
62. See note 60
63. Ibid.
64. JM, letter to CM, 11 Feb 1916 (CBS p.144)
65. JM, letter to CM, 3 Feb 1916 (CBS p.149)
66. Unidentified source (*LftF*, p.106)
67. JM, letter to CM, undated within *LftF*, p.108
68. N.P.D., 'Mr. Masefield Lectures', unidentified newspaper source (CBSA and see also CBS pp.141–42)
69. Corliss Lamont, 'Introduction', *LtoFL*, p.2
70. JM, letter to FL, 21 Mar [1916], (*LtoFL*, p.10)
71. Gilbert Parker, letter to JM, 30 Mar 1916 (HRC, University of Texas)
72. See note 60
73. See note 54
74. *The Times*, 22 Sep 1916, p.9
75. *The Times*, 27 Oct 1916, p.4 and 9 Mar 1917, p.11
76. JM, 'The *Wanderer*', *Philip the King and other poems*, London: Heinemann, 1914, pp.61–71
77. Sanford Sternlicht, *John Masefield*, Boston: Twayne, 1977, p.124
78. Henry W. Nevinson, *Fire of Life*, London: Nisbet, 1935, p.344
79. Ian Hamilton, letter to JM, 18 Jul 1916 (Bodleian)
80. JM, letter to William Rothenstein, 9 Nov 1916 (Houghton Library, University of Harvard)
81. JM, letter to HM, 16 Aug 1916 (TS copy within CBSA)
82. C.F.G. Masterman to M.W. Lampson, 18 Aug 1916 (National Archives)
83. See note 13
84. JM, letter to CM, 21 Oct 1916 (*LftF*, pp.190–91)
85. JM, letter to CM, 21 Oct 1916 (*LftF*, p.189)
86. JM, letter to CM, 4 Sep 1916 (*LftF*, p.123)
87. JM, letter to CM, 9 Oct 1916 (*LftF*, p.177)
88. JM, letter to CM, 12 Oct 1916 (*LftF*, p.180)
89. JM, letter to CM, 4 Oct 1916 (*LftF*, p.170)
90. JM, letter to CM, 16 Oct 1916 (*LftF*, p.187)
91. JM, letter to CM, 21 Oct 1916 (*LftF*, p.192)
92. JM, letter to CM, 22 Oct 1916 (*LftF*, p.193)
93. Lytton, p.81

94. It is assumed Masefield does not refer to *Sonnets* (published in America by Macmillan in February 1916). This was a specifically American publication (with the dedication 'To My American Friends'). It is more likely that Masefield refers to *Sonnets and Poems* of August / September 1916. *Sonnets and Poems* was published by The Garden City Press, Letchworth, in an edition of 200 copies and in a regular edition by Masefield ('printed at Letchworth by the Garden City Press'). The editions were not a strictly commercial enterprise although they caused concern to Masefield's commercial publisher, William Heinemann (see Philip W. Errington, *John Masefield – The 'Great Auk' of English Literature*, London: The British Library, 2004, p.150). A gift of this book should be considered significant since it was not merely a copy of Masefield's latest offering from Heinemann.

95. JM, letter to CM, 12 Mar 1917 (*LftF*, pp.212–13)

96. JM, letter to CM, 21 Mar 1917 (*LftF*, p.224)

97. JM, letter to CM, 3 Mar 1917 (*LftF*, p.202)

98. JM, letter to CM, 20 Mar 1917 (*LftF*, p.222)

99. JM, letter to CM, 23 Mar 1917 (*LftF*, p.226)

100. JM, letter to CM, 31 Mar 1917 (*LftF*, p.234)

101. JM, letter to CM, 16 Apr 1917 (*LftF*, p.247)

102. JM, letter to CM, 18 Apr 1917 (*LftF*, p.250)

103. JM, letter to CM, 15 Mar 1917 (*LftF*, p.216)

104. JM, letter to CM, 7 Mar 1917 (*LftF*, p.207)

105. JM, letter to CM, 29 Apr 1917 (*LftF*, p.264)

106. JM, letter to CM, 16 May 1917 (*LftF*, p.283)

107. JM, letter to CM, 8 (or 9) May 1917 (*LftF*, p.275)

108. JM, letter to CM, 12 May 1917 (*LftF*, p.277)

109. JM, letter to CM, 23 May 1917 (*LftF*, p.293)

110. Contained in the archives of The Society of Authors as the literary representatives of the estate of John Masefield. I am extremely grateful to W.H. Masefield and The Society of Authors for permission to consult these documents.

111. JM, 'Foreword', *The Battle of the Somme*, London: Heinemann, 1919, pp.2–3

112. Lytton, pp.80–81

113. JM, letter to Annie Horniman, 10 Mar 1918 (Beinecke Rare Book and Manuscript Library, Yale University)

114. JM, letter to J.B. Pond, 20 Nov 1916 (University of Iowa)

115. JM, letter to FL, 16 Apr [1917] (*LtoFL*, p.36)

116. J.B. Pond, letter to A.P. Saunders, 12 Feb 1918 (Hamilton College)

117. JM, letter to Margaret Bridges (MB), 24 Jan 1918 (*ed.* Donald Stanford, *John Masefield Letters to Margaret Bridges (1915–1919)*, Manchester: Carcanet, 1984 (*LtoMB*), p.81)

118. JM, letter to FL, 15 Jul [1918] (*LtoFL*, p.71)

119. JM, letter to MB, 9 Feb 1918 (*LtoMB*, p.82)

120. JM, letter to MB, 13 Feb 1918 (*LtoMB*, p.83)

121. See note 54

122. JM, letter to FL, 5 Mar [1918] (*LtoFL*, p.61)

123. JM, letter to FL, 27 Mar 1918 (*LtoFL*, p.62)

124. See J.B. Pond advertisement published within *The New York Times*, 17 Apr 1918, p.11

125. JM, letter to FL, 27 Mar 1918 (*LtoFL*, pp.62–63)
126. Ibid.
127. *The New York Times*, 2 Jun 1918, p.41
128. JM, letter to MB, 27 May 1918 (*LtoMB*, p.97)
129. JM, letter to MB, 1 Jun 1918 (*LtoMB*, p.98)
130. *Manchester Guardian*, 7 July 1917, p.26
131. See Corliss Lamont, *Remembering John Masefield*, London: Kaye & Ward, 1972, pp.83–84
132. JM, letter to FL, 20 Jul [1918] (*LtoFL*, p.72)
133. JM, letter to A.G. Gardiner, 27 Sep 1918 (British Library of Political and Economic Science)
134. JM, letter to Siegfried Sassoon, 5 Sep 1918 (Cambridge University Library)
135. See Sotheby's auction catalogue, 18 July 1991, lot 90
136. JM, letter to Ronald Ross, 7 Oct 1918 (London School of Hygiene and Tropical Medicine)
137. JM, letter to FL, 13 Nov [1918] (*LtoFL*, p.74)
138. JM, letter to HWN, (Bodleian)
139. JM, letter to Cecil Roberts, 3 Dec 1918 (Churchill College, Cambridge)
140. *Answers*, 14 December 1918, p.43
141. JM, 'Note', *Reynard the Fox . . . with Selected Sonnets and Lyrics*, London: Heinemann, 1946, p.[v]
142. Ibid.

A Note on the Texts

This edition collects together for the first time Masefield's four books on the First World War: *Gallipoli*, *The Old Front Line*, *St. George and the Dragon* (first published in America as *The War and the Future*) and *The Battle of the Somme*.

The first three were printed in England by William Heinemann and in the United States by Macmillan. Each edition presents a number of editorial choices. The texts of *Gallipoli* are, for example, very slightly different with the American text probably comprising a slightly earlier version than the English text. I have followed the English text except when minor punctuation changes from the American version are to be preferred. *The Old Front Line* was first published by Macmillan and it is the later Heinemann printing that comprises a slightly later textual state with the inclusion of chapter headings and this has been used here as the copy-text. *St. George and the Dragon* was probably set from a copy of *The War and the Future* and I have therefore used the American version as my copy-text except where the text in *St. George and the Dragon* has evidently been corrected. *The Battle of the Somme* was published only in an English edition (limited to 250 copies) and this is the only printed source. This is the first commercial printing of the text.

Of the other texts, many are taken from contemporary periodicals from both England and the United States: five are from *The New York Times*, four are from the *Manchester Guardian* and others are taken from *The English Review*, the *Daily Chronicle*, *Harper's Monthly Magazine*, *The Saturday Evening Post*, *The Nation*, *Answers* and *The Times*. The limited distribution of *Yale Alumni Weekly* deserves special mention and I am grateful to Yale University for providing me with a copy.

Other contributions are taken from their appearance in other volumes by Masefield (*Good Friday and other poems* and a new edition of *Gallipoli*) or from volumes with contributions by Masefield (see *The Queen's Book of the Red Cross* and works by Edward G.D. Liveing and E.J. Rule). The Yale Review's 1928 publication of Masefield's *Any Dead to Any Living* is an oddity in Masefield bibliography and it is a pleasure to include it here.

Finally Masefield's 'A Report on American Opinion and Some Suggestion' was printed within Foreign Office war papers (see National Archives FO 371/2835 pp 62922).

Texts have been edited to provide English renderings of words throughout, together with modern usage ('to-day' becomes 'today', for example). To provide consistency across such a disparate group of texts has been challenging and I ask for the reader's patience for any errors. My choice and location of texts has been informed by my bibliographical work on Masefield and I refer any interested readers to *John Masefield – The 'Great Auk' of English Literature*, London: The British Library, 2004.

August, 1914

How still this quiet cornfield is tonight;
By an intenser glow the evening falls,
Bringing, not darkness, but a deeper light;
Among the stooks a partridge covey calls.

The windows glitter on the distant hill;
Beyond the hedge the sheep-bells in the fold
Stumble on sudden music and are still;
The forlorn pinewoods droop above the wold.

An endless quiet valley reaches out
Past the blue hills into the evening sky;
Over the stubble, cawing, goes a rout
Of rooks from harvest, flagging as they fly.

So beautiful it is, I never saw
So great a beauty on these English fields,
Touched by the twilight's coming, into awe,
Ripe to the soul and rich with summer's yields.

       *   *   *   *   *

These homes, this valley spread below me here,
The rooks, the tilted stacks, the beasts in pen,
Have been the heartfelt things, past-speaking dear
To unknown generations of dead men,

Who, century after century, held these farms,
And, looking out to watch the changing sky,
Heard, as we hear, the rumours and alarms
Of war at hand and danger pressing nigh,

And knew, as we know, that the message meant
The breaking-off of ties, the loss of friends,
Death like a miser getting in his rent
And no new stones laid where the trackway ends.

The harvest not yet won, the empty bin,
The friendly horses taken from the stalls,
The fallow on the hill not yet brought in,
The cracks unplastered in the leaking walls;

Yet heard the news, and went discouraged home,
And brooded by the fire with heavy mind,
With such dumb loving of the Berkshire loam
As breaks the dumb hearts of the English kind,

Then sadly rose and left the well-loved Downs
And so, by ship to sea, and knew no more
The fields of home, the byres, the market towns,
Nor the dear outline of the English shore,

But knew the misery of the soaking trench,
The freezing in the rigging, the despair
In the revolting second of the wrench
When the blind soul is flung against the air,

And died (uncouthly, most) in foreign lands
For some idea but dimly understood
Of an English city never built by hands,
Which love of England prompted and made good.

        *   *   *   *   *

If there be any life beyond the grave
It must be near the men and things we love,
Some power of quick suggestion how to save,
Touching the living soul as from above,

An influence from the Earth from those dead hearts
So passionate once, so deep, so truly kind,
That in the living child the spirit starts
Feeling companioned still, not left behind.

Surely above these fields a spirit broods,
A sense of many watchers muttering near,
Of the lone Downland with the forlorn woods
Loved to the death, inestimably dear.

A muttering from beyond the veils of Death
From long dead men, to whom this quiet scene
Came among blinding tears with the last breath,
The dying soldier's vision of his queen.

All the unspoken worship of those lives
Spent in forgotten wars at other calls
Glimmers upon these fields where evening drives
Beauty like breath so gently darkness falls.

Darkness that makes the meadows holier still,
The elm trees sadden in the hedge, a sigh
Moves in the beech-clump on the haunted hill,
The rising planets deepen in the sky,

And silence broods like spirit on the brae;
A glimmering moon begins, the moonlight runs
Over the grasses of the ancient way,
Rutted this morning by the passing guns.

[source: 'August, 1914', *The English Review*, September 1914, pp.145–147]

John Masefield's Sale

To the Editor of *The New York Times:*

In your issue of May 16 you give some particulars of the sale of manuscripts and autograph books for the benefit of Belgian sufferers.

I have come back from a French hospital to organize a nursing unit to go out to the front behind the army of the Argonne, and to keep near enough to the front to save some of the wounded the journey in the train. I need funds for this purpose, and therefore ask you to let me state in your columns that I shall be happy to sell manuscripts, typescripts and autograph copies of my books and poems to any of my American readers who may wish to buy them. Any money so made will go to the equipment of the hospital, and any surplus to the purchase of artificial limbs for maimed French soldiers. I shall be greatly obliged if you will help me by printing this letter.

JOHN MASEFIELD.
Cholsey, Berkshire, England, June 16, 1915.

[source: *The New York Times*, 30 June 1915, p.10]

A Red Cross Lighter

To the Editor of *The New York Times:*

Some months ago you kindly allowed me to print an appeal for contributions to a Red Cross scheme in which I was interested. Will you allow me to say here that the money sent to me by American well-wishers in response to this appeal has been expended in equipping a lighter ambulance for the towing of French and English wounded in the Ægean Sea? The lighter is now in the Ægean, actively employed in this work. The small remaining surplus of less than £5 is being sent to a French hospital to help in the purchase of some artificial limbs.

   I wish to thank your readers for their help.

J. MASEFIELD.
Hampstead, England, Nov. 13, 1915.

[source: *The New York Times*, 28 November 1915, p.16]

Untitled Sonnet

Here, where we stood together, we three men,
Before the war had swept us to the East
Three thousand miles away, I stand again
And hear the bells, and breathe, and go to feast.
We trod the same path, to the self-same place,
Yet here I stand, having beheld their graves,
Skyros whose shadows the great seas erase,
And Seddul Bahr that ever more blood craves.
So, since we communed here, our bones have been
Nearer, perhaps, than they again will be,
Earth and the world-wide battle lie between,
Death lies between, and friend-destroying sea.
Yet here, a year ago, we talked and stood
As I stand now, with pulses beating blood.

[source: *Good Friday and other poems*, New York:
Macmillan, 1916, p.96]

Untitled Sonnet

I saw her like a shadow on the sky
In the last light, a blur upon the sea,
Then the gale's darkness put the shadow by,
But from one grave that island talked to me;
And, in the midnight, in the breaking storm,
I saw its blackness and a blinking light,
And thought, "So death obscures your gentle form,
So memory strives to make the darkness bright;
And, in that heap of rocks, your body lies,
Part of the island till the planet ends,
My gentle comrade, beautiful and wise,
Part of this crag this bitter surge offends,
While I, who pass, a little obscure thing,
War with this force, and breathe, and am its king."

[source: *Good Friday and other poems*, New York: Macmillan, 1916, p.97]

A Report on American Opinion
and Some Suggestions

Sir Gilbert Parker has received the following report from Mr. John Masefield, who has lately finished a lecturing tour in the United States, and has returned to this country with clear ideas of the condition of American public opinion concerning the war and our international relations. Mr. Masefield has written a considerable number of letters, which Sir Gilbert has passed on to the Government; but the following report presents a bird's-eye view of the whole prospect. Mr. Masefield's suggestions will command the interest of all who read them:–

March 28, 1916

I have the honour to present to you my report of things noticed during my stay in the United States between the 13th January and the 18th March. During that time I visited some thirty towns in the East, the South, and the Middle West, and had the fortune to meet and talk with many people of every sort and condition, from millionaires to day labourers.

I will divide my report into three portions – the first, a general survey; the second, some account of things which should be done soon, or might with advantage be done presently; and the third, a suggestion of steps which might now be taken to make the friendship between the two countries a lasting and deep bond or national reconciliation.

(I.) – The United States may be divided roughly into four distinct provinces – Eastern, Southern, Middle Western, and Western. I did not visit the Western province; it is some thousands of miles from the war, absorbed in its own affairs, and, on the whole, indifferent to the outcome.

(a.) In the East the feeling is very generally pro-Ally. The feeling is strongest where the cultivation is greatest, as in Boston, Philadelphia, and New York, from which towns a number of men and women have gone to take an active part in the war, but it is fairly general, and in some Eastern societies Germans have been ostracised, or forced by public opinion to adopt cringing and apologetic airs as though ashamed of their country.

It must, however, be remembered that, for many years, throughout America, the schools, the press, and public oratory have proclaimed the iniquities of England. England has been held up as the traditional enemy much more vigorously than she has been extolled (if ever she has been) as the mother country, and there is, therefore, in this pro-Ally Eastern province, a multitude of Americans who hate the English and lose no opportunity to malign them. These people are kept upon our side by the traditional national friendship with France; their sympathies are with the French, not with us, and however much they may hate the Germans, they are loth to admit any merit in our share in the undertaking. Side by side with this very large body is the very large, well-organised, and malignant body of the Irish-Americans, who are bitterly anti-English, and work the Catholic communities against us.

(b.) In the South, the feeling is more warmly and perhaps more generally pro-Ally, the people being more impulsive, more kindly towards English ideals, and still remembering England's sympathy with the Southern cause in the Secession War. The old antagonism between North and South crops out occasionally, and one meets the feeling that the South would have gone to war with Germany long ago had not the North directed otherwise. At the same time, the sympathy is less practical here. I had not the fortune to hear of any Southerner who had actually gone to the war to help in any way with personal service.

(c.) In the Middle West, the American feeling, even if it be, as it may be, in the main, pro-Ally, is overshadowed and subdued by fear of the great German organisations centred in Milwaukee, Chicago, and St. Louis. German influence dominates and cowes the Middle West. In this province, the anti-Ally lies, insinuations, and rumours are first set going, to spread abroad wherever emptiness will repeat and ignorance credit what malice has invented. These unresting organisations poison the minds of multitudes against us. No means is left unused by them, from buying or intimidating the press to the telling of lies to school girls. Their methods are seldom subtle, but with an audience so uncritical this does not matter. These organisations have their emissaries in the East, including some dozen clever and versatile journalists whose daily tasks provide letters (signed 'True American,' 'Mayflower,' '1776,' 'Boston Tea Party,' etc.) for the Eastern press, pointing out the iniquity of England, and the danger of departing from the great American doctrines laid down by George Washington, etc. Sometimes these dozen, or half dozen, souls will write 100 different letters in a day and scatter them through the national press, which guilelessly prints them.

(II.) – (a.) It is most important that some authoritative loyal Irish member, preferably a Catholic, should go over as soon as may be, before the summer fighting begins, to silence the Irish-American party, who exude poison from every pore. If Mr. Redmond would do this, it would be the work of his life. But let some good man do it, without delay, for these snakes are at work daily, with a great priesthood and a skilled journalism to back them, in those Eastern towns which would otherwise be ours. This is most important.

(b.) Many people in the cultivated Eastern centres feel that their marked pro-Ally feelings might be rewarded by a more generous supply of news from the front, not so much news of the actual military events, which, as they realise, cannot be divulged, as of the life in the trenches, vivid personal letters, with drawings and photographs. If such letters could be sent continuously, from the Belgian, English, and French fronts, in much greater variety than heretofore, they would have a very good effect. As there is a prejudice against the English in many American minds, the letters from the English front ought to be edited by men who know America. Much good might be done by writing-up Belgium and the devastated parts of France rather more particularly than has been done.

(c.) Cinemas, or moving picture shows, are much more thronged, and have far greater influence, in America than in this country. The Germans use them to exalt their points of view, and more might be done by our own side. Good films of life in the Belgian, English, and French camps, and in the trenches or dugouts, would have a very good effect. Films of Stratford and of other places dear to Americans, such as the old Washington home, with troops passing, etc., might be shown. Of course, now that they have their own little war in Mexico these things may prove less attractive.

(d.) Taking the hint from German agents, but perhaps prompted in part by their ignorance of war and hatred of the English, various men ask 'What have the English done?' or 'What has the English army done?' My own reply to such has been that we and the army have not been too proud to fight, but the answer has not been perfect as a begetter of good relations. It might be well to turn various writers to answering these questions in the big American monthlies, pointing out the obvious parallel of the raising of the Northern armies in 1861, and showing how very much more creditable our own achievements have been. Our help to France and Belgium might be insisted on. Our best brains might be turned onto this task.

(e.) There can be no doubt that the failure in the Dardanelles has damaged us in America in many ways. Americans neither understand nor pity failure, worshipping success, as they do, they dread it. The Germans, realising this, have emphasised our failure there, and the results are unpleasant. Much has been, and is being, said about 'failure of generalship,' 'useless slaughter of men,' 'divided counsels,' etc. I gather that Mr. Ashmead-Bartlett has been lecturing in America on this campaign (I know not from what point of view nor with what success), but more than one voice ought to be raised in the matter. I was myself in the Dardanelles, after the Suvla Bay landing, for a brief while, and would most respectfully suggest that I be allowed to prepare an article upon the venture, for publication in America. I could at least convince them of the difficulties which we overcame.

(III.) – Apart from the fact that German agents are everywhere spreading the belief that the English hate and despise the Americans, the present would be a good time to attempt a real linking together of the English-speaking peoples. Americans are perturbed by the increase of the Slav elements in their populations and by the persistence with which their German settlers cling to their Fatherland. They would welcome anything which would strengthen the bond between their race and the traditional English culture. If there could be a constant and liberal exchange of college professors, and (especially) a big application of the idea of the Rhodes Scholarships to our advanced schools of technology, the effect, in a short time, would be very marked. The immediate evil might be remedied effectually and easily. It would probably suffice if the universities, for instance, could give to the Universities of Yale and Harvard (say) some public mark of thanks to the many Americans who have left those colleges to serve in France. Some few scraps of autograph by famous English writers would be ample for the purpose. Such a gift, gracefully made, would be publicly exhibited, universally acclaimed in the press, and lastingly remembered. In any case, many Americans would welcome any sign, however slight, that they are not, as they fear, hated and wholly despised by the country of their traditional culture.

[source: 'A Report on American Opinion and some Suggestions',
A Supplement to the American Press Résumé (April 7, 1916)
[FO 371/2835 pp 62922]]

Gallipoli

DEDICATED WITH THE
DEEPEST ADMIRATION AND RESPECT
TO
GENERAL SIR IAN HAMILTON, G.C.B., D.S.O.,
AND THE
OFFICERS AND MEN UNDER HIS COMMAND
MARCH TO OCTOBER, 1915

I

Oliver said: "I have seen the Saracens: the valley and the mountains are covered with them; and the lowlands and all the plains; great are the hosts of that strange people; we have here a very little company."

Roland answered: "My heart is the bigger for that. Please God and His holiest angels, France shall never lose her name through me." – *The Song of Roland*.

A little while ago, during a short visit to America, I was often questioned about the Dardanelles Campaign. People asked me why that attempt had been made, why it had been made in that particular manner, why other courses had not been taken, why this had been done and that either neglected or forgotten, and whether a little more persistence, here or there, would not have given us the victory.

These questions were often followed by criticism of various kinds, some of it plainly suggested by our enemies, some of it shrewd, and some the honest opinion of men and women happily ignorant of modern war. I answered questions and criticism as best I could, but in the next town they were repeated to me, and in the town beyond reiterated, until I wished that I had a printed leaflet, giving my views of the matter, to distribute among my questioners.

Later, when there was leisure, I began to consider the Dardanelles Campaign, not as a tragedy, nor as a mistake, but as a great human effort, which came, more than once, very near to triumph, achieved the impossible many times, and failed, in the end, as many great deeds of arms have failed, from something which had nothing to do with arms nor with the men who bore them. That the effort failed is not against it; much that is most splendid in military history failed, many great things and noble men have failed. To myself, this failure is the second grand event of the war; the first was Belgium's answer to the German ultimatum.

The Peninsula of Gallipoli, or Thracian Chersonese, from its beginning in the Gulf of Xeros to its extremity at Cape Helles, is a tongue of hilly land, about fifty-three miles long, between the Ægean Sea and the Straits of the Dardanelles. At its north-eastern, Gulf of Xeros, or European end, it is four or five miles broad; then, a little to the south of the town of

Bulair, it narrows to three miles, in a contraction or neck which was fortified during the Crimean War by French and English soldiers. This fortification is known as the Lines of Bulair. Beyond these lines, to the south-west, the Peninsula broadens in a westward direction and attains its maximum breadth, of about twelve miles, some twenty-four miles from Bulair, between the two points of Cape Suvla, on the sea, and Cape Uzun, within the Straits. Beyond this broad part is a second contraction or neck, less than five miles across, and beyond this, pointing roughly west-south-westerly, is the final tongue or finger of the Peninsula, an isosceles triangle of land with a base of some seven miles, and two sides of thirteen miles each, converging in the blunt tip (perhaps a mile and a half across) between Cape Helles and Cape Tekke. There is no railway within the Peninsula, but bad roads, possible for wheeled traffic, wind in the valleys, skirting the hills and linking up the principal villages. Most of the travelling and commerce of the Peninsula is done by boat, along the Straits, between the little port of Maidos, near the Narrows, and the town of Gallipoli (the chief town) near the Sea of Marmora. From Gallipoli there is a fair road to Bulair and beyond. Some twenty other small towns or hamlets are scattered here and there in the well-watered valleys in the central broad portion of the Peninsula. The inhabitants are mostly small cultivators with olive and currant orchards, a few vineyards and patches of beans and grains; but not a hundredth part of the land is under cultivation.

The seashore, like the Straits shore, is mainly steep-to, with abrupt sandy cliffs rising from the sea to a height of from one hundred to three hundred feet. At irregular and rare intervals these cliffs are broken by the ravines or gullies down which the autumnal and winter rains escape; at the sea mouths of these gullies are sometimes narrow strips of stony or sandy beach.

Viewed from the sea, the Peninsula is singularly beautiful. It rises and falls in gentle and stately hills between four hundred and eleven hundred feet high, the highest being at about the centre. In its colour (after the brief spring), in its gentle beauty, and the grace and austerity of its line, it resembles those parts of Cornwall to the north of Padstow from which one can see Brown Willie. Some Irish hills recall it. I know no American landscape like it.

In the brief spring the open ground is covered with flowers, but there is not much open ground. In the Cape Helles district it is mainly poor land growing heather and thyme; farther north there is abundant scrub, low shrubs and brushwood, from two to four feet high, frequently very thick. The trees are mostly stunted firs, not very numerous in the south, where the fighting was, but more frequent north of Suvla. In one or two of the villages there are fruit trees; on some of the hills there are small clumps of pine. Viewed from the sea the Peninsula looks waterless and sun-smitten; the few watercourses are deep ravines showing no water. Outwardly, from a distance, it is a stately land of beautiful graceful hills rolling in suave yet austere lines and covered with a fleece of brushwood. In reality the suave and graceful hills are exceedingly steep, much broken and roughly indented with gullies, clefts, and narrow irregular valleys. The soil is something between a sand and a marl, loose and apt to blow about in dry weather when not bound down by the roots of brushwood, but sticky when wet.

Those who look at the south-western end of the Peninsula, between Cape Suvla and Cape Helles, will see three heights greater than the rolling wold or downland around them. Seven miles south-east from Cape Suvla is the great and beautiful peaked hill of Sari Bair, 970 feet high, very steep on its sea side and thickly fleeced with scrub. This hill commands the landing-place at Suvla. Seven miles south from Sari Bair is the long dominating plateau of Kilid Bahr, which runs inland from the Straits, at heights varying between five and seven hundred feet, to within two miles of the sea. This plateau commands the Narrows of the Hellespont. Five miles farther to the south-west and less than six miles from Cape Helles is the bare and lonely lump of Achi Baba, 590 feet high. This hill commands the landing-place at Cape Helles. These hills and the ground commanded by them were the scenes of some of the noblest heroism which ever went far to atone for the infamy of war. Here the efforts of our men were made.

Those who wish to imagine the scene must think of twenty miles of any rough and steep sea coast known to them, picturing it as roadless, waterless, much broken with gullies, covered with scrub, sandy, loose and difficult to walk on, and without more than two miles of accessible landing throughout its length. Let them picture this familiar twenty miles as dominated at intervals by three hills bigger than the hills about them, the north hill a peak, the centre a ridge or plateau, and the south hill a lump. Then let them imagine the hills entrenched, the landing mined, the beaches tangled with barbed wire, ranged by howitzers and swept by machine guns, and themselves three thousand miles from home, going out before dawn, with rifles, packs, and water-bottles, to pass the mines under shellfire, cut through the wire under machine gun fire, clamber up the hills under the fire of all arms, by the glare of shell-bursts, in the withering and crashing tumult of modern war, and then to dig themselves in in a waterless and burning hill while a more numerous enemy charge them with the bayonet. And let them imagine themselves enduring this night after night, day after day, without rest or solace, nor respite from the peril of death, seeing their friends killed, and their position imperilled, getting their food, their munitions, even their drink, from the jaws of death, and their breath from the taint of death, and their brief sleep upon the dust of death. Let them imagine themselves driven mad by heat and toil and thirst by day, shaken by frost at midnight, weakened by disease and broken by pestilence, yet rising on the word with a shout and going forward to die in exultation in a cause foredoomed and almost hopeless. Only then will they begin, even dimly, to understand what our seizing and holding of the landings meant.

All down the south-eastern coast of this Peninsula or outlier from Europe is a channel of sea, known, anciently, as the Hellespont, but in modern times more generally as the Dardanelles, from old fortifications of that name near the south-western end of the Strait. This channel, two or three miles across at its south-western end, broadens rapidly to four or five, then narrows to two, then, for a short reach, to one mile or less, after which (with one more contraction) it maintains a steady breadth of two or three miles till it opens into the great salt lake of the Sea of Marmora, and thence by another narrow reach into the Black Sea, or Euxine.

It is a deep-water channel, with from twenty-five to fifty fathoms of water in it throughout its length. The Gallipoli, or European, shore is steep-to, with a couple of fathoms of water close inshore, save in one or two beaches where it shoals. On the Asian shore, where the ground is lower and the coast more shelving, the water is shallower. A swift current of from two to three knots an hour runs always down the channel from the Sea of Marmora; and this with a south-westerly gale against it makes a nasty sea.

This water of the Hellespont is the most important channel of water in the world. It is the one entrance and exit to the Black Sea, the mouths of the Danube, Dniester, Dnieper, and Don, and the great ports of Constantinople, Odessa, and Sebastopol. He who controls the channel controls those ports, with their wealth and their power to affect great conflicts. The most famous war of all time was fought, not for any human Helen, but to control that channel. Our Dardanelles Campaign was undertaken to win through it a free passage for the ships of the Allied Powers.

While the war was still young it became necessary to attempt this passage for five reasons: (1) To break the link by which Turkey keeps her hold as a European Power. (2) To divert a large part of the Turkish army from operations against our Russian Allies in the Caucasus and elsewhere. (3) To pass into Russia, at a time when her northern ports were closed by ice, the rifles and munitions of war of which her armies were in need. (4) To bring out of Southern Russia the great stores of wheat lying there waiting shipment. (5) If possible, to prevent, by a successful deed of arms in the Near East, any new alliance against us among the Balkan peoples.

In its simplest form the problem was to force a passage through the defended channel of the Dardanelles into the Sea of Marmora, to attack the capital of Turkey in Europe, to win through the Bosphorus into the Black Sea, securing each step in the advance against reconquest by the Turks, so that ships might pass from the Ægean to the Russian ports in the Black Sea, bringing to the Russians arms for their unequipped troops and taking from them the corn of the harvests of Southern Russia. The main problem was to force a passage through the defended channel of the Hellespont.

This passage had been forced in the past by a British naval squadron. In February, 1807, Sir John Duckworth sailed through with seven ships of the line and some smaller vessels, silenced the forts at Sestos and Abydos and destroyed some Turkish ships, and then, fearing that the Turks, helped by French engineers, would so improve the fortifications that he would never be able to get back, he returned. On his return, one of his ships, the *Endymion* frigate, 40 guns, received in her hull two stone shot each twenty-six inches in diameter.

The permanent fortifications guarding the channel were added to and improved during the nineteenth century. At the outbreak of the war with Italy, four years ago, they were equipped (perhaps by German officers) with modern weapons. An attempt made by Italian torpedo-boats to rush the Straits by night was discovered by searchlights and checked by a heavy fire from quick-firing and other guns. All the torpedo-boats engaged in the operations were hit and compelled to return.

When Turkey entered the war against the Allied Powers, her officers had every reason to expect that the British or French fleets would attempt to force the channel. The military prize, Constantinople and the control of the Black Sea (whether for peace or for offence), was too great a temptation to be resisted. Helped by their German allies, they prepared for this attack with skill, knowledge, and determination. The Turks had no effective battle fleet, as in the sixteenth century, when they sought their enemies upon their own coasts, and had they had one they could not have passed the British fleet blockading the Dardanelles; but they prepared the channel and its shores so that no enemy ship might pass to seek them.

More than the two great wars, in South Africa and Manchuria, the present war has shown:

(a) That in modern war, defence is easier and less costly in men and munitions, however much less decisive, than attack;

(b) That the ancient type of permanent fortress, built of steel, concrete, and heavy masonry, is much less easy to defend against the fire of heavy modern howitzers and high-explosives than temporary field works, dug into the earth and protected by earth and sandbags;

(c) That the fire of modern long-range guns is wasteful and ineffective unless the object fired at can be accurately ranged, and the fire controlled by officers who can watch the bursting of the shells on or near the target;

(d) That in restricted waters the fixed or floating mine, filled with high-explosive, is a sure defence against enemy ships.

Beginning with proposition (a), the Turks argued that (unlike most defences) a defence of the passage of the Dardanelles against naval attack might well be decisive (*i.e.*, that it might well cause the attack to be abandoned or even destroy the attacking ships), since ships engaged in the attack would be under every disadvantage.

(b) Their guns, however heavy, would not be overwhelmingly successful against temporary field works and gun emplacements.

(c) Their officers, unable in the first place to locate the guns hidden on the shore, would be unable to observe the effect of their fire, and therefore unable to direct it, and this disadvantage would become greater as the ships advanced within the channel and became shut in by the banks.

(d) They would be unable to enter the channel until the waters had been dragged for mines by minesweepers. The batteries of field guns hidden on the coast would perhaps be sufficient to stop the progress of the minesweepers. If not, floating mines, alongshore torpedo-tubes, and the accurately ranged and directed fire of heavy howitzers, would perhaps sink the ships of war as they advanced.

(e) A ship, if damaged, would be five hundred miles from any friendly dock and seven hundred miles from any friendly arsenal. Replenishments of ammunition, fuel, food and water would have to be brought to the attacking fleet across these distances of sea, past many islands, and through one or two channels well-suited to be the lurking grounds for enemy submarines.

On the other hand, there was the possibility that the heavy naval guns would make the field works untenable; that observers in aeroplanes and seaplanes would locate, range, and observe the fire upon the hidden batteries; that thus the minesweepers would be able to clear a passage up the Straits without undue interruption, and complete the task demanded of them without military assistance.

Before operations could be begun by the Allied Fleets it was necessary to secure some harbour, as close as possible to the Straits, to serve as what is called an advanced or subsidiary base, where large stores of necessaries, such as fuel and munitions, could be accumulated for future use by the ships engaged.

The port of Mudros, in Lemnos, was selected as this subsidiary base. This great natural harbour, measuring some two by three miles across, provides good holding ground in from five to seven fathoms of water for half the ships in the world. Two islands in the fairway divide the entrance into three passages, and make it more easy for the naval officer to defend the approaches. It is a safe harbour for ocean-going ships in all weathers; but with northerly or southerly gales, such as spring up very rapidly there in the changeable seasons of the year, and blow with great violence for some hours at a time, the port is much wind-swept, and the sea makes it dangerous for boats to lie alongside ships. Mudros itself, the town from which the port is named, is a small collection of wretched houses inhabited by Levantines, who live by fishery, petty commerce, and a few olive gardens and vineyards. It has a cathedral or largish church, and a small wooden pier, without appliances, for the use of the native boatmen. The town lies to the east of the harbour, on some rising ground or sand which stands up a little higher than the surrounding country. Behind it, rather more than a mile away, are barren hills of some eight hundred or nine hundred feet. The port is ringed in with these hills; it looks like a great extinct crater flooded by the sea. Over the hills in fair weather the peaks of Samothrace can be seen. When the spring flowers have withered the island is of the colour of a lion's skin. Its only beauty then is that of changing light.

Mudros in itself offered nothing to the Allied Fleets but a safe anchorage. It could not even supply the ships with fresh water, let alone meat, bread, and vegetables. The island produces little for its few inhabitants; its wealth of a few goats, fish, olives, and currants could be bought up in a week by the crew of one battleship. Everything necessary for the operations had therefore to be brought by sea and stored in Mudros till wanted. When this is grasped, the difficulties of the undertaking will be understood. There was no dock, wharf, nor crane in Mudros, nor any place in the harbour where a dock or wharf could be built without an immense labour of dredging. Ships could not be repaired nor dry-docked there, nor could they discharge and receive heavy stores save by their own winches and derricks. Throughout the operations ships had to serve as wharves, and ships' derricks as cranes, and goods were shipped, reshipped, and transhipped by that incessant manual labour which is the larger half of war.

Early in 1915, it was decided that a naval force should attempt the passage of the Straits.

On the 18th of February and following days, the Allied Fleets attacked the forts at the entrance to the Straits and soon silenced them. These were old-fashioned stone structures of great strength; they were knocked about and made untenable by the fire from the ships, but not destroyed. After this first easy success came delay, for the real obstacles lay within the Straits, between Cape Helles and the Narrows. Here, at intervals, very skilfully laid, commanded by many guns, ranged to the inch, were eight big minefields, stretching almost across the navigable channel in different directions. No ships could pass this part of the Straits until the mines had been groped for and removed. In thick and violent weather, under heavy fire, and troubled by the strong current, the minesweepers began to remove them, helped by the guns of the fleet. But the fleet's fire could not destroy the mobile field guns and howitzers hidden in the gullies and nullahs (invisible from the ships) on the Asian shore and to the east of Achi Baba. The Boers, and, later, the Japanese, had shown how difficult it is to locate well-concealed guns. Even when sea and aeroplanes had seen and signalled the whereabouts of the hidden guns, the ships could only fire at the flashes and at most hit some of the gunners; if their fire became too accurate, the gunners would retire to their shelters, or withdraw their guns to new hidden emplacements. These hidden guns, firing continually upon the minesweepers, made the clearing of the minefields towards the Narrows a slow and bloody task.

On the 18th of March, the ships developed a fierce fire upon the shore defences, and in the midst of the engagement the Turks floated some large mines upon the attacking ships, and by these means sank three battleships, one French, two English, the French ship with all her crew.

Heavy and unsettled weather, which made minesweeping impossible, broke off serious operations for some days. During these days it was decided, though with grave misgivings among the counsellors, that an army should be landed on the Peninsula to second the next naval attack.

It was now a month since the operations had begun, and the original decision, to leave the issue solely to the ships, had delayed the concentration of the troops needed for the task. The army, under the supreme command of General Sir Ian Hamilton, was assembling, but not yet concentrated nor on the scene. Some of it was in Egypt, some in transports at sea. When it was decided to use the army in the venture, much necessary work had still to be done. The Turks had now been given so much time to defend the landing-places that to get our troops ashore at all called for the most elaborate preparation and the working out of careful schemes with the naval officers. The Germans boasted that our troops would never be able to land; possibly at first thought many soldiers would have agreed with them. But English soldiers and sailors are not Germans; they are, as Carlyle says, "far other"; our Admirals and General felt that with courage and a brave face our troops could land. It was true that the well-armed Turks were amply ready, and could easily concentrate against any army which we could land and supply a far larger force, more easily supplied and supported. But in the narrow Peninsula they could not move their larger forces so as to outflank us. Our flanks could be protected always by the fleet. And besides, in war, fortune plays a large part, and skill, courage, and resolution, and that fine blending of all three in the uncommon sense called genius, have often triumphed even where common sense has failed. It was necessary that we should divert large armies of Turks from our Russian allies in the Caucasus; it was desirable to strike the imaginations of the Balkan States by some daring feat of arms close to them; it was vital to our enterprise in Mesopotamia and to the safety of Egypt that we should alarm the Turks for their capital and make them withdraw their armies from their frontiers. This operation, striking at the heart of the Turkish Empire, was the readiest way to do all these things.

The army designed for this honourable and dangerous task consisted of the following:

A division of French soldiers, the Corps Expéditionnaire de l'Orient, under M. le General d'Amade. This division was made up of French Territorial soldiers and Senegalese.
The 29th Division of British regular troops.
The Royal Naval Division.
The Australian and New Zealand Army Corps.

The French Division and the 29th Division of British Regular soldiers were men who had been fully trained in time of peace, but the Australian and New Zealand Army Corps and the Royal Naval Division, who together made up more than half the army, were almost all men who had enlisted since the declaration of war, and had had not more than six months' active training. They were, however, the finest body of young men ever brought together in modern times. For physical beauty and nobility of bearing they surpassed any men I have ever seen; they walked and looked like the kings in old poems, and reminded me of the line in Shakespeare:

"Baited like eagles having lately bathed."

As their officers put it, "they were in the pink of condition and didn't care a damn for anybody." Most of these new and irregular formations were going into action for the first time, to receive their baptism of fire in "a feat of arms only possible to the flower of a very fine army."

Having decided to use the army, the question how to use it was left to the commanding General, whose task was to help the British fleet through the Narrows. Those who have criticized the operations to me, even those who knew or pretended to know the country and military matters (but who were, for the most part, the gulls or agents of German propaganda), raised, nearly always, one or both of the following alternatives to the attack used by Sir Ian Hamilton. They have asked:

(1) Why did he not attack at or to the north of Bulair in the Gulf of Xeros, or
(2) Why did he not attack along the Asiatic coast instead of where he did, at Cape Helles and Anzac?

Those who have asked these questions have always insisted to me that had he chosen either alternative his efforts must have been successful. It may be well to set down here the final and sufficient reasons against either folly.

Firstly, then, the reasons against landing the army at or to the north of Bulair in the Gulf of Xeros.

The task demanded of the army was to second the naval attack in the Straits – *i.e.*, by seizing and occupying, if possible, that high ground in the Peninsula from which the Turkish guns molested the minesweepers. As this high ground commanded the Asiatic shore, its occupation by the British troops would have made possible the passage of the Straits. This and this alone was the task demanded of the army; no adventure upon Constantinople was designed or possible with the numbers of men available. How the army could have seconded the naval attack by landing three or four days' march from the Narrows within easy reach of the large Turkish armies in European Turkey is not clear.

Nevertheless, our task was to land the army, and all landing-places had to be examined. Pass now to –

(a) Bulair was carefully reconnoitred, and found to be a natural stronghold, so fortified with earthworks that there was no chance of taking it. Ten thousand Turks had been digging there for a month, and had made it impregnable. There are only two landing-places near Bulair: one (a very bad one) in a swamp or salt marsh to the east, the other in a kind of death-trap ravine to the west, both dominated by high ground in front, and one (the eastward) commanded also from the rear. Had the army, or any large part of it, landed at either beach, it would have been decimated in the act and then held up by the fortress.

(b) Had the army landed to the north of Bulair on the coast of European Turkey, it would have been in grave danger of destruction. Large Turkish armies could have marched upon its left and front from Adrianople and Rodosto, while, as it advanced, the large army in Gallipoli, reinforced from Asia across the Straits, could have marched from Bulair and fallen upon its right flank and rear.

(c) But even had it beaten these armies, some four times its own strength, it would none the less have perished, through failure of supplies, since no European army could hope to live upon a Turkish province in the spring, and European supplies could have been brought to it only with the utmost difficulty and danger. There is no port upon that part of the Turkish coast; no shelter from the violent southerly gales, and no depth of water near the shore. In consequence, no transports of any size could approach within some miles of the coast to land either troops or stores. Even had there been depth of water for them, transports could not have discharged upon the coast because of the danger from submarines. They would have been compelled to discharge in the safe harbour of the subsidiary base at Mudros in Lemnos, and (as happened with the fighting where it was) their freight, whether men or stores, reshipped into small ships of too light draught to be in danger from submarines, and by them conveyed to the landing-places. But this system, which never quite failed at Anzac and Cape Helles, would have failed on the Xeros coast. Anzac is some forty miles from Mudros, the Xeros coast is eighty, or twice the distance. Had the army landed at Xeros, it would have been upon an unproductive enemy territory in an unsettled season of the year, from eight to twenty hours' steam from their one safe subsidiary base. A stormy week might have cut them off at any time from all possibility of obtaining a man, a biscuit, a cartridge, or even a drink of water, and this upon ground where they could with little trouble be outnumbered by armies four times their strength with sound communications.

Secondly, for the reasons against attacking along the Asiatic coast –

(a) The coast is commanded from the Gallipoli coast, and therefore less important to those trying to second a naval attack upon the Narrows.

(b) An army advancing from Kum Kale along the Asiatic shore would be forced to draw its supplies from overseas. As it advanced, its communications could be cut with great ease at any point by the hordes of armed Turks in Asia Minor.

(c) The Turkish armies in Asia Minor would have attacked it in the right and rear, those from Bulair and Rodosto would have ferried over and attacked it in front, the guns in Gallipoli would have shelled its left, and the task made impracticable.

Some of those who raised these alternatives raised a third when the first two had been disposed of. They asked, "Even if the army could not have landed at Bulair or on the Asian coast, why did it land where it did land, on those suicidal beaches?" The answer to this criticism is as follows: It landed on those beaches because there were no others on the Peninsula, because the only landing-places at which troops could be got ashore with any prospect of success, however slight, were just those three or four small beaches near Cape Helles, at the south-west end of the Peninsula, and the one rather longer beach to the north of Gaba or Kaba Tepe. All these beaches were seen to be strongly defended, with barbed wire entanglements on the shore and under the water, with sea and land mines, with strongly entrenched riflemen, many machine guns, and an ample artillery. In addition, the beaches close to Cape Helles were within range of big guns mounted near Troy on the Asian shore, and the beach near Gaba Tepe was ranged by the guns in the olive-groves to the south and on the hills to the north of it. A strong Turkish army held the Peninsula, and very powerful reserves were at Bulair, all well-supplied (chiefly by boat from the Asian shore) with food and munitions. German officers had organized the defence of the Peninsula with great professional skill. They had made it a fortress of great strength, differing from all other fortresses in this, that besides being almost impregnable it was almost unapproachable. But our army had its task to do, there was no other means of doing it, and our men had to do what they could. Anyone trying to land, to besiege that fortress, had to do so by boat or lighter under every gun in the Turkish army. The Turks and the Germans knew, better than we, what few and narrow landing-places were possible to our men; they had had more than two months of time in which to make those landing-places fatal to any enemy within a mile of them, yet our men came from three thousand miles away, passed that mile of massacre, landed and held on with all their guns, stores, animals, and appliances, in spite of the Turk and his ally, who outnumbered them at every point.

No army in history has made a more heroic attack; no army in history has been set such a task. No other body of men in any modern war has been called upon to land over mined and wired waters under the cross-fire of machine guns. The Japanese at Chinampo and Chemulpho were not opposed, the Russians at Pitzewo were not prepared, the Spaniards at Daiquiri made no fight. Our men achieved a feat without parallel in war, and no other troops in the world (not even Japanese or Ghazis in the hope of heaven) would have made good those beaches on the 25th of April.

II

Then said Roland: "Oliver, companion, brother . . . we shall have a strong and tough battle, such as man never saw fought. But I shall strike with my sword, and you, comrade, will strike with yours; we have borne our swords in so many lands, we have ended so many battles with them, that no evil song shall be sung of them . . . " At these words the Franks went forward gladly. – *The Song of Roland.*

Let the reader now try to imagine the nature of the landing. In order to puzzle the Turkish commander, to make him hesitate and divide his forces, it was necessary to land or pretend to land, in some force, simultaneously at various places. A feint of landing was to be made near Bulair; the French Corps Expéditionnaire was to land at Kum Kale, to attack and silence the Asiatic fortifications and batteries; the Australian and New Zealand Army Corps was to land at or near Gaba Tepe; while men of the 29th and Royal Naval Divisions landed at or near Cape Helles, some towards Krithia on the north, others nearer Sedd-el-Bahr on the south-west and south. The main attacks were to be those near Gaba Tepe and Cape Helles.

At Cape Helles three principal landings were to be made at the following places:

1. At Beach V, a small semicircular sandy bay, three hundred yards across, just west of the ruins of Sedd-el-Bahr castle. The ground rises steeply round the half-circle of the bay exactly as the seats rise in an amphitheatre. Modern defence could not ask for a more perfect site.
2. At Beach W (to the west of V), where a small sandy bay, under Cape Tekke, offered a landing upon a strip of sand about the size of Beach V. The slope upward from this beach is more gentle than at V, through a succession of sand-dunes, above which the ground was strongly entrenched. The cliffs north and south are precipitous, and make the beach a kind of gully or ravine. The Turks had placed machine guns in holes in the cliff, had wired and mined both beach and bay, and thrown up strong redoubts to flank them. Beach W was a death trap.
3. At Beach X (north of W, on the other or northern side of Cape Tekke), a narrow strip of sand, two hundred yards long, at the foot of a low cliff. This, though too small to serve for the quick passage ashore of

many men at a time, was a slightly easier landing-place than the other two, owing to the lie of the ground.

Besides these main landings, two minor landings were to be made as follows:

4. At Beach S, a small beach, within the Straits, beyond Sedd-el-Bahr.
5. At Beach Y (on the Ægean, to the west of Krithia), a strip of sand below a precipitous cliff, gashed with steep, crumbling, and scrub-covered gullies.

These two minor landings were to protect the flanks of the main landing parties, "to disseminate the forces of the enemy and to interrupt the arrival of his reinforcements." They were to take place at dawn (at about 5 a.m. or half an hour before the main attacks), without any preliminary bombardment from the fleet upon the landing-places.

Near Gaba Tepe only one landing was to be made, upon a small beach, two hundred yards across, a mile to the north of Gaba Tepe promontory. The ground beyond this beach is abrupt sandy cliff, covered with scrub, flanked by Gaba Tepe, and commanded by the land to shoreward.

For some days before the landing the army lay at Mudros, in Lemnos, aboard its transports, or engaged in tactical exercises ashore and in the harbour. Much bitter and ignorant criticism has been passed upon this delay, which was, unfortunately, very necessary. The month of April, 1915, in the Ægean, was a month of unusually unsettled weather; it was quite impossible to attempt the landing without calm water and the like-lihood of fine weather for some days. In rough weather it would have been impossible to land laden soldiers with their stores through the surf of open beaches under heavy fire, and those who maintain that "other soldiers" (*i.e.*, themselves) would have made the attempt can have no knowledge of what wading ashore from a boat, in bad weather, in the Ægean or any other sea, even without a pack and with no enemy ahead, is like. But in unsettled weather the Gallipoli coast is not only difficult, but exceedingly dangerous for small vessels. The currents are fierce, and a short and ugly sea gets up quickly and makes towing hazardous. Had the attempt been made in foul weather a great many men would have been drowned, some few would have reached the shore, and then the ships would have been forced off the coast. The few men left on the shore would have had to fight there with neither supplies nor supports till the enemy overwhelmed them.

Another reason for delay was the need for the most minute prepara-tion. Many armies have been landed from boats from the time of Pharaoh's invasion of Punt until the present; but no men, not even Cæsar's army of invasion in Britain, have had to land in an enemy's country with such a prospect of difficulty before them. They were going to land on a foodless cliff, five hundred miles from a store, in a place and at a season in which the sea's rising might cut them from supply. They had to take with them all things – munitions, guns, entrenching tools, sandbags, provisions, clothing, medical stores, hospital equipment, mules, horses, fodder, even water to drink, for the land produced not even that. These military supplies had to be arranged in boats and lighters in such a way that they might be thrust ashore with many thousands of men in all haste but without confusion. All this world of preparation, which made each unit landed a self-supporting army, took time and labour – how much can only be judged by those who have done similar work.

On Friday, the 23rd of April, the weather cleared so that the work could be begun. In fine weather in Mudros a haze of beauty comes upon the hills and water till their loveliness is unearthly, it is so rare. Then the bay is like a blue jewel, and the hills lose their savagery, and glow, and are gentle, and the sun comes up from Troy, and the peaks of Samothrace change colour, and all the marvellous ships in the harbour are transfigured. The land of Lemnos was beautiful with flowers at that season, in the brief Ægean spring, and to seawards always, in the bay, were the ships, more ships, perhaps, than any port of modern times has known; they seemed like half the ships of the world. In this crowd of shipping, strange beautiful Greek vessels passed, under rigs of old time, with sheep and goats and fish for sale, and the tugs of the Thames and Mersey met again the ships they had towed of old, bearing a new freight, of human courage. The transports (all painted black) lay in tiers, well within the harbour, the men-of-war nearer Mudros and the entrance. Now in all that city of ships, so busy with passing picket-boats, and noisy with the labour of men, the getting of the anchors began. Ship after ship, crammed with soldiers, moved slowly out of harbour in the lovely day, and felt again the heave of the sea. No such gathering of fine ships has ever been seen upon this earth, and the beauty and the exultation of the youth upon them made them like sacred things as they moved away. All the thousands of men aboard them gathered on deck to see, till each rail was thronged. These men had come from all parts of the British world, from Africa, Australia, Canada, India, the Mother Country, New Zealand, and remote islands in the sea. They had said goodbye to home that they might offer their lives in the cause we stand for. In a few hours at most, as they well-knew, perhaps a tenth of them would have looked their last on the sun, and be a part of foreign earth or dumb things that the tides push. Many of them would have disappeared for ever from the knowledge of man, blotted from the book of life none would know how – by a fall or chance shot in the darkness, in the blast of a shell, or alone, like a hurt beast, in some scrub or gully, far from comrades and the English speech and the English singing. And perhaps a third of them would be mangled, blinded or broken, lamed, made imbecile or disfigured, with the colour and the taste of life taken from them, so that they would never more move with comrades nor exult in the sun. And those not taken thus would be under the ground, sweating in the trench, carrying sandbags up the sap, dodging death and danger, without rest or food or drink, in the blazing sun or the frost of the Gallipoli night, till death seemed relaxation and a wound a luxury. But as they moved out these things were but the end they asked, the reward they had come for, the unseen cross upon the breast. All that they felt was a gladness of exultation that their young courage was to be used. They went like kings in a pageant to the imminent death.

As they passed from moorings to the man-of-war anchorage on their way to the sea, their feeling that they had done with life and were going out to something new welled up in those battalions; they cheered and cheered till the harbour rang with cheering. As each ship crammed with soldiers drew near the battleships, the men swung their caps and cheered again, and the sailors answered, and the noise of cheering swelled, and the men in the ships not yet moving joined in, and the men ashore, till all the life in the harbour was giving thanks that it could go to death rejoicing. All was beautiful in that gladness of men about to die, but the most moving thing was the greatness of their generous hearts. As they passed the French ships, the memory of old quarrels healed, and the sense of what sacred France has done and endured in this great war, and the pride of having such men as the French for comrades, rose up in their warm souls, and they cheered the French ships more, even, than their own.

They left the harbour very, very slowly; this tumult of cheering lasted a long time; no one who heard it will ever forget it, or think of it unshaken. It broke the hearts of all there with pity and pride: it went beyond the guard of the English heart. Presently all were out, and the fleet stood across for Tenedos, and the sun went down with marvellous colour, lighting island after island and the Asian peaks, and those left behind in Mudros trimmed their lamps knowing that they had been for a little brought near to the heart of things.

The next day, the 24th of April, the troops of the landing parties went on board the warships and minesweepers which were to take them ashore. At midnight the fleet got under way from Tenedos and stood out for the Peninsula. Dawn was to be at five; the landings on the flanks were to take place then, the others at half-past five, after the fleet had bombarded the beaches. Very few of the soldiers of the landing parties slept that night; the excitement of the morrow kept them awake, as happened to Nelson's sailors before Trafalgar. It was a very still fine night, slightly hazy, with a sea so still that the ships had no trouble with their long tows of boats and launches. As it began to grow light the men went down into the boats, and the two flanking parties started for the outer beaches S and Y. The guns of the fleet now opened a heavy fire upon the Turkish positions, and the big guns on the Asian shore sent over a few shells in answer; but the Turks near the landing-places reserved their fire. During the intense bombardment by the fleet, when the ships were trembling like animals with the blasts of the explosions, the picket-boats towing the lighters went ahead, and the tow-loads of crowded men started for the main landings on beaches V, W, and X.

It was now light, and the haze on Sedd-el-Bahr was clearing away, so that those in charge of the boats could see what they were doing. Had they attempted an attack in the dark on those unsurveyed beaches among the fierce and dangerous tide rips, the loss of life would have been very great. As it was, the exceeding fierceness of the currents added much to the difficulty and danger of the task. We will take the landings in succession.

The Landing at V beach, near Sedd-el-Bahr

The men told off for this landing were: The Dublin Fusiliers, the Munster Fusiliers, half a battalion of the Hampshire Regiment, and the West Riding Field Company.

Three companies of the Dublin Fusiliers were to land from towed lighters, the rest of the party from a tramp steamer, the collier *River Clyde*. This ship, a conspicuous seamark at Cape Helles throughout the rest of the campaign, had been altered to carry and land troops. Great gangways or entry ports had been cut in her sides on the level of her between decks, and platforms had been built out upon her sides below these, so that men might run from her in a hurry. The plan was to beach her as near the shore as possible, and then drag or sweep the lighters, which she towed, into position between her and the shore, so as to make a kind of boat bridge from her to the beach. When the lighters were so moored as to make this bridge, the entry ports were to be opened, the waiting troops were to rush out onto the external platforms, run from them onto the lighters, and so to the shore. The ship's upper deck and bridge were protected with boiler plate and sandbags, and a casemate for machine guns was built upon her fo'c'sle, so that she might reply to the enemy's fire.

Five picket-boats, each towing five boats or launches full of men, steamed alongside the *River Clyde* and went ahead when she grounded. She took the ground rather to the right of the little beach, some four hundred yards from the ruins of Sedd-el-Bahr Castle, before the Turks had opened fire; but almost as she grounded, when the picket-boats with their tows were ahead of her, only twenty or thirty yards from the beach, every rifle and machine gun in the castle, the town above it, and in the curved, low, strongly trenched hill along the bay, began a murderous fire upon ship and boats. There was no question of their missing. They had their target on the front and both flanks at ranges between a hundred and three hundred yards in clear daylight, thirty boats bunched together and crammed with men and a good big ship. The first outbreak of fire made the bay as white as a rapid, for the Turks fired not less than ten thousand shots a minute for the first few minutes of that attack. Those not killed in the boats at the first discharge jumped overboard to wade or swim ashore. Many were killed in the water, many, who were wounded, were swept away and drowned; others, trying to swim in the fierce current, were drowned by the weight of their equipment. But some reached the shore, and these instantly doubled out to cut the wire entanglements, and were killed, or dashed for the cover of a bank of sand or raised beach which runs along the curve of the bay. Those very few who reached this cover were out of immediate danger, but they were only a handful. The boats were destroyed where they grounded.

Meanwhile the men of the *River Clyde* tried to make their bridge of boats by sweeping the lighters into position and mooring them between the ship and the shore. They were killed as they worked, but others took their places; the bridge was made, and some of the Munsters dashed along it from the ship and fell in heaps as they ran. As a second company followed, the moorings of the lighters broke or were shot; the men leaped into the water, and were drowned or killed, or reached the beach and were killed, or fell wounded there, and lay under fire, getting wound after wound till they died; very, very few reached the sandbank. More brave men jumped aboard the lighters to remake the bridge; they were swept away or shot to pieces. The average life on those boats was some three minutes long, but they remade the bridge, and the third company of the Munsters doubled down to death along it under a storm of shrapnel which scarcely a man survived. The big guns in Asia were now shelling the *River Clyde*, and the hell of rapid fire never paused. More men tried to land, headed by Brigadier-General Napier, who was instantly killed, with nearly all his followers. Then for long hours the remainder stayed on board, down below in the grounded steamer, while the shots beat on her plates with a rattling clang which never stopped. Her twelve machine gun fired back, killing any Turk who showed; but nothing could be done to support the few survivors of the landing, who now lay under cover of the sandbank on the other side of the beach. It was almost certain death to try to leave the ship, but all through the day men leaped from her (with leave or without it) to bring water or succour to the wounded on the boats or beach. A hundred brave men gave their lives thus; every man there earned the Cross that day. A boy earned it by one of the bravest deeds of the war, leaping into the sea with a rope in his teeth to try to secure a drifting lighter.

The day passed thus, but at nightfall the Turks' fire paused, and the men came ashore from the *River Clyde*, almost unharmed. They joined the survivors on the beach, and at once attacked the old fort and the village above it. These works were strongly held by the enemy. All had been ruined by the fire from the fleet, but in the rubble and ruin of old masonry there were thousands of hidden riflemen backed by machine guns. Again and again they beat off our attacks, for there was a bright moon and they knew the ground, and our men had to attack uphill over wire and broken earth and heaped stones in all the wreck and confusion and strangeness of war at night in a new place. Some of the Dublins and Munsters went astray in the ruins, and were wounded far from their fellows, and so lost. The Turks became more daring after dark; while the light lasted they were checked by the *River Clyde*'s machine guns, but at midnight they gathered unobserved and charged. They came right down onto the beach, and in the darkness and moonlight much terrible and confused fighting followed. Many were bayoneted, many shot, there was wild firing and crying, and then the Turk attack melted away, and their machine guns began again. When day dawned, the survivors of the landing party were crouched under the shelter of the sandbank; they had had no rest; most of them had been fighting all night; all had landed across the corpses of their friends. No retreat was possible, nor was it dreamed of, but to stay there was hopeless. Lieut.-Colonel Doughty-Wylie gathered them together for an attack; the fleet opened a terrific fire upon the ruins of the fort and village, and the landing party went forward again, fighting from bush to bush and from stone to stone, till the ruins were in their hands. Shells still fell among them, single Turks, lurking under cover, sniped them and shot them; but the landing had been made good, and V beach was secured to us.

This was the worst and the bloodiest of all the landings.

The Landing at W beach, under Cape Tekke

The men told off for this landing were the 1st Battalion Lancashire Fusiliers, supported (later) by the Worcester Regiment.

The men were landed at six in the morning from ships' boats run ashore by picket-boats. On landing, they rushed the wire entanglements, broke through them, with heavy loss, and won to the dead ground under the cliffs. The ships drew nearer to the beach and opened heavy fire upon the Turks, and the landing party stormed the cliffs and won the trenches.

The Worcester Regiment having landed, attempts were made to break a way to the right, so as to join hands with the men on V beach. All the land between the two beaches was heavily wired and so broken that it gave much cover to the enemy. Many brave Worcesters went out to cut the wires and were killed; the fire was intense, there was no getting farther. The trenches already won were secured and improved, the few available reserves were hurried up, and by dark, when the Turks attacked again and again, in great force, our men were able to beat them off, and hold on to what they had won.

The Landing at X beach (sometimes called Implacable Landing), towards Krithia

The men told off for this landing were the 1st Royal Fusiliers, with a working-party of the Anson Battalion, R.N.D.

These men were towed ashore from H.M.S. *Implacable* about an hour after dawn. The ship stood close in to the beach, and opened rapid fire on the enemy trenches; under cover of this fire the men got ashore fairly easily. On moving inland, they were attacked by a great force of Turks and checked; but they made good the ground won, and opened up communications with the Lancashires who had landed at W beach. This landing was the least bloody of all.

Of the two flank landings, that on the right, within the Straits, to the right of Sedd-el-Bahr, got ashore without great loss and held on; that on the left, to the left of X beach, got ashore, fought a desperate and bloody battle against five times its strength, and finally had to re-embark. The men got ashore upon a cliff so steep that the Turks had not troubled to defend it; but on landing they were unable to link up with the men on X beach, as had been planned. They were attacked in great force by an ever-growing Turkish army, fought all day and all through the night in such trenches as they had been able to dig under fire, and at last in the morning of the next day went down the cliffs and re-embarked, most nobly covered to the end by a party from the King's Own Scottish Borderers and the Plymouth Battalion.

During the forenoon of the 25th, a regiment of the French Corps landed at Kum Kale, under cover of the guns of the French warships, and engaged the enemy throughout the day and night. Their progress was held up by a strongly entrenched force during the afternoon, and after sharp fighting all through the night they re-embarked in the forenoon of the 26th with some 400 Turkish prisoners. This landing of the French diverted from us on the 25th the fire of the howitzers emplaced on the Asiatic shore. Had these been free to fire upon us, the landings near Sedd-el-Bahr would have been made even more hazardous than they were.

At Bulair, one man, Lieutenant Freyberg, swam ashore from a destroyer towing a little raft of flares. Near the shore he lit two of these flares, then, wading on to the land, he lit others at intervals along the coast; then he wandered inland, naked, on a personal reconnaissance, and soon found a large Turkish army strongly entrenched. Modesty forbade further intrusion. He went back to the beach and swam off to his destroyer; could not find her in the dark, and swam for several miles, was exhausted and cramped, and was at last picked up, nearly dead. This magnificent act of courage and endurance, done by one unarmed man, kept a large Turkish army at Bulair during the critical hours of the landing. "The Constantinople papers were filled with accounts of the repulse of the great attack at Bulair." The flares deceived the Turks even more completely than had been hoped.

While these operations were securing our hold upon the extreme end of the Peninsula, the Australian and New Zealand Army Corps were making good their landing on the Ægean coast, to the north of Gaba Tepe. They sailed from Mudros on the 24th, arrived off the coast of the Peninsula at about half-past one on the morning of the 25th, and there under a setting moon, in calm weather, they went on board the boats which were to take them ashore. At about half-past three the tows left the ships, and proceeded in darkness to the coast.

Gaba or Kaba Tepe is a steep cliff or promontory about ninety feet high, with a whitish nose and something the look of a blunt-nosed torpedo or porpoise. It is a forbidding-looking snout of land, covered with scrub where it is not too steep for roots to hold, and washed by deep water. About a mile to the north of it there is a possible landing-place, and north of that again a long and narrow strip of beach between two little headlands. This latter beach cannot be seen from Gaba Tepe. The ground above these beaches is exceedingly steep sandy cliff, broken by two great gulleys or ravines, which run inland. All the ground, except in one patch in the southern ravine, where there is a sort of meadow of grass, is densely covered with scrub, mostly between two and three feet high. Inland from the beach, the land of the Peninsula rises in steep, broken hills and spurs, with clumps of pine upon them, and dense undergrowths of scrub. The men selected for this landing were the 3rd Brigade of the Australian and New Zealand Army Corps, followed and supported by the 1st and 2nd Brigades.

The place selected for the landing was the southern beach, the nearer of the two to Gaba Tepe. This, like the other landing-places near Cape Helles, was strongly defended, and most difficult of approach. Large forces of Turks were entrenched there, well-prepared. But in the darkness of the early morning after the moon had set, the tows stood a little farther to the north than they should have done, perhaps because some high ground to their left made a convenient steering mark against the stars. They headed in towards the northern beach between the two little head-lands, where the Turks were not expecting them. However, they were soon seen, and very heavy independent rifle fire was concentrated on them. As they neared the beach, "about one battalion of Turks" doubled along the land to intercept them. These men came from nearer Gaba Tepe, firing, as they ran, into the mass of the boats at short range. A great many men were killed in the boats, but the dead men's oars were taken by survivors, and the boats forced into the shingle. The men jumped out, waded ashore, charged the enemy with the bayonet, and broke the Turk attack to pieces. The Turks scattered and were pursued, and now the steep scrub-covered cliffs became the scene of the most desperate fighting.

The scattered Turks dropped into the scrub and disappeared. Hidden all over the rough cliffs, under every kind of cover, they sniped the beach or ambushed the little parties of the 3rd Brigade who had rushed the landing. All over the broken hills there were isolated fights to the death, men falling into gullies and being bayoneted; sudden duels, point blank, where men crawling through the scrub met each other, and life went to the quicker finger; heroic deaths, where some half-section which had lost touch were caught by ten times their strength and charged and died. No man of our side knew that cracked and fissured jungle. Men broke through it onto machine guns, or showed up on a crest and were blown to pieces, or leaped down from it into some sap or trench, to catch the bombs flung at them and hurl them at the thrower. Going as they did, up cliffs through scrub over ground which would have broken the alignment of the Tenth Legion, they passed many hidden Turks who were thus left to shoot them in the back or to fire down at the boats, from perhaps only fifty yards away. It was only just light, theirs was the first British survey of that wild country; only now, as it showed up clear, could they realize its difficulty. They pressed on up the hill; they dropped and fired and died; they drove the Turks back; they flung their packs away, wormed through the bush, and stalked the snipers from the flash. As they went, the words of their song supported them, the ribald and proud chorus of "Australia will be there" which the men on the torpedoed *Southland* sang as they fell in expecting death. Presently, as it grew lighter, the Turks' big howitzers began shelling the beach, and their field guns, well-hidden, opened on the transports, now busy disembarking the 1st and 2nd Brigades. They forced the transports to stand farther out to sea, and shelled the tows, as they came in, with shrapnel and high-explosive. As the boats drew near the shore, every gun on Gaba Tepe took them in flank, and the snipers concentrated on them from the shore. More and more Turks were coming up at the double to stop the attack up the hill. The fighting in the scrub grew fiercer; shells burst continually upon the beach, boats were sunk, men were killed in the water. The boatmen and beach working-parties were the unsung heroes of that landing. The boatmen came in with the tows, under fire, waited with them under intense and concentrated fire of every kind until they were unloaded, and then shoved off, and put slowly back for more, and then came back again. The beach parties were wading to and from that shell-smitten beach all day unloading, carrying ashore, and sorting the munitions and necessaries for many thousands of men. They worked in a strip of beach and sea some five hundred yards long by forty broad, and the fire directed on that strip was such that every box brought ashore had one or more shells and not less than fifty bullets directed at it before it was flung upon the sand. More men came in and went on up the hill in support; but as yet there were no guns ashore, and the Turks' fire became intenser. By ten o'clock the Turks had had time to bring up enough men from their prepared positions to hold up the advance. Scattered parties of our men who had gone too far in the scrub were cut off and killed, for there was no thought of surrender in those marvellous young men; they were the flower of this world's manhood, and died as they had lived, owning no master on this earth. More and more Turks came up with big and field artillery, and now our attack had to hold on to what it had won, against more than twice its numbers. We had won a rough bow of ground, in which the beach represented the bow-string, the beach near Gaba Tepe the south end, and the hovel known as Fisherman's Hut the north. Against this position, held by at most 8,000 of our men, who had had no rest and had fought hard since dawn under every kind of fire in a savage rough country unknown to them, came an overwhelming army of Turks to drive them into the sea. For four hours the Turks attacked and again attacked, with a terrific fire of artillery and waves of men in succession. They came fresh from superior positions, with many guns, to break a disorganized line of breathless men not yet dug in. The guns of the ships opened on them, and the scattered units in the scrub rolled them back again and again by rifle and machine gun fire, and by charge after counter-charge. More of the Army Corps landed to meet the Turks, the fire upon the beach never slackened, and they came ashore across corpses and wrecked boats and a path like a road in hell with ruin and blasts and burning. They went up the cliff to their fellows under an ever-growing fire, that lit the scrub and burned the wounded and the dead. Darkness came, but there was no rest nor lull. Wave after wave of Turks came out of the night, crying the proclamation of their faith; others stole up in the dark through the scrub and shot or stabbed and crept back, or were seen and stalked and killed. Flares went up, to light with their blue and ghastly glare the wild glens peopled by the enemy. Men worked at the digging in till they dropped asleep upon the soil, and more Turks charged, and they woke and fired and again dug. It was cruelly cold after the sun had gone, but there was no chance of warmth or proper food; to dig in and beat back the Turk or die were all that men could think of. In the darkness, among the blasts of the shells, men scrambled up and down the pathless cliffs bringing up tins of water and boxes of cartridges, hauling up guns and shells, and bringing down the wounded. The beach was heaped with wounded, placed as close under the cliff as might be, in such yard or so of dead ground as the cliffs gave. The doctors worked among them and shells fell among them, and doctors and wounded were blown to pieces, and the survivors sang their song of "Australia will be there," and cheered the newcomers still landing on the beach. Sometimes our fire seemed to cease, and then the Turk shells filled the night with their scream and blast and the pattering of their fragments. With all the fury and the crying of the shells, and the shouts and cries and cursing on the beach, the rattle of the small arms and the cheers and defiance up the hill, and the roar of the great guns far away, at sea, or in the olive-groves, the night seemed in travail of a new age. All the blackness was shot with little spurts of fire, and streaks of fire, and malignant bursts of fire, and arcs and glows and crawling snakes of fire, and the moon rose, and looked down upon it all. In the fiercer hours of that night shells fell in that contested mile of ground and on the beach beyond it at the rate of one a second, and the air whimpered with passing bullets, or fluttered with the rush of the big shells, or struck the head of the passer like a moving wall with the shock of the explosion. All through the night the Turks attacked, and in the early hours their fire of shrapnel became so hellish that the Australians soon had not men enough left to hold the line. Orders were given to fall back to a shorter line, but in the

70

darkness, uproar, and confusion, with many sections refusing to fall back, others falling back and losing touch, others losing their way in gully or precipice, and shrapnel hailing on all, as it had hailed for hours, the falling back was mistaken by some for an order to re-embark. Many men who had lost their officers and non-commissioned officers fell back to the beach, where the confusion of wounded men, boxes of stores, field dressing-stations, corpses, and the litter and the waste of battle, had already blocked the going. The shells bursting in this clutter made the beach, in the words of an eyewitness, "like bloody hell, and nothing else." But at this breaking of the wave of victory, this panting moment in the race, when some of the runners had lost their first wind, encouragement reached our men: a message came to the beach from Sir Ian Hamilton, to say that help was coming, and that an Australian submarine had entered the Narrows and had sunk a Turkish transport off Chanak.

This word of victory, coming to men who thought for the moment that their efforts had been made in vain, had the effect of a fresh brigade. The men rallied back up the hill; bearing the news to the firing-line, the new, constricted line was made good, and the rest of the night was never anything but continued victory to those weary ones in the scrub. But twenty-four hours of continual battle exhausts men, and by dawn the Turks, knowing the weariness of our men, resolved to beat them down into the sea. When the sun was well in our men's eyes they attacked again, with not less than twice our entire strength of fresh men, and with an overwhelming superiority in field artillery. Something in the Turk commander, and the knowledge that a success there would bring our men across the Peninsula within a day, made the Turks more desperate enemies there than elsewhere. They came at us with a determination which might have triumphed against other troops. As they came on they opened a terrific fire of shrapnel upon our position, pouring in such a hail that months afterwards one could see their round shrapnel bullets stuck in bare patches of ground, or in earth thrown up from the trenches, as thickly as plums in a pudding. Their multitudes of men pressed through the scrub as skirmishers, and sniped at every moving thing; for they were on higher ground, and could see over most of our position, and every man we had was under direct fire for hours of each day. As the attack developed, the promised help arrived; our warships stood in and opened on the Turks with every gun that would bear. Some kept down the guns of Gaba Tepe, others searched the line of the Turk advance, till the hills over which they came were swathed with yellow smoke and dust, the white clouds of shrapnel, and the drifting darkness of conflagration. All the scrub was in a blaze before them, but they pressed on, falling in heaps and lines; and their guns dropped a never-ceasing rain of shells on trenches, beach, and shipping. The landing of stores and ammunition never ceased during the battle. The work of the beach parties in that scene of burning and massacre was beyond all praise; so was the work of the fatigue parties, who passed up and down the hill with water, ammunition, and food, or dug sheltered roads to the trenches; so was the work of the Medical Service, who got the wounded out of cuts in the earth, so narrow and so twisted that there was no using a stretcher, and men had to be carried on stretcher-bearers' backs or on improvised chairs made out of packing-cases.

At a little before noon the Turk attack reached its height in a blaze and uproar of fire and the swaying forward of their multitudes. The guns of the warships swept them from flank to flank with every engine of death: they died by hundreds, and the attack withered as it came. Our men saw the enemy fade and slacken and halt; then with their cheer they charged him and beat him home, seized new ground from him, and dug themselves in in front of him. All through the day there was fighting up and down the line, partial attacks, and never-ceasing shellfire, but no other great attack: the Turks had suffered too much. At night their snipers came out in the scrub in multitudes and shot at anything they could see, and all night long their men dragged up field guns and piles of shrapnel, and worked at the trenches which were to contain ours. When day dawned, they opened with shrapnel upon the beach, with a *feu de barrage* designed to stop all landing of men and stores. They whipped the bay with shrapnel bullets. Where their fire was concentrated, the water was lashed as with hail all day long; but the boats passed through it, and men worked in it, building jetties for the boats to land at, using a big Turk shell as a pile-driver. When they got too hot they bathed in it, for no fire shook those men. It was said that when a big shell was coming men of other races would go into their dugouts, but that these men paused only to call it a bastard, and then went on with their work.

By the night of the second day the Australian and New Zealand Army Corps had won and fortified their position. Men writing or reporting on service about them referred to them as the A.N.Z.A.C., and these letters soon came to mean the place in which they were, unnamed till then, probably, save by some rough Turkish place-name, but now likely to be printed on all English maps, with the other names, of Brighton Beach and Hell Spit, which mark a great passage of arms.

III

King Marsilies parted his army: ten columns he kept by him, and the other ten rode in to fight. The Franks said: "God, what ruin we shall have here! What will become of the twelve Peers?" The Archbishop Turpin answered first: "Good knights, you are the friends of God; today you will be crowned and flowered, resting in the holy flowers of Paradise, where no coward will ever come."

The Franks answered: "We will not fail. If it be God's will, we will not murmur. We will fight against our enemies; we are few men, but well-hardened."

They spurred forward to fight the pagans. The Franks and Saracens are mingled. – *The Song of Roland.*

This early fighting, which lasted from dawn on the 25th of April till noon on the following day, won us a footing, not more than that, on the Peninsula; it settled the German brag that we should never be able to land. We had landed upon, had taken, and were holding, the whole of the south-western extremity of the Peninsula and a strip of the Ægean coast, in the face of an army never less than twice our strength, strongly entrenched and well-supplied. We had lost very heavily in the attack, our men were weary from the exceedingly severe service of the landing, but the morrow began the second passage in the campaign, the advance from the sea, before the Turks should have recovered.

Many have said to me, with a naïveté that would be touching if it were not so plainly inspired by our enemies: "Why did not the troops press on at once the day they landed? The Japanese pressed on the day they landed, so did the Americans in Cuba. If you had pressed on at once, you would have won the whole Peninsula. The Turks were at their last cartridge, and would have surrendered."

It is quite true that the Japanese moved inland immediately from their transports at Chemulpho and Chinampo. Those ports were seized before the Russians knew that war was declared; they were not defended by Russian soldiers, and the two small Russian cruisers caught there by the Japanese fleet were put out of action before the transports discharged. The Japanese were free to land as they chose on beaches prepared, not with machine guns and mines, but with cranes, gangways, and good roads. Even so, they did not press on. The Japanese do not press on unless they are attacking; they are as prudent as they are brave; they waited till they were ready, and then marched on. The Americans landed at Daiquiri and at Guanica unopposed, and in neither case engaged the enemy till next day.

In the preceding chapter I have tried to show why we did not press on at once after landing. We did not because we could not, because two fresh men strongly entrenched, with machine guns, will stop one tired man with a rifle in nine cases out of ten. Our men had done the unimaginable in getting ashore at all; they could not do the impossible on the same day. I used to say this to draw the answer, "Well, other troops would have done it," so that I might say, what I know to be the truth, that no other men on this earth either would have or could have made good the landing; and that the men have not yet been born who could have advanced after such a feat of arms. The efforts of men are limited by their strength. The strength of men, always easily exhausted, is the only strength at the disposal of a General; it is the money to be spent by him in the purchase of victory, whether by hours of marching in the mud, digging in the field, or in attack. Losses in attack are great, though occasional; losses from other causes are great and constant. All armies in the field have to be supplied constantly with fresh drafts to make good the losses from attack and exhaustion. No armies can move without these replenishments, just as no individual man can go on working, after excessive labour, without rest and food. Our losses in the landings were severe, even for modern war, even for the Dardanelles. The bloodiest battle of modern times is said to have been the Antietam or Sharpsburg, in the American Civil War, where the losses were perhaps nearly one-third of the men engaged. At V beach the Munsters lost more than one-third, and the Dublins more than three-fifths, of their total strength. The Lancashires at W beach lost nearly as heavily as the Dublins. At Anzac, one Australian battalion lost 422 out of 900. At X beach, the Royals lost 487 out of 979. All these battalions had lost more than half their officers – indeed, by the 28th of April the Dublins had only one officer left. How could these dwindled battalions press on?

Then for the individual exhaustion. Those engaged in the first landing were clambering and fighting in great heat, without proper food, and in many cases without water, for the first twenty-four or thirty-six hours, varying the fighting with hurried but deep digging in marl or clay, getting no sleep, nor any moment's respite from the peril of death. Then, at the end of the first phase, when the fact that they had won the landing was plain, some of these same men, unrested, improperly fed, and wet through with rain, sweat, and the sea, had to hold what they had won, while the others went down to the beach to make piers, quarry roads, dig shelters, and wade out to carry or drag on shore food, drink, munitions, and heavy guns, and to do this without appliances, by the strength of their arms. Then, when these things had been done almost to the limit of human endurance, they carried water, food, and ammunition to the trenches, not in carts, but on their backs, and then relieved their fellows in the trenches, and withstood the Turk attacks and replied to the Turks' fire for hours on end. At Anzac, the A.N.Z. Army Corps had "ninety-six hours continuous fighting in the trenches, with little or no sleep," and "at no time during the ninety-six hours did the Turks' firing cease, although it varied in volume; at times the fusillade was simply deafening." Men worked like this, to the limit of physical endurance, under every possible exposure to wet, heat, cold, death, hunger, thirst, and want of rest, become exhausted, and their nerves shattered, not from fear, which was a thing those men did not understand, but because the machine breaks. On the top of the misery, exhaustion, and never-ceasing peril, is "the dreadful anxiety of not knowing how the battle is progressing," and the still worse anxiety of vigilance. To the strain of keeping awake, when dead-beat, is added the strain of watching men, peering for spies, stalking for snipers, and listening for bombing parties. Under all these strains the minds of strong men give way. They are the intensest strains ever put upon intelligences. Men subjected to them for many hours at a time cannot at once "press on," however brave their hearts may be. Those who are unjust enough to think that they can, or could, should work for a summer's day, without food or drink, at digging, then work for a night in the rain carrying heavy boxes, then dig for some hours longer, and at the end ask me to fire a machine gun at them while they "press on," across barbed wire, in what they presume to be the proper manner.

Our men could not "press on" at once. They had not enough unwounded men to do more than hold the hordes of fresh Turks continually brought up against them. They had no guns ashore to prepare an advance, nor enough rifle ammunition to stand a siege. They had the rations in their packs and the water in their bottles, and no other supplies but the seven days' food, water, and rifle ammunition put into each boat at the landing. To get men, stores, water, and guns ashore under fire, on beaches without wharves, cranes, or derricks of any kind, takes time, and until men and goods were landed no advance was possible. Until then our task was not to press on, but to hang on, like grim death. It was for the enemy to press on, to beat our tired troops before their supports could be landed, and this the Turks very well understood, as their captured orders show, and as their behaviour showed only too clearly. During the days which followed the landing, the Turks, far from being at their last cartridge and eager to surrender, prevented our pressing on by pressing on themselves, in immense force and with a great artillery, till our men were dying of fatigue in driving back their attacks.

One point more may be discussed before resuming the story. The legend, "that the Turks were at their last cartridge, and would have surrendered had we advanced," is very widely spread abroad by German emissaries. It appears in many forms, in print, in the lecture, and in conversation. Sometimes place and date are given, sometimes the authority, all confidently, but always differently. It is well to state here the truth, so that the lie may be known. The Turks were never at the end of their supplies. They were always better and more certainly supplied with shells and cartridges than we were. If they were ever (as perhaps they sometimes were) rather short of big gun ammunition, so were we. If they were sometimes rather short of rifles and rifle ammunition, so were we. If they were often short of food and all-precious water, so were we, and more so, and doubly more so. For all our supplies came over hundreds of miles of stormy water infested by submarines, and were landed on open beaches under shellfire, and their supplies came along the Asiatic coast and by ferry across the Hellespont, and thence, in comparative safety, by road to the trenches. The Turkish army was well-supplied, well-equipped, more numerous, and in better positions than our own. There was neither talk nor thought among them at any time of surrender, nor could there have been in an army so placed and so valiant. There was some little disaffection among them. They hated their German officers and the German methods of discipline so much that many prisoners when taken expressed pleasure at being taken, spat at the name of German, and said, "English good, German bad." Some of this, however, may have been Levantine tact.

Late on the 26th of April, the French corps landed men at V beach, and took over the trenches on the right of the ground won – *i.e.*, towards the Straits. At noon the next day the whole force advanced inland, without much opposition, for rather more than a mile. At nightfall on the 27th, they held a line across the Peninsula from the mouth of the Sighir watercourse (on the Ægean) to Eski Hissarlik (on the Straits). The men were very weary from the incessant digging of trenches, fighting, and dragging up of stores from the beach. They dug themselves in under shell and rifle fire, stood to their arms to repel Turk attacks for most of the night, and at eight next morning began the battle of the 28th of April. The French corps was on the right, the 29th Division (with one battalion of the R.N. Division) on the left. They advanced across rough moorland and little cultivated patches to attack the Turk town of Krithia. All the ground over which they advanced gave cover of the best kind to the defence. All through the morning, at odd times, the creeping companies going over that broken country came suddenly under the fire of machine guns, and lost men before they could fling themselves down. In the heather and torrent-beds of that Scotch-looking moorland, the Turk had only to wait in cover till his targets appeared, climbing a wall or getting out of a gully, then he could turn on his machine guns, at six hundred shots a minute each, and hold up the advance. From time to time the Turks attacked in great numbers. Early in the afternoon our advance reached its farthest point, about three-quarters of a mile from Krithia. Our artillery, short of ammunition at the best of times, and in these early days short of guns too, did what it could, though it had only shrapnel, which is of small service against an entrenched enemy. Those who were there have said that nothing depressed them more than the occasional shells from our guns in answer to the continual fire from the Turk artillery. They felt themselves out-gunned and without support. Rifle cartridges were running short, for, in spite of desperate efforts, in that roadless wild land with the beaches jammed with dead, wounded, stores, the wrecks of boats, and parties trying to build piers under shellfire, it was not possible to land or to send up cartridges in the quantity needed. There were not yet enough mules ashore to take the cartridge-boxes, and men could not be spared: there were too few men to hold the line. Gradually our men fell back a little from the ground they had won. The Turks brought up more men, charged us, and drove us back a little more, and were then themselves held. Our men dug themselves in as best they could and passed another anxious night, in bitter cold and driving rain, staving off a Turk attack, which was pressed with resolute courage against our centre and the French corps to the right of it. There were very heavy losses on both sides, but the Turks were killed in companies at every point of attack, and failed to drive us farther.

The next two days were passed in comparative quiet, in strengthening the lines, landing men, guns, and stores, and preparing for the next advance. This war has shown what an immense reserve of shell is needed to prepare a modern advance. Our men never had that immense reserve, nor, indeed, a large reserve, and in those early days they had no reserve at all, but a day to day allowance, and before a reserve was formed the Turks came down upon us with every man and gun they had, in the desperate night attack of the 1st of May. This began with shellfire at 10 p.m., and was followed half an hour later by a succession of charges in close order. The Turk front ranks crept up on hands and knees without firing (their cartridges had been taken from them), and charged our trenches with the bayonet. They got into our trenches in the dark, bayoneted the men in them, broke our line, got through to the second line, and were there mixed up in the night in a welter of killing and firing beyond description. The moon had not risen when the attack came home. The fighting took place in the dark: men fired and stabbed in all directions, at flashes, at shouts, by the burning of the flares, by the coloured lights of the Turk officers, and by the gleams of the shells on our right. There were 9,000 Turks in the first line, 12,000 more behind them. They advanced, yelling for God and Enver Pasha, amid the roar of every gun and rifle in range. They broke through the French, were held, then driven back, then came again, bore everything before them, and then met the British supports, and went no farther. Our supports charged the Turks and beat them back; at dawn our entire line advanced and beat them back in a rout, till their machine guns stopped us.

Upon many of the dead Turks in front of the French and English trenches were copies of an address issued by a German officer, one Van Zowenstern, calling on the Turks to destroy the enemy, since their only hope of salvation was to win the battle or die in the attempt. On some bodies were other orders, for the Mahometan priests to encourage the men to advance, for officers to shoot those soldiers who hung back, and for prisoners to be left with the reserves, not taken to the rear. In this early part of the campaign there were many German officers in the Turkish army. In these early night attacks they endeavoured to confuse our men by shouting orders to them in English. One, on the day of the landing, walked up to one of the trenches of the 29th Division, and cried out: "Surrender, you English, we ten to one." "He was thereupon hit on the head with a spade by a man who was improving his trench with it."

This battle never ceased for five days. The artillery was never silent. Our men were shelled, sniped, and shrapnelled every day and all day long, and at night the Turks attacked with the bayonet. By the evening of the 5th of May the 29th Division, which had won the end of the Peninsula, had been reduced by one-half and its officers by two-thirds. The proportion of officers to men in a British battalion is as one to thirty-seven, but in the list of killed the proportion was as one to eleven. The officers of that wonderful company poured out their lives like water; they brought their weary men forward hour after hour in all that sleepless ten days, and at the end led them on once more in the great attack of the 6th–8th of May.

This attack was designed to push the Allied lines farther forward into the Peninsula, so as to win a little more ground, and ease the growing congestion on the beaches near Cape Helles. The main Turkish position lay on and about the hump of Achi Baba, and on the high ground stretching down from it. It was hoped that even if Achi Baba could not be carried, the ground below him, including the village of Krithia, might be taken. The movement was to be a general advance, with the French on the right attacking the high ground nearer to the Straits, the 29th Division on the left, between the French and the sea, attacking the slowly sloping ground which leads past Krithia up to Achi Baba. Krithia stands high upon the slope, among orchards and gardens, and makes a good artillery target; but the slope on which it stands, being much broken, covered with dense scrub (some of it thorny) and with clumps of trees, is excellent for defence. The Turks had protected that square mile of ground with many machine guns and trenches so skilfully concealed that they could not be seen either from close in front or from aeroplanes. The French line of attack was over ground equally difficult, but steeper, and therefore giving more "dead ground," or patches upon which no direct fire can be turned by the defence. The line of battle from the French right to the English left stretched right across the Peninsula with a front (owing to bends and salients) of about five miles. It was nearly everywhere commanded by the guns of Achi Baba, and in certain places the enemy batteries on the Turk left, near the Straits, could enfilade it. Our men were weary, but the Turks were expecting strong reinforcements: the attack could not be delayed.

Few people who have not seen modern war can understand what it is like. They look at a map, which is a small flat surface, and find it difficult to believe that a body of men could have had difficulty in passing from one point upon it to another. They think that they themselves would have found no difficulty, that they would not have been weary nor thirsty, the distance demanded of them being only a mile, possibly a mile and a quarter, and the reward a very great one. They think that troops who failed to pass across that mile must have been in some way wanting, and that had *they* been there, either in command or in the attack, the results would have been different.

One can only answer, that in modern war it is not easy to carry a well-defended site by direct attack. In modern war you may not know, till fire breaks out upon you, where the defence, which you have to attack, is hidden. You may not know (in darkness, in a strange land) more than vaguely which is your "front," and you may pass by your enemy, or over him, or under him without seeing him. You may not see your enemy at all. You may fight for days and never see an enemy. In modern war troops see no enemy till he attacks them; then, in most cases if they are well-entrenched with many guns behind them, they can destroy him.

The Allied officers, looking through their field-glasses at the ground to be attacked, could see only rough, sloping ground, much gullied, much overgrown, with a few clumps of trees, a few walls, orchards, and houses, but no guns, no trenches, no enemy. Aeroplanes scouting over the Turks could see men but not the trenches nor the guns; they could only report that they suspected them to be in such a place. Sometimes in the mornings men would notice that the earth was turned newly on some bare patch on the hill, but none could be sure that this digging was not a ruse to draw fire. The trenches were hidden cunningly, often with a head cover of planks so strewn with earth and planted with scrub as to be indistinguishable from the ground about. The big guns were coloured cunningly, like a bird or snake upon the ground. From above in an aeroplane an observer could not pick them out so as to be certain, if they were not in action at the time. Brave men scouting forward at night to reconnoitre brought back some information, but not more than enough to show that the Turks were there in force. No man in the Allied army expected less than a desperate battle; no officer in the world could have made it anything but that, with all the odds against us. Nothing could be done, but cover the Turk position with the fire of every gun on shore or in the ships, and then send the men forward, to creep or dash as far as they could go, and then dig themselves in.

Let the reader imagine himself to be facing three miles of any very rough broken sloping ground known to him, ground for the most part gorse-, thyme-, and scrub-covered, being poor soil, but in some places beautiful with flowers (especially "a spiked yellow flower with a whitish leaf"), and in others green from cultivation. Let him say to himself that he and an army of his friends are about to advance up the slope towards the top, and that as they will be advancing in a line along the whole length of the three miles, he will only see the advance of those comparatively near to him, since folds or dips in the ground will hide the others. Let him, before he advances, look earnestly along the line of the hill, as it shows up clear, in blazing sunlight, only a mile from him, to see his tactical objective, one little clump of pines three hundred yards away, across what seem to be fields. Let him see in the whole length of the hill no single human being – nothing but scrub, earth, a few scattered buildings of the Levantine type (dirty white with roofs of dirty red), and some patches of dark Scotch pine, growing, as the pine loves, on bleak crests. Let him imagine himself to be more weary than he has ever been in his life before, and dirtier than he has ever believed it possible to be, and parched with thirst, nervous, wild-eyed, and rather lousy. Let him think that he has not slept for more than a few minutes together for eleven days and nights, and that in all his waking hours he has been fighting for his life, often hand to hand in the dark with a fierce enemy, and that after each fight he has had to dig himself a hole in the ground, often with his hands, and then walk three or four roadless miles to bring up heavy boxes under fire. Let him think, too, that in all those eleven days he has never for an instant been out of the thunder of cannon, that waking or sleeping their devastating crash has been blasting the air across within a mile or two, and this from an artillery so terrible that each discharge beats, as it were, a wedge of shock between the skull-bone and the brain. Let him think, too, that never for an instant, in all that time, has he been free or even partly free from the peril of death in its most sudden and savage forms, and that hourly in all that time he has seen his friends blown to pieces at his side, or dismembered, or drowned, or driven mad, or stabbed, or sniped by some unseen stalker, or bombed in the dark sap with a handful of dynamite in a beef-tin, till their blood is caked upon his clothes and thick upon his face, and that he knows, as he stares at the hill, that in a few moments, more of that dwindling band, already too few, God knows how many too few, for the task to be done, will be gone the same way, and that he himself may reckon that he has done with life, tasted and spoken and loved his last, and that in a few minutes more he may be blasted dead, or lying bleeding in the scrub, with perhaps his face gone and a leg and an arm broken, unable to move but still alive, unable to drive away the flies or screen the ever-dropping rain, in a place where none will find him, or be able to help him – a place where he will die and rot and shrivel, till nothing is left of him but a few rags and a few remnants and a little identification disc flapping on his bones in the wind. Then let him hear the intermittent crash and rattle of the fire augment suddenly and awfully in a roaring, blasting roll, unspeakable and un-thinkable, while the air above, that has long been whining and whistling, becomes filled with the scream of shells passing like great cats of death in the air; let him see the slope of the hill vanish in a few moments into the white, yellow, and black smokes of great explosions shot with fire, and watch the lines of white puffs marking the hill in streaks where the shrapnel searches a suspected trench; and then, in the height of the tumult, when his brain is shaking in his head, let him pull himself together with his friends, and clamber up out of the trench, to go forward against an invisible enemy, safe in some unseen trench expecting him.

The 29th Division went forward under these conditions on the 6th of May. They dashed on, or crawled, for a few yards at a time, then dropped for a few instants before squirming on again. In such an advance men do not see the battlefield. They see the world as the rabbit sees it, crouching on the ground, just their own little patch. On broken ground like that, full of dips and rises, men may be able to see nothing but perhaps the ridge of a bank ten feet ahead, with the dust flying in spouts all along it, as bullets hit it, some thousand a minute, and looking back or to their flanks they may see no one but perhaps a few men of their own platoon lying tense but expectant, ready for the sign to advance, while the bullets pipe over them in a never-ending bird-like croon. They may be shut off by some all-important foot of ground from seeing how they are fronting, and from all knowledge of what the next platoon is doing or suffering. It may be quite certain death to peep over that foot of ground in order to find out, and while they wait for a few instants, shells may burst in their midst and destroy a half of them. Then the rest, nerving themselves, rush up the ridge, and fall in a line dead under machine gun fire. The supports come up, creeping over their corpses, get past the ridge, into scrub which some shell has set on fire. Men fall wounded in the fire, and the cartridges in their bandoliers explode and slowly kill them. The survivors crawl through the scrub, half choked, and come out on a field full of flowers tangled three feet high with strong barbed wire. They wait for a while, to try to make out where the enemy is. They may see nothing but the slope of the field running up to a skyline, and a flash of distant sea on a flank, but no sign of any enemy, only the crash of guns and the pipe and croon and spurt of bullets. Gathering themselves together, their brave men dash out to cut the wire, and are killed; others take their places, and are killed; others step out with too great a pride even to stoop, and pull up the supports of the wires and fling them down, and fall dead on top of them, having perhaps cleared a couple of yards. Then a couple of machine guns open on the survivors, and kill them all in thirty seconds, with the concentrated fire of a battalion.

The supports come up, and hear about the wire from some wounded man who has crawled back through the scrub. They send back word, "Held up by wire," and in time the message comes to the telephone which has just been blown to pieces by a shell. Presently, when the telephone is repaired, the message reaches the gunners, who fire high-explosive shells onto the wire, and onto the slopes where the machine guns may be hidden. Then the supports go on over the flowers, and are met midway by a concentrated fire of shells, shrapnel, machine guns, and rifles. Those who are not killed lie down among the flowers, and begin to scrape little heaps of earth with their hands to give protection to their heads. In the light sandy marl this does not take long, though many are blown to pieces or hit in the back as they scrape. As before, they cannot see how the rest of the attack is faring, nor even where the other platoons of the battalion are; they lie scraping in the roots of daffodils and lilies, while bullets sing and shriek a foot or two over their heads. A man peering from his place in the flowers may make out that the man next to him, some three yards away, is dead, and that the man beyond is praying, the man beyond him cursing, and the man beyond him out of his mind from nerves or thirst.

Long hours pass, but the air above them never ceases to cry like a live thing with bullets flying. Men are killed or maimed, and the wounded cry for water. Men get up to give them water, and are killed. Shells fall at regular intervals along the field. The waiting men count the seconds between the shells to check the precision of the battery's fire. Some of the bursts fling the blossoms and bulbs of flowers into the bodies of men, where they are found long afterwards by the X-rays. Bursts and roars of fire on either flank tell of some intense moment in other parts of the line. Every feeling of terror and mental anguish and anxiety goes through the mind of each man there, and is put down by resolve.

The supports come up, they rise with a cheer, and get out of the accursed flowers, into a gully where some men of their regiment are already lying dead. There is a little wood to their front; they make for that, and suddenly come upon a deep and narrow Turk trench full of men. This is their first sight of the enemy. They leap down into the trench, and fight hand to hand, kill and are killed, in the long grave already dug. They take the trench, but opening from the trench are saps, which the Turks still hold. Men are shot dead at these saps by Turk sharpshooters cunningly screened within them. Bullets fall in particular places in the trench from snipers hidden in the trees of the wood. The men send back for bombs; others try to find out where the rest of the battalion lies, or send word that from the noise of the fire there must be a battery of machine guns beyond the wood, if the guns would shell it.

Presently, before the bombs come, bombs begin to drop among them from the Turks. Creeping up, the men catch them in their hands before they explode, and fling them back so that they burst among the Turks. Some have their hands blown off, others their heads, in doing this, but the bloody game of catch goes on till no Turks are left in the sap, only a few wounded groaning men who slowly bleed to death there. After long hours the supports come up, and a storm of high-explosives searches the little wood, and then with a cheer the remnant goes forward out of the trench into the darkness of the pines. Fire opens on them from snipers in the trees and from machine guns everywhere; they drop and die, and the survivors see no enemy, only their friends falling and a place where no living thing can pass. Men find themselves suddenly alone, with all their friends dead, and no enemy in sight, but the rush of bullets filling the air. They go back to the trench, not afraid, but in a kind of maze, and as they take stock and count their strength there comes the roar of the Turkish war-cry, the drum-like proclamation of the faith, and the Turks come at them with the bayonet. Then that lonely remnant of a platoon stands to it with rapid fire, and the machine gun rattles like a motor bicycle, and some ribald or silly song goes up, and the Turks fail to get home, but die or waver and retreat, and are themselves charged as they turn. It is evening now; the day has passed in long hours of deep experience, and the men have made two hundred yards. They send back for supports and orders, link up, if they are lucky, with some other part of their battalion, whose adventures, fifty yards away, have been as intense, but wholly different, and prepare the Turk trench for the night. Presently word reaches them from some far-away headquarters (some dugout five hundred yards back, in what seems, by comparison, like peaceful England) that there are no supports, and that the orders are to hold the line at all costs and prepare for a fresh advance on the morrow. Darkness falls, and ammunition and water come up, and the stretcher-bearers hunt for the wounded by the groans, while the Turks search the entire field with shell to kill the supports which are not there. Some of the men in the trench creep out to their front, and are killed there as they fix a wire entanglement. The survivors make ready for the Turk attack, certain soon to come. There is no thought of sleep: it is too cold for sleep; the men shiver as they stare into the night. They take the coats of the dead, and try to get a little warmth. There is no moon, and the rain begins. The marl at the bottom of the trench is soon a sticky mud, and the one dry patch is continually being sniped. A few exhausted ones fall not into sleep, but into nervous dreams, full of twitches and cries, like dogs' nightmares, and away at sea some ship opens with her great guns at an unseen target up the hill. The terrific crashes shake the air; someone sees a movement in the grass and fires; others start up and fire. The whole irregular line starts up and fires, and machine guns rattle, the officers curse, and the guns behind, expecting an attack, send shells into the wood. Then slowly the fire drops and dies, and stray Turks, creeping up, fling bombs into the trench.

This kind of fighting, between isolated bodies of men advancing in a great concerted tactical movement stretching right across the Peninsula, went on throughout the 6th, the 7th, and the 8th of May, and ended on the evening of the 8th in a terrific onslaught of the whole line, covered by a great artillery. The final stage of the battle was a sight of stirring and awful beauty. The Allied line went forward steadily behind the moving barrier of the explosions of their shells. Every gun on both sides opened and maintained a fire dreadful to hear and see. Our men were fighting for a little patch of ground vital not so much to the success of the undertaking, the clearing of the Narrows, as to their existence on the Peninsula. In such a battle, each platoon, each section, each private soldier, influences the result, and "pays as current coin in that red purchase" as the

Brigadier. The working-parties on the beaches left their work (it is said) to watch and cheer that last advance. It was a day of the unmatchable clear Ægean spring. Samothrace and Eubœa were stretched out in the sunset like giants watching the chess, waiting, it seemed, almost like human things, as they had waited for the fall of Troy and the bale-fires of Agamemnon. Those watchers saw the dotted order of our advance stretching across the Peninsula, moving slowly forward, and halting and withering away, among fields of flowers of spring and the young corn that would never come to harvest. They saw the hump of Achi Baba flicker and burn and roll up to heaven in a swathe of blackness, and multitudinous brightness changing the face of the earth, and the dots of our line still coming, still moving forward, and halting and withering away, but still moving up among the flashes and the darkness, more men, and yet more men, from the fields of sacred France, from the darkness of Senegal, from sheep-runs at the ends of the earth, from blue-gum forests, and sunny islands, places of horses and good fellows, from Irish pastures and glens, and from many a Scotch and English city and village and quiet farm; they went on and they went on, up ridges blazing with explosion into the darkness of death. Sometimes, as the light failed, and peak after peak that had been burning against the sky grew rigid as the colour faded, the darkness of the great blasts hid sections of the line; but when the darkness cleared they were still there, line after line of dots, still more, still moving forward and halting and withering away, and others coming, and halting and withering away, and others following, as though those lines were not flesh and blood and breaking nerve, but some tide of the sea coming in waves that fell yet advanced, that broke a little farther, and gained some yard in breaking, and were then followed, and slowly grew, that halted and seemed to wither, and then gathered and went on, till night covered those moving dots, and the great slope was nothing but a blackness spangled with the flashes of awful fire.

What can be said of that advance? The French were on the right, the 29th Division on the left, some Australians and New Zealanders (brought down from Anzac) in support. It was their thirteenth day of continual battle, and who will ever write the story of even one half-hour of that thirteenth day? Who will ever know one-hundredth part of the deeds of heroism done in them, by platoons and sections and private soldiers, who offered their lives without a thought to help some other part of the line, who went out to cut wire, or brought up water and ammunition, or cheered on some bleeding remnant of a regiment, halting on that hill of death, and kept their faces to the shrapnel and the never-ceasing pelt of bullets as long as they had strength to go and light to see? They brought the line forward from a quarter of a mile to six hundred yards farther into the Peninsula; they dug in after dark on the line they had won, and for the next thirty-six hours they stood to arms to beat back the charges of the Turks, who felt themselves threatened at the heart.

Our army had won their hold upon the Peninsula. On the body of a dead Turk officer was a letter written the night before to his wife, a tender letter, filled mostly with personal matters. In it was the phrase, "These British are the finest fighters in the world. We have chosen the wrong friends."

IV

"So great is the heat that the dust rises." – *The Song of Roland.*

During the next three weeks the Allied troops made small advances in parts of the lines held by them at Anzac and Cape Helles. Fighting was continuous in both zones; there was always much (and sometimes intense) artillery fire. The Turks frequently attacked in force, sometimes in very great force, but were repulsed. Our efforts were usually concentrated on some redoubt, stronghold, or salient, in the nearer Turkish lines, the fire from which galled our trenches or threatened any possible advance. These posts were either heavily bombarded and then rushed under the cover of a *feu de barrage*, or carried by surprise attack. Great skill and much dashing courage were shown in these assaults. The emplacements of machine guns were seized and the guns destroyed, dangerous trenches or parts of trenches were carried and filled in, and many roosts or hiding-places of snipers were made untenable. These operations were on a small scale, and were designed to improve the position then held by us, rather than to carry the whole line farther up the Peninsula. Sometimes they failed, but by far the greater number succeeded, so that by these methods, eked out by ruses, mines, clever invention, and the most dare-devil bravery, parts of our lines were advanced by more than a hundred yards.

On the 4th of June a second great attack was made by the Allied troops near Cape Helles. Like the attack of the 6th–8th May, it was an advance on the whole line, from the Straits to the sea, against the enemy's front line trenches. As before, the French were on the right and the 29th Division on the left, but between them, in this advance, were the R.N. Division and the newly arrived 42nd Division. Our men advanced after a prolonged and terrible bombardment, which so broke down the Turk defence that the works were carried all along the line, except in one place, on the left of the French sector, and in one other place, on our own left, near the sea. Our advance, as before, varied in depth from a quarter of a mile to six hundred yards; all of it carried by a rush, in a short time, owing to the violence of the artillery preparation, though with heavy losses from shrapnel and machine gun fire. In this attack the 42nd or East Lancashire Division received its baptism of fire. Even these who had seen the men of the 29th Division in the battles for the landing admitted that "nothing could have been finer" than the extreme gallantry of these newly landed men. The Manchester Brigade and two companies of the 5th Lancashire Fusiliers advanced with the most glorious and dashing courage, routed the Turks, and carried both their lines of trenches. One battalion, the 6th, very nearly carried the village of Krithia; there was, in fact, no entrenched line between them and the top of Achi Baba.

But in this campaign we were to taste, and be upon the brink of, victory in every battle, yet have the prize dashed from us, by some failure elsewhere, each time. So, in this first rush, when, for the first time, our men felt that they, not the Turks, were the real attackers, the victory was not to remain with us. We had no high-explosive shell and not enough shrapnel shell to deny to the Turks the use of their superior numbers and to hold them in a beaten state. They rallied and made strong counter-attacks, especially upon a redoubt or earthwork-fortress called the "Haricot," on the left of the French sector, which the French had stormed an hour before and garrisoned with Senegalese troops. The Turks heavily shelled this work and then rushed it. The Senegalese could not hold it; the French could not support it; and the Turks won it. Unfortunately the Haricot enfiladed the lines we had won. In a little while the Turks developed from it a deadly enfilade fire upon the R.N. Division, which had won the Turk trenches to the west of it. The R.N. Division was forced to fall back, and in doing so uncovered the right of the brigade of Manchesters beyond it to the westward. The Manchesters were forced to give ground, and the French were unable to make a new attack upon the Haricot, so that by nightfall our position was less good than it had been at half-past twelve.

But for the fall of the Haricot, the day would have been a notable victory for ourselves. Still, over three miles of the Allied front our lines had been pushed forward from two hundred to four hundred yards. This, in modern war, is a big advance, but it brings upon the conquerors a very severe labour of digging. The trenches won from the defence have to be converted to the uses of the attack and linked up, by saps and communication trenches, with the works from which the attack advanced. All this labour had to be done by our men in the midst of bitter fighting, for the Turks fought hard to win back these trenches in many bloody counter-attacks, and (as always happened after each advance) outlying works and trenches, from which fire could be brought to bear upon the newly won ground, had to be carried, filled in, or blown up before the new line was secure.

A little after dawn on the 21st of June the French stormed and won the Haricot redoubt, and advanced the right of the Allied position by six hundred yards. The Turkish counter-attacks were bloodily defeated.

In the forenoon of the 28th of June the English divisions advanced the left of the Allied position by a full one thousand yards. This attack, which was one of the most successful of the campaign, was the first of which it could be said that it was a victory. Of course our presence upon the Peninsula was in itself a victory, but in this battle we were not trying to land nor to secure ourselves, but (for the first time) to force a decision. Three of our divisions challenged the greater part of the Turk army and beat it. And here, for the first time in the operations, we felt, what all our soldiers had expected, that want of fresh men in reserve to make a success decisive, which afterwards lost us the campaign.

Our enemies have often said that the English cannot plan nor execute an attack. In this battle of the 28th of June the attack was a perfect piece of planning and execution. Everything was exactly timed, everything worked smoothly. Ten thousand soldiers, not one of whom had had more than six months' training, advanced uphill after an artillery preparation and won two lines of elaborately fortified trenches, by the bayonet alone. Then, while these men consolidated and made good the ground which they had won, the artillery lengthened their fuses and bombarded the ground beyond them. When the artillery ceased, ten thousand fresh soldiers climbed out of the English lines, ran forward, leaped across the two lines of Turk trench already taken, and took three more lines of trench, each line a fortress in itself. Besides advancing our position a thousand yards, this attack forced back the right of the Turks from the sea, and won a strong position between the sea and Krithia, almost turning Achi Baba. But much more than this was achieved. The great triumph of the day was the certainty then acquired that the Turks were beaten, that they were no longer the fierce and ardent fighters who had rushed V beach in the dark, but a shaken company who had caught the habit of defeat and might break at any moment. They were beaten; we had beaten them at every point, and they knew that they were beaten. Every man in the French and British lines knew that the Turks were at the breaking-point. We had only to strike while the iron was hot to end them.

As happened afterwards, after the battle of August, we could not strike while the iron was hot; we had not the men nor the munitions. Had the fifty thousand men who came there in July and August but been there in June, our men could have kept on striking. But they were not there in June, and our victory of the 28th could not be followed up. More than a month passed before it could be followed up. During that month the Turks dug themselves new fortresses, brought up new guns, made new stores of ammunition, and remade their army. Their beaten troops were withdrawn and replaced by the very pick and flower of the Turkish Empire. When we attacked again we found a very different enemy; the iron was cold, and we had to begin again from the beginning.

Thirty-six hours after our June success, at midnight in the night of June 29th–30th, the Turks made a counter-attack, not at Cape Helles, where their men were shaken, but at Anzac, where perhaps they felt our menace more acutely. A large army of Turks, about 30,000 strong, ordered by Enver Pasha "to drive the foreigners into the sea or never to look upon his face again," attacked the Anzac position under cover of the fire of a great artillery. They were utterly defeated, with the loss of about a quarter of their strength, some seven to eight thousand killed and wounded.

All this fighting proved clearly that the Turks, with all their power of fresh men, their closeness to their reserves, and their superior positions, could not beat us from what we had secured, nor keep us from securing more. Our advance into the Peninsula, though slow and paid for with much life, was sure and becoming less slow. What we had won we had fought hard for and never ceased to fight hard for, but we had won it and could hold it, and with increasing speed add to it; and the Turks knew this as well as we did. But early in May something happened which had a profound result upon the course of the operations. It is necessary to write of it at length, if only to show the reader that this Dardanelles Campaign was not a war in itself, but a part of a war involving most of Europe and half of Asia, and that that being so, it was affected by events in other parts of the war, as deeply as it affected those parts in turn by its own events.

No one of the many who spoke to me about the campaign knew or understood that the campaign, as planned, was not to be solely a French and English venture, but (in its later stages) a double attack upon the Turkish power, by ourselves on the Peninsula and the Hellespont, and by the Russians on the shores of the Black Sea. The double attack, threatening Turkey at the heart, was designed to force the Turks to divide their strength, and, by causing uneasiness among the citizens, to keep in and about Constantinople a large army which might otherwise wreck our Mesopotamian expedition, threaten India and Egypt, and prevent the Grand Duke Nicholas from advancing from the Caucasus on Erzerum. But as the Polish campaign developed adversely to Russia it became clear that it would be impossible for her to give the assistance she had hoped.

Early in May, Sir Ian Hamilton learned that his advance, instead of being a part of a concerted scheme, was to be the only attack upon the Turks in that quarter, and that he would have to withstand the greater part of the Turkish army. This did not mean that the Turks could mass an overwhelming strength against any part of his positions, since in the narrow Peninsula there is not room for great numbers to manœuvre; but it meant that the Turks would have always within easy distance great reserves of fresh men to take the place of those exhausted, and that without a correspondingly great reserve we had little chance of decisive success.

This change in the strategical scheme was made after we were committed to the venture; it made a profound difference to our position. Unfortunately we were so deeply engaged in other theatres that it was impossible to change our plans as swiftly and as profoundly as our chances. The great reserve could not be sent when it became necessary, early in May, nor for more than two months. Until it came, it happened, time after time, that even when we fought and beat back the Turks they could be reinforced before we could. All through the campaign we fought them and beat them back, but always, on the day after the battle, they had a division of fresh men to put in to the defence, while we, who had suffered more, being the attackers, had but a handful with which to follow up the success.

People have said: "But you could have kept fresh divisions in reserve as easily as the Turks. Why did you not send more men, so as to have them ready to follow up a success?" I could never answer this question. It is the vital question. The cry for "fifty thousand more men and plenty of high-explosive" went up daily from every trench in Gallipoli, and we lost the campaign through not sending them in time. On the spot, of course, our Generals knew that war (like life) consists of a struggle with disadvantages, and their struggle with these was a memorable one. Only, when all was done, their situation remained that of the Frank rearguard in the "Song of Roland." In that poem the Franks could and did beat the Saracens, but the Saracens brought up another army before the Franks were reinforced. The Franks could and did beat that army, too, but the Saracens brought up another army before the Franks were reinforced. The Franks could and did beat that army, too, but then they were spent, and Roland had to sound his horn, and Charlemagne would not come to the summons of the horn, and the heroes were abandoned in the dolorous pass.

Summer came upon Gallipoli with a blinding heat only comparable to New York in July. The flowers which had been so gay with beauty in the Helles fields in April soon wilted to stalks. The great slope of Cape Helles took on a savage and African look of desolation. The air quivered over the cracking land. In the blueness of the heat haze the graceful, terrible hills looked even more gentle and beautiful than before; and one who was there said that "there were little birds that droned, rather like the English yellow-hammers." With the heat, which was a new experience to all the young English soldiers there, came a plague of flies beyond all record and belief. Men ate and drank flies; the filthy insects were every-where. The ground in places was so dark with them, that one could not be sure whether the patches were ground or flies. Our camps and trenches were kept clean; they were well-scavenged daily. But only a few yards away were the Turk trenches, which were invariably filthy: there the flies bred undisturbed, perhaps encouraged. There is a fine modern poem which speaks of the Indian sun in summer as "the blazing death star." Men in Gallipoli in the summer of 1915 learned to curse the sun as an enemy more cruel than the Turk. With the sun and the plague of flies came the torment of thirst, one of the greatest torments which life has the power to inflict.

At Cape Helles, in the summer, there was a shortage, but no great scarcity, of water, for the Turk wells supplied more than half the army, and less than half the water needed had to be brought from abroad. At Anzac, however, there was always a scarcity, for even in the spring not more than a third of the water needed could be drawn from wells. At first water could be found by digging shallow pans in the beach, but this method failed when the heats began. Two-thirds (or more) of the water needed at Anzac had always to be brought from abroad, and to bring this two-thirds regularly and land it and store it under shellfire was a difficult task. "When operations were on," as in the August battle, the difficulty of distribution was added to the other difficulties, and then, indeed, want of water brought our troops to death's door. At Anzac, "when operations were on," even in the intensest heat the average ration of water for all purposes was, perhaps, at most, a pint and a half, sometimes only a pint. And though this extremity was as a rule only reached "when operations were on," that is, when there was heavy fighting, then the need was greatest.

In peace, in comfortable homes and in cool weather, civilized people need or consume a little less than three pints of liquid in each day. In hot weather and when doing severe bodily labour they need more, perhaps half a gallon in the day. Thirst, which most of us know solely as a pleasant zest to drinking, soon becomes a hardship, then, in an hour, an obsession, and by high noon a madness, to those who toil in the sun with nothing to drink. Possibly to most of the many thousands who were in the Peninsula last summer the real enemies were not the Turks, but the sun in heaven, shaking "the pestilence of his light," and thirst that withered the heart and cracked the tongue.

Some have said to me: "Yes, but the Turks must have suffered, too, just as much, in that waterless ground." It is not so. The Turks at Cape Helles held the wells at Krithia; inland from Anzac they held the wells near Lonesome Pine and Koja Dere. They had other wells at Maidos and Gallipoli. They had always more water than we, and (what is more) the certainty of it. Most of them came from lands with little water and great heat, ten (or more) degrees farther to the south than any part of England. Heat and thirst were old enemies to them; they were tempered to them. Our men had to serve an apprenticeship to them, and pay for what they learned in bodily hardship. Not that our men minded hardship. They did not; they were volunteers who had chosen their fate and were there of their own choice, and no army in the world has ever faced suffering more cheerily. But this hardship of thirst was a weight upon them throughout the summer; like malaria, it did not kill, but it lowered all vitality. It halved the possible effort of men always too few for the work in hand. Let it now double the honour paid to them.

In the sandy soil of the Peninsula were many minute amœbæ, which played their part in the summer suffering. In the winds of the great droughts of July and August the dust blew about our positions like smoke from burning hills. It fell into food and water, and was eaten and drunk (like the flies) at each meal. Within the human body the amœbæ of the sand set up symptoms like those of dysentery, as a rule slightly less severe than the true dysentery of camps. After July nearly every man in our army in Gallipoli suffered from this evil. Like the thirst, it lowered more vitality than it destroyed. Many died, it is true, but then nearly all were ill; it was the universal sickness, not the occasional death, that mattered.

Pass now to the position of affairs at the end of June. We were left to our own strength in this struggle. The Turks were shaken; it was vital to our chances to attack again before they recovered. We had not the men to attack again, but they were coming, and were due in a few weeks' time. While they were on their way the question how to use them was considered.

As the army's task was to help the fleet through the Narrows, it had to operate in the south-western portion of the Peninsula. Further progress against Achi Baba in the Helles sector was hardly possible; for the Turks had added too greatly to their trenches there since the attacks of April and May. Operations on the Asian coast were hardly possible without a second army; operations against Bulair were not likely to help the fleet. Operations in the Anzac sector offered better chances of success. It was hoped that a thrust south-eastward from Anzac might bring our men across to the Narrows or to the top of the ridges which command the road to Constantinople. It was reasonable to think that such a thrust; backed up by a new landing in force to the north, in Suvla Bay, might turn the Turkish right and destroy it. If the men at Helles attacked, to contain the Turks in the south, and the men on the right of Anzac attacked, to hold the Turks at Anzac, it was possible that men on the left of Anzac, backed up by a new force marching from Suvla, might give a decisive blow. The Turk position on the Peninsula roughly formed a letter L. The plan (as it shaped) was to attack the horizontal line at Cape Helles, press the centre of the vertical line at Anzac, and bend back, crumple, and break the top of the vertical line between the Anzac position and Suvla. At the same time Suvla Bay was to be seized and prepared as a harbour at which supplies might be landed, even in the stormy season.

Some soldier has said, that "the simple thing is the difficult thing." The idea seems simple to us, because the difficulty has been cleared away for us by another person's hard thought. Such a scheme of battle, difficult to think out in the strain of holding on and under the temptation to go slowly, improving what was held, was also difficult to execute. Very few of the great battles of history, not even those in Russia, in Manchuria, and in the Virginian Wilderness have been fought on such difficult ground, under such difficult conditions.

The chosen battlefield (the south-western end of the Peninsula) has already been described; the greater part of it consists of the Cape Helles and Anzac positions, but the vital or decisive point, where, if all went well, the Turk right was to be bent back, broken and routed, lies to the north of Anzac, on the spurs and outlying bastions of Sari Bair.

Suvla Bay, where the new landing was to take place, lies three miles to the north of Anzac. It is a broad, rather shallow, semicircular bay, open to the west and south-west, with a partly practicable beach, some of it (the southern part) fairly flat and sandy, the rest steepish and rocky, though broken by creeks. Above it, one on the north, one on the south horn of the bay, rise two small low knolls or hillocks known as Ghazi Baba and Lala Baba, the latter a clearly marked tactical feature. To the north, beyond the horn of the bay, the coast is high, steep-to sandy cliff, broken with gullies and washed by deep water; but to the south, all the way to Anzac, the coast is a flat, narrow, almost straight sweep of sandy shore shutting a salt marsh and a couple of miles of lowland from the sea; it is a lagoon beach of the common type, with the usual feature of shallow water in the sea that washes it. The northern half of this beach is known as Beach C, the southern as Beach B.

Viewed from the sea, the coast chosen for the new landing seems comparatively flat and gentle, seemingly, though not really, easy to land upon, but with no good military position near it. It looks as though once, long ago, the sea had thrust far inland there, in a big bay or harbour stretching from the high ground to the north of Suvla to the left of the Anzac position. This bay, if it ever existed, must have been four miles long and four miles across, a very noble space of water, ringed by big, broken, precipitous hills, into which it thrust in innumerable creeks and combes. Then (possibly), in the course of ages, silt brought down by the torrents choked the bay, and pushed the sea farther and farther back, till nothing remained of the harbour but the existing Suvla Bay and the salt marsh (dry in summer). The hills ringing Suvla Bay and this flat or slightly rising expanse, which may once have been a part of it, stand (to the fancy) like a rank that has beaten back an attack. They are high and proud to the north; they stand in groups in the centre; but to the south, where they link onto the broken cliffs of the Anzac position, they are heaped in tumbling, precipitous, disordered bulges of hill, cut by every kind of cleft and crumpled into every kind of fold, as though the dry land had there been put to it to keep out the sea. These hills are the scene of the bitterest fighting of the battle.

Although these hills in the Suvla district stand in a rank, yet in the centre of the rank there are two gaps where the ancient harbour of our fancy thrusts creeks far inland. These gaps or creeks open a little to the south of the north and south limits of Suvla Bay. They are watered, culti-vated valleys with roads or tracks in them. In the northern valley is a village of some sixty houses, called Anafarta Sagir, or Little Anafarta. In the southern valley is a rather larger village of some ninety houses, called Biyuk Anafarta, or Great Anafarta. The valleys are called after these villages.

Between these valleys is a big blunt-headed jut or promontory of higher ground, which thrusts out towards the bay. At the Suvla end of this jut, about one thousand yards from the bight of the Salt Marsh, it shoots up in three peaks or top-knots, two of them united in the lump called Chocolate Hill, the other known as Scimitar Hill or Hill 70; all, roughly, one hundred and fifty feet high. About a mile directly inland from Chocolate Hill is a peak of about twice the height, called Ismail Oglu Tepe, an abrupt and savage heap of cliff, dented with chasms, harshly scarped at the top, and covered with dense thorn scrub. This hill is the southern-most feature in the northern half of the battlefield. The valley of Great Anafarta, which runs east and west below it, cuts the battlefield in two.

The southern side of the Great Anafarta valley is just that disarrange-ment of precipitous bulged hill which rises and falls in crags, peaks, and gullies all the way from the valley to Anzac. Few parts of the earth can be more broken and disjointed than this mass of precipice, combes, and ravines. A savage climate has dealt with it since the beginning of time, with great heats, frosts, and torrents. It is not so much a ridge or chain of hills as the manifold outlying bastions and buttresses of Sari Bair, from which they are built out in craggy bulges parted by ravines. It may be said that Sari Bair begins at Gaba Tepe (to the south of the Anzac position), and stretches thence north-easterly towards Great Anafarta in a rolling and confused five miles of hill that has all the features of a mountain. It is not high. Its peaks range from about two hundred and fifty to six hundred feet; its chief peak (Koja Chemen Tepe) is a little more than nine hundred feet. Nearly all of it is trackless, waterless, and confused, densely covered with scrub (sometimes with forest), littered with rocks, an untamed savage country. The south-western half of it made the Anzac position; the north-eastern and higher half was the prize to be fought for.

It is the watershed of that part of the Peninsula. The gullies on its south side drain down to the Hellespont; those upon its north side drain to the flat land which may once have been submerged as a part of Suvla Bay. These northern gullies are great, savage, irregular gashes or glens running westerly or north-westerly from the hill bastions. Three of them, the three nearest to the northern end of the Anzac position, may be mentioned by name: Sazli Beit Dere, Chailak Dere, and Aghyl Dere. The word Dere means watercourse; but all three were bone dry in August when the battle was fought. It must be remembered that in the trackless Peninsula a watercourse of this kind is the nearest approach to a road, and (to a mili-tary force) the nearest approach to a covered way. All these three Deres lead up the heart of the hills to those highlands of Sari Bair where we wished to plant ourselves. From the top of Sari Bair one can look down on the whole Turkish position facing Anzac, and see that position not only dominated, but turned and taken in reverse. One can see, only three miles away, the only road to Constantinople, and, five miles away, the little port of Maidos near the Narrows. To us the taking of Sari Bair meant the closing of that road to the passing of Turk reinforcements and the opening of the Narrows to the fleet. It meant victory, and the begin-ning of the end of this great war, with home and leisure for life again, and all that peace means. Knowing this, our soldiers made a great struggle for Sari Bair, but Fate turned the lot against them. Sari was not to be an English hill, though the flowers on her sides will grow out of English dust forever. Those who lie there thought, as they fell, that over their bodies our race would pass to victory. It may be that their spirits linger there at this moment, waiting for the English bugles and the English singing, and the sound of the English ships passing up the Hellespont.

Among her tumble of hills, from the Anzac position to Great Anafarta, Sari Bair thrusts out several knolls, peaks, and commanding heights. Within the Anzac position is the little plateau of Lone or Lonesome Pine, to be described later. Farther to the north-east are the heights known as Baby 700 and Battleship Hill, and beyond these, still farther to the north-east, the steep peak of Chunuk Bair. All of these before this battle were held by the Turks, whose trenches defended them. Lone Pine is about four hundred feet high, the others rather more, slowly rising as they go north-east, but keeping to about the height of the English Chilterns. Chunuk Bair, the highest of these, is about seven hundred and fifty feet. Beyond Chunuk, half a mile farther to the north-east, is Hill Q, and beyond Hill Q a very steep, deep gully, above which rises the beautiful peak, the summit of Sari, known as Koja Chemen Tepe. One or two Irish hills in the wilder parts of Antrim are like this peak, though less fleeced with brush. In height, as I have said, it is a little more than nine hundred feet, or about the height of our Bredon Hill. One point about it may be noted. It thrusts out a great spur or claw for rather more than a mile due north; this spur, which is much gullied, is called Abd-el-Rahman Bair.

For the moment Chunuk Bair is the most important point to remember, because –

(a) It was the extreme right of the prepared Turk position.
(b) The three Deres previously mentioned have their sources at its foot and start there, like three roads starting from the walls of a city on their way to the sea. They lead past the hills known as Table Top and Rhododendron Spur. Close to their beginnings, at the foot of Chunuk, is a building known as the Farm, round which the fighting was very fierce.

The "idea" or purpose of the battle was "to endeavour to seize a position across the Gallipoli Peninsula from Gaba Tepe to Maidos, with a protected line of supply from Suvla Bay."

The plan of the attack was, that a strong force in Anzac should endeavour to throw back the right wing of the Turks, drive them south towards Kilid Bahr, and thus secure a position commanding the narrow part of the Peninsula.

Meanwhile a large body of troops should secure Suvla, and another large body, landing at Suvla, should clear away any Turkish forces on the hills between the Anafarta valleys, and then help the attacking force from Anzac by storming Sari Bair from the north and west.

The 6th of August was fixed for the first day of the attack from Anzac;

the landing at Suvla was to take place during the dark hours of the night of the 6th–7th. "The 6th was both the earliest and the latest date possible for the battle – the earliest, because it was the first by which the main part of the reinforcements would be ready; the latest, because of the moon." Both in the preparation and the surprise of this attack dark nights were essential.

Sir Ian Hamilton's despatch (reprinted from the *London Gazette* of Tuesday, the 4th of January, 1916) shows that this battle of the 6th to 10th August was perhaps the strangest and most difficult battle ever planned by mortal General. It was to be a triple battle, fought by three separated armies, not in direct communication with each other. There was no place from which the battle, as a whole, could be controlled nearer than the island of Imbros (fourteen miles from any part of the Peninsula), to which telegraphic cables led from Anzac and Cape Helles. The left wing of our army, designed for the landing at Suvla, was not only not landed, when the battle began, but not concentrated. There was no adjacent subsidiary base big enough (or nearly big enough) to hold it. "On the day before the battle, part were at Imbros, part at Mudros, and part at Mitylene, . . . separated respectively by fourteen, sixty, and one hundred and twenty miles of sea from the arena into which they were simultaneously to appear." The vital part of the fight was to be fought by troops from Anzac. The Anzac position was an open book to every Turk aeroplane and every observer on Sari Bair. The reinforcements for this part of the battle had to be landed in the dark, some days before the battle, and kept hidden underground, during daylight, so that the Turks should not see them and suspect what was being planned.

In all wars, but especially in modern wars, great tactical combinations have been betrayed by very little things. In war, as in life, the unusual thing, however little, betrays the unusual thing, however great. An odd bit of paper round some cigars betrayed the hopes of the American Secession; some litter in the sea told Nelson where the French fleet was; one man rising up in the grass by a roadside saved the wealth of Peru from the hands of Drake. The Turks were always expecting an attack from Anzac. It is not too much to say that they searched the Anzac position hourly for the certain signs of an attack, reinforcements, and supplies. They had not even to search the whole position for these signs, since there was only one place (towards Fisherman's Hut) where they could be put. If they had suspected that men and stores were being landed, they would have guessed at once that a thrust was to be made, and our attacks upon their flanks would have met with a prepared defence.

It was vital to our chance of success that nothing unusual, however little, should be visible in Anzac from the Turk positions during the days before the battle. One man staring up at an aeroplane would have been evidence enough to a quick observer that there was a newcomer on the scene. One new water-tank, one new gun, one mule not yet quiet from the shock of landing, might have betrayed all the adventure. Very nearly thirty thousand men, one whole division and one brigade of English soldiers, and a brigade of Gurkhas, with their guns and stores, had to be landed unobserved and hidden.

There was only one place in which they could be hidden, and that was under the ground. The Australians had to dig hiding-places for them before they came.

In this war of digging, the daily life in the trenches gives digging enough to every soldier. Men dig daily even if they do not fight. At Anzac in July the Australians had a double share of digging – their daily share in the front lines, and when that was finished their nightly share, preparing cover for the new troops. During the nights of the latter half of July the Australians at Anzac dug, roofed, and covered not less than twenty miles of dugouts. All of this work was done in their sleep time, after the normal day's work of fighting, digging, and carrying up stores. Besides digging these hiding-places they carried up, fixed, hid, and filled the water-tanks which were to supply the newcomers.

On the night of the 3rd of August, when the landing of the new men began, the work was doubled. Everybody who could be spared from the front trenches went to the piers to help to land, carry inland, and hide the guns, stores, carts, and animals coming ashore. The nights, though lengthening, were still summer nights. There were seven hours of semi-darkness in which to cover up all traces of what came ashore. The newcomers landed at the rate of about 1,500 an hour, during the nights of the 3rd, 4th, and 5th of August. During those nights the Australians landed, carried inland, and hid, not less than one thousand tons of shells, cartridges, and food, some hundreds of horses and mules, many guns, and two or three hundred water-carts and ammunition-carts. All night long, for those three nights, the Australians worked like schoolboys. Often, towards dawn, it was a race against time, but always at dawn the night's tally of new troops were in their billets, the new stores were under-ground, and the new horses hidden. When the morning aeroplanes came over, their observers saw nothing unusual in any part of Anzac. The half-naked men were going up and down the gullies, the wholly naked men were bathing in the sea; everything else was as it had always been, nor were any transports on the coast. For those three nights nearly all the Australians at Anzac gave up most of their sleep. They had begun the work by digging the cover; they took a personal pride and pleasure in playing the game of *cache-cache* to the end.

It is difficult to praise a feat of the kind, and still more difficult to make people understand what the work meant. Those smiling and glorious young giants thought little of it. They loved their chiefs and they liked the fun, and when praised for it looked away with a grin. The labour of the task can only be felt by those who have done hard manual work in hot climates. Digging is one of the hardest kinds of work, even when done in a garden with a fork. When done in a trench with a pick and shovel it is as hard work as threshing with a flail. Carrying heavy weights over uneven ground is harder work still; and to do either of these things on a salt-meat diet, with a scanty allowance of water, is very, very hard; but to do them at night, after a hard day's work, instead of sleeping, is hardest of all. Even farm-labourers would collapse and sailors mutiny when asked to do this last. It may be said that no one could have done this labour but splendid young men splendidly encouraged to do their best. Many of these same young men who had toiled thus almost without sleep for three days and nights fell in with the others and fought all through the battle.

But all this preparation was a setting of precedents and the doing of something new to war. Never before have 25,000 men been kept buried under an enemy's eye until the hour for the attack. Never before have two divisions of all arms been brought up punctually, by ship, over many miles of sea, from different ports, to land under fire, at an appointed time, to fulfil a great tactical scheme.

But all these difficulties were as nothing to the difficulty of making sure that the men fighting in the blinding heat of a Gallipoli August should have enough water to drink. Eighty tons of water a day does not seem very much. It had only to be brought five hundred miles, which does not seem very far, to those who in happy peace can telephone for eighty tons of anything to be sent five hundred miles to anywhere. But in war, weight, distance, and time become terrible and tragic things, involving the lives of armies. The water-supply of that far battlefield, indifferent as it was at the best, was a triumph of resolve and skill unequalled yet in war. It is said that Wellington boasted that, while Napoleon could handle men, he, Wellington, could feed them. Our naval officers can truly say that, while Sir Ian Hamilton can handle men, they can give them drink.

As to the enemy before the battle, it was estimated that (apart from the great strategical reserves within thirty or forty miles) there were 30,000 Turks in the vital part of the battlefield, to the north of Kilid Bahr. Twelve thousand of these were in the trenches opposite Anzac; most of the rest in the villages two or three miles to the south and south-east of Sari Bair. Three battalions were in the Anafarta villages, and one battalion was entrenched on Ismail Oglu Tepe; small outposts held the two Baba hillocks on the bay; and the land north of the bay was patrolled by mounted gendarmerie. These scattered troops on the Turk right had guns with them; it was not known how many. The beach of Suvla was known to be mined.

August began with calm weather. The scattered regiments of the divisions for Suvla, after some weeks of hard exercise ashore, were sent on board their transports. At a little before four o'clock on the afternoon of the 6th of August the 29th Division began the battle by an assault on the Turk positions below Krithia.

V

Roland put the horn to his mouth, gripped it hard, and with great heart blew it. The hills were high, and the sound went very far: thirty leagues wide they heard it echo. Charles heard it and all his comrades; so the King said: "Our men are fighting." Count Guenes answered: "If any other said that, I should call him a liar."

Count Roland, in pain and woe and great weakness, blew his horn. The bright blood was running from his mouth, and the temples of his brains were broken. But the noise of the horn was very great. Charles heard it as he was passing at the ports; Naimes heard it, the Franks listened to it. So the King said: "I hear the horn of Roland; he would never sound it if he were not fighting." Guenes answered: "There is no fighting. You are old and white and hoary. You are like a child when you say such things."

Count Roland's mouth was bleeding; the temples of his brain were broken. He blew his horn in weakness and pain. Charles heard it and his Franks heard it. So the King said: "That horn has long breath." Duke Naimes answered: "Roland is in trouble. He is fighting, on my conscience. Arm yourself. Cry your war-cry. Help the men of your house. You hear plainly that Roland is in trouble."

The Emperor made sound his horns. . . . All the barons of the army mounted their chargers. But what use was that? They had delayed too long. What use was that? It was worth nothing; they had stayed too long; they could not be in time.

Then Roland said: "Here we shall receive martyrdom, and now I know well that we have but a moment to live. But may all be thieves who do not sell themselves dearly first. Strike, knights, with your bright swords; so change your deaths and lives, that sweet France be not ashamed by us. When Charles comes into this field he shall see such discipline upon the Saracens that he shall not fail to bless us." – *The Song of Roland*.

The Cape Helles attack, designed to keep the Turks to the south of Kilid Bahr from reinforcing those near Anzac, became a very desperate struggle. The Turk trenches there were full of men, for the Turks had been preparing a strong attack upon ourselves, which we forestalled by a few hours. The severe fighting lasted for a week along the whole Cape

Helles front, but it was especially bloody and terrible in the centre, in a vineyard to the west of the Krithia road. It has often happened in war that some stubbornness in attack or defence has roused the same quality in the opposer, till the honour of the armies seems pledged to the taking or holding of one patch of ground, perhaps not vital to the battle. It may be that in war one resolute soul can bind the excited minds of multitudes in a kind of bloody mesmerism; but these strange things are not studied as they should be. Near Krithia, the battle, which began as a containing attack, a minor part of a great scheme, became a furious weeklong fight for this vineyard, a little patch of ground "two hundred yards long by a hundred yards broad."

From the 6th to 13th of August, the fight for this vineyard never ceased. Our Lancashire regiments won most of it at the first assault on the 6th. For the rest of the week they held it against all that the Turks could bring against them. It was not a battle in the military textbook sense: it was a fight man to man, between two enemies whose blood was up. It was a weeklong cursing and killing scrimmage, the men lying down to fire and rising up to fight with the bayonet, literally all day long, day after day, the two sides within easy bombing distance all the time. The Turks lost some thousands of men in their attacks upon this vineyard; after a week of fighting they rushed it in a night attack, were soon bombed out of it, and then gave up the struggle for it. This bitter fighting not only kept the Turks at Cape Helles from reinforcing those at Anzac: it caused important Turk reinforcements to be sent to the Helles sector.

Less than an hour after the 29th Division began the containing battle at Krithia, the Australians at Anzac began theirs. This, the attack on the Turk fort at Lone Pine, in the southern half of the Anzac front, was designed to keep large bodies of Turks from reinforcing their right, on Sari Bair, where the decisive blow was to be struck. It was a secondary operation, not the main thrust, but it was in itself important, since to those at Anzac the hill of Lone Pine was the gate into the narrowest part of the Peninsula, and through that gate, as the Turks very well-knew, a rush might be made from Anzac upon Maidos and the Narrows. Such a thrust from Lone Pine, turning all the Turkish works on the range of Sari Bair, was what the Turks expected and feared from us. They had shown us as much, quite plainly, all through the summer. Any movement, feint, or demonstration against Lone Pine brought up their reserves at once. It was the sensitive spot on their not too strong left wing. If we won through there, we had their main water-supply as an immediate prize, and no other position in front of us from which we could be held. Any strong attack there was therefore certain to contain fully half a division of the enemy.

The hill of Lone or Lonesome Pine is a little plateau less than four hundred feet high, running north-west by south-east, and measuring perhaps two hundred and fifty yards long by two hundred across. On its south-western side it drops down in gullies to a col or ridge, known as

Pine Ridge, which gradually declines away to the low ground near Gaba Tepe. On its north-eastern side it joins the high ground known as Johnston's Jolly, which was, alas, neither jolly nor Johnston's, but a strong part of the Turk position.

We already held a little of the Lone Pine plateau. Our trenches bulged out into it in a convexity or salient known as the Pimple; but the Turks held the greater part, and their trenches curved out the other way, in a mouth, concavity, or trap opening towards the Pimple as though ready to swallow it. The opposing lines of trenches ran from north to south across the plateau, with from fifty to a hundred yards between them. Both to the north and south of the plateau are deep gullies. Just beyond these gullies Turk trenches were so placed that the machine guns in them could sweep the whole plateau. The space between the Australian and Turk lines was fairly level hilltop, covered with thyme and short scrub.

For some days before the 6th of August the warships had been shelling the Turk position on Lone Pine to knock away the barbed wire in front of it. On the 5th, the Australian brigade told off for the attack, sharpened bayonets, and prepared their distinguishing marks of white bands for the left arms and white patches for the backs of their right shoulders. In the afternoon of the 6th, the shelling by the ships became more intense; at half-past four it quickened to a very heavy fire; at exactly half-past five it stopped suddenly, "the three short whistle-blasts sounded and were taken up along the line, our men cleared the parapet" in two waves on a front of about one hundred and sixty yards, "and attacked with vigour." The hilltop over which they charged was in a night of smoke and dust from the explosions of the shells, and into that night, already singing with enemy bullets, the Australians disappeared. They had not gone twenty yards before all that dark and blazing hilltop was filled with explosion and flying missiles from every enemy gun. One speaks of a hail of bullets, but no hail is like fire, no hail is a form of death crying aloud a note of death, no hail screams as it strikes a stone, or stops a strong man in his stride. Across that kind of hail the Australians charged on Lone Pine. "It was a grim kind of steeplechase," said one, "but we meant to get to Koja Dere." They reached the crumpled wire of the entanglement, and got through it to the parapet of the Turk trench, where they were held up. Those behind them at the Pimple, peering through the darkness to see if any had survived the rush, saw figures on the parados of the enemy's trench, and wondered what was happening. They sent forward the third wave, with one full company carrying picks and shovels, to make good what was won. The men of this third wave found what was happening.

The Turkish front line trench was not, like most trenches, an open ditch into which men could jump, but covered over along nearly all its length with blinders and beams of pinewood, heaped with sandbags, and in some places with a couple of feet of earth. Under this cover the Turks fired at our men through loopholes, often with their rifles touching their victims. Most of the Australians, after heaving in vain to get these blinders up, under a fire that grew hotter every instant, crossed them, got into the open communication trenches in the rear of the Turk line, and attacked through them; but some, working together, hove up a blinder or two, and down the gaps so made those brave men dropped themselves, to a bayonet fight like a rat fight in a sewer, with an enemy whom they could hardly see, in a narrow dark gash in the earth where they were, at first, as one to five or seven or ten.

More and more men dropped down or rushed in from the rear; the Turks, so penned in, fought hard, but could not beat back the attack. They surrendered, and were disarmed. The survivors were at least as many as their captors, who had too much to do at that time to send them to the rear, even if there had been a safe road by which to send them. They were jammed up there in the trenches with the Australians, packed man to man, suffering from their friends' fire and getting in the way.

The first thing to be done was to block up the communication trenches against the Turkish counter-attack. Every man carried a couple of sand-bags, and with these, breastworks and walls were built. Their work was done in a narrow, dark, sweltering tunnel, heaped with corpses and wounded, and crowded with prisoners who might at any moment have risen. Already the Turks had begun their counter-attacks. At every other moment a little rush of Turks came up the communication trenches, flung their bombs in the workers' faces, and were bayoneted as they threw. The trenches curved and zigzagged in the earth; the men in one section could neither see nor hear what the men in the nearest sections were doing. What went on under the ground there in the making good of those trenches will never be known. From half-past five till midnight every section of the line was searched by bombs and bullets, by stink-pots and sticks of dynamite, by gas-bombs and a falling tumult of shell and shrapnel, which only ceased to let some rush of Turks attack, with knives, grenades, and bayonets, hand to hand and body to body in a blackness like the darkness of a mine. At midnight the wounded were lying all over the trenches; the enemy dead were so thick that our men had to walk on them, and bombs were falling in such numbers that every foot in those galleries was stuck with human flesh. No man slept that night. At half-past seven next morning (the 7th) a small quantity of bread and tea was rushed across the plateau to the fighters, who had more than earned their breakfast. Turk shell had by this time blown up some of the head-cover, and some of the new communication trenches were still only a few feet deep. A Colonel, passing along one of them, told an officer that his section of the trench was too shallow. Half an hour later, in passing back, he found the officer and three men blown to pieces by a shell; in a few minutes more he was himself killed. At noon the bombing became so severe that some sections of the line were held only by one or two wounded men. At one o'clock the enemy attacked furiously with bomb and bayonet, in great force. They came on in a mass, in wave after wave, shoulder to shoulder, heads down, shouting the name of God. They rushed across the plateau, jumped into the trenches, and were mixed up with our men in a hand-to-hand fight, which lasted for five hours. Not many of them could join in the fight at one time, and not many of them went back to the Turk lines; but they killed many of our men, and when their last assault failed our prize was very weakly held. At half-past seven the survivors received a cheering (and truthful) message from the Brigadier, "that no fighters can surpass Australians," and almost with the message came another Turk assault, begun by bomb and shell and rifle fire, and followed by savage rushes with the bayonet, one of which got in, and did much slaughter. No man slept that night. The fight hardly slackened all through the night; at dawn the dead were lying three deep in every part of the line. Bombs fell every minute in some section of the line, and where the wide Turk trenches had been blasted open they were very destructive. The men were "extremely tired, but determined to hold on." They did hold on.

They held on for the next five days and nights, till Lone Pine was ours past question. For those five days and nights the fight for Lone Pine was one long personal scrimmage in the midst of explosion. For those five days and nights the Australians lived and ate and slept in that gallery of the mine of death, in a half-darkness lit by great glares, in filth, heat, and corpses, among rotting and dying and mutilated men, with death blasting at the doors only a few feet away, and intense and bloody fighting, hand to hand, with bombs, bayonets, and knives, for hours together by night and day. When the Turks gave up the struggle, the dead were five to the yard in that line of works; they were heaped in a kind of double wall all along the sides of the trench. Most of them were bodies of Turks, but among them were one-quarter of the total force which ran out from the Pimple on the evening of the 6th.

Like the fight for the vineyard near Krithia, this fight for Lone Pine kept large numbers of Turks from the vital part of the battlefield.

When the sun set upon this battle at Lone Pine on that first evening of the 6th of August, many thousands of brave men fell in for the main battle, which was to strew their glorious bodies in the chasms of the Sari Bair, where none but the crows would ever find them. They fell in at the appointed places in four columns, two to guard the flanks, two to attack. One attacking column, guarded and helped by the column on its right, was to move up the Chailak and Sazli Beit Deres to the storm of Chunuk Bair; the other attacking column, guarded and helped by the column on its left, was to move up the Aghyl Dere to the storm of Sari's peak of Koja Chemen Tepe. The outermost (left) guarding column (though it did not know it) was to link up with the force soon to land at Suvla.

They were going upon a night attack in a country known to be a wilderness, with neither water nor way in it. They had neither light nor guide, nor any exact knowledge of where the darkness would burst into a blaze from the Turk fire. Many armies have gone out into the darkness of a night adventure, but what army has gone out like this, from the hiding-places on a beach to the heart of unknown hills, to wander up crags under fire, to storm a fortress in the dawn? Even in Manchuria there were roads and the traces and the comforts of man. In this savagery there was nothing but the certainty of desolation, where the wounded would lie until they died and the dead be never buried.

Until this campaign the storm of Badajos was the most desperate duty ever given to British soldiers. The men in the forlorn hope of that storm marched to their position to the sound of fifes, "which filled the heart with a melting sweetness," and tuned that rough company to a kind of sacred devotion. No music played away the brave men from Anzac. They answered to their names in the dark, and moved off to take position for what they had to do. Men of many races were banded together there. There were Australians, English, Indians, Maoris and New Zealanders, made one by devotion to a cause, and all willing to die that so their comrades might see the dawn make a steel streak of the Hellespont from the peaked hill now black against the stars. Soon they had turned their backs on friendly little Anzac and the lights in the gullies, and were stepping out with the sea upon their left and the hills of their destiny upon their right, and the shells, star-lights, and battle of Lone Pine far away behind them. Before 9 p.m. the right covering column (of New Zealanders) was in position, ready to open up the Sazli Beit and Chailak Deres to their brothers, who were to storm Chunuk. Half an hour later, cunningly backed by the guns of the destroyer *Colne*, they rushed the Turk position, routed the garrison and its supports, and took the fort known as Old No. 3 Post. It was an immensely strong position, protected by barbed wire, shielded by shell-proof head-cover, and mined in front "with twenty-eight mines electrically connected to a first-rate firing apparatus within." *Sed nisi Dominus.*

This success opened up the Sazli Dere for nearly half of its length.

Inland from Old No. 3 Post, and some seven hundred yards from it, is a crag or precipice which looks like a round table, with a top projecting beyond its legs. This crag, known to our men as Table-Top, is a hill which few would climb for pleasure. Nearly all the last one hundred feet of the peak is precipice, such as no mountaineer would willingly climb without clear daylight and every possible precaution. It is a sort of skull of rock fallen down upon its body of rock, and the great rocky ribs heave out with gullies between them. The Table-Top, or plateau summit, was strongly entrenched and held by the Turks, whose communication trenches ran down the back of the hill to Rhododendron Spur.

While their comrades were rushing Old No. 3 Post, a party of New Zealanders marched to storm this natural fortress. The muscular part of the feat may be likened to the climbing of the Welsh Glyddyrs, the Irish Lurig, or the craggier parts of the American Palisades, in a moonless midnight, under a load of not less than thirty pounds. But the muscular effort was made much greater by the roughness of the unknown approaches, which led over glidders of loose stones into the densest of short, thick, intensely thorny scrub. The New Zealanders advanced under fire through this scrub, went up the rocks in a spirit which no crag could daunt, reached the Table-Top, rushed the Turk trenches, killed some Turks of the garrison, and captured the rest with all their stores.

This success opened up the remainder of the Sazli Beit Dere.

While these attacks were progressing, the remainder of the right covering column marched north to the Chailak Dere. A large body crossed this Dere and marched on, but the rest turned up the Dere, and soon came to a barbed wire entanglement which blocked the ravine. They had met the Turks' barbed wire before, on Anzac Day, and had won through it; but this wire in the Dere was new to their experience: it was meant rather as a permanent work than as an obstruction. It was secured to great balks or blinders of pine, six or eight feet high, which stood in a rank twenty or thirty deep right across the ravine. The wire, which crossed and criss-crossed between these balks, was as thick as a man's thumb and profusely barbed. Beyond it lay a flanking trench, held by a strong outpost of Turks, who at once opened fire. This, though not un-expected, was a difficult barrier to come upon in the darkness of a summer night, and here, as before, at the landing of the Worcester Regiment at W beach, men went forward quietly, without weapons, to cut the wire for the others. They were shot down, but others took their places, though the Turks, thirty steps away on the other side of the gully, had only to hold their rifles steady and pull their triggers to destroy them. This holding up in the darkness by an unseen hidden enemy and an obstacle which needed high-explosive shell in quantity caused heavy loss and great delay. For a time there was no getting through; but then, with the most desperate courage and devotion, a party of Engineers cleared the obstacle, the Turks were routed, and a path made for the attackers.

This success opened up the mouth of the Chailak Dere.

Meanwhile those who had marched across this Dere and gone on towards Suvla swung round to the right to clear the Turks from Bauchop's Hill, which overlooks the Chailak Dere from the north. Bauchop's Hill (a rough country even for Gallipoli) is cleft by not less than twenty great gullies, most of them forked, precipitous, overgrown, and heaped with rocks. The New Zealanders scrambled up it from the north, got into a maze of trenches, not strongly held, beat the Turks out of them, wandered south across the neck or ridge of the hill, discovering Turk trenches by their fire, and at last secured the whole hill.

This success, besides securing the Chailak Dere from any assault from the north, secured the south flank of the Aghyl Dere beyond it.

Meanwhile the left covering column (mainly Welshmen), which for some time had halted at Old No. 3 Post, waiting for the sound of battle to tell them that the Turks on Bauchop's Hill were engaged, marched boldly on the Aghyl Dere, crossed it in a rush, taking every Turk trench in the way, then stormed the Turk outpost on Damakjelik Bair, going on from trench to trench in the dark, guided by the flashes of the rifles, till the whole hill was theirs. This success opened up the Aghyl Dere to the attacking column.

As the troops drew their breath in the still night on the little hill which they had won, they heard about three miles away a noise of battle on the sea coast to their left. This noise was not the nightly "hate" of the monitors and destroyers, but an irregular and growing rifle fire. This, though they did not know it, was the beginning of the landing of the new divisions, with their 30,000 men, at Suvla Bay.

For the moment, Suvla was not the important point in the battle. The three Deres were the important points, for up the three Deres, now cleared of Turks, our attacking columns were advancing to the assault.

By this time, however, the Turks were roused throughout their line. All the Anzac position from Tasmania Post to Table-Top was a blaze of battle to contain them before our trenches; but they knew now that their right was threatened, and their reserves were hurrying out to meet us before we had gained the crests. Our right attacking column (of English and New Zealand troops) went up the Sazli Beit and Chailak Deres, deployed beyond Table-Top, and stormed Rhododendron Spur, fighting for their lives every inch of the way. The left column (mainly Indians and Australians) pressed up the Aghyl, into the stony clefts of its upper forks, and so, by rock, jungle, heart-breaking cliff and fissure, to the attack of Hill Q and the lower slopes of Sari. They, too, were fighting for their lives. Their advance was across a scrub peopled now by little clumps of marksmen firing from hiding. When they deployed out of the Deres, to take up their line of battle, they linked up with the right assaulting column, and formed with them a front of about a mile, stretching from the old Anzac position to within a mile of the crests which were the prize. By this time the night was over, day was breaking, the Turks were in force, and our attacking columns much exhausted, but there was still breath for a last effort. Now, with the breath, came a quick encouragement, for looking down from their hillsides, they could see Suvla Bay full of ships, the moving marks of boats, dotted specks of men on the sand-hills, and more ships on the sea marching like chariots to the cannon. In a flash, as happens when many minds are tense together, they realized the truth. A new landing was being made. All along the coast by the Bay the crackle and the flash of firing was moving from the sea, to show them that the landing was made good, and that the Turks were falling back. Hardening their hearts at this sight of help coming from the sea, the Australians and Sikhs, with the last of their strength, went at Koja Chemen Tepe, and the New Zealanders upon their right rose to the storm of Chunuk.

It was not to be. The guns behind them backed them. They did what mortal men could do, but they were worn out by the night's advance; they could not carry the two summits. They tried a second time to carry Chunuk; but they were too weary and the Turks in too great strength: they could not get to the top. But they held to what they had won; they

106

entrenched themselves on the new line, and there they stayed, making ready for the next attack.

Two or three have said to me: "They ought not to have been exhausted; none of them had marched five miles." It is difficult to answer such critics patiently, doubly difficult to persuade them, without showing them the five miles. There comes into my mind, as I write, the image of some hills in the West of Ireland, a graceful and austere range, not difficult to climb, seemingly, and not unlike these Gallipoli hills, in their look of lying down at rest. The way to those hills is over some miles of scattered limestone blocks, with gaps between them full of scrub, gorse, heather, dwarf-ash, and little hill-thorn, and the traveller proceeds, as the devil went through Athlone, "in standing lepps." This journey to the hills is the likest journey (known to me) to that of the assaulting columns. Like the devil in Athlone, the assaulting columns had often to advance "in standing lepps," but to them the standing lepp came as a solace, a rare, strange, and blessed respite, from forcing through scrub by main strength, or scaling a crag of rotten sandstone, in pitch-darkness, in the presence of an enemy. For an armed force to advance a mile an hour by day over such a country is not only good going, but a great achievement; to advance four miles in a night over such a country, fighting literally all the way, often hand to hand, and to feel the enemy's resistance stiffening and his reserves arriving as the strength fails and the ascent steepens, and yet to make an effort at the end, is a thing unknown in the history of war. And this first fourteen hours of exhausting physical labour was but the beginning. The troops, as they very well-knew, were to have two or three days more of the same toil before the battle could be ended, one way or the other. So after struggling for fourteen hours with every muscle in their bodies, over crags and down gullies in the never-ceasing peril of death, they halted in the blaze of noon and drew their breath. In the evening, as they hoped, the men from Suvla would join hands and go on to victory with them; they had fought the first stage of the battle, the next stage was to be decisive.

The heat of this noon of the 7th of August on those sandy hills was a scarcely bearable torment.

Meanwhile at Suvla, the left of the battle, the 11th Division had landed in the pitch-darkness, by wading ashore, in five feet of water, under rifle fire, onto beaches prepared with land mines. The first boat-loads lost many men from the mines and from the fire of snipers, who came right down to the beach in the darkness, and fired from the midst of our men. These snipers were soon bayoneted; our men formed for the assault in the dark, and stormed the Turk outpost on Lala Baba there and then. While Lala Baba was being cleared, other battalions moved north to clear the Turks from the neighbourhood of the beach on that side. The ground over which they had to move is a sand-dune land, covered with gorse and other scrub, most difficult to advance across in a wide extension. About half a mile from the beach the ground rises in a roll or whale-back, known on the battle plans as Hill 10. This hill is about three hundred yards long and thirty feet high. At this whale-back (which was entrenched) the Turks rallied on their supports; they had, perhaps, a couple of thousand men and (some say) a gun or two, and the dawn broke before they could be rushed. Their first shells upon our men set fire to the gorse, so that our advance against them was through a blazing common, in which many men who fell wounded were burnt to death or suffocated. The Turks, seeing the difficulties of the men in the fire, charged with the bayonet, but were themselves charged and driven back in great disorder; the fire spread to their hill, and burned them out of it. Our men then began to drive the Turks away from the high ridges to the north of Suvla. The 10th Division began to land while this fight was still in progress.

This early fighting had won for us a landing-place at Suvla, and had cleared the ground to the north of the Bay for the deployment for the next attack. This was to be a swinging round of two brigades to the storm of the hills directly to the east of the Salt Lake. These hills are the island-like, double-peaked Chocolate Hill (close to the Lake), and the much higher and more important hills of Scimitar Hill (or Hill 70) and Ismail Oglu Tepe (Hill 100) behind it. The brigade chosen for this attack were the 31st (consisting of Irish Regiments) belonging to the 10th Division, and the 32nd (consisting of Yorkshire and North of England Regiments) belonging to the 11th Division. The 32nd had been hotly engaged since the very early morning, the 31st were only just on shore. The storm was to be pushed from the north, and would, if successful, clear the way for the final thrust, the storm of Koja Chemen Tepe from the north-west.

This thrust from Suvla against Koja Chemen was designed to complete and make decisive the thrust already begun by the right and left attacking columns. The attack on Chocolate Hill, Scimitar Hill, and Ismail Oglu, was to make that thrust possible by destroying forever the power of the Turk to parry it. The Turk could only parry it by firing from those hills on the men making it. It was therefore necessary to seize those hills before the Turk could stop us. If the Turks seized those hills before us, or stopped us from seizing them, our troops could not march from Suvla to take part in the storm of Koja Chemen. If we seized them before the Turks, then the Turks could not stop us from crossing the valley to that storm. The first problem at Suvla, therefore, was not so much to win a battle as to win a race with the Turks for the possession of those hills; the winning of the battle could be arranged later. Our failure to win that race brought with it our loss of the battle. The next chapter in the story of the battle is simply a description of the losing of a race by loss of time.

Now the giving of praise or blame is always easy, but the under-standing of anything is difficult. The understanding of anything so vast, so confused, so full of contradiction, so dependent on little things (them-selves changing from minute to minute, the coward of a moment ago blazing out into a hero at the next turn) as a modern battle, is more than difficult. But some attempt must be made to understand how it came about that time was lost at Suvla between the landing, at midnight, on the 6th–7th of August, and the arrival of the Turks upon the hills, at midnight, on the 8th–9th.

In the first place, it should be said that the beaches of Suvla are not the beaches of seaside resorts, all pleasant, smooth sand and shingle. They are called beaches because they cannot well be called cliffs. They slope into the sea with some abruptness, in *pentes* of rock and tumbles of sand-dune difficult to land upon from boats. From them one climbs on to sand-dune into a sand-dune land, which is like nothing so much as a sea-marsh from which the water has receded. Walking on this soft sand is difficult: it is like walking in feathers; working, hauling, and carrying upon it is very difficult. Upon this coast and country, roadless, wharfless, beachless and unimproved, nearly 30,000 men landed in the first ten hours of the 7th of August. At 10 a.m. on that day, when the sun was in his stride, the difficulty of those beaches began to tell on those upon them. There had been sharp fighting on and near the beaches, and shells were still falling here and there in all the ground which we had won. On and near the beaches there was a congestion of a very hindering kind. With men coming ashore, shells bursting among them; mules landing, biting, kicking, shying, and stampeding; guns limbering up and trying to get out into position; more men coming ashore or seeking for the rest of their battalion in a crowd where all battalions looked alike; shouts, orders, and counter-orders; ammunition boxes being passed along; water-carts and transport being started for the firing-line; wounded coming down, or being helped down, or being loaded into lighters; doctors trying to clear the way for field dressing-stations, with every now and then a shell from Ismail sending the sand in clouds over corpses, wounded men, and fatigue parties; and a blinding August sun over all to exhaust and to madden: it was not possible to avoid congestion. This congestion was the first, but not the most fatal, cause of the loss of time.

Though the congestion was an evil in itself, its first evil effect was that it made it impossible to pass orders quickly from one part of the beach to another. In this first matter of the attack on the hills, the way had been opened for the assault by 10 a.m. at the latest; but to get through the confusion along the beaches (among battalions landing, forming, and defiling, and the waste of wounded momently increasing), to arrange for the assault and to pass the orders to the battalions named for the duty, took a great deal of time. It was nearly 1 p.m. when the 31st moved north from Lala Baba on their march round the head of the Salt Lake into position for the attack. The 32nd Brigade, having fought since dawn at Hill 10, was already to the north of the Salt Lake; but when (at about 3 p.m.) the 31st took position, facing south-east, with its right on the north-east corner of the Salt Lake, the 32nd was not upon its left ready to advance with it. Instead of that guard upon its left the 31st found a vigorous attack of Turks. More time was lost waiting for support to reach the left, and before it arrived word came that the attack upon the hills was to be postponed till after 5 p.m. Seeing the danger of delay, and that Chocolate Hill at least should be seized at once, the Brigadier-General (Hill) telephoned for supports and covering fire, held off the attack on his left with one battalion, and with the rest of his brigade started at once to take Chocolate Hill, cost what it might. The men went forward and stormed Chocolate Hill, the 7th Royal Dublin Fusiliers bearing the brunt of the storm.

At some not specified time, perhaps after this storm, in a general retirement of the Turks, Hill 70, or Scimitar Hill, was abandoned to us, and occupied by an English battalion.

During all this day of the 7th of August all our men suffered acutely from the great heat and from thirst. Several men went raving mad from thirst, others assaulted the water guards, pierced the supply hoses, or swam to the lighters to beg for water. Thirst in great heat is a cruel pain, and this (afflicting some regiments more than others) demoralized some and exhausted all. Efforts were made to send up and to find water; but the distribution system, beginning on a cluttered beach and ending in a rough, unknown country full of confused fighting and firing, without anything like a road, and much of it blazing or smouldering from the scrub fires, broke down, and most of the local wells, when discovered, were filled with corpses put there by the Turk garrison. Some unpolluted wells of drinkable, though brackish, water were found; but most of these were guarded by snipers, who shot at men going to them. Many men were killed thus and many more wounded, for the Turk snipers were good shots, cleverly hidden.

All through the day in the Suvla area thirst, due to the great heat, was another cause of loss of time in the fulfilment of that part of the tactical scheme; but it was not the final and fatal cause.

Chocolate Hill was taken by our men (now utterly exhausted by thirst and heat) just as darkness fell. They were unable to go on against Ismail Oglu Tepe. They made their dispositions for the night on the line they had won, sent back to the beaches for ammunition, food, and water, and tried to forget their thirst. They were in bad case, and still two miles from the Australians below Koja Chemen Tepe. Very late that night word reached them that the Turks were massed in a gully to their front, that no other enemy reserves were anywhere visible, and that the Turks had withdrawn their guns, fearing that they would be taken next morning. Before dawn on the all-important day of the 8th of August, our men at Suvla, after a night of thirst and sniping, stood to arms to help out the vital thrust of the battle.

Had time not been lost on the 7th, their task on the 8th would have been to cross the valley at dawn, join the Australians, and go with them up the spurs to victory, in a strength which the Turks could not oppose.

At dawn on the 8th their path to the valley was still barred by the un-captured Turk fort on Ismail; time had been lost; there could be no crossing the valley till Ismail was taken. There was still time to take it and cross the valley to the storm, but the sands were falling. Up on Chunuk already the battle had begun without them; no time was lost on Chunuk.

Up on Chunuk at that moment a very bitter battle was being fought. On the right, on Chunuk itself, the Gloucester and New Zealand Regiments were storming the hill; in the centre and on the left the Australians, English, and Indians were trying for Hill Q and the south of Koja Chemen. They had passed the night on the hillsides under a never-ceasing fire of shells and bullets; now, before dawn, they were making a terrible attempt. Those on Chunuk went up with a rush, pelted from in front and from both flanks by every engine of death. The Gloucesters were on the left and the New Zealanders on the right in this great assault. They deployed past the Farm, and then went on to the storm of a hill which rises some four hundred feet in as many yards. They were on the top by dawn; Chunuk Bair, the last step but one to victory, was ours, and remained ours all day, but at a cost which few successful attacks have ever known. By four o'clock that afternoon the New Zealanders had dwindled to three officers and fifty men, and the Gloucester battalion, having lost every officer and senior non-commissioned officer, was fighting under section leaders and privates. Still, their attack had succeeded; they were conquerors. In the centre the attack on Hill Q was less successful. There the English and Indian regiments, assaulting together, were held; the Turks were too strong. Our men got up to the top of the lower spurs, and there had to lie down and scrape cover, for there was no going farther. On the left of our attack the Australians tried to storm the Abd-el-Rahman Bair from the big gully of Asma Dere. They went up in the dark with Australian dash to a venture pretty desperate even for Gallipoli. The Turks held the high ground on both sides of the Asma gully, and were there in great force with many machine guns. The Australians were enfiladed, held in front and taken in reverse, and (as soon as it was light enough for the Turks to see) they suffered heavily. As one of the Australians has described it: "The 14th and 15th Battalions moved out in single file and deployed to the storm, and an advance was made under heavy rifle and machine gun fire. After the 15th Battalion had practically withered away, the 14th continued to advance, suffering heavily, and the Turks in great force. As we drove them back, they counter-attacked, several times. The battalion thus got very split up, and it is impossible to say exactly what happened."

It is now possible to say exactly that that 14th Battalion fought like heroes in little bands of wounded and weary men, and at last, with great reluctance, on repeated orders, fell back to the Asma Dere from which they had come, beating off enemy attacks all the way down the hill, and then held on against all that the Turk could do.

By noon, this assault, which would have been decisive had the men from Suvla been engaged with the Australians, was at an end. Its right had won Chunuk, and could just hold on to what it had won; its centre was held, and its left driven back. The fire upon all parts of the line was terrific; our men were lying (for the most part) in scratchings of cover, for they could not entrench under fire so terrible. Often in that rough-and-tumble country the snipers and bombers of both sides were within a few yards of each other, and in the roar and blast of the great battle were countless little battles, or duels, to the death, which made the ground red and set the heather on fire. Half of the hills of that accursed battlefield, too false of soil to be called crags and too savage with deso-lation to be called hills, such as feed the sheep and bees of England, were blazing in sweeps of flame, which cast up smoke to heaven, and swept in great swathes across the gullies. Shells from our ships were screaming and bursting among all that devil's playground; it was an anxious time for the Turks. Many a time throughout that day the Turkish officers must have looked down anxiously upon the Suvla plain to see if our men there were masters of Ismail and on the way to Koja Chemen. For the moment, as they saw, we were held; but not more than held. With a push from Suvla to help us, we could not be held. Our men on the hills, expecting that helping push, drew breath for a new assault.

It was now noon. The battle so far was in our favour. We had won ground, some of it an all-important ground, and for once we had the Turks with their backs against the wall and short of men. At Helles they were pressed, at Lone Pine they were threatened at the heart, under Koja Chemen the knife-point was touching the heart, and at Suvla was the new strength to drive the knife-point home and begin the end of the war. And the Turks could not stop that new strength. Their nearest important reserve of men was at Eski Keui, ten miles away by a road which could scarcely be called a goat track, and these reserves had been called on for the fight at Krithia, and still more for the two days of struggle at Lone Pine. All through that day of the 8th of August Fate waited to see what would happen between Suvla and Koja Chemen. She fingered with her dice, uncertain which side to favour; she waited to be courted by the one who wanted her. Eight hours of daylight had gone by, but there was still no moving forward from Suvla, to seize Ismail and pass from it across the valley to the storm. Noon passed into the afternoon, but there was still no movement. Four hours more went by, and now our aeroplanes brought word that the Turks near Suvla were moving back their guns by ox-teams, and that their foot were on the march, coming along their break-neck road, making perhaps a mile an hour, but marching and drawing steadily nearer to the threatened point. The living act of the battle was due at Ismail; from Ismail the last act, the toppling down of the Turk for ever among the bones of his victims and the ruin of his Ally, would have been prepared and assured. There was a desultory fire around Ismail and the smoke of scrub fires, which blazed and smouldered everywhere as far as the eye could see, but no roar and blaze and outcry of a meant attack. The battle hung fire on the left, the hours were passing, the Turks were coming. It was only five o'clock still; we had still seven hours or more. In the centre we had almost succeeded. We could hang on there and try again, there was still time. The chance which had been plainly ours was still an even chance. It was for the left to seize it for us: the battle waited for the left; the poor dying Gloucesters and Wellingtons hung on to Chunuk for it; the Gurkhas and English in the trampled corn-fields near the Farm died where they lay on the chance of it; the Australians on Abd-el-Rahman held steady in the hope of it, under a fire that filled the air.

If, as men say, the souls of a race, all the company of a nation's dead, rally to the living of their people in a time of storm, those fields of hell below Koja Chemen, won by the sweat and blood and dying agony of our thousands, must have answered with a ghostly muster of English souls in the afternoon of that 8th of August. There was the storm, there was the crisis, the one picked hour, to which this death and mangling and dying misery and exultation had led. Then was the hour for a casting off of self, and a setting aside of every pain and longing and sweet affection, a giving up of all that makes a man to the something which makes a race, and a going forward to death resolvedly to help out their brothers high up above in the shell bursts and the blazing gorse. Surely all through the 8th of August our unseen dead were on that field, blowing the horn of Roland, the unheard, unheeded horn, the horn of heroes in the dolorous pass, asking for the little that heroes ask, but asking in vain. If ever the great of England cried from beyond death to the living they cried then. *De ço qui calt. Demuret i unt trop.*

All through the morning of that day the Commander-in-Chief, on watch at his central station, had waited with growing anxiety for the advance from the Suvla beaches. Till the afternoon the critical thrust on Chunuk and the great Turk pressure at Lone Pine made it impossible for him to leave his post to intervene; but in the afternoon, seeing that neither wireless nor telephone messages could take the place of personal vision and appeal, he took the risk of cutting himself adrift from the main conflict, hurried to Suvla, landed, and found the great battle of the war, that should have brought peace to all that Eastern world, being lost by minutes before his eyes.

Only one question mattered then: "Was there still time?" Had the Turks made good their march and crowned those hills, or could our men forestall them? It was now doubtful, but the point was vital, not only to the battle, but to half the world in travail. It had to be put to the test. A hundred years ago, perhaps even fifty years ago, all could have been saved. Often in those old days a Commander-in-Chief could pull a battle out of the fire and bring halted or broken troops to victory. Then, by waving a sword, and shouting a personal appeal, the resolute soul could pluck the hearts of his men forward in a rush that nothing could stem.

So Wolfe took Quebec; so Desaix won Marengo; so Bonaparte swept the bridge at Lodi, and won at Arcola; so Cæsar overcame the Nervii in the terrible day, and wrecked the Republic at Pharsalia; so Sherman held the landing at Shiloh, and Farragut pitted his iron heart against iron ships at Fort Jackson; so Sir Ian Hamilton himself snatched victory from the hesitation at Elandslaagte. Then the individual's will could take instant effect. But then the individual's front was not a five-mile front of wilderness; the men were under his hand, within sight and sound of him, and not committed by order to another tactical project. There, at Suvla, was no chance for these heroic methods. Suvla was the modern battle-field, where nothing can be done quickly except the firing of a machine gun. On the modern field, especially on such a field as Suvla, where the troops were scattered in the wilderness, it may take several hours for an order to pass from one wing to the other. In this case it was not an order that was to pass, but a counter-order; the order had already gone, for an attack at dawn on the morrow.

All soldiers seem agreed, that even with authority to back it, a counter-order, on a modern battlefield, to urge forward halted troops, takes time to execute. Sir Ian Hamilton's determination to seize those hills could not spare the time; too much time had already gone. He ordered an advance at all costs with whatever troops were not scattered, but only four battalions could be found in any way ready to move. It was now 5 p.m.: there were perhaps three more hours of light. The four battalions were ordered to advance at once to make good what they could of the hills fronting the bay before the Turks forestalled them. At dawn the general attack, as already planned, was to support them. Unfortunately, the four battalions were less ready than was thought; they were not able to advance at once, nor for ten all-precious hours. They did not begin to advance till four o'clock the next morning (the 9th of August), and even then the rest of the division which was to support them was not in concert with them. They attacked the hills to the north of Anafarta Sagir, but they were now too late; the Turks were there before them, in great force, with their guns, and the thrust, which the day before could have been met by (at most) five Turk battalions without artillery, was now parried and thwarted. Presently the division attacked, with great gallantry, over burning scrub, seized Ismail, and was then checked and forced back to the Chocolate Hills. The left had failed. The main blow of the battle on Sari Bair was to have no support from Suvla.

The main blow was given, none the less, by the troops near Chunuk. Three columns were formed in the pitchy blackness of the very early morning of the 9th, two to seize and clear Chunuk and Hill Q, the third to pass from Hill Q on the wave of the assault to the peak of Koja Chemen. The first two columns were on the lower slopes of Chunuk and in the fields about the Farm, with orders to attack at dawn. The third column, consisting wholly of English troops, was not yet on the ground, but moving during the night up the Chailak Dere. The Dere was jammed

114

with pack-mules, ammunition, and wounded men; it was pitch-dark, and the column made bad going, and those leading it were doubtful of the way. Brigadier-General Baldwin, who commanded, left his brigade in the Dere, went to the headquarters of the first column, and brought back guides to lead his brigade into position. The guides led him on in the darkness, till they realized that they were lost. The Brigadier marched his men back to the Chailak, and then, still in pitch-darkness, up a nullah into the Aghyl Dere, and from there, in growing light, towards the Farm. This wandering in the darkness had tragical results.

At half-past four the guns from the ships and the army opened on Chunuk, and the columns moved to the assault. Soon the peaks of their objective were burning like the hills of hell to light them on their climb to death, and they went up in the half-darkness to the storm of a volcano spouting fire, driving the Turks before them. Some of the Warwicks and South Lancashires were the first upon the top of Chunuk; Major Allanson, leading the 6th Gurkhas, was the first on the ridge between Chunuk and Hill Q. Up on to the crests came the crowding sections; the Turks were breaking and falling back. Our men passed over the crests, and drove the Turks down on the other side. Victory was flooding up over Chunuk like the Severn tide; our men had scaled the scarp, and there below them lay the ditch, the long grey streak of the Hellespont, the victory and the reward of victory. The battle lay like a field ripe to the harvest: our men had but to put in the sickle. The third column was the sickle of that field, that third column which had lost its way in the blackness of the wilderness. Even now that third column was coming up the hill below; in a few minutes it would have been over the crest, going on to victory with the others. Then, at that moment of time, while our handful on the hilltop waited for the weight of the third column to make its thrust a death-blow, came the most tragical thing in all that tragical campaign.

It was barely daylight when our men won the hilltop. The story is that our men moving on the crest were mistaken for Turks, or (as some think) that there was some difference in the officers' watches – some few minutes' delay in beginning the fire of the guns, and therefore some few minutes' delay in stopping the bombardment, which had been ordered to continue upon the crest for three-quarters of an hour from 4.30 a.m. Whatever the cause, whether accident, fate, mistake, or the daily waste and confusion of battle, our own guns searched the hilltop for some minutes too long, and thinned out our brave handful with a terrible fire. They were caught in the open and destroyed there; the Turks charged back upon the remnant, and beat them off the greater part of the crest. Only a few minutes after this the third column came into action in support: too late.

The Turks beat them down the hill to the Farm, but could not drive the men of the first column from the south-western half of the top of the Chunuk. All through the hard and bloody day of the 9th of August the

Turks tried to carry this peak, but never quite could, though the day was one long succession of Turk attacks, the Turks fresh and in great strength, our men weary from three terrible days and nights and only a battalion strong, since the peak would not hold more. The New Zealanders and some of the 13th Division held that end of Chunuk. They were in trenches which had been dug under fire, partly by themselves, partly by the Turks. In most places these trenches were only scratchings in the ground, since neither side on that blazing and stricken hill could stand to dig. Here and there, in sheltered patches, the trenches were three feet deep, but whether three feet deep or three inches, all were badly sited, and in some parts had only ten yards' field of fire. In these pans or scratchings our men fought all day, often hand to hand, usually under a pelt of every kind of fire, often amid a shower of bombs, since the Turks could creep up under cover to within so few yards. Our men lost very heavily during the day, but at nightfall we still held the peak. After dark the 6th Loyal North Lancashires relieved the garrison, took over the trenches, did what they could to strengthen them, and advanced them by some yards here and there. At four o'clock on the morning of the 10th, the 5th Wiltshires came up to support them, and lay down behind the trenches in the ashes, sand, and scattered rubble of the hilltop. Both battalions were exhausted from four days and nights of continual fighting, but in very good heart. At this time these two battalions marked the extreme right of our new line; on their left, stretching down to the Farm, were the 10th Hampshires, and near the Farm the remains of the third column under General Baldwin. There may have been in all some 5,000 men on Chunuk and within a quarter of a mile of it round the Farm.

In the darkness before dawn, when our men on the hill were busy digging themselves better cover for the day's battle, the Turks, now strongly reinforced from Bulair and Asia, assaulted Chunuk with not less than 15,000 men. They came on in a monstrous mass, packed shoulder to shoulder, in some places eight deep, in others three or four deep. Practically all their first line were shot by our men, practically all the second line were bayoneted, but the third line got into our trenches and overwhelmed the garrison. Our men fell back to the second line of trenches, and rallied and fired; but the Turks overwhelmed that line too, and then with their packed multitude they paused and gathered like a wave, burst down on the Wiltshire Regiment, and destroyed it almost to a man. Even so, the survivors, outnumbered forty to one, formed and charged with the bayonet, and formed and charged a second time, with a courage which makes the charge of the Light Brigade seem like a dream. But it was a hopeless position. The Turks came on like the sea, beat back all before them, paused for a moment, set rolling down the hill upon our men a number of enormous round bombs, which bounded into our lines and burst, and then following up this artillery they fell on the men round the Farm in the most bloody and desperate fight of the campaign.

Even as they topped Chunuk and swarmed down to engulf our right, our guns opened upon them in a fire truly awful; but thousands came alive over the crest, and went down to the battle below. Stragglers running from the first rush put a panic in the Aghyl Dere, where bearers, doctors, mules, and a multitude of wounded were jammed up with soldiers trying to get up to the fight. Some of our men held up against this thrust of the Turks, and in that first brave stand General Baldwin was killed. Then our line broke, the Turks got fairly in among our men with a weight which bore all before it, and what followed was a long succession of British rallies to a tussle body to body, with knives and stones and teeth – a fight of wild beasts in the ruined cornfields of the Farm. Nothing can be said of that fight, no words can describe nor any mind imagine it, except as a roaring and blazing hour of killing. Our last reserves came up to it, and the Turks were beaten back; very few of their men reached their lines alive. The Turk dead lay in thousands all down the slopes of the hill; but the crest of the hill, the prize, remained in Turk hands, not in ours.

That ended the battle of the 6th to 10th of August. We had beaten off the Turks, but our men were too much exhausted to do more. They could not go up the hill again. Our thrust at Sari Bair had failed. It had just failed, by a few minutes, though unsupported from the left. Even then, at the eleventh hour, two fresh battalions and a ton of water would have made Chunuk ours; but we had neither the men nor the water. Sari was not to be our hill. Our men fought for four days and nights in a wilderness of gorse and precipice to make her ours. They fought in a blazing sun, without rest, with little food and with almost no water, on hills on fire and on crags rotting to the tread. They went, like all their brothers in that Peninsula, on a forlorn hope, and by bloody pain they won the image and the taste of victory; and then, when their reeling bodies had burst the bars, so that our race might pass through, there were none to pass; the door was open, but there were none to go through it to triumph. And then, slowly, as strength failed, the door was shut again, the bars were forged again, victory was hidden again, all was to do again, and our brave men were but the fewer and the bitterer for all their bloody sacrifice for the land they served. All was to do again after the 10th of August; the great battle of the campaign was over. We had made our fight, we had seen our enemy beaten and the prize displayed, and then (as before at Helles) we had to stop for want of men, till the enemy had remade his army and rebuilt his fort.

VI

The day passed, the night came, the King lay down in his vaulted room. St. Gabriel came from God to call him. "Charles, summon the army of your Empire, and go by forced marches into the land of Bire, to the city that the pagans have besieged. The Christians call and cry for you." The Emperor wished not to go. "God," he said. "How painful is my life!" He wept from his eyes, he tore his white beard. – *The End of the Song of Roland.*

That, in a way, was the end of the campaign, for no other attempt to win through was made. The Turks were shaken to the heart. Another battle following at once might well have broken them. But we had not the men nor the shells for another battle. In the five days' battle on the front of twelve miles we had lost very little less than a quarter of our entire army, and we had shot away most of our always scanty supply of ammunition. We could not attack again till 50,000 more men were landed and the store of shells replenished. Those men and shells were not near Gallipoli, but in England, where the war as a whole had to be considered. The question to be decided, by those directing the war as a whole, was, "Should those men and shells be sent?" It was decided by the High Direction that they should not be sent; the effort, therefore, could not be made.

Since the effort could not be made, the campaign declined into a secondary operation – to contain large reserves of Turks, with their guns and munitions, from use elsewhere, in Mesopotamia or in the Caucasus. But before it became this, a well-planned and well-fought effort was made from Suvla to secure our position by seizing the hills to the east of the Bay. This attack took place on the 21st of August, in intense heat, across an open plain without cover of any kind, blazing throughout nearly all its length with scrub fires. The 29th Division (brought up from Cape Helles) carried Scimitar Hill with great dash, and was then held up. The attack on Ismail Oglu failed. Two thrusts, made by the men of Anzac in the latter days of August, secured an important well and the Turk stronghold of Hill 60. This last success made the line from Anzac to Suvla impregnable.

After this, since no big attempt could be made by the Allied troops, and no big attempt was made by the enemy, the fighting settled down into trench warfare on both sides. There was some shelling every day and night, some machine gun and rifle fire, much sniping, great vigilance, and occasional bombing and mining. The dysentery, which had been present ever since the heats began, increased beyond all measure: very few men in all that army were not attacked and weakened by it. Many thousands went down with it; Mudros, Alexandria, and Malta were filled with cases; many died.

Those who remained, besides carrying on the war by daily and nightly fire, worked continually with pick and shovel to improve the lines. Long after the war, the goatherd on Gallipoli will lose his way in the miles of trenches which zigzag from Cape Helles to Achi Baba and from Gaba Tepe to Ejelmer Bay. They run to and fro in all that expanse of land, some of them shallow, others deep cuttings in the marl, many of them paved with stone or faced with concrete, most of them sided with little caverns, leading far down (in a few cases) to rooms twenty feet under the ground. Long after we are all dust, the goats of Gallipoli will break their legs in those pits and ditches, and over their coffee round the fire the elders will say that they were dug by devils and the sons of devils, and antiquarians will come from the West to dig there, and will bring away shards of iron and empty tins and bones. Fifty years ago some French staff officers traced out the works round Durazzo, where Pompey the Great fought just such another campaign, two thousand years ago. Two thousand years hence, when this war is forgotten, those lines under the ground will draw the staff officers of whatever country is then the most cried for brains.

Those lines were the homes of thousands of our soldiers for half a year and more. There they lived and did their cooking and washing, made their jokes and sang their songs. There they sweated under their burdens, and slept, and fell in to die. There they marched up the burning hill, where the sand devils flung by the shells were blackening heaven; there they lay in their dirty rags awaiting death; and there by thousands up and down they lie buried, in little lonely graves where they fell, or in the pits of the great engagements.

Those lines at Cape Helles, Anzac, and Suvla, were once busy towns, thronged by thousands of citizens, whose going and coming and daily labour were cheerful with singing, as though those places were mining camps during a gold rush, instead of a perilous front where the fire never ceased and the risk of death was constant. But for the noise of war, coming in an irregular rattle, with solitary big explosions, the screams of shells, or the wild whistling crying of ricochets, they seemed busy but very peaceful places. At night, from the sea, the lamps of the dugouts on the cliffs were like the lights of sea-coast towns in summer, and the places seemingly as peaceful, but for the pop and rattle of fire and the streaks of glare from the shells. There was always singing, sometimes very good and always beautiful, coming in the crash of war; and always one heard the noises of the work of men – the beat of pile-drivers, wheels going over

119

stones, and the little solid pobbing noises, from bullets dropping in the sea.

I have said that those positions were like mining camps during a gold rush. Ballarat, the Sacramento, and the camps of the Transvaal, must have looked strangely like those camps at Suvla and Cape Helles. Anzac at night was like those crags of old building over the Arno at Florence; by day it was a city of cliff dwellers, stirring memories of the race's past. An immense expanse was visible from all these places: at Cape Helles there was the plain rising gradually to Achi Baba, at Anzac a wilderness of hills, at Suvla the same hills seen from below. Over all these places came a strangeness of light, unlike anything to be seen in the West, a light which made the hills clear and unreal at the same time, softening their savagery into peace, till they seemed not hills but swellings of the land, as though the land there had breathed in and risen a little. All the places were dust-coloured as soon as the flowers had withered, a dark dust-colour where the scrub grew (often almost wine-dark like our own hills where heather grows), a pale sand colour where the scrub gave out, and elsewhere a paleness and a greyness as of moss and lichen and old stone. On this sandy and dusty land, where even the trees were grey and ghostly (olive and Eastern currant), the camps were scattered, a little and a little, never much in one place on account of shelling, till the impression given was one of multitude.

The signs of the occupation began far out at sea, where the hospital ships lay waiting for their freight. There were always some there, painted white and green, lying outside the range of the big guns. Nearer to the shore were the wrecks of ships, some of them sunk by our men, to make breakwaters, some sunk by the Turk shells, some knocked to pieces or washed ashore by foul weather. Nearly all these wrecks were of small size, trawlers, drifters, and little coastwise vessels such as peddle and bring home fish on the English coasts. Closer in, right on the beaches, were the bones of still smaller boats, pinnaces, cutters, and lighters, whose crews had been the men of the first landings. Men could not see those wrecks without a thrill. There were piers at all the beaches, all built under shellfire, to stand both shellfire and the sea, and at the piers there was always much busy life, men singing at their work, horses and mules disembarking, food and munitions and water discharging, wounded going home and drafts coming ashore. On the beaches were the hiero-glyphs of the whole bloody and splendid story; there were the marks and signs, which no one could mistake nor see unmoved.

Even after months of our occupation the traces were there off the main tracks. A man had but to step from one of the roads into the scrub, and there they lay, relics of barbed wire (blown aside in tangles), round shrapnel-bullets in the sand, empty cartridge-cases, clips of cartridge-cases bent double by a blow yet undischarged, pieces of flattened rifle barrel, rags of leather, broken bayonets, jags and hacks of shell, and, in little hollows, little heaps of cartridge-cases where some man had lain to fire for hour after hour, often until he died at his post, on the 25th of April. Here, too, one came upon the graves of soldiers, sometimes alone, sometimes three or four together, each with an inscribed cross and border of stones from the beach. Privates, sergeants, and officers lay in those graves, and by them, all day long, the work, which they had made possible by that sacrifice on the 25th, went on in a stream, men and munitions going up to the front, and wounded and the dying coming down, while the explosions of the cannon trembled through the earth to them, and the bullets piped and fell over their heads.

But the cities of those camps were not cities of the dead, they were cities of intense life, cities of comradeship and resolve, unlike the cities of peace. At Mudros, all things seemed little, for there men were dwarfed by their setting; they were there in ships, which made even a full battalion seem only a cluster of heads. On the Peninsula they seemed to have come for the first time to full stature. There they were bigger than their surroundings. There they were naked manhood pitted against death in the desert, and more than holding their own.

All those sun-smitten hills and gullies, growing nothing but crackling scrub, were peopled by crowds. On all the roads, on the plain, which lay white like salt in the glare, and on the sides of the gullies, strange, sunburned, half-naked men moved at their work with the bronze bodies of gods. Like Egyptians building a city, they passed and repassed with boxes from the walls of stores built on the beach. Dust had toned their uniforms even with the land. Their half-nakedness made them more grand than clad men. Very few of them were less than beautiful; whole battalions were magnificent, the very flower of the world's men. They had a look in their eyes which those who saw them will never forget.

Sometimes, as one watched, one heard a noise of cheering from the ships, and this, the herald of good news, passed inland, till men would rise from sleep in their dugouts, come to the door, blinking in the sun, to pass on the cheer. In some strange way the news, the cause of the cheering, passed inland with the cheer, a submarine had sunk a transport off Constantinople, or an aeroplane had bombed a powder factory. One heard the news pass on and on, till it rang from the front trenches ten yards from the Turk line. Sometimes the cheering was very loud, mingled with singing; then it was a new battalion, coming from England, giving thanks that they were there, after their months of training, to help the fleet through. Men who heard those battalions singing will never hear those songs of "Tipperary," "Let's all go down the Strand," or "We'll all go the same way home," without a quickening at the heart.

Everywhere in the three positions there were the homes of men. In gashes or clefts of the earth were long lines of mules or horses with Indian grooms. On the beaches were offices, with typewriters clicking and telephone bells ringing. Stacked on one side were ammunition-carts so covered with bushes that they looked like the scrub they stood on. Here and there were strangely painted guns, and everywhere the work of men, armourers' forges, farriers' anvils, the noise and clink and bustle of a multitude. Everywhere, too, but especially in the gullies, were the cave-dwellings of the dugouts, which so dotted the cliffs with their doors that one seemed put back to Cro-Magnon or Tampa, into some swarming tribe of cave-dwellers. All the dugouts were different, though all were built upon the same principle, first a scooping in the earth, then a raised earth ledge for a bed, then (if one were lucky) a corrugated iron roof propped by balks, lastly a topping of sandbags strewn with scrub. For doors, if one had a door or sunshade, men used sacking, burlap, a bit of canvas, or a blanket. Then, when the work was finished, the builder entered in, to bathe in his quarter of a pint of water, smoke his pipe, greet his comrades, and think foul scorn of the Turk, whose bullets piped and droned overhead, all day and night, like the little finches of home. Looking out from the upper dugouts, one saw the dusty, swarming warren of men, going and coming, with a kind of swift slouch, carrying boxes from the beach. Mules and men passed; songs went up and down the gullies, and were taken up by those at rest; men washed and mended clothes, or wandered naked and sun-reddened along the beach, bathing among dropping bullets. Wounded men came down on stretchers, sick men babbled in pain or cursed the flies, the forges clinked, the pile-drivers beat in the balks of the piers, the bullets droned and piped, or rushed savagely, or pobbed into a sandbag. Up in the trenches the rifles made the irregular snaps of fire-crackers, sometimes almost ceasing, then popping, then running along a section in a rattle, then quickening down the line and drawing the enemy, then pausing and slowly ceasing and beginning again. From time to time, with a whistle and a wailing, some Asian shell came over, and drooped and seemed to multiply, and gathered to herself the shriek of all the devils of hell, and burst like a devil, and filled a great space with blackness and dust and falling fragments. Then another and another came, almost in the same place, till the gunners had had enough. Then the dust settled, the ruin was made good, and all went on as before, men carrying and toiling and singing, bullets piping, and the flies settling and swarming on whatever was obscene in what the shell had scattered.

Everywhere in those positions there was gaiety and courage and devoted brotherhood; but there was also another thing, which brooded over all, and struck right home to the heart. It was a tragical feeling, a taint or flavour in the mind, such as men often feel in hospitals when many are dying, the sense that Death was at work there, that Death lived there, that Death wandered up and down there and fed on Life.

Since the main object of the campaign, to help the fleet through the Narrows, had been abandoned (in mid-August), and no further thrust was to be made against the Turks, the questions, "Were our 100,000 men in Gallipoli containing a sufficiently large army of Turks to justify their continuance on the Peninsula?" and "Could they be more profitably used

122

elsewhere?" arose in the minds of the High Direction from week to week as the war changed and increased.

In the early autumn, when the Central Powers combined with Bulgaria to crush Serbia and open a road to Constantinople, these questions became acute. During October, owing to the radical change in the Balkan situation, which was produced by the treachery of Bulgaria and the bewildering indecision of Greece, the advantage of our continuing the campaign became more and more doubtful; and in November, after full consideration, it was decided to evacuate the Peninsula. Preparations were made and the work begun.

Late in November something happened which had perhaps some influence in hurrying on the date of the evacuation. This was the blizzard of the 26th to 28th, which lost us about a tenth of our whole army from cold, frostbite, exposure, and the sicknesses which follow them. The 26th began as a cold, dour Gallipoli day with a bitter north-easterly wind, which increased in the afternoon to a fresh gale, with sleet. Later, it increased still more, and blew hard, with thunder; and with the thunder came a rain more violent than any man of our army had ever seen. Water pours off very quickly from that land of abrupt slopes. In a few minutes every gully was a raging torrent, and every trench a river. By an ill-chance this storm fell with cruel violence upon the ever famous 29th Division, then holding trenches at Suvla. The water poured down into their trenches as though it were a tidal wave. It came in with a rush, with a head upon it like the tide advancing, so quickly that men were one minute dry and the next moment drowned at their posts. They were caught so suddenly that those who escaped had to leap from their trenches for dear life, leaving coats, haversacks, food, and sometimes even their rifles, behind them.

Our trenches were in nearly every case below those of the Turks, who therefore suffered from the water far less than our men did. The Turks saw our men leaping from their trenches, and, either guessing the reason or fearing an attack, opened a very heavy rifle and shrapnel fire upon them. Our men had to shelter behind the parados of their trenches, where they scraped themselves shallow pans in the mud under a heavy fire. At dark the sleet increased, the mud froze, and there our men lay, most of them without overcoats, and many of them without food. In one trench when the flood rose, a pony, a mule, a pig, and two dead Turks were washed over a barricade together.

Before the night fell, many of our men were frostbitten, and started limping to the ambulances, under continual shrapnel fire and in blinding sleet. A good many fell down by the way, and were frozen to death. The gale increased slowly all through the night, blowing hard and steadily from the north, making a great sea upon the coast, and driving the spray far inland. At dawn it grew colder, and the sleet hardened into snow, with an ever-increasing wind, which struck through our men to the marrow. "They fell ill," said one who was there, "in heaps." The water from the flood had fallen in the night, but it was still four feet deep in many of the trenches, and our men passed the morning under fire in their shelter pans, fishing for food and rifles in their drowned lines. All through the day the wind gathered, till it was blowing a full gale, vicious and bitter cold; and on the 28th it reached its worst. The 28th was spoken of afterwards as "Frozen Foot Day"; it was a day more terrible than any battle. But now it was taking toll of the Turks, and the fire slackened. Probably either side could have had the other's position for the taking on the 28th, had there been enough unfrosted feet to advance. It was a day so blind with snow and driving storm that neither side could see to fire, and this brought the advantage, that our men, hopping to the ambulances, had not to go through a pelt of shrapnel bullets. On the 29th, the limits of human strength were reached. Some of those frozen three days before were able to return to duty, but "a great number of officers and men who had done their best to stick it out were forced to go to hospital." The water fell during this day, but it left on an average two and a half feet of thick, slushy mud, into which many trenches collapsed. After this the weather was fine and warm.

At Helles and Anzac the fall of the ground gave some protection from this gale, but at Suvla there was none. When the weather cleared, the beaches were heaped with the wreck of piers, piles, boats and lighters, all broken and jammed together. But great as this wreck was, the wreck of men was even greater. The 29th Division had lost two-thirds of its strength. In the three sectors over 200 men were dead, over 10,000 were unfit for further service, and not less than 30,000 others were sickened and made old by it.

The Turk loss was much more serious even than this, for though they suffered less from the wet, they suffered more from the cold, through being on the higher ground. The snow lay upon their trenches long after it had gone from ours, and the Turk equipment, though very good as far as it went, was only good for the summer. Their men wore thin clothes, and many of them had neither overcoat nor blanket. The blizzard, which was a discouragement to us, took nearly all the heart out of the Turks; and this fact must be borne in mind in the reading of the next few pages.

The gale had one good effect: either the cold or the rain destroyed or removed the cause of the dysentery, which had taken nearly a thousand victims a day for some months. The disease stopped at once, and no more fresh cases were reported.

This storm made any attempt to land or to leave the land impossible for four days together. Coming, as it did, upon the decision to evacuate, it gave the prompting, that the evacuation should be hurried, lest such weather should prevent it. On the 8th of December, the evacuation of Anzac and Suvla was ordered to begin.

It was not an easy task to remove large numbers of men, guns, and animals from positions commanded by the Turk observers, and open to every cruising aeroplane. But by ruse and skill, and the use of the dark, favoured by fine weather, the work was done, almost without loss, and, as far as one could judge, unsuspected.

German agents, eager to discredit those whom they could not defeat, have said "that we bribed the Turks to let us go"; next year, perhaps, they will say "that the Turks bribed us to go"; the year after that, perhaps, they will invent something equally false and even sillier. But putting aside the foulness and the folly of this bribery lie, it is interesting to inquire how it happened that the Turks did not attack our men while they were embarking.

The Turks were very good fighters, furious in attack and resolute in defence, but among their qualities of mind were some which greatly puzzled our commanders. Their minds would sometimes work in ways very strange to Europeans. They did, or refrained from doing, certain things in ways for which neither we nor our Allies could account. Someday, long hence, when the war is over, the Turk story of our withdrawal will be made known. Until then, we can only guess why it was that the embarkation, which many had thought would lose us half our army, was made good from Anzac and Suvla with the loss of only four or five men (or less than the normal loss of a night in the trenches). Only two explanations are possible. Either (1) the Turks knew that we were going, and wanted to be rid of us; or (2) they did not know that we were going, and were entirely deceived by our ruses.

Had they known that we were going from Anzac and Suvla, it is at least likely that they would have hastened our going, partly that they might win some booty, which they much needed, or take a large number of prisoners, whose appearance would have greatly cheered the citizens of Constantinople. But nearly all those of our army who were there felt, both from observation and intelligence, that the Turks did not know that we were going. As far as men on one side in a war can judge of their enemies, they felt that the Turks were deceived, completely deceived, by the ruses employed by us, and that they believed that we were being strongly reinforced for a new attack. Our soldiers took great pains to make them believe this. Looking down upon us from their heights, the Turks saw boats leaving the shore apparently empty, and returning, apparently, full of soldiers. Looking up at them; from our position our men saw how the sight affected them. For the twelve days during which the evacuation was in progress at Anzac and Suvla, the Turks were plainly to be seen, digging everywhere to secure themselves from the feared attack. They dug new lines, they brought up new guns, they made ready for us in every way. On the night of the 19th–20th December, in hazy weather, at full moon, our men left Suvla and Anzac unmolested.

It was said by Dr. Johnson that "no man does anything, consciously for the last time, without a feeling of sadness." No man of all that force passed down those trenches, the scenes of so much misery and pain and joy and valour and devoted brotherhood, without a deep feeling of sadness. Even those who had been loudest in their joy at going were sad.

Many there did not want to go, but felt that it was better to stay, and that then, with another 50,000 men, the task could be done, and their bodies and their blood buy victory for us. This was the feeling even at Suvla, where the men were shaken and sick still from the storm; but at Anzac, the friendly little kindly city, which had been won at such cost in the ever-glorious charge of the 25th, and held since with such pain, and built with such sweat and toil and anguish, in thirst, and weakness, and bodily suffering, which had seen the thousands of the 13th Division land in the dark and hide, and had seen them fall in with the others to go to Chunuk, and had known all the hope and fervour, all the glorious resolve, and all the bitterness and disappointment of the unhelped attempt, the feeling was far deeper. Officers and men went up and down the well-known gullies moved almost to tears by the thought that the next day those narrow acres so hardly won and all those graves of our people so long defended would be in Turk hands.

For some weeks our men had accustomed the Turks to sudden cessations of fire for half an hour or more. At first the Turks had been made suspicious by these silences, but they were now used to them, and perhaps glad of them. They were not made suspicious by the slackening of the fire on the night of the withdrawal. The mules and guns had all gone from Suvla. A few mules and a few destroyed guns were left at Anzac; in both places a pile of stores was left, all soaked in oil and ready for firing. The ships of war drew near to the coast, and trained their guns on the hills. In the haze of the full moon the men filed off from the trenches down to the beaches, and passed away from Gallipoli, from the unhelped attempt which they had given their bodies and their blood to make. They had lost no honour. They were not to blame, that they were creeping off in the dark, like thieves in the night. Had others (not of their profession), many hundreds of miles away, but been as they, as generous, as wise, as foreseeing, as full of sacrifice, those thinned companies with the looks of pain in their faces, and the mud of the hills thick upon their bodies, would have given thanks in Santa Sophia three months before. They had failed to take Gallipoli, and the minefields still barred the Hellespont, but they had fought a battle such as has never been seen upon this earth. What they had done will become a glory for ever, wherever the deeds of heroic unhelped men are honoured and pitied and understood. They went up at the call of duty, with a bright banner of a battle-cry, against an impregnable fort. Without guns, without munitions, without help, and without drink, they climbed the scarp, and held it by their own glorious manhood, quickened by a word from their chief. Now they were giving back the scarp, and going out into new adventures, wherever the war might turn.

Those going down to the beaches wondered in a kind of awe whether the Turks would discover them and attack. The minutes passed, and boat after boat left the shore, but no attack came. The arranged rifles fired mechanically in the outer trenches at long intervals, and the crackle of the Turk reply followed. At Anzac, a rearguard of honour had been formed. The last two hundred men to leave Anzac were survivors of those who had landed in the first charge, so glorious and so full of hope, on the 25th of April. They had fought through the whole campaign from the very beginning; they had seen it all. It was only just that they should be the last to leave. As they, too, moved down, one of their number saw a solitary Turk, black against the sky, hard at work upon his trench. That was the last enemy to be seen from Anzac.

At half-past five in the winter morning of the 20th of December the last boat pushed off, and the last of our men had gone from Suvla and Anzac. Those who had been there from the first were deeply touched. There was a longing that it might be to do again, with the same comrades, under the same chiefs, but with better luck and better backing. Some distance from the shore the boats paused to watch the last act in the withdrawal. It was dead calm weather, with just that ruffle of wind which comes before the morning. The Turk fire crackled along the lines as usual, but the withdrawal was still not suspected. Then from the beaches within the stacks of abandoned stores came the noise of explosion; the charges had been fired, and soon immense flames were licking up those boxes and reddening the hills. As the flames grew, there came a stir in the Turk lines, and then every Turk gun that could be brought to bear opened with shrapnel and high-explosive on the area of the bonfires. It was plain that the Turks misread the signs. They thought that some lucky shell had fired our stores, and that they could stop us from putting out the flames. Helped by the blasts of many shells, the burning rose like bale-fire, crowned by wreaths and streaks and spouts of flame. The stores were either ashes or in a blaze which none could quench before the Turks guessed the meaning of that burning. Long before the fires had died and before the Turks were wandering in joy among our trenches, our men were aboard their ships standing over to Mudros.

Some have said: "Even if the Turks were deceived at Anzac and Suvla, they must have known that you were leaving Cape Helles. Why did they not attack you while you were embarking there?" I do not know the answer to this question. But it is possible that they did not know that we were leaving. It is possible that they believed that we should hold Cape Helles like an Eastern Gibraltar. It is possible, on the other hand, that they were deceived again by our ruses. It is, however, certain that they watched us far more narrowly at Cape Helles after the Anzac evacuation. Aeroplanes cruised over our position frequently, and shellfire increased and became very heavy. Still, when the time came, the burning of our stores, after our men had embarked, seemed to be the first warning that the Turks had that we were going.

This was a mystery to our soldiers at the time, and seems strange now. It is possible that at Cape Helles the Turks' shaken, frozen, and out-of-heart soldiers may have known that we were going, yet had no life left in them for an attack. Many things are possible in this world, and the darkness is strange, and the heart of a fellow-man is darkness to us. There were things in the Turk heart very dark indeed to those who tried to read it. The storm had dealt with them cruelly, that is all that we know. Let us wait till we know their story.

The Cape Helles position was held for twenty days after we had left Anzac and Suvla. On the 8th–9th of January in the present year, it was abandoned, with slight loss, though in breaking weather. By four o'clock on the morning of the 9th of January, the last man had passed the graves of those who had won the beaches. They climbed on board their boats and pushed off. They had said goodbye to the English dead, whose blood had given them those acres, now being given back. Some felt, as they passed those graves, that the stones were living men, who cast a long look after them when they had passed, and sighed, and turned landward, as they had turned of old. Then in a rising sea, whipped with spray, among the noise of ships weltering to the rails, the battalions left Cape Helles; the *River Clyde* dimmed into the gale and became a memory, and the Gallipoli campaign was over.

Many people have asked me what the campaign achieved. It achieved much. It destroyed and put out of action many more of the enemy than of our own men. Our own losses in killed, wounded, and missing were, roughly speaking, 115,000 men, and in sick about 100,000 more, or (in all) more than two and one-half times as many as the army which made the landing. The Turk losses from all causes were far greater; they had men to waste, and wasted them, like water, at Cape Helles, Lone Pine, and Chunuk. The real Turk losses will never be tabled and published, but at the five battles of the Landings, the 6th of May, the 4th of June, the 28th of June, and the 6th to 10th of August, they lost in counted killed alone very nearly as many as were killed on our side in the whole campaign. Then, though we did not do what we hoped to do, our presence in Gallipoli contained large armies of Turks in and near the Peninsula. They had always from 15,000 to 20,000 more men than we had on the Peninsula itself, and at least as many more, ready to move, on the Asian shore and at Rodosto. In all, we disabled, or held from action elsewhere, not less than 400,000 Turks, that is, a very large army of men who might have been used else-where, with disastrous advantage, in the Caucasus, when Russia was hard-pressed, or, as they were used later, in Mesopotamia.

So much for the soldiers' side. But politically, the campaign achieved much. In the beginning, it had a profound effect upon Italy; it was, perhaps, one of the causes which brought Italy into her war with Austria. In the beginning, too, it had a profound effect upon the Balkan States. Bulgaria made no move against us until five months after our landings. Had we not gone to Gallipoli, she would have joined our enemies in the late spring instead of in the middle autumn.

Some of our enemies have said that "the campaign was a defeat for the British navy." It is true that we lost two capital ships, from mines, in the early part of the campaign, and I think, in all, two others, from torpedoes, during the campaign. Such loss is not very serious in eleven months of naval war. For the campaign was a naval war; it depended utterly and solely upon the power of the navy. By our navy we went there and were kept there, and by our navy we came away. During the nine months of our hold on the Peninsula, over 300,000 men were brought by the navy from places three, four, or even six thousand miles away. During the operations some half of these were removed by our navy, as sick and wounded, to ports from five hundred to three thousand miles away. Every day, for eleven months, ships of our navy moved up and down the Gallipoli coast bombarding the Turk positions. Every day during the operations our navy kept our armies in food, drink, and supplies. Every day, in all that time, if weather permitted, ships of our navy cruised in the Narrows and off Constantinople, and the seaplanes of our navy raided and scouted within the Turk lines. If there had been, I will not say any defeat of, but any check to, the navy, we could not have begun the campaign or continued it. Every moment of those eleven months of war was an illustration of the silent and unceasing victory of our navy's power. As Sir Ian Hamilton has put it, "the navy was our father and our mother."

"Still," our enemies say, "you did not win the Peninsula." We did not; and someday, when truth will walk clear-eyed, it will be known why we did not. Until then, let our enemies say this: "They did not win, but they came across three thousand miles of sea, a little army without reserves and short of munitions, a band of brothers, not half of them half-trained, and nearly all of them new to war. They came to what we said was an impregnable fort, on which our veterans of war and massacre had laboured for two months, and by sheer naked manhood they beat us, and drove us out of it. Then rallying, but without reserves, they beat us again, and drove us farther. Then rallying once more, but still without reserves, they beat us again, this time to our knees. Then, had they had reserves, they would have conquered, but by God's pity they had none. Then, after a lapse of time, when we were men again, they had reserves, and they hit us a staggering blow, which needed but a push to end us, but God again had pity. After that our God was indeed pitiful, for England made no further thrust, and they went away."

> Even so was wisdom proven blind,
> So courage failed, so strength was chained;
> Even so the gods, whose seeing mind
> Is not as ours, ordained.

Lollingdon
June 29, 1916

[source: *Gallipoli*, London: William Heinemann, 1916]

An Anglo-American Entente

Sir, – Will you allow me to back Mr. Whelpley's plea for friendship with the United States by a brief account of what America has done since the war began, and is now doing, for the cause of the Allies?

It is sometimes said, especially by Americans in the belligerent countries, that America should have entered the war upon the side of the Allies. But this course, though it may seem natural to many here, now in the fever of the war, must seem less obvious four, five, or even six thousand miles away, across an ocean and a continent. At those great distances from any part of the war the mind of a nation, as a whole, cannot grasp the war, and the passion of a nation, as a whole, cannot be roused by it. Besides this, the tradition of the nation, always a strong thing in a young community, is against all entanglement in European affairs.

But though America has not entered the war (and should we enter the war if, say, United South America suddenly ignored the Monroe Doctrine, tore up all existing treaties, and overwhelmed Colombia with fire and rape?), the most thoughtful and feeling of her people have helped our cause with a persistent largeness of generous effort. By their help the funds given for the relief of Belgium and Serbia are administered and applied, within the enemy lines, to the salvation of millions of lives. By their efforts the condition of British prisoners of war in the hands of the enemy, in Central Europe and in Turkey, is made endurable. By their efforts many thousands of our Allies have been healed, helped, and comforted with every circumstance of kindness.

It is well-known that some thousands of generous young Americans are serving in our Canadian regiments; others, like Mr. Hall, have enlisted in our own Army; others (certainly many) have enlisted in the French Foreign Legion. Among these latter was the brilliant young poet, Alan Seeger, who has since given his life for France. Ever since the war began some hundreds of the finest young men in America, the very pick and flower of the graduates and undergraduates of the universities, have been serving under fire with the French armies in the Field Service sections of the American Ambulance, a devoted service, in which two of their number have been killed, many maimed, and many decorated. The courage and devotion of these young men have been praised repeatedly in the French Army and Divisional Orders. Very nearly half the members of their company have won either the military medal or the cross of war.

Hospital Work in France

Apart from this service, there are other American institutions now in France for the healing and helping of wounded men, French and English. There is the Harvard Unit serving with the British Army under the orders of the R.A.M.C. There is the American Ambulance in the Lycée Pasteur at Neuilly, near Paris. This ambulance, or military hospital, has been open since September 1914 to French and British soldiers. It is one of the most beautiful and most thorough of the many large military hospitals now in France. It is wholly the work of American and Franco-American lovers of France. Many of the most famous American surgeons have given their services to its different departments, and have done notable work, especially in facial and dental surgery, face restoration, and in the treatment of gaseous gangrene. This hospital fills a large lycée, an annexe at Juilly, not far from Paris, and several convalescent homes, mostly in the care of sisters of charity, in the district of St. Cloud.

Besides these hospitals there are several others, at Versailles, Limoges, and near Compiégne, managed by Americans bound to France by long and tender associations. There are others at Valéry-en-Caux, at Passy par Veron, and at Nice. At Ris Orangis an English hospital has a most noteworthy American surgical staff. In the earlier stages of the war there were other American hospitals at Pau and at Aix-les-Bains, but these have now been discontinued. In this country Americans have founded and now support at least three hospitals for soldiers of our own Armies.

There are now in France many other expressions of American sympathy for the cause of the Allies. There are in Paris alone several distributing centres for the gifts of goods, comforts and hospital equipment which reach France from America daily. One of these centres (in the Alcazar d'Eté) is the depot of the American Fund for French Wounded; another is the truly great business organisation of the American Clearing House, which is now a sorting and delivery business as big as the clearing house of a department store.

Among other charitable works begun and maintained in France by Americans since the beginning of the war are some private workshops where poor women may earn a living by sewing; some church schools and orphanages for destitute children; a big depot for the issue of clothing to refugees; an association for rebuilding in the devastated districts; a society for supplying delicacies to the severely wounded; a society for providing French soldiers with "marraines," and an excellent studio or workshop, imagined, planned and conducted by an American lady, for the invention, manufacture and supply of surgical apparatus for the extension and flexion of wounded limbs.

As this makes a fair record for a neutral country, and may not be well-known here, where there are fewer American institutions than in France, the land bound to America by long traditions of friendship, it may be of interest to your readers.

JOHN MASEFIELD.
13, Well-Walk, London, N.W.

[source: *Daily Chronicle*, 29 January 1917, p.4]

The Harvest of the Night

[PREFATORY NOTE. – This article on the work of the American Ambulance Field Service in France is one of the results of a visit paid by Mr. John Masefield to France for the purpose of studying the work of the corps on the spot. Deeply interested in and grateful for the work done by Americans in this European conflict, which is the struggle of democratic civilization against aggressive and barbarous militarism, the British Government suggested that Mr. Masefield should go and see the American Ambulance men at work. Mr. Masefield had had experience in Red Cross work both under the British Red Cross and under the French Red Cross at Gallipoli, and he went to France as a Red Cross man. He was rarely well-qualified for his task, and he approached it with enthusiasm and devotion. Always a student of our armed services, and the writer of a famous book, *The British Navy in Nelson's Time*, [sic] Mr. Masefield approached his work with the instinct of an outdoor man, with the capacity of a scholar and the skill of a poet. Above everything else, thoroughness and sanity, balance and charm, make Mr. Masefield's study of the American Ambulance Field Service notable and most accurate in description. Mr. Masefield received no instructions from the British Government further than that he was to set down honestly and fairly the result of his observation, and his opinions. It is for the readers of *Harper's Magazine* to decide whether he has done it interestingly. I think their answer will be in the affirmative. – GILBERT PARKER.]

It is perhaps unnecessary to describe the daily life of the members of the American Field Service. It must have been described many times already. One need only say here, that in ordinary times, when there is not much fighting in the sector, a day in camp with an American Ambulance Section is quiet enough. Those men who are not for duty lead, in the main, a life like that of a sailor in a watch below. There is nothing doing; they can wash or mend clothes, sleep, read, write, or work about the camp, as they prefer. Dinner comes at noon and supper in the evening. The real work of the section begins with darkness, when the roads can no longer be seen by observers in the sky.

After supper, in the last of the light, the ambulance-cars are made ready; the two drivers in each car put on their steel helmets and take their gas masks, and the convoy (or a part of it, according to the need of the service and the severity of the fighting) moves out, car by car, toward the Postes de Secours, where they will find the wounded. Some camps are so far from the front that the first part of the journey up can be done with headlights. All roads leading to the front are crowded with men or wagons going up or coming down. In a little while after leaving camp the ambulances run into the full stream of the relief and revictualing. It is the rule upon all roads in France that troops and vehicles shall keep well to the right, so that there shall be room for the column going as well as for the column returning. The day is busy enough upon the roads well back from the front, though those farther up are quiet. But at night this changes, and in the darkness the life on the real roads begins. It is difficult to describe this night life on the roads, since so little of it can be seen; yet on first moving out with the cars, before darkness has fallen and the headlights are doused, enough is caught to show that in modern war there is no splendour of movement or of position, as in the old wars, when divisions of cavalry charged and the front of a battle advanced as one man, but that there is still something distinctive about it by which it will be remembered. Old wars are remembered, perhaps, for their glitter or their crash, for something big in their commanders or fatal in their results. This war will perhaps be remembered for the monotony and the patience behind the lines. There alone is the imagination struck. There, on the midnight roads, is the visible struggle; there the nations are passing and repassing to the defence of the gates, and, to many, the image of this war will be not, as before, a spangled man or anything splendid, but simply the convoy of many wagons, driven by tired men, going on and on along the darkness of a road, in a cloud of dust or in the welter of a swill of mud, each man seeing no more of the war than the tail-board of the wagon in front, or the flash of faces where men light their pipes by the roadside, or the glow of some lantern where there is a guard to pass.

So, in moving out of the camp into this life upon the roads, a man passes into the heart of modern war, which is, in the main, a war of supply. Twilight and the dust together make the wagons and the soldiers the colour of a far horizon. Dust wavers and settles on the moving things, the smell of dust is in the breath, and the taste of it on the lips. The old men who work by the roadside night and day, cracking stones for road metal, disappear, as each wagon passes, in a smoke of dust; the dust is thick upon them; when it rains the mud is caked upon them. They work slowly, as all men work who have to work all day. They are all past their prime, but their work is precious, for the safety of their country depends upon the roads, and over the stones broken by them the means of victory go on up to the front. Almost the last things seen in the twilight, as the cars move out, are these men cracking stones by the roadside in mists of dust. Some of them have peaked hoods drawn over their heads; some of them have lanterns by them.

Soon the light dies. In open parts of the road, where things passing show against the sky, the convoys of wagons, twenty in a section, move and are black. The road is noisy with their rumble. Some of them, driven by men who are perhaps asleep, sway out of line into the middle of the road. Then the ambulance-drivers, trying to get past, sound their klaxons and shout, "*A droit!*" till the sleeper wakes and turns his wagon aside. Sometimes, as the ambulance shoots ahead of a string of wagons, there is an empty stretch of road running through empty fields and the night is as in peacetime. Then something big, black, and flopping shows ahead, making the darkness darker; there comes a jingling and the snort of horses, and out of the night comes, perhaps, a battery going down, gun after gun, some quickening, some staying, or empty horse-wagons with spare horses tied to the tail-board and the chains rattling on the slats and the drivers riding. They pass and drop down into the night like ships gone hull down; but others and others come, some walking, some with their men walking, calling to their horses, some rattling quick and empty, some slipping or shying or kicking at the passers. At times, as the ambulances go, something like a caterpillar appears ahead, moving slowly with a caterpillar's humping wriggle, and filling one half of the road. This blackness is lower than the other blacknesses, and unlike anything met with hitherto. At the sound of the klaxon it shogs a little to one side, stray blacknesses break from it, and the humping wriggle pauses in some disorder. It is a column of the *relève* going up to the front. It is a company of foot-soldiers marching in column of twos, each man bent under his load, which makes him twice the size of a man, and all walking slowly, many of them with walking-staffs, like pilgrims. All men doing hard work welcome an excuse to stop. The passing of the ambulance brings many men of the column to a halt; they turn to peer at the passing cars; faces show up under the helmets, like palenesses with dark marks upon them, and voices come from the column asking for a lift. They drop behind into the night, and then ahead comes a whinny and a clatter and the car runs alongside a squadron of trotting cavalry, and the horses toss their heads and blow foam or shy away from the car, and the men, a little out of breath, speak or curse and cry aloud to the drivers. They, too, drop behind, and on in front are wagons again, many sections together; and beyond them are columns of foot, all heaving forward, not like soldiers in peacetime, but like ploughmen coming home from ploughing, bent under their loads and silent from the labour. Presently the rumble ahead slackens and ceases, and the wagons ahead halt and the clatter of the chains stops. There is a block on the road; wagons continue to come down; the stream up is checked; then the stream down stops, too, and the night becomes suddenly very still but for the noise of the shifting of feet and the blowing or the rattle of the horses.

In the silence, the drivers get down to stretch their legs; some near-by soldier accepts a cigarette and lights it with his briquet, or flint and steel, and says something about the chance of the division moving, or the duration of the war, or tells how in the earlier fighting he found three dead men without visible wounds in some dugout in a far-away part of the line. Another soldier, drawn by the talk, says that they are going to attack down there, and that it will be hot, and that his brother is there. The moon rises during the talk; the men look at the moon for some hint of the coming weather.

The block, whatever it was, breaks up or is removed, and the column moves forward again in a strangeness of moonlight. It moves through the street of a village where there was fighting in the early part of the war. It is now a village of the dead; half of the houses are roofless, others lie in heaps of stone, the rest are barred and dark. On one side of the street some of the wreckage of the war lies – a broken cannon, part of a cart with the wheels gone, and a child's wooden horse. Near it is a drinking-fountain with running water in it, making a gurgle to the night. The street is as silent as the grave, but for the noise of the column on the road and the lead and chuckle of the water. In one part of the street some light glimmers up from a cellar; a man emerges, drops a curtain behind him, and the light disappears. Sometimes these villages seem to be lying sick of the plague and the column, the people fleeing. At other times the shut houses seem to be full of life, brooding and about to burst out upon the column as it goes.

All the way, at odd times, far off, with neither sense nor sequence, the guns have sounded almost like the noises of peace – blasting or pile-driving. Now, outside the village, as the ambulance comes out upon the hill, they sound for the first time like the noise of battle, much nearer and much more terrible. Now, too, far off, as the car runs in the open, the drivers see the star-shells going up and up, and bursting into white stars, and pausing and drifting slowly down, very, very slowly, pausing as they come, far apart, yet so many that there are always more than one aloft. They are the most beautiful things in modern war and almost the most terrible. Often they pause so long before dying that they look like the lights of peace in lighthouse and city beacon, or like planets in the sky.

In this open space the drivers can see for some miles over the battle-field. Over it all, as far as the eye can see, the lights are rising and falling. There is not much noise, almost no continual noise, but a sort of mutter of battle with explosions now and then. Very far away, perhaps ten miles away, there is fighting, for in that quarter the sky glimmers as though with summer lightning; the winks and flashes of the guns shake and die across heaven.

One side of the road here is screened with burlap stretched upon posts for half a mile together; otherwise daytime traffic on it would be seen by the enemy. Some of the burlap is in rags and some of the posts are broken; the wreck of a cart lies beside the road, and in the road itself are roundish patches of new stones where shell-holes have been mended, perhaps a few minutes before. This part of the road jingles like the rest with traffic, though here, for some reason, there are fewer motor-lorries and more horse-wagons. Here and there are working parties filling up shell-holes with stones. That piece of the road is always much shelled in the daytime.

By this time the moon is riding the night in beauty. The ambulance passes from the danger patch into a desert with neither hedge nor tree upon it. In the moonlight one can see the fields on each side of the road for perhaps a quarter of a mile, as in a summer dusk. One glance at the fields is enough to show that they have been bedevilled by the hand of war. All the countryside shows like a warren, with holes and tossed-up earth, as though rabbits as big as horses had been burrowing there for years. The earth lies scooped up in lines and heaps and hillocks, paler than the grass in this light, but all irregular and meaningless and useless. Near the road the pits and tossings of the earth run into one another at every yard, and out of them project the bones of their victims – carts with their wheels in air, the skulls of horses, the bonnets of ambulances, and splinters that might have been anything. Once, for three weeks on end, day and night, all that road and the land beside it was rained upon by shells of every kind till it became as it is now, blasted from all likeness to land. There are not five consecutive unscarred yards upon any part of it. It is torn and burrowed in and pitted with the pox of war; the flesh of the earth is eaten and blown away and the bones of the solid world laid bare. At seeing this for the first time in its fullness a man has just that sense of infamous desecration which comes to him when he first sees wounded men brought in from the battlefield. During the weeks of that fury the men and horses that were killed upon that land were buried and unburied daily many times, and torn at last to dust and laid with the dust. That fury has long since ceased. It was the effort of a nation and it failed. It gives a man a sense of his littleness in this world to see that the effort of a nation made so small a wreck upon the world it outraged.

Passing this desolation the ambulances come to another, perhaps sadder. Here the road runs through woodland, but such woodland; it is like that wood in hell where the trees are the souls of suicides. No single tree stands. All are torn off short and burned black. It is a wood of rampikes about five feet high, each tree ending in a bunch of splinters, or rayed down, or split. Some are uprooted, some tossed up and flung across their fellows, but all are shorn and pollarded by hours and weeks of shellfire. All the ground of the wood is dug into shell-holes and some rats are scuttling and squeaking among the wreck and running across the road. Some men are in the wood, probably they have their dugouts there; one man, perhaps a curé, cries goodnight as the cars pass. He is half seen among the stumps as the cars turn a corner. Lovers must have gone to that place in peacetime, when the primroses were out and the blackbird built and sang there; now . . .

Just overhead as the car passes comes a blasting, shattering crash which is like sudden death. Then another and another follow, one on the other, right overhead. On the ground above, the slope of the little hill, a battery of soixante-quinze guns has just opened fire. On the tail of each crash comes the crying of the shell, passing overhead like a screech-owl, till it is far away in the enemy lines, where it bursts. Another round follows, but by this time the ambulance is a hundred yards away, and now, on the heels of the affront, comes the answer. Rather to the right and very near in the stillness of the moonlight an enemy battery replies, one, two, three guns in as many seconds, a fourth gun a little late, and the shells come with a scream across and burst behind the ambulances, somewhere near the battery. Then a starlight goes up near enough to dazzle the eyes, and near enough, one would think, to show the ambulance to the world; and as the starlight goes down a second round comes from the battery, aimed God knows at what, but so as to *arroser* the district. The noise of the engine stifles the noise of the shells, but above the engines one shell's noise is heard; the screech of its rush comes very near, there is a flash ahead, a burst, and the patter of falling fragments. Long afterward, perhaps six seconds afterward, a tiny piece of shell drops upon the ambulance. Another shell bursts behind the car, and another on the road in front; the car goes round the new shell-hole and passes on. The firing ceases for the moment. The land ahead is quiet, moonlit country, seemingly at peace, however much shell-torn, though the starlights still rise and burst and pause, white and beautiful, over the valley beyond.

The cars come to a crossroads where a train of fifty pack-mules has halted. They are all laden with ammunition, and war has made them quiet (for mules), though many of them show the yellows of their eyes as the cars pass. Beyond them is a wayside cross, with a cluster of soldiers' graves about it. Shells have dug up the graves and broken the memorials on them; they lie scattered here and there, little wooden crosses and wreaths of coloured wire, under the Christ upon the cross. All the neighbourhood of the crossways is blasted with shells. Some shell-holes lie in regular lines along the roads there, perhaps twenty feet apart, just as they were sown in methodical bombardment; others are scattered broadcast; some, old ones partly filled, little more than a foot deep; others big enough to hold half a dozen men and deep enough to hide them. This crossways is, in its way, a famous place. It is called Golgotha in that part of the front. Four hundred yards from it some of the bloodiest fighting in all this war took place. The cross is the Calvary of Golgotha, past which thousands of brave men marched to their deaths.

The cars are now close to the enemy and very close to the Poste de Secours. The noise of the war runs up and down the front, but not at all like war as it is imagined in peacetime. It is a popping and banging, more like fireworks on the Fourth than something ordered and deadly. Then with their shattering bang the guns of a battery begin, and the shells rush screaming overhead and pass away and burst, and the enemy replies with heavier shells, so loud and so near that men expect to see them against the sky. With the bursts of these enemy shells comes a noise of collapse; a few ruined houses behind there have fallen to them.

The cars go slowly now, for the road is full of shell-holes. All the trees in the hedgerows have been shot to rampikes. Two lonely walls of houses stand up white in the moonlight over the ruins of their roofs. What were once gardens show up whitish as heaps of rubble. The cars jolt over a dead horse from which the rats scatter; beyond it is another dead horse with part of his cart still harnessed to him; beyond that lie two dead mules and about half of a Red Cross ambulance. This is a bad part of the road, not three hundred yards from the enemy. Very many men have been killed at just this point.

At the moment it is more beautiful than words can say. With the light of the moon upon them the walls of the ruins are like obelisks in some garden of the gods. Bats are flitting up and down above the road, and the shadows of the trees make patterns and an owl is calling. Then from in front comes a pattering of little feet, and a drove of donkeys comes along, tiny donkeys hardly bigger than sheep, and pattering with their little hooves like sheep. A man is in charge of them. They come here night after night; they are safer than these wagons and cars which make a noise. For tonight they have done their task; they have brought up their loads and now are going back to safety. They patter by with that air of patience and wisdom which the donkey has. The man in charge calls to them and they shift to their side of the road, stumbling, slackening, and quickening, with their little feet beating out of time.

The ambulances have to go very slowly here, for the road is so full of shell-holes. Some of the worst of these have been roughly filled with ruin, but even so they are still nearly a foot deep. A brook runs across the road in one place. It once ran under the road through a culvert, but the culvert has been blown to pieces and the masonry merged with the road, and now the water flows across and runs into the shell-holes. The taint of corruption hangs about this place and the rats are busy there, for dead horses lie in the water, just as they were killed a few days since when they stooped there to drink after the dusty journey. The ambulances splash across the swamp and turn a bend into the Place of what was once a big village.

All the Place shows up brightly in the moonlight. It was once the Place, the central square, the heart and market-place of a community. Now it is like a cemetery or place of death. All the houses surrounding it are ruins, all are roofless, most of the walls are down, the few walls still standing are pierced with holes, or toppling, or half-razed, or propped by the wreck of their floors which have fallen sideways and now support them. The trees are wrenched off six feet from the ground and end in bunches of twisted splinters. A bed or two, the sticks of chairs, some broken carts, some garden gates, a mess of straw and a travelling soup-kitchen are littered up and down in the road. Disemboweled houses, with their fronts gone, pour out their treasures of broken plaster. A pile of coils of barbed wire lies on one side, and two stretcher-bearers are seated beside it, talking in low tones. In the centre of the Place is the village Calvary, famous in its way among the Calvarys of France. Shells have fallen round it and burst against it and pitted it with marks, but have not destroyed it. One shell (said now to have been the last of the great attack) tore an arm from it and slued the whole cross round, so that now the figure of Christ leans toward the enemy and points with his one arm forward, as though showing France the way.

This is "the front." Two hundred and fifty yards away, a seventh part of a mile, two minutes' walk, are the enemy lines. Dead ahead, in what looks like a big rubbish-heap, such as one may see in suburbs where builders have been putting up a row of villas, is the Poste de Secours. The rubbish-heap was once a farm, though no man, not even the farmer, could now say where his buildings lay. The cellars, where once the farmer matured his vintage, make the Poste; the rising ground beyond, once the vineyard, is dug across by "our" support trenches, "our" outermost line is somewhere beyond the ridge, under a star which does not float down, but is steady, being Vega. Someone has fixed a Red Cross mark on the rubbish-heap as a guide to the ambulance, and a pile of bloody old stretchers lies beside it. The cellar entrance has been adapted. The approach is down a gentle slope, barred across with battens to keep the feet of the stretcher-bearers from slipping. The entrance is hung across with canvas so that no gleam of light may pass.

The drivers leave their cars and go toward the entrance, where a stretcher-bearer stands. He welcomes them, and the usual talk begins of how long the war will last, and how it will end. There are several cases inside, he says, and more are coming, for the enemy has been firing trench torpedoes. He says that the cases will not be ready for an hour, and then at one in the morning some sick are coming; the cars will have to wait for instructions. The drivers go down the sloping path into the cellars. The cellar roof has been propped and heaped with layers of timber balks interspersed with sandbags, and the cellar itself, shored up, is like a mine. It is a vast place with several rooms in it, from one of which, strongly lighted, comes the sound of voices and of people moving. Looking round near at hand, as the eye becomes accustomed to the darkness, one sees some loaded stretchers on the floor near the doorway. Three dead men, who were alive an hour ago, lie there awaiting burial. They were all hit by one torpedo, says the stretcher-bearer, these and five others, but these three died on their way to the Poste. Some say that the dead look as though they were asleep, but no sleep ever looked like death. These men are not asleep; they are dead, whatever that may mean. Their uniforms are clean; there is no mud on their boots. By their clean equipment it is easy to see that they were men of this night's relief; probably they were only an hour in the trenches, and now they are relieved forever.

Farther from the door, in a darkness like that of an old ship's forecastle, are stands of bunks for the stretcher-bearers. Those who are off duty lie asleep there, "like a trooper's horse, all standing"; that is, with their clothes on. Beyond them is a kind of office where two men are playing draughts, one man is writing a letter, and a fourth is reading a newspaper.

Away to the right, where the voices and the movement are, is a larger room. Men move about in it, softly, and one man with his side to the door is bending over something. He is the *Médecin Chef* of the Poste watching a dying soldier in the very article of death. He and his assistant are dressed in white sterilized operating robes. The orderlies stand about the table, intent upon their tasks. A saline injection is at work. There is a smell of ether and a blinding presence of iodine. One man has his hand on the patient's wrist, and all eyes are turned upon the poor fellow's face, as his breath fails. "Both his legs were broken by the torpedo," says the doctor, "and we have done all we could, but he had lost too much blood." The man dies, even as he speaks; tender hands very gently order his body and lay it on its stretcher with the three others near the door. Another wounded man, lying on a stretcher, is lifted onto the operating-table. One of his legs is shattered; but this man is a grizzled country labourer, much stronger than the man who has just gone. He looks round on the people with a look of terror, like an animal's terror. Someone says, "*N'ayez pas peur.*" The anaesthetist lowers a mask upon his face, pours ether, and murmers, "*Respirez.*" The man breathes hard for two minutes, and then in the drunkenness of the fumes struggles up, claws at the orderlies, and swears and calls upon the Holy Ghost. The orderlies grin and glance at each other; the man falls into unconsciousness, and his wound is laid bare and searched. The doctors shake their heads and cut off the leg below the knee, and an orderly plobs it into a tin bucket, foot uppermost. Before the man has completely recovered consciousness he is off the table, wrapped up upon his stretcher, and another wounded man takes his place. This man has a piece of the torpedo in his ankle, but with help he is able to hobble to the table and to swing himself onto it. He casts a frightened grin at the men about him, but tries to see the operation, such as it is. The other wounded men have been treated. They are sitting silent and motionless, absorbed in their own pain, in semi-darkness on a bench at the back. One can see their three white faces, much swathed in bandages, and the droop of their three bodies. They do not want to talk. It is labour enough to them to keep from crying out. They do not move, they regard nothing; they sit as though dazed, and as though they belonged to a different species, as though they were in a different world. The world of pain is a different world.

The work goes on in a sort of sequence of smells – first the smell of ether, then the smell of iodine, then ether again. All the time, outside, the shells are passing and bursting; but the noise seems unreal down in the cellar, and very far away. Sometimes the strangeness of it strikes deeply home, that this down in the cellar is the height of man's skill, done many feet underground at midnight because of the depth of man's deficiency. The drivers sit on a bench beside the buckets of legs and fall asleep there, and wake up from time to time to see men bending over the table, and great shadows falling and shifting on the ceiling, and limbs turning yellow from the iodine. The iodine gets into the eyes, and a certain quietness in people's movements gets into the nerves, and one feels that it all happened long ago, in some old tower – not now at all – and that it is part of a dream which once had a meaning.

Once or twice, as the drivers wake, men come into the cellars, and presently the sick arrive, haggard and white, but able to walk, and the gathering breaks up and the ambulances are free to go. The moon is blotted by this time; it is darker and beginning to rain, the men say. On leaving the operating-room, one hears again as a real thing the scream of the rush of the big shells, the thump of the bursts, and the crash of the great guns. The stretchers are passed into the ambulances, the sick are helped onto seats, they are covered with blankets, and the doors are closed. It is much darker now and the rain has already made the ground sticky; and with the rain the smell of corruption has become heavier, and the ruin is like what it is – a graveyard laid bare. Shells from the enemy rush overhead and burst in a village which lies on the road home. They are strafing the village; the cars have a fair chance of being blown to pieces; it is as dark as pitch and the road will be full of new shell-holes. The drivers start their engines and turn the cars for home; the rain drives in their faces as they go, and along the road in front of them the shells flash at intervals, lighting the tree-stumps.

This is a quiet evening's work in a quiet time, but it is not always thus. Often there is no moon, but a blinding snow and a road on fire with shell-bursts. Then the drivers grope forward by such glimmers as they can get from searchlights; they butt into the side of the road and lurch across craters, and perhaps break down on a road being searched by shells, and do their repairs in the scattering of the shrapnel.

These drivers (there are now, and have been, some hundreds of them) are men of high education. They are the very pick and flower of American life, some of them professional men, but the greater number of them young men on the threshold of life, lads just down from college or in their last student years. All life lies before them in their own country, but they have put that aside for an idea, and have come to help France in her hour of need. Two of them have died and many of them have been maimed for France, and all live a life of danger and risk death nightly. To this company of splendid and gentle and chivalrous Americans be all thanks and greetings from the friends and allies of sacred France.

[source: *Harper's Monthly Magazine*, May 1917, pp.[801]–810]

The Irony of Battle

Irony is difficult to define, for it has many kinds and many depths; it may be light, evil and bitter, artificial and profound; it is sometimes noble in persons, as in the three or four recorded words of Dante; and it is always strange and suggestive in circumstance. In the ironical suggestion of circumstances, if ever, men catch a hint of some working behind Life upon the surface of Life; one sees glimpses of a game being played, and wonders, for a moment, if all be accidental, the working of our own wills.

The stories of wars (which often centre about the persons of great ideas) are full of ironical circumstance, most of them, no doubt, the inventions of the poets, but some of them true. The tale that, before his defeat, Mark Antony heard in the air the music of troops passing from him, and knew that his god, Hercules, was giving him over, is probably poetical, like Pompey's dream before Pharsalia. But it is true, and strange, that Cromwell died, knowing that his effort had failed, on the anniversary of the day which made it for the time successful. After the battle of Sedan, Napoleon the Third surrendered to the enemy in a room hung with prints of the successes of the great Napoleon. It may be that in this present war, the end will come with some strangeness and mockery of circumstance humbling to the proud.

Probably everyone who has seen the fields of this present war has seen cases and instances of irony. Not far from one of the most famous battle-fields of this war, there is a military cemetery, containing some two thousand dead. Just beside it is a village Calvary with the inscription:– "C'EST AINSI QUE DIEU A AIMÉ LE MONDE."

On another battlefield, in a field fortress, stubbornly defended by the enemy and at last won by the English, there is the crater of a mine, sprung by the English under a strong part of the defence. When the fortress was at last won, this crater was found to be littered with enemy dead. One of them was found lying on his face gripping a handful of papers. The papers were little tracts or leaflets sent round (apparently) for distribution to the men, and perhaps this man had been killed in the act of distributing them. The leaflets each bore a rough woodcut, representing a sinking steamer, with a naval cutter rowing towards her. The title underneath the woodcut was:– "THE U BOAT'S REWARD."

Close to this crater, in another part of the same fortress, where the fighting was close and desperate for several days together, the bodies of two men were found clutching each other as though wrestling. They had evidently grappled each other without weapons of any kind, and had then been killed by a shell or bomb. One of these men was a Bavarian, the other a man of some Scottish regiment. The Scotsman's field service Bible had fallen from his pocket and lay open on the ground at a little distance from him. It was open at the 22nd Chapter of Deuteronomy, under the page headings "Humanity towards Brethren," and "An uncertain Murder."

A more significant and more touching instance of the same thing may be seen in a distant part of the old battlefield of the Somme, in a part of the field where the attack of the English was a containing attack, not meant to do more than to hold the enemy while he was attacked and defeated in the main battle some miles away. Here, where the bombardment was not so terrible as in other parts of that awful moorland of battle, the spring has already begun to cover the desolation, the birds are singing and the grass pushing. The story of the battle is written plainly on the earth for anyone to read. There is the English line, just as the English held it when the battle began. In front of it is the greenish strip of No Man's Land, with the English wire intact, save for lanes left in it for the passage of the troops in the charge. Two hundred yards down the slope is the dark, rusty tangle of the enemy wire, cut into rags and flung into heaps by the English shrapnel, which plied it for the whole of one terrible week, in the storm of fire which made the enemy speak of the Somme battle as the Blood Bath. All the way, from the English trench to the enemy wire, the English graves are heaped on the ground, just where the men fell in the minute of their leaving their trench. It is possible that they knew, as they went over the parapet, that their charge was but a secondary affair in the tactical scheme, and would not be decisive and glorious in the day's history, so that the graves of these men are deeply pathetic. The marks of the graves stand up all the way to the enemy, almost like the men charging. Some are marked with crosses, others with rifles thrust into the ground by their bayonets, others with standing shells, or with strips of packing-case or bits of equipment. These last are nearly always the graves of the unknown or unrecognizable.

Near one of these graves of the unknown a field prayer-book lies open in the mud at the Psalms appointed for the seventeenth day of the month. The mud and the rain have obliterated nearly all the print upon the page, but for one verse, which says, "Thou hast broken his hedge, thou hast torn down his strong places." The enemy's hedge is indeed broken there, and his strong place is now many miles away; so far that the guns cannot be heard from where this dead man lies.

[source: *The Nation*, 16 June 1917, p.272]

Messages of Greeting . . .
. . . From England to Russia . . .

I wish the Russian revolution all glorious and complete success. That a great country, for so many years past the leader of the world in all the arts, should have at last cast out the government, at once devilish and incompetent, which broke Dostoievsky, exiled Kropotkin, threatened Tolstoy, bullied Tchaikovsky, and cramped, killed, blinded, and dwarfed every intelligence it could reach, throughout its continent of possessions; which, although the granary of the world, allowed its millions to go breadless, and although linked with us in arms betrayed its armies and its allies to the enemy, is the profoundest and most living event of our time. In greeting the new Russia we greet a new world and a new way of life for the world.

[source: *Manchester Guardian*, 7 July 1917, p.26]

In the Vosges

The Story of an American Driver's First Night Under Fire

It is a year ago now. I was twenty at the time and had only just come out; in fact, I reached Paris on the thirteenth day after leaving home. When I reached Paris they sent me across France to join my section, which was down in the Vosges. I did not know then that trains in wartime are few and crowded; I came late and had to stand in the corridor all the way to Lorraine.

The train made ———, in Lorraine, on time, but there came a *changement* and delay; I could go no farther till the next morning. I had difficulty in getting permission to leave the station so as to sleep at an inn. During the night there was an air raid. In the morning there was another difficulty. The usual civilian train to ——— was suspended, owing to the movements of troops. The commandant of the station was too busy to attend to me. I went to his office to ask what I was to do, but it was crowded with officers, and his orderly kept me back. One officer who was writing at a desk told me that I could not go.

I suppose that the men were nearly off their heads with work. I was on the platform for three hours, and in all that time men were bringing them papers, and officers were coming up for instructions. The line was busy, soldiers were cheering, trains full of troops came past, with windows full of shouting heads, and in the midst of all the noise they started loading the horses of a battery into some cars at a siding.

While they were doing this I had another go at the commandant, and this time one of his officers said that I might go on with the battery. His orderly took me along and left me in charge of some *artilleurs*, who led me in to the dirty straw on the floor of a horse box, where I lay among the crowd, with my head on my bag.

By and by we started and crawled along the line to where we stopped at a siding – for hours, it seemed. It was bitterly cold December weather, with snow overhead, and a flake or two blowing in the air. I don't know that I have ever known a more evil day. None of the *artilleurs* knew where they were going – except vaguely, that there was to be a push on the right. We kept the doors closed and tried to keep warm. One of the men, who had just parted from his wife, was weeping; the others sang a little, and smoked and chaffed and cursed the cold.

The Men in the Hospital Train

Presently we heard a noise of shouting, so we opened the door and looked out, and saw a trainload of infantry going in the direction of the frontier. One of our *artilleurs* said, "*Cà chauffe*," which means, I suppose, "Things are beginning to get a move on." I was excited at this, yet anxious, for I did not much know what being in a battle would be like, or how much scared I should be. After this train had passed us we were allowed to proceed, and crawled on for an hour or two, when we stopped at a little station where there was a halted train that I shall never forget. One of the *artilleurs* pointed it out to me, with the remark that there was work for me.

It was what is called a *train sanitaire*, or train for carrying the wounded. Part of it was divided up, so to speak, into residential blocks or compartments for the surgeons, cooks and orderlies, who lived and slept on board her day in, day out; the rest of it was for the wounded. I had never seen wounded men before; this was my first view of them. Of course the seriously hurt were lying on their stretchers inside the train; I could not see them. But I could see the others.

By a chance the others were nearly all men suffering from shell shock, and on seeing them my first thought was that I was looking at a train-load of gibbering lunatics. All the windows were filled with faces full of terror and horror, with staring eyes and dribbling mouths.

They were all white, and all ghastly; and none of them could stand being touched, or the sound of the train.

They must have come out of the trenches during the night.

The mud was caked thick upon them everywhere, except where they were bandaged, and one man, for some reason, stared at me in a way that I shall remember. It is possible that he never saw me, but his eyes were turned upon me all the time that I stood there. God knows what agony of terror and pain had brought that look upon him. It was the face of a man who for hours on hours has had to watch death coming nearer and nearer in its most awful form, and had at last been struck by death, and yet could not tell how badly. His arms and shoulder were all swathed in bandages, but I know now that he was not dangerously hit. By his look, he had been a clerk or shop assistant before the war, and a game of dominoes was about as much contest as he was fit for. Now he stared, as though the horror of what he had seen would never pass from his memory. His look had a kind of pity and a kind of ghastly envy in it for me who was young, and still clean and unwounded.

After this we passed on out of the station to other stations, all full of the confusion and the bustle of war. There was certainly going to be a push on the right. At last we reached the terminus, where we all got out, and my friends, the *artilleurs*, bade me goodbye. They got out their horses and their guns and limbered up and away, in quick time. I never saw any of them again.

When I got out I was numb with cold; snow was falling and we were well up among the foothills of the Vosges. It was about five o'clock in the evening, very dark, with no glimmer of a moon. As far as one could see we were in a kind of glen, with a sort of blackness, which might be hills, on both sides of the line. I had hoped some member of my section might be there to meet me, but when I saw there was none I realized that they had expected me by the earlier train, half a dozen hours before, and had now given me up.

I went to the commandant of the depot to ask about it. He told me that a man had come down to meet me, but had long since given me up and gone. It was seven miles to the village where the section was billeted; I could walk it, he thought, unless stopped by the guards; or perhaps someone would give me a lift.

Some First Impressions

He was called away before I could ask him how I could get a lift. I waited for him to come back, but he did not come. His office was a little room, with a red-hot stove in it, and two tables, one his own and the other for his clerks. The clerks were two old soldiers, both intently busy, making three copies of everything on paper of different colours with pens that scratched. I wondered what it was they were doing and what would happen if they left out, say, a yellow copy or a dark-red one, in any of their sets of three.

There were some prints upon the wall; a big coloured map of France with "the line" drawn across it in blue chalk; a map of the Vosges, with big red wafers stuck upon it to mark I know not what; and the famous yellow print of the Crown Prince, *Le Raté*, or The Thwarted, on the battlefield of the Marne. Men came in from time to time to leave papers on the commandant's desk.

By and by, after I had waited a long time, an officer who entered asked who I was. He looked at me pretty narrowly and asked to see my papers, which he studied with care, especially the photograph on my passport. This photograph was not very like me; it had been taken at home, before I put on my uniform, and my uniform had greatly changed my appearance. He asked if I had no photograph showing me in uniform, and when I said "No" he seemed displeased. My papers were *en règle*, but I had been told about the danger of spies, and the man's manner made me anxious. He asked how I had come on from ———, and then took my *ordre de mission* out of the room.

As he went out the two clerks stopped writing and looked up at me. They were two nice old soldiers, but the look had about it something of the police court and the firing party. It made me wonder what they would do if I stepped toward the door. I stood still where I was, and gazed at the pictures and maps, and they dropped their eyes and went on with their writing.

148

The officer was gone for ten minutes. As I had imagined, he had gone to telephone to my section about me. When he came back he was very nice to me; he even tried his English on me. "We wish you good luck!" he said. Then in French he said that some *camions* were about to start for my village and that I could go in one of them. He gave back my papers, smiled, shook hands, again wished me good luck and sent one of the old clerks with me to the *place* of the town, where the *camion* convoy stood.

When I went out of the hot office the cold seemed to go right through me. Snow was blowing about in those little dry aimless pellets, too tiny to be called flakes, which come at the beginning of a fall. We went out of the station and round a block of buildings into the *place*, which had a light or two in it. Just as we came round the corner I heard quite plainly a noise of distant explosions – not, perhaps, many together, but coming in a run, one after the other, pretty continually. "*Les canons*," said my guide. They seemed to come from somewhere above, to the east of me.

On the south side of the *place* was a big building with a kind of veranda in front of it. Men were moving about with lanterns near this veranda, and presently I saw that it was not a veranda but a convoy of big, roofed, motor wagons getting ready to start. My guide explained to someone who I was and where I was to go; he then bade me goodnight and turned away. He was a little elderly man from a village in Haute-Savoie; I met him afterward. The convoy man put me into one of his wagons, which was full of sacks of potatoes; I curled myself up out of the drafts, with my baggage round me; presently we started and I fell asleep.

When I got down from the wagon we were in a pitch-dark village street, where a mountain torrent ran in front of the houses. The roar of the water almost drowned the noise of the guns, which were still going on somewhere above me. The snow was blowing about, there was a smell of sauerkraut and a dog was howling. My driver helped me to take my baggage to a door from which a light streamed. The wagons went on after that; and as they started the commandant of my section welcomed me in.

I went into a long, narrow room where about thirty weary men were eating supper. A place was made for me near the stove, so that I thawed and ate at the same time. The food was exceedingly good, it being near the Front, and there is a saying: "The nearer the Front the sweeter the meat." But the men there had the air of eating so as to be done with it. They were tipping food into themselves exactly as one tips letters into a letter-box. One or two men, as they finished, got up and went out. A minute or two later I heard their ambulances starting in the street outside.

There was not much need to ask questions, for what I had seen and heard among the soldiers during the day had taught me that there was fighting in the mountains. Now I could see that the fighting was hard and that these men were in it. The fighting had lasted for two days and nights, so they told me, and this was the third night, and the ambulances had been going and coming all the time till the drivers were nearly worn out.

149

Both sides were attacking. Far up, above us on the ridges, there was a battle of hell for the possession of the peaks, and no man could say which way the fight would turn.

A Journey in Darkness

From the manner of the men I gathered that there was a chance that our side might not win. I will not say that I was scared; but there I was, just arrived, and the battle was going on, and it was dark, and I knew nothing about a battle anyway. One man fell fast asleep at his food, even as he ate. I had read of exhausted soldiers doing this; now I saw it done.

The commandant asked if I were too weary to go right away in one of the ambulances, so as to give the driver a night's rest. He said that he would drive, so as to show me the road, and that I should be the assistant. I said that of course I would come. He said: "We'll start directly after supper. We'll go to the topmost *poste*, right up among the hills. I hope the snow will keep off."

I asked if it were far to where the fighting was. He said: "About four miles, all uphill, and in forest as dark as pitch. Wrap yourself, for it's going to be cold, though the engine will warm you up when she gets going."

I talked jauntily enough, but I did not feel jaunty. I had come all that way, four thousand miles, without really thinking what it would be like at the end. The excitement of helping France, and the pleasure of being in uniform, and the vanity of being thought a hero, had kept me from seeing the truth. Now here it was, in the dark and cold, only four miles away, and it made me anxious in a new kind of way. We went out of the mess room to the street where the ambulance cars were parked.

As soon as my eyes were accustomed to the darkness I made out some blackness of buildings, with chinks of light at windows and doors. Beyond these in one place I made out a bigger blackness, which was a mountain. Snow was still drifting about in pellets. Not enough was on the ground to cover it; there was just a dust of snow, powdering about in a stillness that foretold a big fall. If the snow had been on the ground it would have made the night lighter. As it was, it was one of the darkest nights I could remember, and as cold as the Banks.

The commandant climbed into his seat; I sat beside him, and we started.

For the first few minutes it was not so bad, because the road lay along the valley of the brook for a fairly open stretch. Then we ran into a village where the darkness was utter. I could scarcely catch the blackness of the houses against the blackness of the sky. There was not even a gleam of light in this village. "It has been shot up," said the commandant. "Nobody lives at this end. They shoot it up still from time to time, just at this end, trying to catch the crossroads."

We took a turning at the crossroads and came into what seemed a wider place. I could see nothing, but the commandant slowed down here,

150

and when the engine quieted I could hear other engines moving beside us and see a sort of moving blackness in the blackness, where something was wallowing along. I heard a horse walking past us, then rather a lot of horses, and I caught a whiff of stables and horse sweat and heard a clack of chain. Straining to see, the dust of snow blew into my eyes; and the pellets pitted gently on my face and against the screen.

We went on a little, and the noise of the torrent fell away, and I heard a noise of men marching, and cries in the road and the rumble of wagons. How the commandant could see to drive I could not imagine. I do not know even now how one drives on those roads in the dark nights. We were in a road with convoys of wagons and moving troops going in both directions, and I could see nothing but blackness that might have been anything, full of noises from everywhere.

Presently in front of us a shaft of light fell across the road from a door suddenly opened and left wide. I saw men on a sidewalk at my left, and, on my right, going across the shaft of light, in the same direction as ourselves, a column of soldiers marching. Someone on a white horse crossed the shaft, and glittered as he crossed; then rank after rank of men, all grey in the light and all alike, with their rifles and their packs and their tin dishes on their packs, and their buttoned-back coat skirts and shifting gaiters, went on and on.

At first they were invisible, then they loomed up black and rather big, then became grey in the light, then darkened and passed into the darkness, and others and others came. We went slowly there, for men were going into the doorway from the road. One of them shouted "*Bon repos!*" to us, and another, seeing the car with the Red Cross upon it, knew that we were Americans and called out, in good Virginian: "Well! What's the matter?" After that the blackness shut down upon us and I knew neither where we were nor how long we were going.

Up the Mountain Slopes

We turned to the left and went up a slope where there was a glow of light from a double doorway. It was the door of a big house in use as a hospital. An ambulance was near the door and some *brancardiers* were unloading the wounded from it and carrying them up the steps. When we were clear of that house we saw no more light for a long time. We began to zigzag up the road that leads to the peaks. My companion told me that there were vineyards on both sides of us and that the enemy used to shell the vineyards when the grapes were ripe. I was glad that it was now long after grape harvest. Afterward I made that journey many times by daylight, and got to know it pretty well. It is a bad road even in daylight; its surface curves and gradients are all bad. At the beginning of the war it was a charcoal-burner's cart track. They had made it a passable road for wartime. Perhaps the very best road comes down to that in wartime, from the traffic on it.

We swung round a kind of bastion or bulge in the mountain, and one of the gusts that blow down glens pelted the dust of snow on our front and flank, with malice, as we came round. My eyes were stung with it so that I had to shut them, and as I shut them I heard the roar of water from a torrent that went under the road. I could not make anything out of the road, except that we were on the flank of a glen, and I learned that from the way the wind was blowing. I could see nothing but blackness and what I imagined to be in the blackness.

It may partly have been the rhythm of the engines, partly the strain of not being able to see through the blackness and the snow dust, but all the time I felt that the road beside us was full of voices. I seemed to hear men talking as they marched, or singing those marching songs like

C'est pour la Patrie
Et pour la Nation,

or sometimes bursting into laughter. Then I would crane out from behind the screen, expecting to find a column on the road, at my elbow, but there was no one there. Looking out like that, I saw a light very far below me; and realized that the light was in the valley and that we had already climbed, and were up among the hills.

The car stopped for a moment; we had to get out to lift the bonnet. The noise of the men marching, with their laughter and songs, stopped with us, and instantly the peace of the night was in its place, with the ripple of a brook, trotting downhill, and a murmur like the noise of a beach where the sea falls upon sand. For an instant I felt that we were beside the sea or that we were on an island in the sea, for the noise of waves fell all round us and died and rose and strengthened, and then gathered as though the tide were upon us.

"Is not that like the sea?"

"It's the pine beginning. It is all pine forest on from here."

"Listen!"

There was no noise of cannon. One of the great owls of the forest was crying near by, and his mate was hunting in the valley. Somewhere, very far away, a motor horn sounded, and near at hand the pellets of snow pitted on our coats, and the breathing in the trees was made louder by them. The commandant flashed his torch, so as to show the road, just dusted with snow, running behind us between bare banks, and running on before us into what looked like an army of giants drawn up and halted on the path; these were the pines.

When we were in the forest the noise of the voices began and I felt again all the impotence of blindness. The dust of the snow drove into my eyes, and I could see nothing but blackness, peopled – as it seemed – by voices and by bulks of blackness that would seem to be wagons or guns or marching columns and then prove to be nothing. We wound up the hill in a zigzag, like a beast nosing on a trail.

After rounding each turn the commandant let her out and she ran uphill for a minute or two, hugging the inner bank. Then, as he judged her to be near the next turn, he edged her over, slowed her and crept along till we were round. I did not then know what lay beyond on the outside edge of the road. Afterward I saw it by daylight. The hill tips down on a slope that is the steepest a man can climb without having to use his hands. Out of this slope the pine trees shoot like the columns of a cathedral. There is nothing but the pine trees to keep a falling car from rolling over and over into the scree, and from the scree into the river at the bottom.

We had groped our way round one or two turns when the car lurched, nosed into the bank, scraped along it, dropped her hind wheel with another lurch and then went on. The jolt gave me a pang, for I thought we were over. We slackened a bit and felt our way; and then from right ahead came the cry "*Attention!*" which in French means "Look out!" or "Mind what you're playing at!"

We stopped dead, and there came a shogging of feet; it was a column of the *relève* going up; we had overtaken the rear company, and now they were shifting to the right to let us go past. By a flash torch I could see the great packs upon the men's shoulders and the droop of weary bodies. The men were not what you would call marching. They were plodding forward, much as pack slaves must have plodded on the road between Panama and Porto Bello.

Batteries Open Fire

We went warily on, sounding the horn; we heard the crunching of the road under the feet, and the strain of leather and the voices, though not the words, of those who cried for a lift. Presently we passed the rear company, and the voices died away, and we came to some gap or glen that let in the roar of the battle, and I heard the crashing of the guns and saw a glimmer in the sky. It did not last for more than a minute, but it went right through me, it was so much nearer. Then we passed again into the heart of the forest and that noise of the sea shut the battle away, except for an occasional crash from the French heavy guns on our side of the hill.

All the time the snow was falling. It came from nowhere, over the screen into my eyes, almost as though someone were throwing it. Whenever I shut my eyes I heard voices and the noise of wagons ahead; whenever I opened them I saw blackness, with a sort of dance of greyness in it. Then the specks of the snow came into my eyes and made me shut them again. I cannot tell you the trouble of not being able to see. We crept forward, rubbing our nose in the bank and edging one wheel in the ditch, while the snow came pit-pit-pitter-pit and the crunch of the wagons filled the road. And the surf overhead was full of laughter.

Then there were lights in among the tree boles – or, rather, streaks of light – with men's bodies moving across the streaks and hurrying across the road. We had to wait while some hundreds of men came down at the *pas de charge* – a sort of heavy-laden trot – and went away to our left.

They were out of breath, and their officers, being younger, called to them, and one or two of the men joked. The noise of the guns could be heard again, but somehow they seemed far off; the near-at-hand things were what mattered – these men in the road, the snow-like dust, and not being able to see.

When we had gone some distance farther I had the shock of my life. Two hidden batteries in the wood beside us suddenly opened a rapid fire, with a succession of crashes and screams that sent my heart into my boots. Then over the noise of our engines came a wailing whistle; I saw a blinding light with a tree bole in it; there was a bang and a sound of something falling. Then another blinding light burst with a bang on the road in front of us; then another and another and another, each one glimmering nearer to us and screaming.

The Shells in the Forest

I did not need to be told that these were enemy shells and that they were meant to kill me. I made that out for myself. Was I scared? No; I was not scared. I was terrified out of my wits! Laying down my life for France seemed sweet and fitting four thousand miles away; but here it was being blown to bits by something unseen that rushed on you out of the dark. There came one awful thing; I felt the wind of it, it screamed right at us and flung earth over us.

"That was a dud," said the commandant. "It would have about put us west if it had burst. They have this bit of road down fine."

I got a bit of a hold of myself, though I felt my heart shaking like a buzzer. My tongue seemed too big for my mouth and all dried up at the roots, and my chest seemed so tight that I could hardly breathe. Ow-ow! Ow-ow!! Bong!!! came a shell in front. I swore with terror; and I remember the thought: "These damned artists don't give you any idea of it!" Then I heard a bong behind us, and heard a pellet hit the ambulance. Then came another dud fairly close, and then a succession of howling in the air that made me really sick.

"They're only our *départs*," said the commandant. "But, golly, here's an *arrivée!* Golly, he's a big one!"

Right ahead there was a roaring scream, louder than anything that had come. There was a blast on the road in front and a droning aloft from the shell shards spinning in the air; then a noise of collapsing and the gallop of a runaway horse. I heard the hoofs and the noise of chain and something slatting and dragging on the road, and then a half-mad *ravitaillement* horse came tearing downhill with a bit of his wagon still hitched to him. His chain hit our bonnet a good clip, and then he was gone. I got one thing from that horse – that this life of ours, man's and horse's, is pretty much of a piece in the main. I knew what he was feeling, and I felt the same way myself.

By the time the last of the shell was down we were at the shell-hole in the middle of the road. I suppose it was four feet deep and six feet across. My first thought, as I flashed the torch so that we could dodge it, was: "Suppose another comes while we are here!" Then as our engine slackened I heard a man groaning and saw a piece of a horse and a sort of tumble of planks lying in the road. The groans came from among the planks, so we stopped and got down, and I just saw the face of an old man change into a dead face.

"It got him on the head," said the commandant, "and blew the one horse to pieces and cut the other loose. Here come some *génies*; they'll clear the road."

The snow was drifting about still, but what there was of it was blowing up off the ground, not falling. The ground was powdered over with it. My flash torch made a circle of light round the dead man in the wreck; beyond the circle were a dimness, the road, tree boles, and then blackness. Out of the blackness came some men with a lantern. They were bearded men and moved slowly. They were the *génies*, or engineers, in charge of that section of the road.

Another shell and then another burst in the forest beyond us. After one of them there were a pause, a splitting crack, and a swoosh and collapse as a big tree came down. Its fall scared up some little animal, a rabbit or squirrel, which pattered about and seemed lost, and bolted into the road and then saw us and bolted back. My one thought was: "O God, why don't these *génies* hustle and clear the road, so that we can get past? Do they want to keep us here till we are blown to pieces?"

They bent down at the wreck, lifted some planks of the wagon and hove them aside, so as to free the body of the driver.

"He got it on the brow," said one. "That's bad, that!"

"Yes," said another. "They killed my cousin so, in Champagne, in the Battle of the Marne."

"He's dead," said a third to me. "You needn't take him to the *poste*." They pitched some of the wreck into the shell-hole, and presently the road was clear, but for parts of the horse; an engineer waved us forward. About half a dozen shells burst right over the road in front of us, and at each burst there came a whi-i-i-i-ng in the air that I had not heard before. One of the *génies* laughed.

"Shrapnel!" he said. "That's pretty, that!"

"That's the bullets of the shrapnel scattering," said the commandant; "and I can't get her to start. It's a hell of a place to go *en panne* in!" *En panne* means hove-to, stopped, without way, and, at the Front, broken down.

I thought "Now I am done! I shall be killed here. I shall be blown to pieces here in this road. Damn this dirty enemy who began this war; I shan't even see them!"

There came a shrapnel fairly close. If it had been high-explosive I might have bolted, but shrapnel seemed quite friendly, and I got hold of myself and I said:

"Did she get a bit of *éclat* in front?"

When I had said that I found that I could turn my back on the enemy and see about patching the car. It was nothing; we had her going in a minute.

"*Bonne chance!*" said one of the *génies*; a little dud shell went into the wood and nosed the earth about.

"Some shooting tonight!" said the commandant.

The Attack

When we were away from the engineers the darkness closed in upon us for what seemed a long time; we went uphill as before, as blind as the dead. The shells seemed to miss the next bit of road; they went over it and burst in the wood beyond, thirty yards below us. It seemed very safe after the last piece. We came up on to what was a kind of neck between two bulges of mountain, and as we came round onto it we caught the roar of the battle, now dead near and banging like the Fourth. I had never heard such a racket, but even as we went it quickened to a rolling drumming, and immediately every gun within miles took up the song and let out for all it was worth, and every hill and valley and *col* sent back a different echo, till the roar shook and rocked and hit the head.

"That's an attack," said the commandant. "Do you hear the mitrailleuses? Here we are at the *poste*."

I could see nothing, but by the flash torch I could make out a cleared space with a kind of cave built into the hill, and a very neat pine railing in front of it. There was a garden there, with little paved alleys and a summerhouse in it – all made by the soldiers. Someone cried out "*Attention!*" and I got out of the way of two stretcher-bearers who were carrying a man who kept saying: "*Oh, là là! Oh, là là.*"

I thought, when they had passed, that that was over; but it was only the beginning of a procession of stretcher-bearers, all coming very slowly, in the midnight, step by cautious step, on their plod from the trenches to the road and down to the *poste*. I cannot describe their plod. It was slower than a funeral march. First the bearers groped with their feet for a footing in the dark, then made good the footing with their other feet. I thought: "Imagine travelling like that, in the front communication trenches, with shells bursting all round! And these stretcher-bearers are elderly men – married men with families, or priests and monks. They go right up to the first line day in, day out; in a midnight attack like this they work all night as well. I should be a cur to be afraid simply to go along a road in an ambulance."

All this time many shells were passing overhead, so many that I could not think of each one; there was some comfort in that. Then a fair number failed to burst, which was a great comfort; but even so the racket was terrific. There were a lot of ambulances parked at the roadside in a line, ready to go down when filled. I put my hand on the side of one of them

– it was trembling, just like an animal. The commandant asked me if I would like to see the *poste*.

We went into the mouth of the cave to a low hall or cellar, vaulted with iron, and ceiled above the iron with many feet of timber balks, sandbags, earth and stones. The floor of the hall was already covered with stretchers. I suppose there were twenty stretchers at my feet; in the room beyond, where they were operating, there were others; and outside, in the terrace or kind of garden, they were laying down more. The place was lit with an oil lamp. The light seemed to have an attraction for the wounded men. Many of them stared at it. No doubt it caught their eyes when they were brought in out of the dark, and they were still too dazed to be able to look away.

I don't know that I was shocked or horrified or terrified, but I was moved right down to the heart. Nothing that I could say was any good, nothing I could do to help. Then I looked at those men and heard a sort of whimper of pain pass like a message across them, and I thought: "There are beautiful human beings, finer fellows than I; and some devils have been doing this to them."

What the Sign Meant

The médecin-chef – surgeon in charge – of the *poste* came from his operating table to peer at us. He waved to the commandant, called out that he was too busy, and went back to the table. There was a smell of ether, and the air seemed full of iodine. I don't know what they were doing in there, but I saw great shadows moving and heard a thick voice cursing; I suppose someone was being anaesthetized. It was my first sight of surgery of war. These things cannot be described; they have to be felt.

Outside they were loading up the ambulances, so we bore a hand and soon loaded up ours. Ours were three bad cases who lay very still. One of them was a head case, whom we had to lift with the extreme of care, since one touch might be death to him. We were told to take another road down the mountain; so we set off.

Going down was like going up – a groping in a blackness – but that there was less forest by this road. The first part of the way was fairly clear, open moorland, with a kind of lightness or snow blink on it, so that we could see. It was not a snow blink, though, but the glare of war. In all the sky above this moorland was a ruddy running glimmer of flashes, which never really stopped. It was like summer lightning, only ruddier and more constant. Then at intervals, all along it, star shells went up, and stopped in the air like the toys tossed up by a conjurer. I liked the star shells, for when they were aloft I could see where we were going; but they were dreadful for all that, and the racket from where they came, always slackening and quickening, was terrible.

When we had gone about a quarter of a mile we came to a crossways where some companies of soldiers were halted. Right at the crossways there was a lantern on the stump of a tree. A sergeant was standing by the light calling a roll, and men were answering to it. On the top of the stump was a big white placard or direction pointer, pointing toward the battle.

We stopped there for some minutes while the troops mustered and took their several roads. While we waited I read the writing on the pointer. It was *Centre de Résistance*. I asked the commandant what it meant.

"That?" he said. "It means that that bit of hill over there must be held at all costs, and that these men going to it must not leave it alive. Every man must die at his post, rather!"

Presently we were able to move forward on our way down to the valley. Once or twice, on our way down, the cocks in the hen-roosts, roused by our passing, flapped their wings on their perches and crowed at us.

[source: *The Saturday Evening Post*, 21 July 1917, pp.8–9 and pp.58–59]

The Old Front Line
or
The Beginning of
The Battle of The Somme

TO
NEVILLE LYTTON

Chapter I

This description of the old front line, as it was when the Battle of the Somme began, may someday be of use. All wars end; even this war will someday end, and the ruins will be rebuilt and the field full of death will grow food, and all this frontier of trouble will be forgotten. When the trenches are filled in, and the plough has gone over them, the ground will not long keep the look of war. One summer with its flowers will cover most of the ruin that man can make, and then these places, from which the driving back of the enemy began, will be hard indeed to trace, even with maps. It is said that even now in some places the wire has been removed, the explosive salved, the trenches filled, and the ground ploughed with tractors. In a few years' time, when this war is a romance in memory, the soldier looking for his battlefield will find his marks gone. Centre Way, Peel Trench, Munster Alley, and these other paths to glory will be deep under the corn, and gleaners will sing at Dead Mule Corner.

It is hoped that this description of the line will be followed by an account of our people's share in the battle. The old front line was the base from which the battle proceeded. It was the starting-place. The thing began there. It was the biggest battle in which our people were ever engaged, and so far it has led to bigger results than any battle of this war since the Battle of the Marne. It caused a great falling back of the enemy armies. It freed a great tract of France, seventy miles long, by from ten to twenty-five miles broad. It first gave the enemy the knowledge that he was beaten.

Very many of our people never lived to know the result of even the first day's fighting. For them the old front line was the battlefield, and the No Man's Land the prize of the battle. They never heard the cheer of victory nor looked into an enemy trench. Some among them never even saw the No Man's Land, but died in the summer morning from some shell in the trench in the old front line here described.

It is a difficult thing to describe without monotony, for it varies so little. It is like describing the course of the Thames from Oxford to Reading, or of the Severn from Deerhurst to Lydney, or of the Hudson from New York to Tarrytown. Whatever country the rivers pass they remain water, bordered by shore. So our front line trenches, wherever they lie, are only gashes in the earth, fenced by wire, beside a greenish strip of ground, pitted with shell-holes, which is fenced with thicker, blacker, but more

161

tumbled wire on the other side. Behind this further wire is the parapet of the enemy front line trench, which swerves to take in a hillock or to flank a dip, or to crown a slope, but remains roughly parallel with ours, from seventy to five hundred yards from it, for miles and miles, up hill and down dale. All the advantages of position and observation were in the enemy's hands, not in ours. They took up their lines when they were strong and our side weak, and in no place in all the old Somme position is our line better sited than theirs, though in one or two places the sites are nearly equal. Almost in every part of this old front our men had to go up hill to attack.

If the description of this old line be dull to read, it should be remembered that it was dull to hold. The enemy had the lookout posts, with the fine views over France, and the sense of domination. Our men were down below with no view of anything but of stronghold after stronghold, just up above, being made stronger daily. And if the enemy had strength of position he had also strength of equipment, of men, of guns, and explosives of all kinds. He had all the advantages for nearly two years of war, and in all that time our old front line, whether held by the French or by ourselves, was nothing but a post to be endured, day in day out, in all weathers and under all fires, in doubt, difficulty, and danger, with bluff and makeshift and improvisation, till the tide could be turned. If it be dull to read about and to see, it was, at least, the old line which kept back the tide and stood the siege. It was the line from which, after all those months of war, the tide turned and the besieged became the attackers.

To most of the British soldiers who took part in the Battle of the Somme, the town of Albert must be a central point in a reckoning of distances. It lies, roughly speaking, behind the middle of the line of that battle. It is a knot of roads, so that supports and supplies could and did move from it to all parts of the line during the battle. It is on the main road, and on the direct railway line from Amiens. It is by much the most important town within an easy march of the battlefield. It will be, quite certainly, the centre from which, in time to come, travellers will start to see the battlefield where such deeds were done by men of our race.

It is not now (after three years of war and many bombardments) an attractive town; probably it never was. It is a small straggling town built of red brick along a knot of crossroads at a point where the swift chalk-river Ancre, hardly more than a brook, is bridged and so channelled that it can be used for power. Before the war it contained a few small factories, including one for the making of sewing-machines. Its most important building was a big church built a few years ago, through the energy of a priest, as a shrine for the Virgin of Albert, a small, probably not very old image, about which strange stories are told. Before the war it was thought that this church would become a northern rival to Lourdes for the working of miraculous cures during the September pilgrimage. A gilded statue of the Virgin and Child stood on an iron stalk on the summit of the church tower. During a bombardment of the town at a little after three o'clock in the afternoon of Friday, January 15, 1915, a shell so bent the stalk that the statue bent down over the Place as though diving. Perhaps few of our soldiers will remember Albert for anything except this diving Virgin. Perhaps half of the men engaged in the Battle of the Somme passed underneath her as they marched up to the line, and, glancing up, hoped that she might not come down till they were past. From someone, French or English, a word has gone about that when she does fall the war will end. Others have said that French engineers have so fixed her with wire ropes that she cannot fall.

From Albert four roads lead to the battlefield of the Somme:

1. In a north-westerly direction to Auchonvillers and Hébuterne.
2. In a northerly direction to Authuille and Hamel.
3. In a north-easterly direction to Pozières.
4. In an easterly direction to Fricourt and Maricourt.

Between the second and the third of these the little river Ancre runs down its broad, flat, well-wooded valley, much of which is a marsh through which the river (and man) have forced more than one channel. This river, which is a swift, clear, chalk stream, sometimes too deep and swift to ford, cuts the English sector of the battlefield into two nearly equal portions.

Following the first of the four roads, one passes the wooded village of Martinsart, to the village of Auchonvillers, which lies among a clump of trees upon a ridge or plateau top. The road dips here, but soon rises again, and so, by a flat tableland, to the large village of Hébuterne. Most of this road, with the exception of one little stretch near Auchonvillers, is hidden by high ground from every part of the battlefield. Men moving upon it cannot see the field.

Hébuterne, although close to the line and shelled daily and nightly for more than two years, was never the object of an attack in force, so that much of it remains. Many of its walls and parts of some of its roofs still stand, the church tower is in fair order, and no one walking in the streets can doubt that he is in a village. Before the war it was a prosperous village; then, for more than two years, it rang with the roar of battle and with the business of an army. Presently the tide of the war ebbed away from it and left it deserted, so that one may walk in it now, from end to end, without seeing a human being. It is as though the place had been smitten by the plague. Villages during the Black Death must have looked thus. One walks in the village expecting at every turn to meet a survivor, but there is none; the village is dead; the grass is growing in the street; the bells are silent; the beasts are gone from the byre and the ghosts from the church. Stealing about among the ruins and the gardens are the cats of the village, who have eaten too much man to fear him, but are now too wild to come to him. They creep about and eye him from cover and look like evil spirits.

The second of the four roads passes out of Albert, crosses the railway at a sharp turn, over a bridge called Marmont Bridge, and runs northward along the valley of the Ancre within sight of the railway. Just beyond the Marmont Bridge there is a sort of lake or reservoir or catchment of the Ancre overflows, a little to the right of the road. By looking across this lake as he walks northward, the traveller can see some rolls of gentle chalk hill, just beyond which the English front line ran at the beginning of the battle.

A little further on, at the top of a rise, the road passes the village of Aveluy, where there is a bridge or causeway over the Ancre valley. Aveluy itself, being within a mile and a half of enemy gun positions for nearly two years of war, is knocked about, and rather roofless and windowless. A crossroad leading to the causeway across the valley once gave the place some little importance.

Not far to the north of Aveluy, the road runs for more than a mile through the Wood of Aveluy, which is a well-grown plantation of trees and shrubs. This wood hides the marsh of the river from the traveller. Tracks from the road lead down to the marsh and across it by military causeways.

On emerging from the wood, the road runs within hail of the railway, under a steep and high chalk bank partly copsed with scrub. Three-quarters of a mile from the wood it passes through the skeleton of the village of Hamel, which is now a few ruined walls of brick standing in orchards on a hillside. Just north of this village, crossing the road, the railway, and the river-valley, is the old English front line.

The third of the four roads is one of the main roads of France. It is the state highway, laid on the line of a Roman road, from Albert to Bapaume. It is by far the most used and the most important of the roads crossing the battlefield. As it leads directly to Bapaume, which was one of the prizes of the victory, and points like a sword through the heart of the enemy positions it will stay in the memories of our soldiers as the main avenue of the battle.

The road leaves Albert in a street of dingy and rather broken red brick houses. After passing a corner crucifix it shakes itself free of the houses and rises slowly up a ridge of chalk hill about three hundred feet high. On the left of the road, this ridge, which is much withered and trodden by troops and horses, is called Usna Hill. On the right, where the grass is green and the chalk of the old communication trenches still white and clean, it is called Tara Hill. Far away on the left, along the line of the Usna Hill, one can see the Aveluy Wood.

Looking northward from the top of the Usna-Tara Hill to the dip below it and along the road for a few yards up the opposite slope, one sees where the old English front line crossed the road at right angles. The

164

enemy front line faced it at a few yards' distance, just about two miles from Albert town.

The fourth of the four roads runs for about a mile eastwards from Albert, and then slopes down into a kind of gully or shallow valley, through which a brook once ran and now dribbles. The road crosses the brook-course, and runs parallel with it for a little while to a place where the ground on the left comes down in a slanting tongue and on the right rises steeply into a big hill. The ground of the tongue bears traces of human habitation on it, all much smashed and discoloured. This is the once pretty village of Fricourt. The hill on the right front at this point is the Fricourt Salient. The lines run round the salient and the road cuts across them.

Beyond Fricourt, the road leaves another slanting tongue at some distance to its left. On this second tongue the village of Mametz once stood. Near here the road, having now cut across the salient, again crosses both sets of lines, and begins a long, slow ascent to a ridge or crest. From this point, for a couple of miles, the road is planted on each side with well-grown plane-trees, in some of which magpies have built their nests ever since the war began. At the top of the rise the road runs along the plateau top (under trees which show more and more plainly the marks of war) to a village so planted that it seems to stand in a wood. The village is built of red brick, and is rather badly broken by enemy shellfire, though some of the houses in it are still habitable. This is the village of Maricourt. Three or four hundred yards beyond Maricourt the road reaches the old English front line, at the eastern extremity of the English sector, as it was at the beginning of the battle.

Chapter II

These four roads which lead to the centre and the wings of the battle-field were all, throughout the battle and for the months of war which preceded it, dangerous by daylight. All could be shelled by the map, and all, even the first, which was by much the best hidden of the four, could be seen, in places, from the enemy position. On some of the trees or tree stumps by the sides of the roads one may still see the "camouflage" by which these exposed places were screened from the enemy observers. The four roads were not greatly used in the months of war which preceded the battle. In those months, the front was too near to them, and other lines of supply and approach were more direct and safer. But there was always some traffic upon them of men going into the line or coming out, of ration parties, munition and water carriers, and ambulances. On all four roads many men of our race were killed. All, at some time, or many times, rang and flashed with explosions. Danger, death, shocking escape and firm resolve, went up and down those roads daily and nightly. Our men slept and ate and sweated and dug and died along them after all hardships and in all weathers. On parts of them, no traffic moved, even at night, so that the grass grew high upon them. Presently, they will be quiet country roads again, and tourists will walk at ease, where brave men once ran and dodged and cursed their luck, when the Battle of the Somme was raging.

Then, indeed, those roads were used. Then the grass that had grown on some of them was trodden and crushed under. The trees and banks by the waysides were used to hide batteries, which roared all day and all night. At all hours and in all weathers the convoys of horses slipped and stamped along those roads with more shells for the ever-greedy cannon. At night, from every part of those roads, one saw a twilight of summer lightning winking over the high ground from the never-ceasing flashes of guns and shells. Then there was no quiet, but a roaring, a crashing, and a screaming from guns, from shells bursting and from shells passing in the air. Then, too, on the two roads to the east of the Ancre River, the troops for the battle moved up to the line. The battalions were played by their bands through Albert, and up the slope of Usna Hill to Pozières and beyond, or past Fricourt and the wreck of Mametz to Montauban and the bloody woodland near it. Those roads then were indeed paths of glory leading to the grave.

During the months which preceded the Battle of the Somme, other roads behind our front lines were more used than these. Little villages, out of shellfire, some miles from the lines, were then of more use to us than Albert. Long after we are gone, perhaps, stray English tourists, wandering in Picardy, will see names scratched in a barn, some mark or notice on a door, some signpost, some little line of graves, or hear, on the lips of a native, some slang phrase of English, learned long before in the war-time, in childhood, when the English were there. All the villages behind our front were thronged with our people. There they rested after being in the line and there they established their hospitals and magazines. It may be said, that men of our race died in our cause in every village within five miles of the front. Wherever the traveller comes upon a little company of our graves, he will know that he is near the site of some old hospital or clearing station, where our men were brought in from the line.

So much for the roads by which our men marched to this battlefield. Near the lines they had to leave the roads for the shelter of some communication trench or deep cut in the mud, revetted at the sides with wire to hinder it from collapsing inwards. By these deep narrow roads, only broad enough for marching in single file, our men passed to "the front," to the line itself. Here and there, in recesses in the trench, under roofs of corrugated iron covered with sandbags, they passed the offices and the stores of war, telephonists, battalion headquarters, dumps of bombs, barbed wire, rockets, lights, machine gun ammunition, tins, jars, and cases. Many men, passing these things as they went "in" for the first time, felt with a sinking of the heart, that they were leaving all ordered and arranged things, perhaps for ever, and that the men in charge of these stores enjoyed, by comparison, a life like a life at home.

Much of the relief and munitioning of the fighting lines was done at night. Men going into the lines saw little of where they were going. They entered the gash of the communication trench, following the load on the back of the man in front, but seeing perhaps nothing but the shape in front, the black walls of the trench, and now and then some gleam of a star in the water under foot. Sometimes as they marched they would see the starshells, going up and bursting like rockets, and coming down with a wavering slow settling motion, as white and bright as burning magnesium wire, shedding a kind of dust of light upon the trench and making the blackness intense when they went out. These lights, the glimmer in the sky from the enemy's guns, and now and then the flash of a shell, were the things seen by most of our men on their first going in.

In the fire trench they saw little more than the parapet. If work were being done in the No Man's Land, they still saw little save by these lights that floated and fell from the enemy and from ourselves. They could see only an array of stakes tangled with wire, and something distant and dark which might be similar stakes, or bushes, or men, in front of what could only be the enemy line. When the night passed, and those working outside the trench had to take shelter, they could see nothing, even at a loophole or periscope, but the greenish strip of ground, pitted with shell-holes and fenced with wire, running up to the enemy line. There was little else for them to see, looking to the front, for miles and miles, up hill and down dale.

The soldiers who held this old front line of ours saw this grass and wire day after day, perhaps, for many months. It was the limit of their world, the horizon of their landscape, the boundary. What interest there was in their life was the speculation, what lay beyond that wire, and what the enemy was doing there. They seldom saw an enemy. They heard his songs and they were stricken by his missiles, but seldom saw more than, perhaps, a swiftly moving cap at a gap in the broken parapet, or a grey figure flitting from the light of a star-shell. Aeroplanes brought back photographs of those unseen lines. Sometimes, in raids in the night, our men visited them and brought back prisoners; but they remained mysteries and unknown.

In the early morning of the 1st of July, 1916, our men looked at them as they showed among the bursts of our shells. Those familiar heaps, the lines, were then in a smoke of dust full of flying clods and shards and gleams of fire. Our men felt that now, in a few minutes, they would see the enemy and know what lay beyond those parapets and probe the heart of that mystery. So, for the last half-hour, they watched and held themselves ready, while the screaming of the shells grew wilder and the roar of the bursts quickened into a drumming. Then as the time drew near, they looked a last look at that unknown country, now almost blotted in the fog of war, and saw the flash of our shells, breaking a little further off as the gunners "lifted," and knew that the moment had come. Then for one wild confused moment they knew that they were running towards that unknown land, which they could still see in the dust ahead. For a moment, they saw the parapet with the wire in front of it, and began, as they ran, to pick out in their minds a path through that wire. Then, too often, to many of them, the grass that they were crossing flew up in shards and sods and gleams of fire from the enemy shells, and those runners never reached the wire, but saw, perhaps, a flash, and the earth rushing nearer, and grasses against the sky, and then saw nothing more at all, for ever and for ever and for ever.

It may be some years before those whose fathers, husbands and brothers were killed in this great battle, may be able to visit the battlefield where their dead are buried. Perhaps many of them, from brooding on the map, and from dreams and visions in the night, have in their minds an image or picture of that place. The following pages may help some few others, who have not already formed that image, to see the scene as it appears today. What it was like on the day of battle cannot be imagined by those who were not there.

It was a day of an intense blue summer beauty, full of roaring, violence, and confusion of death, agony, and triumph, from dawn till dark. All through that day, little rushes of the men of our race went towards that No Man's Land from the bloody shelter of our trenches. Some hardly left our trenches, many never crossed the green space, many died in the enemy wire, many had to fall back. Others won across and went further, and drove the enemy from his fort, and then back from line to line and from one hasty trenching to another, till the Battle of the Somme ended in the falling back of the enemy army.

Chapter III

Those of our men who were in the line at Hébuterne, at the extreme northern end of the battlefield of the Somme, were opposite the enemy salient of Gommecourt. This was one of those projecting fortresses or flankers, like the Leipzig, Ovillers, and Fricourt, with which the enemy studded and strengthened his front line. It is doubtful if any point in the line in France was stronger than this point of Gommecourt. Those who visit it in future times may be surprised that such a place was so strong.

All the country there is gentler and less decided than in the southern parts of the batttlefield. Hébuterne stands on a plateau-top; to the east of it there is a gentle dip down to a shallow hollow or valley; to the east of this again there is a gentle rise to higher ground, on which the village of Gommecourt stood. The church of Gommecourt is almost exactly one mile north-east and by north from the church at Hébuterne; both churches being at the hearts of their villages.

Seen from our front line at Hébuterne, Gommecourt is little more than a few red brick buildings, standing in woodland on a rise of ground. Wood hides the village to the north, the west, and the south-west. A big spur of woodland, known as Gommecourt Park, thrusts out boldly from the village towards the plateau on which the English lines stood. This spur, strongly fortified by the enemy, made the greater part of the salient in the enemy line. The landscape away from the wood is not in any way remarkable, except that it is open, and gentle, and on a generous scale. Looking north from our position at Hébuterne there is the snout of the woodland salient; looking south there is the green shallow shelving hollow or valley which made the No Man's Land for rather more than a mile. It is just such a gentle waterless hollow, like a dried-up river-bed, as one may see in several places in chalk country in England, but it is unenclosed land, and therefore more open and seemingly on a bigger scale than such a landscape would be in England, where most fields are small and fenced. Our old front line runs where the ground shelves or glides down into the valley; the enemy front line runs along the gentle rise up from the valley. The lines face each other across the slopes. To the south, the slope on which the enemy line stands is very slight.

The impression given by this tract of land once held by the enemy is one of graceful gentleness. The wood on the little spur, even now, has something green about it. The village, once almost within the wood, wrecked to shatters as it is, has still a charm of situation. In the distance

170

behind Gommecourt there is some ill-defined rising ground forming gullies and ravines. On these rises are some dark clumps of woodland, one of them called after the nightingales, which perhaps sing there this year, in what is left of their home. There is nothing now to show that this quiet landscape was one of the tragical places of this war.

The whole field of the Somme is chalk hill and downland, like similar formations in England. It has about it, in every part of it, certain features well-known to everyone who has ever lived or travelled in a chalk country. These features occur even in the gentle, rolling, and not strongly marked sector near Hébuterne. Two are very noticeable, the formation almost everywhere of those steep, regular banks or terraces, which the French call *remblais* and our own farmers lynchets, and the presence, in nearly all parts of the field, of roads sunken between two such banks into a kind of narrow gully or ravine. It is said, that these *remblais*, or lynchets, which may be seen in English chalk counties, as in the Dunstable Downs, in the Chiltern Hills, and in many parts of Berkshire and Wiltshire, are made in each instance, in a short time, by the ploughing away from the top and bottom of any difficult slope. Where two slopes adjoin, such ploughing steepens the valley between them into a gully, which, being always unsown, makes a track through the crops when they are up. Sometimes, though less frequently, the farmer ploughs away from a used track on quite flat land, and by doing this on both sides of the track, he makes the track a causeway or ridgeway, slightly raised above the adjoining fields. This type of raised road or track can be seen in one or two parts of the battlefield (just above Hamel and near Pozières, for instance), but the hollow or sunken road and the steep *remblai*, or lynchet, are everywhere. One may say that no quarter of a mile of the whole field is without one or other of them. The sunken roads are sometimes very deep. Many of our soldiers, on seeing them, have thought that they were cuttings made, with great labour, through the chalk, and that the *remblais*, or lynchets, were piled up and smoothed for some unknown purpose by primitive man. Probably it will be found, that in every case they are natural slopes made sharper by cultivation. Two or three of these lynchets and sunken roads cross the shallow valley of the No Man's Land near Hébuterne. By the side of one of them, a line of Sixteen Poplars, now ruined, made a landmark between the lines.

The line continues (with some slight eastward trendings, but without a change in its gentle quiet) southwards from this point for about a mile to a slight jut, or salient in the enemy line. This jut was known by our men as the Point, and a very spiky point it was to handle. From near the Point on our side of No Man's Land, a bank or lynchet, topped along its edge with trees, runs southwards for about a mile. In four places, the trees about this lynchet grow in clumps or copses, which our men called after the four Evangelists, John, Luke, Mark, and Matthew. This bank marks the old English front line between the Point and the Serre Road a mile to the south of it. Behind this English line are several small copses, on ground which very gently rises towards the crest of the plateau a mile to the west. In front of most of this part of our line, the ground rises towards the enemy trenches, so that one can see little to the front, but the slope up. The No Man's Land here is not green, but as full of shell-holes and the ruin of battle as any piece of the field. Directly between Serre and the Matthew Copse, where the lines cross a rough lump of ground, the enemy parapet is whitish from the chalk. The whitish parapet makes the skyline to observers in the English line. Over that parapet, some English battalions made one of the most splendid charges of the battle, in the heroic attack on Serre four hundred yards beyond.

To the right of our front at Matthew Copse the ground slopes south-ward a little, past what may once have been a pond or quarry, but is now a pit in the mud, to the Serre road. Here one can look up the muddy road to the hamlet of Serre, where the wrecks of some brick buildings stand in a clump of tree stumps, or half-right down a God-forgotten kind of glen, blasted by fire to the look of a moor in hell. A few rampikes of trees standing on one side of this glen give the place its name of Ten Tree Alley. Immediately to the south of the Serre road, the ground rises into one of the many big chalk spurs, which thrust from the main Hébuterne plateau towards the Ancre Valley. The spur at this point runs east and west, and the lines cross it from north and south. They go up it side by side, a hundred and fifty yards apart, with a greenish No Man's Land between them. The No Man's Land, as usual, is the only part of all this chalk spur that is not burnt, gouged, pocked, and pitted with shellfire. It is, however, enough marked by the war to be bad going. When they are well up the spur, the lines draw nearer, and at the highest point of the spur they converge in one of the terrible places of the battlefield.

For months before the battle began, it was a question here, which side should hold the highest point of the spur. Right at the top of the spur there is one patch of ground, measuring, it may be, two hundred yards each way, from which one can see a long way in every direction. From this patch, the ground droops a little towards the English side and stretches away fairly flat towards the enemy side, but one can see far either way, and to have this power of seeing, both sides fought desperately.

Until the beginning of the war, this spur of ground was corn-land, like most of the battlefield. Unfenced country roads crossed it. It was a quiet, lonely, prosperous ploughland, stretching for miles, up and down, in great sweeping rolls and folds, like our own chalk downlands. It had one feature common to all chalk countries; it was a land of smooth expanses. Before the war, all this spur was a smooth expanse, which passed in a sweep from the slope to the plateau, over this crown of summit.

Today, the whole of the summit (which is called the Redan Ridge), for all its two hundred yards, is blown into pits and craters from twenty to fifty feet deep, and sometimes fifty yards long. These pits and ponds in rainy weather fill up with water, which pours from one pond into another, so that the hilltop is loud with the noise of the brooks. For many weeks, the armies fought for this patch of hill. It was all mined, counter-mined, and re-mined, and at each explosion the crater was fought for and lost and won. It cannot be said that either side won that summit till the enemy was finally beaten from all that field, for both sides conquered enough to see from. On the enemy side, a fortification of heaped earth was made; on our side, castles were built of sandbags filled with flint. These strongholds gave both sides enough observation. The works face each other across the ponds. The sandbags of the English works have now rotted, and flag about like the rags of uniform or like withered grass. The flint and chalk laid bare by their rotting look like the grey of weath-ered stone, so that, at a little distance, the English works look old and noble, as though they were the foundations of some castle long since fallen under Time.

To the right, that is to the southward, from these English castles there is a slope of six hundred yards into a valley or gully. The slope is not in any way remarkable or seems not to be, except that the ruin of a road, now barely to be distinguished from the field, runs across it. The opposing lines of trenches go down the slope, much as usual, with the enemy line above on a slight natural glacis. Behind this enemy line is the bulk of the spur, which is partly white from up-blown chalk, partly burnt from months of fire, and partly faintly green from recovering grass. A little to the right or south, on this bulk of spur, there are the stumps of trees and no grass at all, nothing but upturned chalk and burnt earth. On the battlefield of the Somme, these are the marks of a famous place.

The valley into which the slope descends is a broadish gentle opening in the chalk hills, with a road running at right angles to the lines of trenches at the bottom of it. As the road descends, the valley tightens in, and just where the enemy line crosses it, it becomes a narrow deep glen or gash, between high and steep banks of chalk. Well within the enemy position and fully seven hundred yards from our line, another such glen or gash runs into this glen, at right angles. At this meeting place of the glens is or was the village of Beaumont Hamel, which the enemy said could never be taken.

For the moment it need not be described; for it was not seen by many of our men in the early stages of the battle. In fact our old line was at least five hundred yards outside it. But all our line in the valley here was opposed to the village defences, and the fighting at this point was fierce and terrible, and there are some features in the No Man's Land just outside the village which must be described. These features run parallel with our line right down to the road in the valley, and though they are not features of great tactical importance, like the patch of summit above, where the craters are, or like the windmill at Pozières, they were the last things seen by many brave Irish and Englishmen, and cannot be passed lightly by.

The features are a lane, fifty or sixty yards in front of the front trench, and a *remblai*, or lynchet, fifty or sixty yards in front of the lane.

The lane is a farmer's track leading from the road in the valley to the road on the spur. It runs almost north and south, like the lines of trenches, and is about five hundred yards long. From its start in the valley-road to a point about two hundred yards up the spur it is sunken below the level of the field on each side of it. At first the sinking is slight, but it swiftly deepens as it goes up hill. For more than a hundred yards it lies between banks twelve or fifteen feet deep. After this part the banks die down into insignificance, so that the road is nearly open. The deep part, which is like a very deep, broad, natural trench, was known to our men as the Sunken Road. The banks of this sunken part are perpendicular. Until recently, they were grown over with a scrub of dwarf beech, ash, and sturdy saplings, now mostly razed by fire. In the road itself our men built up walls of sandbags to limit the effects of enemy shellfire. From these defences steps cut in the chalk of the bank lead to the field above, where there were machine gun pits.

The field in front of the lane (where these pits were) is a fairly smooth slope for about fifty yards. Then there is the lynchet, or *remblai*, like a steep cliff, from three to twelve feet high, hardly to be noticed from above until the traveller is upon it. Below this lynchet is a fairly smooth slope, so tilted that it slopes down to the right towards the valley road, and slopes up to the front towards the enemy line. Looking straight to the front from the Sunken Road our men saw no sudden dip down at the lynchet, but a continuous grassy field, at first flat, then slowly rising towards the enemy parapet. The line of the lynchet-top merges into the slope behind it, so that it is not seen. The enemy line thrusts out in a little salient here, so as to make the most of a little bulge of ground which was once wooded and still has stumps. The bulge is now a heap and ruin of burnt and tumbled mud and chalk. To reach it our men had to run across the flat from the Sunken Road, slide down the bank of the lynchet, and then run up the glacis to the parapet.

The Sunken Road was only held by our men as an advanced post and "jumping off" (or attacking) point. Our line lay behind it on a higher part of the spur, which does not decline gradually into the valley road, but breaks off in a steep bank cut by our soldiers into a flight of chalk steps. These steps gave to all this part of the line the name of Jacob's Ladder. From the top of Jacob's Ladder there is a good view of the valley road running down into Beaumont Hamel. To the right there is a big steep knoll of green hill bulking up to the south of the valley, and very well-fenced with enemy wire. All the land to the right or south of Jacob's Ladder is this big green hill, which is very steep, irregular, and broken with banks, and so ill-adapted for trenching that we were forced to make our line further from the enemy than is usual on the front. The front trenches here are nearly five hundred yards apart. As far as the hilltop the enemy line has a great advantage of position. To reach it our men had to cross the open and ascend a slope which gave neither dead ground nor cover to front or flank. Low down the hill, running parallel with the road, is a little lynchet, topped by a few old hawthorn bushes. All this bit of the old front line was the scene of a most gallant attack by our men on the 1st of July. Those who care may see it in the official cinematograph films of the Battle of the Somme.

Right at the top of the hill there is a dark enclosure of wood, orchard, and plantation, with several fairly well-preserved red brick buildings in it. This is the plateau-village of Auchonvillers. On the slopes below it, a couple of hundred yards behind Jacob's Ladder, there is a little round clump of trees. Both village and clump make conspicuous landmarks. The clump was once the famous English machine gun post of the Bowery, from which our men could shoot down the valley into Beaumont Hamel.

Chapter IV

The English line goes up the big green hill, in trenches and saps of reddish clay, to the plateau or tableland at the top. Right up on the top, well behind our front line and close to one of our communication trenches, there is a good big hawthorn bush, in which a magpie has built her nest. This bush, which is strangely beautiful in the spring, has given to the plateau the name of the Hawthorn Ridge.

Just where the opposing lines reach the top of the Ridge they both bend from their main north and south direction towards the south-east, and continue in that course for several miles. At the point or salient of the bending, in the old enemy position, there is a crater of a mine which the English sprang in the early morning of the 1st of July. This is the crater of the mine of Beaumont Hamel. Until recently it was supposed to be the biggest crater ever blown by one explosion. It is not the deepest: one or two others near La Boisselle are deeper, but none on the Somme field comes near it in bigness and squalor. It is like the crater of a volcano, vast, ragged and irregular, about one hundred and fifty yards long, one hundred yards across, and twenty-five yards deep. It is crusted and scabbed with yellowish tetter, like sulphur or the rancid fat on meat. The inside has rather the look of meat, for it is reddish and all streaked and scabbed with this pox and with discoloured chalk. A lot of it trickles and oozes like sores discharging pus, and this liquid gathers in holes near the bottom, and is greenish and foul and has the look of dead eyes staring upwards.

All that can be seen of it from the English line is a disarrangement of the enemy wire and parapet. It is a hole in the ground which cannot be seen except from quite close at hand. At first sight, on looking into it, it is difficult to believe that it was the work of man; it looks so like nature in her evil mood. It is hard to imagine that only three years ago that hill was cornfield, and the site of the chasm grew bread. After that happy time, the enemy bent his line there and made the salient a stronghold, and dug deep shelters for his men in the walls of his trenches; the marks of the dugouts are still plain in the sides of the pit. Then, on the 1st of July, when the explosion was to be a signal for the attack, and our men waited in the trenches for the spring, the belly of the chalk was heaved, and chalk, clay, dugouts, gear, and enemy, went up in a dome of blackness full of pieces, and spread aloft like a toadstool, and floated, and fell down.

From the top of the Hawthorn Ridge, our soldiers could see a great expanse of chalk downland, though the falling of the hill kept them from seeing the enemy's position. That lay on the slope of the ridge, somewhere behind the wire, quite out of sight from our lines. Looking out from our front line at this salient, our men saw the enemy wire almost as a skyline. Beyond this line, the ground dipped towards Beaumont Hamel (which was quite out of sight in the valley) and rose again sharply in the steep bulk of Beaucourt spur. Beyond this lonely spur, the hills ranked and ran, like the masses of a moor, first the high ground above Miraumont, and beyond that the high ground of the Loupart Wood, and away to the east the bulk that makes the left bank of the Ancre River. What trees there are in this moorland were not then all blasted. Even in Beaumont Hamel some of the trees were green. The trees in the Ancre River Valley made all that marshy meadow like a forest. Looking out on all this the first thought of the soldier was that here he could really see something of the enemy's ground.

It is true, that from this hilltop much land, then held by the enemy, could be seen, but very little that was vital to the enemy could be observed. His lines of supply and support ran in ravines which we could not see; his batteries lay beyond crests, his men were in hiding-places. Just below us on the lower slopes of this Hawthorn Ridge he had one vast hiding-place which gave us a great deal of trouble. This was a gully or ravine, about five hundred yards long, well within his position, running (roughly speaking) at right angles with his front line. Probably it was a steep and deep natural fold made steeper and deeper by years of cultivation. It is from thirty to forty feet deep, and about as much across at the top; it has abrupt sides, and thrusts out two forks to its southern side. These forks give it the look of a letter Y upon the maps, for which reason both the French and ourselves called the place the "Ravin en Y" or "Y Ravine." Part of the southernmost fork was slightly open to observation from our lines; the main bulk of the gully was invisible, to us, except from the air.

Whenever the enemy has had a bank of any kind, at all screened from fire, he has dug into it for shelter. In the Y Ravine, which provided these great expanses of banks, he dug himself shelters of unusual strength and size. He sank shafts into the banks, tunnelled long living rooms, both above and below the gully-bottom, linked the rooms together with galleries, and cut hatchways and bolting holes to lead to the surface as well as to the gully. All this work was securely done, with baulks of seasoned wood, iron girders, and concreting. Much of it was destroyed by shellfire during the battle, but much not hit by shells is in good condition today even after the autumn rains and the spring thaw. The galleries which lead upwards and outwards from this underground barracks to the observation posts and machine gun emplacements in the open air, are cunningly planned and solidly made. The posts and emplacements to which they led are now, however, (nearly all) utterly destroyed by our shellfire.

In this gully barracks, and in similar shelters cut in the chalk of the steeper banks near Beaumont Hamel, the enemy could hold ready large numbers of men to repel an attack or to make a counter-attack. They lived in these dugouts in comparative safety and in moderate comfort. When our attacks came during the early months of the battle, they were able to pass rapidly and safely by these underground galleries from one part of the position to another, bringing their machine guns with them. However, the Ravine was presently taken and the galleries and underground shelters were cleared. In one underground room in that barracks, nearly fifty of the enemy were found lying dead in their bunks, all unwounded, and as though asleep. They had been killed by the concussion of the air following on the burst of a big shell at the entrance.

One other thing may be mentioned about this Hawthorn Ridge. It runs parallel with the next spur (the Beaucourt spur) immediately to the north of it, then in the enemy's hands. Just over the crest of this spur, out of sight from our lines, is a country road, well-banked and screened, leading from Beaucourt to Serre. This road was known by our men as Artillery Lane, because it was used as a battery position by the enemy. The wrecks of several of his guns lie in the mud there still. From the crest in front of this road there is a view to the westward, so wonderful that those who see it realize at once that the enemy position on the Ridge, which, at a first glance, seems badly sited for observation, is, really, well-placed. From this crest, the Ridge-top, all our old front line, and nearly all the No Man's Land upon it, is exposed, and plainly to be seen. On a reasonably clear day, no man could leave our old line unseen from this crest. No artillery officer, correcting the fire of a battery, could ask for a better place from which to watch the bursts of his shells. This crest, in front of the lane of enemy guns, made it possible for the enemy batteries to drop shells upon our front line trenches before all the men were out of them at the instant of the great attack.

The old English line runs along the Hawthorn Ridge-top for some hundreds of yards, and then crosses a dip or valley, which is the broad, fan-shaped, southern end of a fork of Y Ravine. A road runs, or ran, down this dip into the Y Ravine. It is not now recognizable as a road, but the steep banks at each side of it, and some bluish metalling in the shell-holes, show that one once ran there. These banks are covered with hawthorn bushes. A *remblai*, also topped with hawthorn, lies a little to the north of this road.

From this lynchet, looking down the valley into the Y Ravine, the enemy position is saddle-shaped, low in the middle, where the Y Ravine narrows, and rising to right and left to a good height. Chalk hills from their form often seem higher than they really are, especially in any kind of haze. Often they have mystery and nearly always beauty. For some reason, the lumping rolls of chalk hill rising up on each side of this valley have a menace and a horror about them. One sees little of the enemy position from the English line. It is now nothing but a track of black wire in front of some burnt and battered heapings of the ground, upon which the grass and the flowers have only now begun to push. At the beginning of the battle it must have been greener and fresher, for then the fire of hell had not come upon it; but even then, even in the summer day, that dent in the chalk leading to the Y Ravine must have seemed a threatening and forbidding place.

Our line goes along the top of the ridge here, at a good distance from the enemy line. It is dug on the brow of the plateau in reddish earth on the top of chalk. It is now much as our men left it for the last time. The trench-ladders by which they left it are still in place in the bays of the trenches. All the outer, or jumping-off, trenches, are much destroyed by enemy shellfire, which was very heavy here from both sides of the Ancre River. A quarter of a mile to the south-east of the Y Ravine the line comes within sight of the great gap which cuts the battlefield in two. This gap is the valley of the Ancre River, which runs here beneath great spurs of chalk, as the Thames runs at Goring and Pangbourne. On the lonely hill, where this first comes plainly into view, as one travels south along the line, there used to be two bodies of English soldiers, buried once, and then unburied by the rain. They lay in the No Man's Land, outside the English wire, in what was then one of the loneliest places in the field. The ruin of war lay all round them.

There are many English graves (marked, then, hurriedly, by the man's rifle thrust into the ground) in that piece of the line. On a windy day, these rifles shook in the wind as the bayonets bent to the blast. The field testaments of both men lay open beside them in the mud. The rain and the mud together had nearly destroyed the little books, but in each case it was possible to read one text. In both cases, the text which remained, read with a strange irony. The one book, beside a splendid youth, cut off in his promise, was open at a text which ran, "And Moses was learned in all the wisdom of the Egyptians and mighty in word and in deed." The other book, beside one who had been killed in an attack which did not succeed at the moment, but which led to the falling back of the enemy nation from many miles of conquered ground, read even more strangely. It was open at the eighty-ninth Psalm, and the only legible words were, "Thou hast broken down all his hedges; thou hast brought his strong-holds to ruin."

From the hilltop where these graves are the lines droop down towards the second of the four roads, which runs here in the Ancre valley parallel with the river and the railway. The slope is steep and the ground broken with shallow gullies and lynchets. Well down towards the river, just above the road, a flattish piece of land leads to a ravine with steep and high banks. This flattish land, well within the enemy line, was the scene of very desperate fighting on the 1st of July.

Looking at the enemy line in front of our own line here, one sees little but a gentle crest, protected by wire, in front of another gentle crest, also wired, with other gentle crests beyond and to the left. To the right there is a blur of gentle crests behind treetops. It is plain from a glance that gullies run irregularly into the spurs here, and make the defence easy. All through the fighting here, it happened too often that the taking of one crest only meant that the winners were taken in flank by machine guns in the crest beyond, and (in this bit of the line) by other guns on the other side of the river.

Well to the back of the English line here, on the top of the plateau, level with Auchonvillers, some trees stand upon the skyline, with the tower of a church, battered, but not destroyed, like the banner of some dauntless one, a little to the west of the wood. The wood shows marks of shelling, but nothing like the marks on the woods attacked by our own men. There are signs of houses among the trees, and the line of a big wood to the east of them.

This church and the buildings near it are parts of Mesnil village, most of which lies out of sight on the further side of the crest. They are conspicuous landmarks, and can be made out from many parts of the field. The chalk scarp on which they stand is by much the most beautiful thing on the battlefield, and the sight of Mesnil church tower on the top of it is most pleasant. That little banner stood all through the war, and not all the guns of the enemy could bring it down. Many men in the field near Mesnil, enduring the mud of the thaw, and the lice, wet, and squalor of dugouts near the front, were cheered by that church tower. "For all their bloody talk the bastards couldn't bring it down."

The hill with the lines upon it slopes steeply down to the valley of the Ancre. Just where the lines come to the valley, the ground drops abruptly, in a cliff or steep bank, twenty-five feet high, to the road.

Our line on this slope covers the village of Hamel, which lies just behind the line, along the road and on the hill-slopes above it. The church and churchyard of Hamel, both utterly ruined, lie well up the hill in such a position that they made good posts from which our snipers could shoot across the river at men in the Schwaben Redoubt. Crocuses, snowdrops, and a purple flower once planted on the graves of the churchyard, but now escaped into the field, blossomed here in this wintry spring, long before any other plant on the battlefield was in bud.

Hamel in peacetime may have contained forty houses, some shatters of which still stand. There are a few red brick walls, some frames of wood from which the plaster has been blown, some gardens gone wild, fruit trees unpruned and more or less ragged from fire, and an air of desecration and desertion. In some of the ruins there are signs of use. The lower windows are filled with sandbags, the lower stories are strengthened with girders and baulks. From the main road in the valley, a country track or road, muddy even for the Somme, leads up the hill, through the heart of the village, past the church, towards our old line and Auchonvillers.

Not much can be seen from the valley road in Hamel, for it is only a few feet above the level of the river-bed, which is well-grown with timber not yet completely destroyed. The general view to the eastward from this low-lying road is that of a lake, five hundred yards across, in some wild land not yet settled. The lake is shallow, blind with reeds, vivid with water-grass, and lively with moor-fowl. The trees grow out of the water, or lie in it, just as they fell when they were shot. On the whole, the trees just here, though chipped and knocked about, have not suffered badly; they have the look of trees, and are leafy in summer. Beyond the trees, on the other side of the marsh, is the steep and high eastern bank of the Ancre, on which a battered wood, called Thiepval Wood, stands like an army of black and haggard rampikes. But for this stricken wood, the eastern bank of the Ancre is a gentle, sloping hill, bare of trees. On the top of this hill is the famous Schwaben Redoubt.

The Ancre River and the marshy valley through which it runs are crossed by several causeways. One most famous causeway crosses just in front of Hamel on the line of the old Mill Road. The Mill from which it takes its name lies to the left of the causeway on a sort of green island. The wheel, which is not destroyed, still shows among the ruins. The enemy had a dressing station there at one time.

The marshy valley of the Ancre splits up the river here into several channels besides the mill stream. The channels are swift and deep, full of exquisitely clear water just out of the chalk. The marsh is rather blind with snags cut off by shells. For some years past the moor-fowl in the marsh have been little molested. They are very numerous here; their cries make the place lonely and romantic.

When one stands on this causeway over the Ancre one is almost at the middle point of the battlefield, for the river cuts the field in two. Roughly speaking, the ground to the west of the river was the scene of continuous fighting, the ground to the east of the river the scene of our advance. At the eastern end of the causeway the Old Mill Road rises towards the Schwaben Redoubt.

Chapter V

All the way up the hill the road is steep, rather deep, and bad. It is worn into the chalk and shows up very white in sunny weather. Before the battle it lay about midway between the lines, but it was always patrolled at night by our men. The ground on both sides of it is almost more killed and awful than anywhere in the field. On the English or south side of it, distant from one hundred to two hundred yards, is the shattered wood, burnt, dead, and desolate. On the enemy side, at about the same distance, is the usual black enemy wire, much tossed and bunched by our shells, covering a tossed and tumbled chalky and filthy parapet. Our own old line is an array of rotted sandbags, filled with chalk-flint, covering the burnt wood. One need only look at the ground to know that the fighting here was very grim, and to the death. Near the road and up the slope to the enemy the ground is littered with relics of our charges, mouldy packs, old shattered scabbards, rifles, bayonets, helmets curled, torn, rolled, and starred, clips of cartridges, and very many graves. Many of the graves are marked with strips of wood torn from packing cases, with pencilled inscriptions, "An unknown British Hero"; "In loving memory of Pte. ——"; "Two unknown British heroes"; "An unknown British soldier"; "A dead Fritz." That gentle slope to the Schwaben is covered with such things.

Passing these things, by some lane through the wire and clambering over the heaps of earth which were once the parapet, one enters the Schwaben, where so much life was spent. As in so many places on this old battlefield, the first thought is: "Why, they were in an eyrie here; our fellows had no chance at all." There is no wonder, then, that the approach is strewn with graves. The line stands at the top of a smooth, open slope, commanding our old position and the Ancre Valley. There is no cover of any kind upon the slope except the rims of the shell-holes, which make rings of mud among the grass. Just outside the highest point of the front line there is a little clump of our graves. Just inside there is a still unshattered concrete fortlet, built for the machine gun by which those men were killed.

All along that front trench of the Schwaben, lying on the parapet, half buried in the mud, are the belts of machine guns, still full of cartridges. There were many machine guns on that earthen wall last year. When our men scrambled over the tumbled chalky line of old sandbags, so plain just down the hill, and came into view on the slope, running and stumbling in the hour of the attack, the machine gunners in the fortress felt indeed that they were in an eyrie, and that our fellows had no chance at all.

For the moment one thinks this, as the enemy gunners must have thought it; then, looking up the hill at the inner works of the great fort, the thought comes that it was not so happy a fate to have to hold this eyrie. Sometimes, in winter storms, the Atlantic is heaved aloft and tossed and tumbled under an evil heaven till all its wilderness is hideous. This hilltop is exactly as though some such welter of water had suddenly become mud. It is all heaped and tossed and tumbled as though the earth there had been a cross-sea. In one place some great earth wave of a trench has been bitten into and beaten back and turned blind into an eddy by great pits and chasms and running heaps. Then in another place, where the crown of the work once reared itself aloft over the hill, the heaps of mud are all blurred and pounded together, so that there is no design, no trace, no visible plan of any fortress, only a mess of mud bedevilled and bewildered. All this mess of heaps and hillocks is strung and filthied over with broken bodies and ruined gear. There is nothing whole, nor alive, nor clean, in all its extent; it is a place of ruin and death, blown and blasted out of any likeness to any work of man, and so smashed that there is no shelter on it, save for the one machine gunner in his box. On all that desolate hill our fire fell like rain for days and nights and weeks, till the watchers in our line could see no hill at all, but a great, vague, wreathing devil of darkness in which little sudden fires winked and glimmered and disappeared.

Once in a lull of the firing a woman appeared upon the enemy parapet and started to walk along it. Our men held their fire and watched her. She walked steadily along the whole front of the Schwaben and then jumped down into her trench. Many thought at the time that she was a man masquerading for a bet, but long afterwards, when our men took the Schwaben, they found her lying in the ruins dead. They buried her there, up on the top of the hill. God alone knows who she was and what she was doing there.

Looking back across the Ancre from the Schwaben the hill of the right bank of the river is clear from the woods near Mesnil to Beaucourt. All along that graceful chalk hill our communication trenches thrust up like long white mole-runs, or like the comb of rollers on a reef. At right angles to these long white lines are black streaks which mark the enemy's successive front lines. The later ones are visibly more ragged than those near our old line.

There are few more lonely places than that scene of old battles. One may stand on the Schwaben for many days together and look west over the moor, or east over the wilderness, without seeing any sign of human life, save perhaps some solitary guarding a dump of stores.

The hill on which the Schwaben is built is like a great thumb laid down beside the Ancre River. There is a little valley on its eastern side exactly like the space between a great thumb and a great forefinger. It is called Crucifix Valley, from an iron Calvary that stood in it in the early days of the war. It must once have been a lovely and romantic glen, strangely beautiful throughout. Even now its lower reach between a steep bank of scrub and Thiepval Wood is as lovely as a place can be after the passing of a cyclone. Its upper reach, which makes the eastern boundary of the Schwaben, is as ghastly a scene of smash as the world can show. It is nothing but a collection of irregular pools dug by big shells during months of battle. The pools are long enough and deep enough to dive into, and full to overflowing with filthy water. Sometimes the pressure of the water bursts the mud banks of one of these pools and a rush of water comes, and the pools below it overflow, and a noise of water rises in that solitude which is like the mud and water of the beginning of the world before any green thing appeared.

Our line runs across this Crucifix Valley in a strong sandbag barricade. The enemy line crosses it higher up in a continuation of the front line of the Schwaben. As soon as the lines are across the valley they turn sharply to the south at an important point.

The Schwaben spur is like a thumb; Crucifix Valley is like the space between a thumb and a forefinger. Just to the east of Crucifix Valley a second spur thrusts away down to the south like a forefinger. It is a long sloping spur, wooded at the lower end. It is known on the maps as Thiepval Hill or the Leipzig Salient. When the lines turn to the south after crossing Crucifix Valley they run along the side of this hill and pass out of sight round the end. The lines are quite regular and distinct. From the top of the Schwaben it looks as though the side of the hill were fenced into a neat green track or racecourse. This track is the No Man's Land, which lies like a broad green regular stripe between brown expanses along the hillside. All this hill was of the greatest importance to the enemy. It was as strong an eyrie as the Schwaben; it turned and made very dangerous our works in front of Hamel; and it was the key to a covered way to the plateau from which all these spurs thrust southward.

It is a bolder, more regular spur than the others which thrust from this plateau. The top slopes so slightly as to be almost level, the two flanks are rather steep.

Right at the top of it, just where it springs from the plateau, much where the knuckle of the imagined hand would be, and perhaps five hundred yards east from our old sandbag barricade in Crucifix Valley, there is a redness in the battered earth and upon the chalk of the road. The redness is patchy over a good big stretch of this part of the spur, but it is all within the enemy lines and well above our own. Where the shattered hillside slopes towards our lines there are many remnants of trees, some of them fruit trees arranged in a kind of order behind the burnt relics of a hedge, others dotted about at random. All are burnt, blasted, and killed. One need only glance at the hill on which they stand to see that it has been more burnt and shell-smitten than most parts of the lines.

It is as though the fight here had been more than to the death, to beyond death, to the bones and skeleton of the corpse which was yet unkillable. This is the site of the little hill village of Thiepval, which once stood at a crossroads here among apple orchards and the trees of a park. It had a church, just at the junction of the roads, and a fine seigneurial château, in a garden, beside the church; otherwise it was a little lonely mean place, built of brick and plaster on a great lonely heap of chalk downland. It had no importance and no history before the war, except that a Seigneur of Thiepval is mentioned as having once attended a meeting at Amiens. It was of great military importance at the time of the Battle of the Somme. In the old days it may have had a beauty of position.

It is worthwhile to clamber up to Thiepval from our lines. The road runs through the site of the village in a deep cutting, which may once have been lovely. The road is reddish with the smashed bricks of the village. Here and there in the mud are perhaps three courses of brick where a house once stood, or some hideous hole bricked at the bottom for the vault of a cellar. Blasted, dead, pitted stumps of trees, with their bark in rags, grow here and there in a collection of vast holes, ten feet deep and fifteen feet across, with filthy water in them. There is nothing left of the church; a big reddish mound of brick, that seems mainly powder round a core of cement, still marks where the château stood. The château garden, the round village pond, the pine-tree which was once a landmark there, are all blown out of recognition.

The mud of the Somme, which will be remembered by our soldiers long after they have forgotten the shelling, was worse at Thiepval than elsewhere, or, at least, could not have been worse elsewhere. The road through Thiepval was a bog, the village was a quagmire. Near the château there were bits where one sank to the knee. In the great battle for Thiepval, on the 26th of last September, one of our Tanks charged an enemy trench here. It plunged and stuck fast and remained in the mud, like a great animal stricken dead in its spring. It was one of the sights of Thiepval during the winter, for it looked most splendid; afterwards, it was salved and went to fight again.

From this part of Thiepval one can look along the top of the Leipzig Spur, which begins here and thrusts to the south for a thousand yards.

There are two big enemy works on the Leipzig Spur: one, well to the south of the village, is (or was, for it is all blown out of shape) a six-angled star-shaped redoubt called the Wonder Work; the other, still further to the south, about a big, disused, and very evil-looking quarry, towards the end of the spur, is, or was, called the Leipzig Salient, or, by some people, the Hohenzollern, from the Hohenzollern Trench, which ran straight across the spur about halfway down the salient.

In these two fortresses the enemy had two strong, evil eyries, high above us. They look down upon our line, which runs along the side of the hill below them. Though, in the end, our guns blasted the enemy off the hill, our line along that slope was a costly one to hold, since fire upon it could be observed and directed from so many points – from the rear (above Hamel), from the left flank (on the Schwaben and near Thiepval), and from the hill itself. The hill is all skinned and scarred, and the trace of the great works can no longer be followed. At the top of the hill, in the middle of a filthy big pool, is a ruined enemy trench-mortar, sitting up like a swollen toad.

At the end of the spur the lines curve round to the east to shut in the hill. A grass-grown road crosses the lines here, goes up to the hilltop, and then along it. The slopes at this end of the hill are gentle, and from low down, where our lines are, it is a pleasant and graceful brae, where the larks never cease to sing and where you may always put up partridges and sometimes even a hare. It is a deserted hill at this time, but for the wild things. The No Man's Land is littered with the relics of a charge; for many brave Dorsetshire and Wiltshire men died in the rush up that slope. On the highest point of the enemy parapet, at the end of the hill, is a lonely white cross, which stands out like a banner planted by a conqueror. It marks the grave of an officer of the Wilts, who was killed there, among the ruin, in the July attack.

Below the lines, where the ground droops away towards the river, the oddly shaped, deeply valleyed Wood of Authuille begins. It makes a sort of socket of woodland so curved as to take the end of the spur.

It is a romantic and very lovely wood, pleasant with the noise of water and not badly damaged by the fighting. The trees are alive and leafy, the shrubs are pushing, and the spring flowers, wood anemones, violets, and the oxlip (which in this country takes the place of the primrose and the cowslip) flower beautifully among the shell-holes, rags, and old tins of war. But at the north-eastern end it runs out in a straggling spinney along the Leipzig's east flank, and this horn of wood is almost as badly shattered as if the shellfire upon it had been English. Here the enemy, fearing for his salient, kept up a terrible barrage. The trees are burnt, ragged, unbarked, topped, and cut off short, the trenches are blown in and jumbled, and the ground blasted and gouged.

Standing in the old English front line just to the north of Authuille Wood, one sees the usual slow gradual grassy rise to the dark enemy wire. Mesnil stands out among its trees to the left; to the right is this shattered stretch of wood, with a valley beyond it, and a rather big, steep, green hill topped by a few trees beyond the valley. The jut of the Leipzig shuts out the view to the flanks, so that one can see little more than this.

The Leipzig, itself, like the Schwaben, is a hawk's nest or eyrie. Up there one can look down by Authuille Wood to Albert church and chimneys, the uplands of the Somme, the Amiens road, down which the enemy marched in triumph and afterwards retreated in a hurry, and the fair fields that were to have been the booty of this war. Away to the left of this is the wooded clump of Bécourt, and, beyond it, One Tree Hill with its forlorn mound, like the burial place of a King. On the right flank is the Ancre Valley, with the English position round Hamel like an open book under the eye; on the left flank is the rather big, steep, green hill, topped by a few trees, before mentioned. These trees grow in and about what was once the village of Ovillers-la-Boisselle. The hill does not seem to have a name; it may be called here Middle Finger Hill or Ovillers Hill.

Like the Schwaben and the Leipzig Hills this hill thrusts out from the knuckle of the big chalk plateau to the north of it like the finger of a hand, in this case the middle finger. It is longer and less regularly defined than the Leipzig Hill; because instead of ending, it merges into other hills not quite so high. The valley which parts it from the Leipzig is steeply sided, with the banks of great lynchets. The lines cross the valley obliquely and run north and south along the flank of this hill, keeping their old relative positions, the enemy line well above our own, so that the approach to it is up a glacis.

As one climbs up along our old line here, the great flank of Ovillers Hill is before one in a noble, bare sweep of grass, running up to the enemy line. Something in the make of this hill, in its shape, or in the way it catches the light, gives it a strangeness which other parts of the battle-field have not. The rise between the lines of the trenches is fully two hundred yards across, perhaps more. Nearly all over it, in no sort of order, now singly, now in twos or threes, just as the men fell, are the crosses of the graves of the men who were killed in the attack there. Here and there among the little crosses is one bigger than the rest, to some man specially loved or to the men of some battalion. It is difficult to stand in the old English line from which those men started without the feeling that the crosses are the men alive, still going forward, as they went in the July morning a year ago.

Just within the enemy line, three-quarters of the way up the hill, there is a sort of small flat field about fifty yards across where the enemy lost very heavily. They must have gathered there for some rush and then been caught by our guns.

At the top of the hill the lines curve to the south-east, drawing closer together. The crest of the hill, such as it is, was not bitterly disputed here, for we could see all that we wished to see of the hill from the eastern flank. Our line passes over the spur slightly below it, the enemy line takes in as much of it as the enemy needed. From it, he has a fair view of Albert town and of the country to the east and west of it, the wooded hill of Bécourt, and the hill above Fricourt. From our line, we see his line and a few treetops. From the eastern flank of the hill, our line gives a glimpse of the site of the village of Ovillers-la-Boisselle, once one of the strong places of the enemy, and now a few heaps of bricks, and one spike of burnt ruin where the church stood.

Like most Picardy villages, Ovillers was compactly built of red brick along a country road, with trees and orchards surrounding it. It had a lofty and pretentious brick church of a modern type. Below and beyond it to the east is a long and not very broad valley which lies between the eastern flank of Ovillers Hill and the next spur. It is called Mash Valley on the maps. The lines go down Ovillers Hill into this valley and then across it.

Right at the upper end of this valley, rather more than a mile away, yet plainly visible from our lines near Ovillers, at the time of the beginning of the battle, were a few red brick ruins in an irregular row across the valley-head. A clump of small fir and cypress trees stood up dark on the hill at the western end of this row, and behind the trees was a line of green hill topped with the ruins of a windmill. The ruins, now gone, were the end of Pozières village, the dark trees grew in Pozières cemetery, and the mill was the famous windmill of Pozières, which marked the crest that was one of the prizes of the battle. All these things were then clearly to be seen, though in the distance.

The main hollow of the valley is not remarkable except that it is crossed by enormous trenches and very steeply hedged by a hill on its eastern flank. This eastern hill which has such a steep side is a spur or finger of chalk thrusting southward from Pozières, like the ring-finger of the imagined hand. Mash Valley curves round its finger-tip, and just at the spring of the curve the third of the four Albert roads crosses it, and goes up the spur towards Pozières and Bapaume. The line of the road, which is rather banked up, so as to be a raised way, like so many Roman roads, can be plainly seen, going along the spur, almost to Pozières. In many places, it makes the eastern skyline to observers down in the valley.

Behind our front line in this Mash Valley is the pleasant green Usna Hill, which runs across the hollow and shuts it in to the south. From this hill, seamed right across with our reserve and support trenches, one can look down at the enemy position, which crosses Mash Valley in six great lines all very deep, strong, and dug into for underground shelter.

Chapter VI

Standing in Mash Valley, at the foot of Ring Finger Spur, just where the Roman Road starts its long rise to Pozières, one sees a lesser road forking off to the right, towards a village called Contalmaison, a couple of miles away. The fork of the road marks where our old front line ran. The trenches are filled in at this point now, so that the roads may be used, but the place was once an exceedingly hot corner. In the old days, all the space between the two roads at the fork was filled with the village or hamlet of La Boisselle, which, though a tiny place, had once a church and perhaps a hundred inhabitants. The enemy fortified the village till it was an exceedingly strong place. We held a part of the village cemetery. Some of the broken crosses of the graves still show among the chalk here.

To the left of the Roman Road, only a stone's-throw from this ruined graveyard, a part of our line is built up with now rotting sandbags full of chalk, so that it looks like a mound of grey rocks. Opposite the mound, perhaps a hundred yards up the hill, is another, much bigger, irregular mound, of chalk that has become dirty, with some relics of battered black wire at its base. The space between the two mounds is now green with grass, though pitted with shell-holes, and marked in many places with the crosses of graves. The space is the old No Man's Land, and the graves are of men who started to charge across that field on the 1st of July. The big grey mound is the outer wall or casting of a mine thirty yards deep in the chalk and a hundred yards across, which we sprang under the enemy line there on that summer morning, just before our men went over.

La Boisselle, after being battered by us in our attack, was destroyed by enemy fire after we had taken it, and then cleared by our men who wished to use the roads. It offers no sight of any interest; but just outside it, between the old lines, there is a stretch of spur, useful for observation, for which both sides fought bitterly. For about 200 yards, the No Man's Land is a succession of pits in the chalk where mines have been sprung. Chalk, wire, stakes, friends, and enemies seem here to have been all blown to powder.

The lines cross this debated bit, and go across a small, ill-defined bulk of chalk, known as Chapes Spur, on the top of which there is a vast heap of dazzlingly white chalk, so bright that it is painful to look at. Beyond it is the pit of a mine, evenly and cleanly blown, thirty-five yards deep, and more than a hundred yards across, in the pure chalk of the upland, as white as cherry blossom. This is the finest, though not the biggest, mine in the battlefield. It was the work of many months, for the shafts by which it was approached began more than a quarter of a mile away. It was sprung on the 1st of July as a signal for the attack. Quite close to it are the graves of an officer and a sergeant, both English, who were killed in the attack a few minutes after that chasm in the chalk had opened. The sergeant was killed while trying to save his officer.

The lines bend down south-eastward from Chapes Spur, and cross a long, curving, shallow valley, known as Sausage Valley, famous, later in the battle, as an assembly place for men going up against Pozières. Here the men in our line could see nothing but chalk slope to right, left, or front, except the last tree of La Boisselle, rising gaunt and black above the line of the hill. Just behind them, however, at the foot of the Sausage Valley they had a pleasant wooded hill, the hill of Bécourt, which was for nearly two years within a mile of the front line, yet remained a green and leafy hill, covered with living trees, among which the château of Bécourt remained a habitable house.

The lines slant in a south-easterly direction across the Sausage Valley; they mount the spur to the east of it, and proceed, in the same direction, across a bare field, like the top of a slightly tilted table, in the long slope down to Fricourt. Here, the men in our front lines could see rather more from their position. In front of them was a smooth space of grass slightly rising to the enemy lines two hundred yards away. Behind the enemy lines is a grassy space, and behind this, there shows what seems to be a gully or ravine, beyond which the high ground of another spur rises, much as the citadel of an old encampment rises out of its walled ditch. This high ground of this other spur is not more than a few feet above the ground near it, but it is higher; it commands it. All the high ground is wooded. To the southern or lower end of it the trees are occasional and much broken by fire. To the northern or upper end they grow in a kind of wood though all are much destroyed. Right up to the wood, all the high ground bears traces of building; there are little tumbles of bricks and something of the colour of brick all over the pilled, poxed, and blasted heap that is so like an old citadel. The ravine in front of it is the gully between the two spurs; it shelters the sunken road to Contalmaison; the heap is Fricourt village, and the woodland to the north is Fricourt Wood. A glance is enough to show that it is a strong position.

To the left of Fricourt, the spur rises slowly into a skyline. To the right the lines droop down the spur to a valley, across a brook and a road in the valley, and up a big bare humping chalk hill placed at right angles to the spur on which Fricourt stands.

The spur on which Fricourt stands and the spur down which the lines run both end at the valley in a steep drop. Just above the steep fall our men fought very hard to push back the enemy a little towards Fricourt, so that he might not see the lower part of the valley, or be able to enfilade our lines on the other side of it. For about three hundred yards here the space between the lines is filled with the craters of mines exploded under the enemy's front line. In some cases, we seized and held the craters; in others the craters were untenable by either side. Under one of those held by us it was found that the enemy had sunk a big counter-mine, which was excavated and ready for charging at the time of the beginning of the battle, when Fricourt fell. This part of the line is more thickly coated with earth than most of the chalk hills of the battlefield. The craters lie in a blown and dug up wilderness of heaps of reddish earth, pocked with shell-holes, and tumbled with wire. The enemy lines are much broken and ruined, their parapets thrown down, the mouths of their dugouts blown in, and their pride abased.

The Fricourt position was one of the boasts of the enemy on this front. Other places on the line, such as the Leipzig, the Schwaben, and the trenches near Hamel, were strong, because they could be supported by works behind them or on their flanks. Fricourt was strong in itself, like Gommecourt. It was perhaps the only place in the field of which it could be said that it was as strong as Gommecourt. As at Gommecourt, it had a good natural glacis up to the front line, which was deep, strong, and well-wired. Behind the front line was a wired second line, and behind that, the rising spur on which the village stood, commanding both with machine gun emplacements.

Fricourt was not captured by storm, but swiftly isolated and forced to surrender. It held out not quite two days. It was the first first-rate fortress taken by our men from the enemy in this engagement. In the ruins, they saw for the first time the work which the enemy puts into his main defences, and the skill and craft with which he provides for his comfort. For some weeks, the underground arrangements of Fricourt, the stairs with wired treads, the bolting holes, the air and escape shafts, the living rooms with electric light, the panelled walls, covered with cretonnes of the smartest Berlin patterns, the neat bunks and the signs of female visitors, were written of in the press, so that some may think that Fricourt was better fitted than other places on the line. It is not so. The work at Fricourt was well done, but it was no better than that at other places, where a village with cellars in it had to be converted into a fortress. Our men took Fricourt at the beginning of the battle, in a fair state of preservation. Such work was then new to our men, and this good example was made much of.

In the valley below the village, in great, deep, and powerfully revetted works, the enemy had built himself gun emplacements, so weighted with timber balks that they collapsed soon after his men ceased to attend them. The line of these great works ran (as so many of his important lines have run) at the foot of a steep bank or lynchet, so that at a little distance the parapet of the work merged into the bank behind it and was almost invisible. This line of guns ran about east and west across the neck of the Fricourt Salient, which thrust still further south, across the little valley and up the hill on the other side.

Chapter VII

Our old line crosses the valley just to the east of the Fricourt Station on the little railway which once ran in the valley past Fricourt and Mametz to Montauban. It then crossed the fourth of the roads from Albert, at Fricourt cemetery, which is a small, raised forlorn garden of broken tombs at a crossroads, under the hill facing Fricourt. Here our line began to go diagonally up the lower slopes of the hill. The enemy line climbed it further to the east, round the bulging snout of the hill, at a steep and difficult point above the bank of a sunken road. Towards the top of the hill the lines converged.

All the way of the hill, the enemy had the stronger position. It was above us almost invisible and unguessable, except from the air, at the top of a steep climb up a clay bank, which in wet weather makes bad going even for the Somme; and though the lie of the ground made it impossible for him to see much of our position, it was impossible for us to see anything of his or to assault him. The hill is a big steep chalk hill, with contours so laid upon it that not much of it can be seen from below. By looking to the left from our trenches on its western lower slopes one can see nothing of Fricourt, for the bulge of the hill's snout covers it. One has a fair view of the old English line on the smoothish big slope between Fricourt and Bécourt, but nothing of the enemy stronghold. One might have lived in those trenches for nearly two years without seeing any enemy except the rain and mud and lice.

Up at the top of the hill, there is an immense prospect over the eastern half of the battlefield, and here, where the lines converge, it was most necessary for us to have the crest and for the enemy to keep us off it. The highest ground is well forward, on the snout, and this point was the only part of the hill which the enemy strove to keep. His line goes up the hill to the highest point, cuts off the highest point, and at once turns eastward, so that his position on the hill is just the northern slope and a narrow line of crest. It is as though an army holding Fleet Street against an army on the Embankment and in Cheapside should have seized Ludgate Hill to the top of the steps of St. Paul's and left the body of the cathedral to its opponent. The lines securing this important salient are of immense strength and intricacy, with many great avenues of approach. The front line is double across the greater part of the crest, and behind it is a very deep, strong, trebly wired support line which is double at important points.

Our old front line runs almost straight across the crest parallel with the enemy front line, and distant from it from forty to one hundred and fifty yards. The crest or highest ground is on both flanks of the hilltop close to the enemy line. Between the lines at both these points are the signs of a struggle which raged for weeks and months for the possession of those lumps of hill, each, perhaps, two hundred yards long, by fifty broad, by five high. Those fifteen feet of height were bartered for with more than their own weight of sweat and blood; the hill can never lose the marks of the struggle.

In those two patches of the hill the space between the lines is a quarry of confluent craters, twenty or thirty yards deep, blown into and under each other till the top of the hill is split apart. No man can now tell which of all these mines were sunk by our men. The quarry runs irregularly in heaps and hollows of chalk and red earth mingled like flesh and blood. On our side of the pits the marks of our occupation are plain. There in several places, as at La Boisselle and on the Beaucourt spur, our men have built up the parapet of our old front line by thousands of sandbags till it is a hilltop or cairn from which they could see beyond. The sandbags have rotted and the chalk and flints within have fallen partly through the rags, and Nature has already begun to change those heaps to her own colours, but they will be there for ever as the mark of our race. Such monuments must be as lasting as Stonehenge. Neither the mines nor the guns of the enemy could destroy them. From among them our soldiers peered through the smoke of burning and explosions at the promised land which the battle made ours.

From those heaps there is a wide view over that part of the field. To the left one sees Albert, the wooded clump of Bécourt, and a high green spur which hides the Sausage Valley. To the front this green spur runs to the higher ground from which the Fricourt spur thrusts. On this higher ground, behind Fricourt and its wood, is a much bigger, thicker, and better grown wood, about a mile and a half away; this is the wood of Mametz. Some short distance to the left of this wood, very plainly visible on the high, rather bare hill, is a clump of pollarded trees near a few heaps of red brick. The trees were once the shade-giving trees about the market-place of Contalmaison, a hamlet at a crossroads at this point. Behind these ruins the skyline is a kind of ridge which runs in a straight line, broken in one place by a few shatters of trees. These trees are the remains of the wood which once grew outside the village of Pozières. The ridge is the Albert-Bapaume Road, here passing over the highest ground on its path.

Turning from these distant places and looking to the right, one sees, just below, twelve hundred yards to the east of Fricourt, across the valley at the foot of this hill of the salient, the end of an irregular spur, on which are the shattered bricks of the village of Mametz before mentioned.

To the north of Mametz the ground rises. From the eyrie of the salient one can look over it and away to the north to big rolling chalk land, most of it wooded. Mametz Wood is a dark expanse to the front; to the right of it are other woods, Bazentin Woods, Big and Little, and beyond them, rather to the right and only just visible as a few sticks upon the skyline, are two other woods, High Wood, like a ghost in the distance, and the famous and terrible Wood of Delville. High Wood is nearly five miles away and a little out of the picture. The other wooded heights are about three miles away. All that line of high ground marked by woods was the enemy second line, which with a few slight exceptions was our front line before the end of the third week of the battle.

From this hilltop of the salient the lines run down the north-eastern snout of the hill and back across the valley, so as to shut in Mametz. Then they run eastward for a couple of miles, up to and across a plateau in front of the hamlet of Carnoy, which was just within our line. From our line, in this bare and hideous field, little could be seen but the slope up to the enemy line. At one point, where the road or lane from Carnoy to Montauban crossed the enemy line, there was a struggle for the power to see, and as a result of the struggle mines and counter-mines were sprung here till the space between the lines is now a chaos of pits and chasms full of water. The country here is an expanse of smoothish tilted slopes, big, empty, and lonely, and crossed (at about the middle point) by a strange narrow gut or gully, up which the railway once ran to Montauban. No doubt there are places in the English chalk counties which resemble this sweep of country, but I know of none so bare or so featureless. The ground is of the reddish earth which makes such bad mud. The slopes are big and gradual, either up or down. Little breaks the monotony of the expanse except a few copses or sites of copses; the eye is always turning to the distance.

In front, more than half a mile away, the ground reaches its highest point in the ridge or bank which marks the road to Montauban. The big gradual sweep up is only broken by lines of trenches and by mud heaped up from the road. Some of the trees which once made Montauban pleasant and shady still stand over the little heaps of brick and solitary iron gate which show where the village used to stand. Rather to the right of this, and nearer to our lines, are some irregular red heaps with girders protruding from them. This is the enemy fortress of the brickworks of Montauban. Beyond this, still further to the right, behind the old enemy line, the ground loses its monotony and passes into lovely and romantic sweeping valleys, which our men could not see from their lines.

Well behind our English lines in this district and above the dip where Carnoy stands, the fourth of the four roads from Albert runs eastward along a ridge-top between a double row of noble trees which have not suffered very severely, except at their eastern end. Just north of this road, and a little below it on the slopes of the ridge, is the village of Maricourt. Our line turns to the south-east opposite Montauban, and curves in towards the ridge so as to run just outside Maricourt, along the border of a little wood to the east of the houses. From all the high ground to the north of it, from the enemy's second line and beyond, the place is useful to give a traveller his bearings. The line of plane-trees along the road on the ridge, and the big clumps of trees round the village, are landmarks which cannot be mistaken from any part of the field.

Little is to be seen from our line outside Maricourt Wood, except the enemy line a little beyond it, and the trees of other woods behind it.

The line turns to the south, parallel with the wood, crosses the fourth road (which goes on towards Peronne) and goes down some difficult, rather lovely, steep chalk slopes, wooded in parts, to the ruins of Fargny Mill on the Somme River.

The Somme River is here a very beautiful expanse of clear chalk water like a long wandering shallow lake. Through this shallow lake the river runs in half a dozen channels, which are parted and thwarted in many places by marsh, reed-beds, osier plots, and tracts of swampy woodland. There is nothing quite like it in England. The river-bed is pretty generally between five and six hundred yards across.

Nearly two miles above the place where the old enemy line comes down to the bank, the river thrusts suddenly north-westward, in a very noble great horse-shoe, the bend of which comes at Fargny where our lines touched it. The enemy line touched the horse-shoe close to our own at a curious wooded bank or slope, known (from its shape on the map, which is like a cocked hat) as the Chapeau de Gendarme. Just behind our lines, at the bend, the horse-shoe sweeps round to the south. The river-bed at once broadens to about two-thirds of a mile, and the river, in four or five main channels, passes under a most beautiful sweep of steep chalk cliff, not unlike some of the chalk country near Arundel. These places marked the end of the British sector at the time of the beginning of the battle. On the south or left bank of the Somme River the ground was held by the French.

Chapter VIII

Such was our old front line at the beginning of the battle, and so the travellers of our race will strive to picture it when they see the ground under the crops of coming Julys. It was never anything but a makeshift, patched together, and held, God knows how, against greater strength. Our strongest places were the half-dozen built-up observation posts at the mines near Fricourt, Serre, and La Boiselle. For the rest, our greatest strength was but a couple of sandbags deep. There was no concrete in any part of the line, very few iron girders and not many iron "humpies" or "elephant backs" to make the roofs of dugouts. The whole line gives the traveller the impression that it was improvised (as it was) by amateurs with few tools, and few resources, as best they could, in a time of need and danger. Like the old, hurriedly built Long Walls at Athens, it sufficed, and like the old camps of Cæsar it served, till our men could take the much finer lines of the enemy. A few words may be said about those enemy lines. They were very different lines from ours.

The defences of the enemy front line varied a little in degree, but hardly at all in kind, throughout the battlefield. The enemy wire was always deep, thick, and securely staked with iron supports, which were either crossed like the letter X, or upright, with loops to take the wire and shaped at one end like corkscrews so as to screw into the ground. The wire stood on these supports on a thick web, about four feet high and from thirty to forty feet across. The wire used was generally as thick as sailors' marline stuff, or two twisted rope-yarns. It contained, as a rule, some sixteen barbs to the foot. The wire used in front of our lines was generally galvanized, and remained grey after months of exposure. The enemy wire, not being galvanized, rusted to a black colour, and shows up black at a great distance. In places this web or barrier was supplemented with trip-wire, or wire placed just above the ground, so that the artillery observing officers might not see it and so not cause it to be destroyed. This trip-wire was as difficult to cross as the wire of the entanglements. In one place (near the Y Ravine at Beaumont Hamel) this trip-wire was used with thin iron spikes a yard long of the kind known as calthrops. The spikes were so placed in the ground that about one foot of spike projected. The scheme was that our men should catch their feet in the trip-wire, fall on the spikes, and be transfixed.

In places, in front of the front line in the midst of his wire, sometimes even in front of the wire, the enemy had carefully hidden snipers and

196

machine gun posts. Sometimes these outside posts were connected with his front line trench by tunnels, sometimes they were simply shell-holes, slightly altered with a spade to take the snipers and the gunners. These outside snipers had some success in the early parts of the battle. They caused losses among our men by firing in the midst of them and by shooting them in the backs after they had passed. Usually the posts were small oblong pans in the mud, in which the men lay. Sometimes they were deep narrow graves in which the men stood to fire through a funnel in the earth. Here and there, where the ground was favourable, especially when there was some little knop, hillock, or bulge of ground just outside their line, as near Gommecourt Park and close to the Sunken Road at Beaumont Hamel, he placed several such posts together. Outside Gommecourt, a slight lynchet near the enemy line was prepared for at least a dozen such posts invisible from any part of our line and not easily to be picked out by photograph, and so placed as to sweep at least a mile of No Man's Land.

When these places had been passed, and the enemy wire, more or less cut by our shrapnel, had been crossed, our men had to attack the enemy fire trenches of the first line. These, like the other defences, varied in degree, but not in kind. They were, in the main, deep, solid trenches, dug with short bays or zigzags in the pattern of the Greek Key or badger's earth. They were seldom less than eight feet and sometimes as much as twelve feet deep. Their sides were revetted, or held from collapsing, by strong wickerwork. They had good, comfortable standing slabs or banquettes on which the men could stand to fire. As a rule, the parapets were not built up with sandbags as ours were.

In some parts of the line, the front trenches were strengthened at intervals of about fifty yards by tiny forts or fortlets made of concrete and so built into the parapet that they could not be seen from without, even five yards away. These fortlets were pierced with a foot-long slip for the muzzle of a machine gun, and were just big enough to hold the gun and one gunner.

In the forward wall of the trenches were the openings of the shafts which led to the front line dugouts. The shafts are all of the same pattern. They have open mouths about four feet high, and slant down into the earth for about twenty feet at an angle of forty-five degrees. At the bottom of the stairs which led down are the living rooms and barracks which communicate with each other so that if a shaft collapse the men below may still escape by another. The shafts and living rooms are strongly propped and panelled with wood, and this has led to the destruction of most of the few which survived our bombardment. While they were needed as billets our men lived in them. Then the wood was removed, and the dugout and shaft collapsed.

During the bombardment before an attack, the enemy kept below in his dugouts. If one shaft were blown in by a shell, they passed to the next. When the fire "lifted" to let the attack begin, they raced up the stairs with their machine guns and had them in action within a minute. Sometimes the fire was too heavy for this, for trench, parapet, shafts, dugouts, wood, and fortlets, were pounded out of existence, so that no man could say that a line had ever run there; and in these cases the garrison was destroyed in the shelters. This happened in several places, though all the enemy dugouts were kept equipped with pioneer tools by which buried men could dig themselves out.

The direction of the front line trenches was so inclined with bends, juts, and angles as to give flanking fire upon attackers.

At some little distance behind the front line (a hundred yards or so) was a second fire line, wired like the first, though less elaborate and generally without concrete fortlets. This second line was usually as well-sited for fire as the front line. There were many communication trenches between the two lines. Half a mile behind the second line was a third support line; and behind this, running along the whole front, a mile or more away, was the prepared second main position, which was in every way like the front line, with wire, concrete fortlets, dugouts, and a difficult glacis for the attacker to climb.

The enemy batteries were generally placed behind banks or lynchets which gave good natural cover; but in many places he mounted guns in strong permanent emplacements, built up of timber balks, within a couple of miles (at Fricourt within a quarter of a mile) of his front line. In woods from the high trees of which he could have clear observation, as in the Bazentin, Bernafay, and Trones Woods, he had several of these emplacements, and also stout concrete fortlets for heavy single guns.

All the enemy position on the battlefield was well-gunned at the time of the beginning of the battle. In modern war, it is not possible to hide preparations for an attack on a wide front. Men have to be brought up, trenches have to be dug, the artillery has to prepare, and men, guns, and trenches have to be supplied with food, water, shells, sandbags, props, and revetments. When the fire on any sector increases tenfold, while the roads behind the lines are thronged with five times the normal traffic of troops and lorries, and new trenches, the attack or "jumping-off" trenches, are being dug in front of the line, a commander cannot fail to know that an attack is preparing. These preparations must be made and cannot be concealed from observers in the air or on the ground. The enemy knew very well that we were about to attack upon the Somme front, but did not know at which point to expect the main thrust. To be ready, in any case, he concentrated guns along the sector. It seems likely that he expected our attack to be an attempt to turn Bapaume by a thrust from the west, by Gommecourt, Puisieux, Grandcourt. In all this difficult sector his observations and arrangements for cross-fire were excellent. He concentrated a great artillery here (it is a legend among our men that he brought up a hundred batteries to defend Gommecourt alone). In this sector, and in one other place a little to the south of it, his barrage upon our trenches, before the battle, was very accurate, terrible, and deadly.

Our attacks were met by a profuse machine gun fire from the trench parapets and from the hidden pits between and outside the lines. There was not very much rifle fire in any part of the battle, but all the hotly-fought-for strongholds were defended by machine guns to the last. It was reported that the bodies of some enemy soldiers were found chained to their guns, and that on the bodies of others were intoxicating pills, designed to madden and infuriate the takers before an attack. The fighting in the trenches was mainly done by bombing with hand-grenades, of which the enemy had several patterns, all effective. His most used type was a grey tin cylinder, holding about a pound of explosive, and screwed to a wooden baton or handle about a foot long for the greater convenience of throwing.

Chapter IX

Early in the spring of 1916, it was determined that an attack should be made by our armies upon these lines of the enemy, so as to bring about a removal of the enemy guns and men, then attacking the French at Verdun and the Russians on the Eastern Front.

Preparations for this attack were made throughout the first half of the year. New roads were cut, old roads were remetalled, new lines of railways were surveyed and laid, and supplies and munitions were accumulated not far from the front. Pumping stations were built and wells were sunk for the supply of water to the troops during the battle. Fresh divisions were brought up and held ready behind the line. An effort was made to check the enemy's use of aeroplanes. In June, our Air Service in the Somme sector made it so difficult for the enemy to take photographs over our lines that his knowledge of our doings along the front of the planned battle was lessened and thwarted. At the same time, many raids were made by our aeroplanes upon the enemy's depots and magazines behind his front. Throughout June, our infantry raided the enemy line in many places to the north of the planned battle. It seems possible that these raids led him to think that our coming attack would be made wholly to the north of the Ancre River.

During the latter half of June, our armies concentrated a very great number of guns behind the front of the battle. The guns were of every kind, from the field gun to the heaviest howitzer. Together they made what was at that time by far the most terrible concentration of artillery ever known upon a battlefield. Vast stores of shells of every known kind were made ready, and hourly increased.

As the guns came into battery, they opened intermittent fire, so that, by the 20th of June, the fire along our front was heavier than it had been before. At the same time, the fire of the machine guns and trench mortars in our trenches became hotter and more constant. On the 24th of June this fire was increased, by system, along the front designed for the battle, and along the French front to the south of the Somme, until it reached the intensity of a fire of preparation. Knowing, as they did, that an attack was to come, the enemy made ready and kept on the alert. Throughout the front, they expected the attack for the next morning.

The fire was maintained throughout the night, but no attack was made in the morning, except by aeroplanes. These raided the enemy observation balloons, destroyed nine of them, and made it impossible for the others to keep in the air. The shelling continued all that day, searching the line and particular spots with intense fire and much asphyxiating gas. Again the enemy prepared for an attack in the morning, and again there was no attack, although the fire of preparation still went on. The enemy said, "Tomorrow will make three whole days of preparation; the English will attack tomorrow." But when the morning came, there was no attack, only the never-ceasing shelling, which seemed to increase as time passed. It was now difficult and dangerous to move within the enemy lines. Relieving exhausted soldiers, carrying out the wounded, and bringing up food and water to the front, became terrible feats of war. The fire continued and increased, all that day and all the next day, and the day after that. It darkened the days with smoke and lit the nights with flashes. It covered the summer landscape with a kind of haze of hell, earth-coloured above fields and reddish above villages, from the dust of blown mud and brick flung up into the air. The tumult of these days and nights cannot be described nor imagined. The air was without wind, yet it seemed in a hurry with the passing of death. Men knew not which they heard, a roaring that was behind and in front, like a presence, or a screaming that never ceased to shriek in the air. No thunder was ever so terrible as that tumult. It broke the drums of the ears when it came singly, but when it rose up along the front and gave tongue together in full cry it humbled the soul. With the roaring, crashing, and shrieking came a racket of hammers from the machine guns till men were dizzy and sick from the noise, which thrust between skull and brain, and beat out thought. With the noise came also a terror and an exultation, that one should hurry, and hurry, and hurry, like the shrieking shells, into the pits of fire opening on the hills. Every night in all this week the enemy said, "The English will attack tomorrow," and in the front lines prayed that the attack might come, that so an end, any end, might come to the shelling.

It was fine, cloudless, summer weather, not very clear, for there was a good deal of heat haze and of mist in the nights and early mornings. It was hot, yet brisk, during the days. The roads were thick in dust. Clouds and streamers of chalk dust floated and rolled over all the roads leading to the front, till men and beasts were grey with it.

At half-past six in the morning of the 1st of July all the guns on our front quickened their fire to a pitch of intensity never before attained. Intermittent darkness and flashing so played on the enemy line from Gommecourt to Maricourt that it looked like a reef on a loppy day. For one instant it could be seen as a white rim above the wire, then some comber of a big shell struck it fair and spouted it black aloft. Then another and another fell, and others of a new kind came and made a different darkness, through which now and then some fat white wreathing devil of explosion came out and danced. Then it would show out, with gaps in it, and with some of it level with the field, till another comber would fall and go up like a breaker and smash it out of sight again. Over all the villages on the field there floated a kind of bloody dust from the blasted bricks.

In our trenches after seven o'clock on that morning, our men waited under a heavy fire for the signal to attack. Just before half-past seven, the mines at half a dozen points went up with a roar that shook the earth and brought down the parapets in our lines. Before the blackness of their burst had thinned or fallen the hand of Time rested on the half-hour mark, and along all that old front line of the English there came a whistling and a crying. The men of the first wave climbed up the parapets, in tumult, darkness, and the presence of death, and having done with all pleasant things, advanced across the No Man's Land to begin the Battle of the Somme.

[source: *The Old Front Line*, London: William Heinemann, 1917]

America's Part to Bring Victory and a Real Peace

I think that in the coming year the United States will play a decisive part in supplying the belligerents while the war continues, and in exercising a sane control upon their councils when the war ends.

[source: *The New York Times*, 1 January 1918, p.3]

Prospect of Labour's Ruling British Parliament

[On *Gallipoli* and the battlefields of France]

The Government put me on the job inasmuch as I had been through part of the campaign, and placed before me all the official records. The book had to be written quickly; there was no time to spare, for I had heard in America rumours about us which would not be well to let grow. No method was too crude, too subtle for the Germans. The Gallipoli book was written and published, and, on the strength of that, the War Office sent me to France to examine more fully the splendid charitable work being done by American organizations.

I had just completed my observation for the Government, and was one day in Paris, when I met a member of the British Military Mission. He told me that he would like to send me immediately to General Headquarters. Evidently they had been reading my book on Gallipoli and had some further work for me. I was taken before General Haig, and he appointed me to the official post of historian and sent me to the Somme.

I saw part of the battle in October, 1916, when the forces were at their highest pitch around Wailencourt. But I had no sooner entered the thick of things than I was forced to return to England to make my report on the activity of the American relief work. It was after this job was done that I returned to the Somme, in January, 1917, and remained there until last June. I got a billet in the town of Albert, which was practically in the middle of the battlefield. I used to go out every day and wander around and see what I could pick up in the way of information.

You know what "booby traps" are; let me give you some idea of the ingenious handiwork of the Germans in these things to deceive. Our soldier is always on the lookout for souvenirs. He prizes especially the brass eagle on the spiked helmet of a German. How often during this Somme campaign have I seen, in German dugouts, such helmets nonchalantly set as bait for our men. How many of our men have taken up these helmets, only to set off a bomb with which they were connected. Sometimes a private has seen a much-coveted revolver resting on the road, and he has picked it up, only to be blown to Kingdom Come. Telescopes left on the parapet of an abandoned trench have, likewise, become devil machines.

So effective did the German find this work that he would go to every extreme to perfect it. Realizing that our soldier likes his rum jar occasionally, the Germans have even sent men into our lines on hunting expeditions for English rum jars, which they have left in their abandoned trenches, knowing full well that they will do their deadly work. For hope springs eternal in the soldier's breast when he sees a rum jar, and he has never learned advantageously to what uses the enemy has put it.

Everyone is in equal danger on the battlefield. I wandered about unarmed. It is easy enough to get weapons at any moment from the dead on the ground. One only has to stoop in order to pick up a hand-grenade that has not gone off. Such are the flowers that bloom on the fields of France.

I remember when we were at Pozières that I innocently walked into a German barrage, and I assure you I had a lively time. The Germans do not think it necessary to open fire when the horizon reveals to them only one or two men emerging from their dugout. On this occasion I went forward with four or five; had we advanced in single file we probably would not have attracted attention; but because of our being bulked together the Germans thought that such activity meant more than it really did. As soon as the firing began I threw myself down into a shell-hole, and suddenly found that I was gripping a dead Prussian guard. Gruesome though it might appear, I lay there without fear or dread, and without moving, until the weather moderated somewhat above me!

[On England and Democracy]

More than ever before, our army is democratic. After this war, I see the possibilities of more kindness and more charity existing between class and class. All of us are in the same boat, and in battle the officer pools supplies with his men. Everywhere there is a greater feeling of equality, and this feeling will result afterward in an equality of opportunity. You know what is taking place in the Labour Party today. I predict that our next Parliament will be a Labour Parliament. It will take unto itself the intellectual workers as well as the hand workers of England. Not many will deny that the pronunciamento of the Labour Party, as published in August, is as fine a document as President Wilson's declaration of war aims. Our Trade Union Congress was responsible for that.

A good many of the Lords (I don't know many) have become democratized. I believe that Henderson will be the controlling factor in the future. England will be saved by the Liberal with his intellect, and the Labour man with his power. Reconstruction committees are now preparing for the remaking of England. I have looked into some of their educational schemes and I cannot say that they go quite far enough to satisfy me. They are not planning to make it sufficiently possible for the clever workingman to get every possible advantage the nation can offer him in the way of intellectual development. The Liberal is still showing class feeling.

I reckon myself as a Liberal and I regard Gilbert Murray as the very soul of cultivated Liberalism. I am among those who believe that when the time comes for talking over lines of policy it is well to ask what Gilbert Murray thinks. But I also believe that the time is ripe for some leader of the Labour Party to come forward with equally as commanding an intellectual point of view. There is no one in the Labour Party at the present comparable with Parnell. There are such men as Ramsay Macdonald and old Gosling, a fine, calm, and charming man, and I have much admiration for the vigour of Henderson. But it seems to me necessary for the Labour Party to ally itself with what is best in Liberalism – the best of the Asquith-Grey type of mind. That is why we have such confidence in Gilbert Murray as one of our most finished intellects.

[On German Accomplishments]

You know, I hear a great deal in America about Germany's efficiency. I cannot see that the Germans are efficient in any very great sense. They have been inventive in deviltry. But our building up of an army is quite as wonderful as anything the Germans have done. I won't deny that from relative heights in an airplane the German can take better photographs than we can. If I were asked what is the German's greatest accomplishment I should say the making of lenses. This war has brought forth, in every direction, the undoubted truth that the German's power of hand is greater than the German's power of mind. The Teutonic diplomatic bungles will show that.

[On Russia and future peace]

There is one good that I believe has come out of this unstable condition in Russia. It has made all the working population in Europe realize that a peace is possible; that it is not necessary for civilized men to keep on cutting their throats. If individuals in a nation would renounce certain greeds and lusts, the honest on the field of battle might go home again and cultivate gardens. But that point of view is all right for the Russians, who are a nation of saints, until lately governed by a squad of natural devils.

But the nation next door to Russia is a nation of natural brutes governed by a small clique of unspeakable scoundrels. And it remains to be seen how far the Russian principles and statements will act upon that nation. They may convert that nation or they may not. But the German soldiers will at least have before their eyes in the future the image of one great nation that has decided that war is not good enough nor worth having in a civilized life. Then, too, the German population must be bitterly disappointed at having the cup of a separate peace suddenly dashed from their lips. They must be sorely distressed at realizing that it was their own Government which dashed it from their lips. Surely such a state of things will have its effect. I am trusting that we are in the final stages of this awful conflict.

Everyone, I believe, now that peace is in the air, must be asking what kind of world will emerge from the ruins of the old one. However difficult it may seem, it is imperative that a means of preventing war by international agreement should be found. For, if it is not found, the old system of competing nationalism, a direct outcome of competing commercialism, will end the world. Man's invention has gone far beyond his social organizations and his governments. We have the case of the mediaeval idea of competing nations – that is, the mediaeval State – endowed with all the powers of the modern scientist at its disposal, to use unscrupulously. If we do not turn the tide of things we may live to see the true barbarian at heart armed with the most finished intellect of modern times at work in some obsolete and barbarous piece of highway robbery.

I am serious about this matter of the safety of the world. If we are not awakened by this enormous conflict, in another twenty years the barbarian will be master, unless the finished intellect can find some means of checking him. Who knows but the day may arrive when the barbarian will have at his disposal some scientific secret that can blast a nation to pieces by touching a button? Who knows but the time may come when man discovers how to tap atomic energy, or is able to direct consuming rays against his antagonist and destroy a nation wholesale and accurately, instead of piecemeal and clumsily, as we are doing at present?

[On feeling in Germany]

It is my belief that the Socialists in the German Reichstag are becoming more powerful every day. There is discontent in Germany over the continuance of this war. If they do make a supreme effort on the Western Front, it will be next month, and it will be the last struggle of the war, it seems to me.

[extracted from *The New York Times Magazine*, 27 January 1918, p.11]

The War and the Future

A Lecture given in America
January – August, 1918

TO
THOMAS W. LAMONT

I have been sent to you, to speak about the war, and about the future, after the war.

You know more than I do about the future. No one can doubt that this country holds the future. I will try to tell you about the war. I've seen it close to, and I've seen its results.

English people who know America, and who have a pride in the fair fame of England, know, that in the old days, we did this country a great wrong. I, here, am very conscious of that. The best thing I can say of that past is that it is the past. We are now associates in a great work which is a forgetting and a putting by of the past, in an effort to make the future.

Whatever this war is, it is a getting rid of the past. The past has gone into the bonfire. We are all in the war now, realizing with more or less surprise and shock and bitterness, that the old delights, the old ideals, the old way of life, with its comfortable loves and hatreds, are gone. We have to remake our lives, forget our old hatreds and learn new ones, and ask ourselves the question: "What kind of a new world am I going to help make?"

This war came gradually to you. You were, as we were, not expecting war, seeing the threat and the preparation of war, but believing, just as we believed, that common sense, or ordinary human sense, and one-thousandth part of goodwill in human intercourse would make war impossible. War to you, as to us, seemed to be out of date in a century which cut the Panama Canal and discovered radium and the wireless telegraph. But it came none the less, and all our ten millions of adults had suddenly to put by their old lives and take on new and dangerous and terrible lives. Now the same thing has happened to you.

When the threat of this war came suddenly to Europe we had nothing to gain by war, except our own soul. That is a big exception. Short of that, we risked everything to keep the peace, as our friends complained, and our enemies agreed.

When the war came to us, and the enemy Ambassador was leaving England, a friend of mine went to say goodbye to him. My friend said to him: "I hope you think that we did our best to prevent this war?" The Ambassador said: "You have done everything that mortals could to prevent the war."

Now the years before the war were very anxious years to everyone. The threat of war hung over every nation in Europe, and every nation in Europe felt and said and wrote that the threat of war was a German threat. The Germans themselves were frank about it. I often used to see German students and German professors in England. They used to say, quite openly, "Our next war will be with England." After the Hague Conference nine years ago, the English delegate said to me that the attitude of Germany could only be explained on the supposition that she meant to have a war. Germany was like an athlete trained to the minute; she was spoiling for a scrap. When boxers are trained to the minute, it is said that their friends always prefer to walk behind them, for when a boxer who is very fit and spoiling for a scrap sees a nice chin the temptation to hit that chin is sometimes more than he can bear.

In the summer of 1914, the European chins looked too tempting to Germany, and she hit out at them. The results are before us.

This war employs all the strength and all the talent of the nations waging it. One of the weapons used by our enemies has been that of lying. They have spread abroad lies about us, which many repeat and some few, perhaps, believe. I wish here to state and answer some of those lies.

Firstly: that we are a decadent people, intent on sports and money-making, and without ideals or any sense of serving the state.

The answer to that is that in England and Scotland alone five million four hundred thousand of our men enlisted as volunteers to fight for our ideals, without compulsion of any kind, while three million more who tried to enlist were rejected as too old, or physically unfit, or needed in other work. That was before we had conscription.

Secondly: that we are a cowardly people, who let other people fight for us.

The answer to that is that had we been a cowardly people we should not have gone to war; but we did; we came into this war and have lost in this war something like two and one-half millions of our best men killed, wounded and missing, and this without counting the losses of the men of our Colonies.

Thirdly: that we are a mean people, who do not take our fair share in the war.

The answer to that is, that we hold one-third of the line in France, much of the line in Italy, nearly all the line in Serbia, all the line in Palestine and Mesopotamia, and all the line on the vast colonial fronts in Africa. We supply or have supplied France, Italy, Serbia, Belgium, Roumania and Russia with millions of tons of equipment of all sorts, guns, shells, uniforms, boots and machines, in all amounting to 3,000 million dollars worth. We feed and clothe and always have fed and clothed since the war began the greater part of the population of Belgium and practically the whole of the population of Serbia. Besides our contributions of men and guns, we have immense hospital organizations working in Russia, in Italy, in Roumania, and with the French. We have had the greater part of the policing of the seas to do, and practically all the submarine hunting. The sea is not an easy place to patrol, and the submarine is not an easy thing to catch, but not much German trade has been done by sea since the war, and not many raiders have got through our guards and we have sunk (I believe) not less than ten times as many submarines as the enemy had at the beginning of the war. We have built ships to make our navy at least half as strong again as it was before the war. We have caused to be made and transported 25,000,000 tons of shells, and we have conveyed to and from different parts of the globe, as soldiers going and coming, well, sick or wounded, some 13,000,000 men. Our policing of the sea has been so done that we have lost by enemy action 2,700 of these 13,000,000 travelling soldiers.

Then in money, we have spent on this war five billion five hundred million dollars, of which rather more than one fifth has been loaned or given to our Allies.

People sometimes say a fourth lie about us: – that we are a grasping people who will profit by this war.

Let me say this, that no one will profit from this war. We in Europe will be beggared by it for years to come; only we want the world to profit by it, by a change of heart, by an understanding among the nations, and by the knowledge which we in Europe needed this war to teach us, that human life is the precious thing on this earth, and that we are here truly linked man to man, and not divided up nation by nation. We are one body of humanity.

There is a fifth lie, that we are a greedy people, who ask you Americans to starve, while we feast on white bread and other delicacies. The answer to that is, that no white bread has been made in England for at least eighteen months, and that there is no feasting there. There is no home in all that land that is not the sadder for this war.

There is no need to lie about a nation any more than there is any need to lie about a man. The truth emerges above any lie.

I know my nation's faults as well as I know my own. They are the faults of a set and of a system. They are faults of head, they are not faults of heart. When I think of those faults I think of a long graveyard in France, a hundred miles long, where simple, good, kind, ignorant Englishmen by the thousand and the hundred thousand lie in every attitude of rest and agony, for ever and for ever and for ever. They did not know where Belgium is, nor what Germany is, nor even what England is. They were told that a great country had taken a little country by the throat, and that it was up to them to help, and they went out by the hundred and the hundred thousand, and by the million, on that word alone, and they stayed there, in the mud, to help that little country, till they were killed.

I've been along many miles of that old line, and seen those graves, many of them not even marked, except by a bayonet, or a bit of packing case, and I've thought, as I went along, what epitaph could be put above that unending graveyard, and I could only think of one epitaph, "*These men came here of their own free will to help their fellow men in trouble.*"

There comes the question, what is the war about? Each nation has its answer to that question, an answer that could be put into twenty words. But in each country, for many years before the war, millions of prejudices, and beliefs, and customs, and ignorances, and blindnesses, and memories, went to make the war. The question, what it is about, does not now so deeply matter, as the question, what the struggle is, now that it is in full swing.

It is a struggle between two conceptions of life, the soldier's and the civilian's. Both conceptions have existed ever since the world began. Much may be said for both.

The soldier says, in theory, "Men are not of much account; it is the man who matters. The man must have power over other men and be able to direct them as he chooses and punish them if they disobey; since men need a strong hand. A State can only be strong if it is so organized as to be obedient within and feared without. Every man within the State owes service to the State, he must be trained to defend it and fight for it. All men of a certain wealth and standing must be officers; the rest are and must be cannon-fodder. The citizens must have good roads fit for the movement of troops, adequate food and housing, a thorough military training and as much schooling as may be good for soldiers." Punctuality, hard work, and cleanliness are made much of; merit of certain kinds is certain of its reward, the citizens are ticketed, looked after, used and pensioned. They are not encouraged to think for themselves nor permitted to break the regulations. Napoleon in France and T'chaka in Zululand both created soldier states in the last century.

The civilian says, in effect, "It is true, that in case of need every man must be ready to fight for his State, and should be trained so that he may do so, but war is not a normal condition, it is an accident which may not occur, and the direction of the State by soldiers is apt to create a privileged class, who will enslave the remainder of the citizens for their own ends, which may be base and probably will be cruel, and which may and very likely will bring about that state of war which soldiers should prevent." So that, in the civilian state, the army is made small, and interferences with personal liberty are bitterly resented and swiftly opposed. The occupation of the civilian state is generally commerce. Its relaxation or amusement is generally the adornment of the individual life, with the arts and sciences which enrich life and make it pleasant. The general feeling is, that men were not meant to be the slaves of other men nor of human systems; but to develop themselves in as loose, easy and pleasant an - organization as a nation can be without collapsing.

Those are the two theories and ways of life, both have been tried and both will work, and both have left great marks in history.

But in working, both are open to grave defects. No nation is perfect, and no system of living will suit all the people all the time; and these ways of life, if persisted in by any nation for three or four generations, intensify themselves, till, in the military state there is too much control and in the civilian state too little.

In the civilian state, where much is left to the individual, much is left undone. Many individuals grow up to be highly educated, pleasant and agreeable men, but more grow up with the feeling that there is nothing to stop them from exploiting their fellow-citizens, and this they do quite as ruthlessly as any soldier, and with far less recompense. The soldier may drive his men, but he feeds, clothes and pensions them. The civilian may drive his men and scrap them as old tools when he has broken them. Very soon, in the civilian state, individualism comes to a point in which the service of the State is left to those who care for that kind of thing.

Those who do care for that kind of thing find that the fear of interference with liberty, which is the main passion in a civilian state, has prevented them from having any power. They can do neither good nor evil, and so they stagnate. They cease to attract the finer and more active kinds of mind. So that in a civilian state though you may find culture, politeness, niceness of feeling, enlightenment, and a wise protection of the individual against certain aggressions by King and State, and a great commerce, strongly protected, you may also find the man of action discountenanced, and the talker in power in his stead.

In the military state, the soldier justifies himself to his subjects by some act which rids the State of a danger or enriches it with a piece of plunder, so that he is able to say, "You see, the Army saved you or enriched you. You see that you must have an Army." When the army is enlarged, he attacks another State and enriches his own State still further; definitely enriches his officers with gifts of other people's property and his surviving men with bits of other people's lands, and at the same time increases his army by conscripting the conquered peoples.

Presently he forgets that the State is anything except himself. He cries out that the State is himself, since he is the head of the Army and the Army is the State. He subordinates everything to the army. He tolerates schools only in so far as they teach military maxims, and women only because they produce cannon-fodder. He encourages bad manners in his officers, because he thinks that it teaches them to dominate; he preaches about duty and his own magnificence in his churches and schools, because he thinks that it teaches people to obey. And at last, when his entire State does obey, and all his officers have bad manners, and a desire to dominate everybody, he has in his hands a terrible instrument of destruction which may be launched anywhere at his caprice. He is that irresponsible autocratic power who has been the main cause of war for twenty centuries.

But for the fact that all the power and blind obedience of a nation may be flung anywhere at the caprice of one man, there is much to be said for the military state. But that fact damns it, and the world has never allowed it to continue. The gunman who may be drunk or mad or savage at any minute is too dangerous to be allowed in the house. Rome, who had nobly held the idea of law, became that kind of State and fell. France, who had nobly held the idea of liberty, became that kind of State, and fell; and the savage Zulus, who made themselves a people and then an exterminating scourge also fell; and I feel that a grosser people, who have upheld neither law nor liberty, but have become exterminating scourges, will also fall. We civilian peoples, flouted, insulted, and taken unawares, are banded together to make that conception of life to fall.

Last April I was in a dirty little town in France. On my right there was a ruined factory containing a pile of smashed sewing-machines, on my left there was a casualty clearing station, in what had once been a rather nice house. Just outside the hospital there was a little old French woman

215

selling newspapers; and dozens of soldiers were buying newspapers and talking about the news. One of the soldiers shouted out, "Hooray, America has declared war," and another, who was older and more thoughtful, said, "Thank God, now we may have a decent world again."

War in one way is very like Mrs. MacGregor.

The poet Swinburne, when he was a young man, was very fond of impassioned conversation and of whisky. One night he met a friend, and suggested that the friend should come to his lodgings for a talk. On their way Swinburne bought a bottle of whisky and with an air of satanic cunning hid it in his tail pocket, and said, "I must be very careful; my landlady is a very troublesome woman." When they reached the door Swinburne said, "We must go in very quietly; my landlady is a very troublesome woman." They opened the door and crept in on tiptoe, and were just creeping upstairs, when a door opened and a stern voice said, "Is that you, Mr. Swinburrrrrne?" "Yes, Mrs. MacGregor," said Swinburne. Then the voice said, "Whattan is yon wee bottle in yeir bit pocket, Mr. Swinburrrne?" "O," said Swinburne, "it's my cough-mixture, Mrs. MacGregor; I'm afraid I've caught cold." "Cough-mixture me nae cough-mixture," said Mrs. MacGregor; "yon is a bottle of whuskey. And ye'll give it heer, Mr. Swinburrrne. Didn't I promise yeir father ye shuld na touch the whuskey?" And she grabbed the bottle and disappeared, and Swinburne was left wringing his hands and saying, "She's a very troublesome woman."

That is a light story, but it reminds me of the war. Many and many a gathering of friends has been interrupted by that savage goddess. All over Europe, quiet, gentle, ordinary men, who were going, as they thought, to the enjoyment of delight, have been seized upon and robbed by her, not only of material things, but of love and leisure and of life itself.

There is a story of a young king of India, who became a leper whom no one could cure. An old man told him that if he went to a certain city and ate bread in a house where there was no sorrow, he would be cured. So he went to the city, and went into every house, but there was no house that had no sorrow, so he was not cured. "There was no house that had not one dead."

There is no house, poor or rich, in any of the countries now fighting in Europe that has not one dead, generally some quite young man.

Many great minds have brooded over war; most of the great minds of the world have taken part in war, and some have tried to understand it. No great mind has ever looked upon it as a good thing, though they see that sometimes in life outrageous, devilish evil can be checked in no other way. To most of them, Homer, Euripides, Shakespeare, Tolstoi, it is nearly the last, greatest and completest evil that can come into human life.

You all know how a fever comes upon the body. Poison must be introduced into it from outside, some living poison of germs; the body must be predisposed to nurture the poison; it must be a little overstrained, restless, tired, bored, cross, or out of sorts. The natural guards of the body must be unable to help. Then the poison germs take hold and the normal life of the man ceases. He becomes a raging incoherent maniac terrible to himself and a danger to all about him, till the poison is at its height and has worked itself out in death or recovery.

Well, you will agree with me perhaps that war comes into the world, in much such a way. The body of a nation does not want it, though it may think about it often and much, the body of a nation is normally busy with its own life. Then, in times of overstrain, of restlessness, or of excitement, or even of busy and pleasant well-being, the poison is introduced, wilfully, by kings and their ministers, and the nation sickens.

The symptoms are always the same. The infected nation becomes, first of all, arrogant. It gets what we call swelled-head. It thinks itself, possibly with reason, the finest nation in the world. As the poison takes hold and the germs multiply, this arrogance leads to a spiritual blindness to whatever may be good or right in any other nation in the world. This blindness leads to an indifference to whatever any other nation may do or care. This indifference leads to the bloody theory, that it is a duty to subjugate any other nation. And at this point, the poison boils over in the system, the nation involved runs up a temperature, and it passes rapidly from acts of injustice to some culminating act of impiety, such as cannot be permitted, and against which a protest has to be made by the outraged world.

Then comes war, which goes on, like a fever, till the nation is dead or cured.

That may not be how all wars begin, but that is how the greatest and longest and most evil wars have begun, in modern times. A nation has caught a fever, run up a temperature, gone mad and bitten, been a danger and a scourge to the world, and has gradually sickened itself out into exhaustion, peace and wisdom. Spain had such a fever three hundred years ago, when her motto was the proud boast, "The world does not suffice for us." France had such a fever a century later. England had such a fever when she forced this country into the Rebellion.

In all three countries, there was just that same irresponsible autocratic power to cultivate the fever for his own ends. And who held that power? The immense power and wealth of Spain were controlled by Philip the Second, one old, miserly, stubborn dotard, a sort of a religious mule. The immense and ordered power of France was controlled by Louis Quatorze, one little man who wore high-heeled shoes and an immense wig to give himself some air of greatness. Afterwards it was held by Napoleon, of whom the French now say that he was as great as any man can be without principles. And who held the power of England? The elderly, pear-headed, self-willed German, often mad and always stupid, who wondered how the apple got inside the dumpling. And working with him were the few, corrupt and evil families engaged in the enslavement of the English poor.

Such were the four irresponsible autocrats who caused the greatest, longest and most evil wars of the past. But all the fever of their wars, multiplied ten-fold, would be as nothing to the fever of arrogance, blindness, wild and bloody thinking, and impious dealing, with which another irresponsible autocrat prepared the present war. No former autocrat took such pains to organize armed force, and to make the evil blood in his nation to run so hotly. No former autocrat had such skill or such clever servants to prepare and direct the outburst. And no former autocrat has reaped such a crop of bloodshed, massacre and destruction.

I'm not here to abuse our present enemies. We are against them today, but we have been with them in the past and we shall have to be with them in the future, if there is to be any future. In this life, collections of men behave worse than individuals, and it is the thought, and the way of life and the irresponsible autocrat that make them behave worse, that are the evil things. This war might have been averted, but that that one irresponsible autocrat was afraid of democracy. Consider what he has let loose upon the world. Consider, too, what he has raised against him.

A few minutes ago, I said that the greatest minds among men looked upon war as nearly (but not quite) the last, greatest and completest evil that can come into human life. Nearly, but not quite. There is one completer evil, that of letting proud, bloody and devilish men to rule this world. While proud, bloody and devilish men strike for power here, free men, who had rather die than serve them, will strike against them. And evil as war is, that resolve of the free soul is beautiful. It is in that resolve that we free peoples are banded, and it is in that resolve that we shall fight, till the proud, bloody and devilish idea is gone.

All of you here have read about this war daily for more than three years. All of you know someone who is taking part in it, and all of you have in your minds some picture of what it is like. The population of these States is said to be nearly a hundred millions. Not less than twenty-five millions of men, or the equivalent of the entire adult male population of these States are or have been engaged in the fighting of this war, and not less than another forty millions are engaged in the making the fighting possible, by the making of arms, equipment and munitions. Then besides those millions there are ten million dead, and twenty million maimed, disabled, blinded or lunatic soldiers who will never fight again.

You begin to meet the war many miles from any part of the fighting. You come upon a village of little huts near a railway siding. A month later you find that the village has become a town. A month later you find that the town has become a city. In that city the picked intellect of your country uses the picked knowledge of the universe to make the picked devilry of this war, some gas that will be deadlier than the other man's, some shell that will kill over a bigger area, some bomb that will go off with a louder bang and blast a bigger hole in a town.

You go elsewhere, and you see miles of chimneys spouting fire, where every known force is pressing every known metal into every known kind of engine of death.

You see the nimblest brains and hands and all the finest courage perfecting our control of the air. You see men gathering and packing food, breaking stones for roads and shaping sleepers for railways. You see men by the million about whom nobody cared, in the old days, in peace, suddenly taken up, and fed and clad and taught, and made much of. You see horses and cars by the hundred thousand, and everything that is swift and strong and clever and destructive, suddenly important and desired and of great account. You see the toil of a nation suddenly intensified sevenfold, and made acute, and better paid than it ever was, and intellect, the searching intellect, that light of the mind which brings us out of the mud, suddenly sought for in the street. And you think, "Is man awakening suddenly to his heritage, and to the knowledge of what life may be here?" Then you say to yourself, "No, this is all due to the war."

You see young men giving up their hopes, and mature men their attainments, and women losing their sons, their husbands and their chance of husbands, and children losing their fathers and their chances of life, and you ask, what earthly endeavour can cause all this sacrifice, into what kind of a hopper is it all being fed? It is being fed into the war.

The war is spread over a tract as big as these States. In many places the tide of war has passed and repassed several times, till the dwellers in those places have died of starvation, or been carried away into slavery. In the East, you can walk for miles along roads peopled with mad, starving and dying men and women; there are heaps of little bones all along the roads. They are all little bones. They are the little bones of little children who have died of starvation there. All the bigger bones have been taken by the enemy to make artificial manure.

In the West, there is a strip of land about four hundred and fifty miles long, by from ten to twenty broad. It is called the Army Zone. With the exception of a few poor people who sell little things, such as fruit and tobacco, to the soldiers, all the inhabitants of that zone are gone. The place is inhabited by the armies. The business there is destruction, and rest, after destruction, so that the destroyers may destroy again.

All that strip of France and Flanders was once happily at peace. All of it was rich and prosperous, with corn and wine and industry. Even the mountains were covered with timber. Today, after the manhood of four nations has fought over it for three and a half years it is a sight which no man can describe.

If one could look down upon that strip from above, it would look like a broad ribbon laid across France. The normal colour of a countryside is green, and green country would appear on both sides of the strip. At the edges however the green would lose its brightness, it would look dull and rather mottled; further from the edges it would look still duller, and in the centre of the strip no trace of green would show, it would all be dark except that the darkness would glitter in many places with little flashes of fire.

219

And if one comes to that strip by any of the roads which lead to it, one sees, at first, simply the normal French landscape, which is tidy, well-cultivated land, on a big scale, with little neat woods and little, compact villages. One notices that many houses are closed, and that very few men are about. Presently one comes to a village, where one or two of the houses are roofless, and perhaps the church tower has a hole in it. And if you ask, you hear, "No, the enemy never got so far as here, but they shelled it." A little further on, you come to a village where every other house is a burnt-out shell, all down the street. And if you ask how this came about, that every other house should be destroyed, you hear, "O, the enemy occupied this place and burnt every other house for punishment." And if you ask, punishment for what? You hear, "O, some of the enemy got drunk here and fired at each other, and they said we did it, so they shot the Maire and burnt every other house."

Then a little further on, you come to a village where there are no roofs nor any big part of a house, but heaps of brick and stone much blackened with fire, and on both sides of the road you see gashes and heapings of the earth and a great many stakes supporting barbed wire, and a general mess and litter as though there had been a fair there in rather rainy weather. And if you ask about this, they say, "Ah, this is where our old support line ran, just along here, and just under the church in what used to be the charnel-house, we had the snuggest little dugout that ever was."

Then if you go on, you come to a landscape where there is no visible living thing; nothing but a blasted bedevilled sea of mud, gouged into great holes and gashed into great trenches, and blown into immense pits, and all littered and heaped with broken iron, and broken leather, and rags and boots and jars and tins, and old barbed wire by the ton and unexploded shells and bombs by the hundred ton, and where there is no building and no road, and no tree and no grass, nothing but desolation and mud and death.

And if you ask, "Is this Hell?" They say, "No, this is the market-place where we are standing. The church is that lump to the right." Then if you look down you see that the ground, though full of holes, is littered with little bits of brick, and you realize that you are standing in a town.

If you go on a little further, you notice that the mud is a little fresher. You come to a deafening noise, which bursts in a succession of shattering crashes, followed by long wailing shrieks, partly like gigantic cats making love, and partly as though the sky were linen being ripped across. The noise makes you sick and dizzy.

If you go on a little further you come to a place where the ground is being whirled aloft in clods and shards, amid clouds of dust and smoke and powdered brick. Screaming shells pass over you or crash beside you, and you realize then that you are at the front. Like Voltaire, you say, "I am among men, because they are fighting. I am among civilized men because they are doing it so savagely." And when the smoke and dust of the shells clear away, you see no men, civilized or savage, nothing but a vast expanse of mud, with a dead mule or two, and great black and white devils of smoke where shells are bursting.

In parts of that strip of France, especially in the broadest part, you come upon places where the ground is almost unmarked with shellfire. There are no traces of fighting, no graves, no litter of broken men or broken equipment, the fields are green and there is no noise of war. Yet all the houses are ruined; they have been gutted, their roofs have been blown off or their fronts pulled out, and in their streets you will sometimes see vast collections of pots, pans, desks, tables, chairs, pictures, all smashed, evidently wantonly smashed; men have evidently defaced them, cut, burnt, and banged them. And you notice that for miles of that country all the best of the trees, especially the fruit trees, have been cut down, not for firewood, for they are all there, with their heads in the mud, but for wanton devilry.

And if you ask about this, you will hear – "O, no; there was no fighting here, but this is the ground the enemy couldn't hold. When he lost the ground to the north, he had to retreat from here in a hurry, but he showed his spite first. First he took away the few remaining boys and girls to work for him at making shells or digging trenches. Then they went from house to house and collected all the furniture and property into the central place of the town; then all that was good or valuable or not too bulky was taken by enemy soldiers, officers as well as men, as prize of war, and sent home to their homes. But all the rest, the things too bulky to pack, were deliberately smashed, defiled and broken, and the fruit trees were systematically killed."

I was in one such town in France last March the day after the enemy left it, and I went into one poor man's garden no bigger than this platform. Five or six little flowering plants had been pulled up by the roots. One little plum tree and two currant bushes had been cut through, and the wall parting this garden from its neighbour had been thrown down. All the wells in this district were poisoned by the enemy before he left. He referred to this in his Orders as being "according to modern theories of war."

Over all that area of the Army Zone, the business of the inhabitants is destruction; they rest not day nor night, not even fog nor snow will stop them. I have watched a raging battle in a snowstorm, and one of our neatest successes was made in a fog. And at night the darkness is lit with starshells, beautiful coloured rockets, flares, searchlights and magnesiums, so that the killing may go on.

You may wonder what kind of a life is lived under such conditions.

I can only say that it is a very attractive kind of life, and that many men who leave it want to go back to it, and few men who have lived that kind of life find it easy to settle down to another. And you will see men at their very best under those conditions. You will find them far more thoughtful of each other; far more generous and self-sacrificing than you

221

will ever see them in time of peace. You will be among men who will die for you without a moment's thought or an instant's hesitation, and who will share their last food or drink with you. You will see dying men giving up their last breath to comfort some other wounded man who may be suffering more at the moment. And living among those men, sharing their hardships and their dangers, you will realize to the full the sense of brotherhood and the unity of life which are among the deepest feelings which can come to men. You will realize the gaity, the courage and the heroism of the mind of man, and you will realize how deeply you love your fellows.

A British officer has defined the life at the front as "damned dull, damned dirty and damned dangerous." It is dull, because you stand in a gash in the earth behind some barbed wire and look through a thing called a periscope at some more barbed wire two hundred yards away, beyond which, somewhere, is the enemy, whom you hardly ever see. Then when you have stood in the trench for a time, you are put to do some digging, and when you have done the digging you are put to dig something else, and when you have done that digging you are put to dig something else. And when you have finished digging for the time, you are put to carrying something heavy and awkward, and when you have carried that, you are given something else to carry, and when you have carried that, you are given something else to carry, and the next morning there will be plenty of other things to carry. The work of soldiers today is not so much fighting, as digging trenches and roads and railways and wells. When they have finished digging, they have to carry up the heavy and awkward things needed at the front lines. Marshal Joffre said that this war is a war of carriers. The Battle of the Marne was won by us because the enemy carriers failed, and Verdun was saved to us because the French carriers did not fail. All the things needed in the front line are heavy and awkward to carry, and all have to be carried up, on the shoulders of men. The image left on the minds of most men by this war is not an image of fighting, nor of men standing in the trenches, nor of attacks, nor even of the gunners at the guns; it is the image of little parties of men plodding along in single file through the mud, carrying up the things needed in the front trenches; barbed wire, trench gratings, trench pumps, machine guns, machine gun ammunition, bombs, Stokes shells, tins of bully beef and tins of water. And by the sides of the gratings which make the roads near the front you will see the graves of hundreds of men who have lost their lives in carrying up these things.

And when it rains, as it has rained for weeks together on the Western Front during the last three years, that task of carrying becomes infinitely more terrible to the men than standing in the trenches to be killed or wounded. All that shot-up field becomes a vast and waveless sea of mud. That mud has to be seen to be believed, it cannot be described. It is more dangerous than any quicksand. I have seen men and horses stuck in it, being pulled out with ropes. I have seen soldiers standing in it up to the

222

waist, fast asleep, and I dare say you have seen that picture of the two soldiers standing in it up to the chin, one of them saying to the other: "If we stay here much longer we shall be submarined." There is nothing like this mud for breaking men's hearts. Any soldier on the Western Front will tell you that the mud is the real enemy. The task of carrying up supplies across that mud, becomes by much the most difficult task which soldiers are called upon to do.

In spite of the danger and the occasional mud, the life at the front is lived with cheerfulness. There is much joking, though many of the jokes are about death and the dead. Very strange and romantic things happen continually, and there are strange escapes. I have not seen any escape quite so wonderful as that escape vouched for during your Civil War. The story goes that a soldier was sitting on the ground eating his supper. Between two mouthfuls he suddenly leaped into the air. While he was in the air, so the story goes, a cannon ball struck the ground where he had been sitting. He could not explain afterwards why it was that he jumped. I dare say that story is true. I have not seen anything quite so wonderful as that, but I know of one very wonderful escape, in Gallipoli. A little party of friends sat together at their dugout door, watching the men swimming on the beach under fire. The beach was continually under fire, but it was no more dangerous than the dry land, and as swimming was the only possible relaxation for the troops, they were allowed to swim. While they watched the swimmers, these friends saw a solitary soldier go into a dugout (some distance down the hill) and draw the sacking which served as a door. Evidently he was settling in for his siesta. About ten minutes later a big Turkish shell came over. There were three big Turkish guns which used to shell the beach. They were known as Beachy Bill, Asiatic Annie, and Lousie Liza. A shell from one of these guns pitched (apparently) right onto the dugout into which this man had gone, and burst. The friends waited for a minute to see if another shell were coming near the same place, but the next shell pitched into the sea. They then went down to see if they could be of any service, though they expected to find the man blown to pieces. As they drew near to the wreck of the dugout, a perfectly naked man emerged, swearing. What had happened was this. He had gone into the dugout, had taken off all his clothes because it was very hot, and had lain down on his bed, which was a raised bank of earth, perhaps three feet above the level of the floor. The shell had come through the roof, had gone into the floor of the dugout, had dug a hole ten feet deep and had then burst. The hole and the raised bank of earth together had protected the man from the concussion and from the chunks of shell. He himself was not touched. Everything which he possessed was blown into little flinders, and he was swearing because his afternoon sleep had been disturbed.

In the same place, in Gallipoli, the day after the landing, the 26th of April, 1915, an Australian Captain was with his platoon of men in a trench up the hill. An Australian Major suddenly appeared to this

223

Captain and said: "Don't let your men fire to their front during the next half hour. An Indian working party has just gone up to your front, you will be hitting some of them." The Captain was a little puzzled at this, because he had seen no Indian working party, so he looked at the Major, and noticed that the Major's shoulder strap bore the number 31. That puzzled him, because he knew that only eighteen Australian battalions had landed on the Peninsula – numbers one to eighteen – and he did not understand what a member of the thirty-first battalion could be doing there. So he looked hard at this Major and said: "Say, are you Fair Dinkum?" That is an Australian slang phrase which means, "Are you the genuine thing? Are you quite all that you pretend to be?" The Major said: "Yes, I'm Major Fair Dinkum."

At the inquest on Major Dinkum, they found that he had taken the uniform from a dead Major of the thirteenth battalion, and had been afraid to wear it just as it was, for fear of being challenged, so he had reversed the numbers on the shoulder straps, and made them thirty-one. The inquest found that he died from lead in the head.

A branch of the service which is very little recognized but exceedingly dangerous is that branch of the messengers who carry messages and carrier pigeons and telephone wires during an attack. One of the most difficult things in modern war is to let your own side know exactly how far an attack has progressed. You send back messengers and the messengers are killed. You run out telephone wires and the wires are cut, as fast as they are laid, by shells or bullets. You send back carrier pigeons and the carrier pigeons are killed. During the Battle of the Somme a friend of mine was up in a tree correcting the fire of his battery. He had a telephone and a telescope. He watched the bursting of the shells and then telephoned back to the guns to correct their fire. While he was doing this, he glanced back at the English lines, and saw a great enemy barrage bursting between himself and his friends, in a kind of wall of explosion. And hopping along through this barrage came one solitary English soldier, who paid no more attention to the shells than if they had been hail. He looked to see this man blown to pieces, but he wasn't blown to pieces; and then he saw that it was his own servant bringing a letter. He wondered what kind of a letter could be brought under such conditions, and what stirring thing made it necessary, so he climbed down the tree and took the letter and read it. The letter ran: "The Veterinary Surgeon-Major begs to report, that your old mare is suffering from a fit of the strangles." The servant saluted and said: "Any answer, sir?" And my friend said: "No, no answer. Acknowledge." The servant saluted and went back with the acknowledgment, hopping through the barrage as though perhaps it were a little wet, but not worth putting on a mackintosh for.

There is another story told of a General (during an attack in the Battle of the Somme) who could not learn how far his division had gone. It was a matter of the most intense anxiety to him. He sent out messengers who never returned, the telephone wires were cut as fast as they were laid, and no pigeons came back. He stood beside the pigeon-loft biting his finger nails. Then at last, out of the battle, came a solitary pigeon, and the General cried: "There she is, there she is. Now we shall know." The pigeon came circling out of the smoke, and came down to the pigeon-loft and went in. The General said, "Go in, man, go in, and get the message!" So the pigeon fancier went into the loft and was gone rather a long time, and the General cried: "Read it out, man, read it out. What do they say?" The man replied, "I'd rather not read it aloud, sir." The General said: "Bring it here, man." The General took the message and read it, and the message ran: "I'm not going to carry this bloody poultry any longer."

I have said something about the dullness and the dirtiness of the life, but there is a kind of dirtiness to which I have not yet alluded. On your way up to the front you are struck by the number of soldiers sitting on the doorsteps of ruined houses studying the tails of their shirts as though they were precious manuscripts. When you are at the front you notice that the men have an uneasy way with their shoulders as though they wished to be scraping along brick walls, and when you have slept one night at the front you realize what the soldier meant when he wrote home to say: "This war isn't a very bloody war, so far as I've seen it, but it does tickle at night." I would like to ask all those who are sending packets of clothing to their friends at the front always to include the strongest insecticide they can find, because, though no insecticide is really strong enough to kill the creatures, a good strong insecticide will take the edge off them. The condition of needing insecticide is known as being "chatty." Not long ago an English actress was playing to the soldiers in a base camp. She was playing a play of Barrie's, in which a lady says of her husband that he was so nice and chatty. She was interrupted by a burst of joy from the troops. She could not understand what she had said to disturb them.

Next as to the danger at the front. In proportion to the numbers engaged, this war is by much the least dangerous war of which we have any record. The great scourges of ancient armies, typhus fever, typhoid, smallpox and measles, have been practically eliminated from this war. The only outbreak of typhus, so far as I know, was the outbreak in Serbia in 1915, and that was due not to the soldiers, but to the filthy conditions in which the Serbian refugees were forced to live. A friend of mine, a Doctor, was in charge of a hospital during that epidemic. The hospital was a big church which was completely filled with misery of every sort; typhus cases, typhoid cases, smallpox cases, maternity cases and children with measles, all jammed up together, and nobody to look after them but my friend and a few Austrian prisoners. The place was very filthy, crawling with vermin, and pretty nearly every known language was spoken there. One day a strange man appeared on the scene of misery. The orderlies asked my friend what they should do with him. My friend looked at the man, and saw that he was pale and shaggy, so he said, "Just wash him and put him into one of the beds." So they washed him. He protested very vigorously, but they did it, and they put him into one of the beds. He protested very vigorously against that, but they put him in and kept him there. My friend, being very busy, was not able to see him for the rest of the day, and didn't get round to him until the next morning. Then he found that he wasn't sick at all, but had come with a message from some neighbouring hospital.

As to the danger from missiles at the front, it is true, that at any minute of the day or night, in any part of the Army Zone, you may become a casualty, and the thing which makes you a casualty may bury you as well, or blow you into such small fragments that nothing of you may ever be seen again, nor anybody know what has become of you. Even if you are away from the front, on some battlefield where there has been no fighting for months, you are still in danger, because the ground is littered with explosives in a more or less dangerous condition. There are bombs which are going off because their safety pins have rusted through, and shells which go off for no apparent cause. You may jump across an open trench and land on a percussion bomb and kill yourself, or you may be riding along, and your horse may kick a percussion bomb and kill you. Or you may meet a souvenir hunter who will be equally deadly. And then some soldiers love to collect shells which have not exploded and then light fires under them for the pleasure of hearing them go Bang! They love to collect bombs and fling them at targets for their amusement. Last summer a General was walking on the old battlefield, when he heard a noise of cheering. There came a Bang, and bits of shrapnel came flying past. Then there came another cheer, and another Bang and some more shrapnel. So, guessing what was the matter, he jumped up onto the trench parapet and looked down. There he saw a burly soldier who had rigged up a target to represent a German and was bowling Mills bombs at it. At each bomb he shouted out: "Every time you hit you get a good cigar!" The General jumped onto this man and said: "Here, what are you doing? Don't you know that's against orders?" The man turned up the face of an innocent child and said: "No sir." "Well," said the General, "at least you know it's very dangerous, don't you?" The man looked at the General and sized him up, and said, "Yes, General. That's just why I was doing it, sir. You know, sir, I'm a family man, sir. I dare say you are yourself, sir. And I was thinking, in a little while the little children will be coming back to these old battlefields. They won't know what these cruel bombs are, sir, they'll go playing with them, poor little things, sir, and they'll blow off their little arms, sir, and their little legs, sir. Then think of their poor mothers' feelings. So I just collected these few bombs, sir, really in order to save those little children, sir." So he was acquitted as a philanthropist.

While I am on the subject of bombs, I may say what happened to a boy of the Gloucester Battalion in Gallipoli. The boy was an agricultural labourer before the war and rather stronger in the arm than in the head.

A friend came to his mother and said: "Oh, Mrs. Brown, what news have you of Bert?" Mrs. Brown beamed all over her face and said: "Oh, our Bert, he have had a narrow escape. He was in Gallipoli and there come a Turk and flung one of they bombs, and the bomb fell just at our Bert's feet, but our Bert he never hesitate, he pick it up, and he flung it right to the other end of the trench, and it burst just as it got there. It killed two of our Bert's best friends, but if our Bert hadn't flung it just when he done, it would have killed our Bert."

During the course of this war some six or seven millions of men have been drawn into the English Army from every rank of society, and have submitted to a pretty rough test. Under that test, thousands of men, who had had no opportunity of showing what was in them in time of peace, have risen to positions of great dignity, trust and authority. And as a result, the Army today is a thoroughly democratic thing. At the beginning of the war it was not so. I know of a case, in which a rich man enlisted with his shepherd. He told the shepherd, when he enlisted, "Of course, I shall pay your wages as my shepherd all the time that we are serving." When they were in the Battalion the shepherd soon proved himself to be the better man. The shepherd became a Sergeant and his master remained a private. Presently, the master did something wrong and the shepherd had him up and got him ten days' fatigue. As he left the court, the master leaned over to the shepherd and said: "Your wages are stopped for these ten days." That was in the early days of the war, when the democratic leaven was not working very well. But it is working very well today. I know of a case of a young man who began life as a stable boy in a racing stable. He didn't like the life, so he became a carpenter; he was a carpenter when the war began. He enlisted in a cavalry regiment, because he was very fond of horses; and as he knew a great deal about the management of horses he was given a commission straight away. He was always a man of great good temper and charm and tact in dealing with other men. He soon rose to a Captain. He went to France with the battalion, served in the trenches, dismounted, and soon rose to be Colonel of the battalion. He handled the battalion with great distinction and was made a Brigadier-General, and he is a Brigadier-General today.

Last summer I was talking with a General about the war, and he said: "Guess what my best staff officer was before the war?" I couldn't guess. He said he was a barber's assistant. "Now what do you think my second best staff officer was before the war?" Again I couldn't guess. He said, "He was a milkman's assistant and went round with the milk cans in the morning. Now what do you think my third best staff officer was before the war? He's the bravest man I've got." Again I could not guess. He said, "He was a milliner's assistant, and sold ribbons over the counter."

When the war is over and these men are disbanded back into every rank of society, they will carry with them this democratic leaven. I am quite sure that England, after the war, will be as democratic a country as this country or France.

If you turn your back upon the Army Zone and walk into the green and pleasant parts of France, you will notice that every big building in France is flying a Red Cross flag, for every big building now in France is a hospital. The business of the care of the wounded is a bigger business than coal or cotton or steel in time of peace. There are hundreds of thousands of orderlies and nurses and all the picked surgeons of the world looking after the wounded. There are miles of Red Cross trains carrying wounded, and there are more ships carrying wounded than carried passengers between England and America in the time of peace. I should like to tell you of one or two things which have been done to better the lot of the wounded. Firstly, about facial surgery. In this war of high-explosives it often happens that men will be brought in with all their faces blown away, with practically no face left beneath their brows, their noses gone, their cheeks gone, their jaws and their tongues gone. In the old days, if those men had survived at all, they could only have survived as objects of pity and horror and disgust. But today the facial surgeon steps in and remakes their faces. The facial surgeon begins by taking a bone from the man's leg. Out of that bone they model him a new jaw-bone, which they graft onto the stumps of the old. Then cunning artists model him a new palate and a new set of teeth. Then, bit by bit, they begin to make him new cheeks. They get little bits of skin from the man's arm, and other little bits from volunteers, and they graft these onto what was left of the man's cheeks. Though it takes a long time to do, they do at last make complete cheeks. Then they take a part of a sheep's tongue and graft it onto the roots of the man's tongue, so that it grows. Then they add artificial lips, an artificial nose, and whiskers, beard and moustaches, if the man chooses. They turn the man out, often handsomer than he ever was before, able to talk, and to earn his own living on equal terms with his fellow-men. In all that work of facial surgery the American surgeons have set a standard for the rest of the world. What they have done is amazing. You can see the men brought in, looking like nothing human, looking like bloody mops on the ends of sticks. Gradually you see them becoming human and at last becoming handsome and at last almost indistinguishable from their fellows. Surgeons not only restore the men fresh from the battlefield, but they remake the faces of those who have been badly patched up in distant parts of this war, such as Mesopotamia, where special treatment has been impossible, and though this re-making takes a very long time, it can still be done.

Another very wonderful treatment is the treatment of the burned men. In this war of high-explosives and flame projectors many men are shockingly burned. You may see men brought in with practically no skin on them above their waist, unable to rest, and suffering torments. They apply the new treatment of Ambrene to these sufferers. Ambrene is said to be a by-product of paraffin mixed with resin and with amber. It is applied in a liquid form with a camel's hair brush. Directly it touches the burned surface all pain ceases and the man is able to rest. In a fortnight the man has an entirely new skin, with no scar and practically no discolouration, and he is able to go back to the trenches, often much disgusted at being cured so soon.

When you have seen the wounded you have seen the fruits of this business. And when you have seen the wounded you resolve within yourself that at whatever cost this must be the last war of this kind. This war is being fought today in order that it may be the last war of its kind. If we succeed in this, as we shall, all the bloodshed and horror and misery of this war will have been very well worthwhile. But even when we have gotten rid of the causes of this war, there will still remain, in all human societies, many potential causes of war. A great deal of cant is talked about war. In all commercial countries there must be some manufacturers who make things that will be of great demand in war, and it is an unfortunate fact that after long periods of peace men begin to think a great deal about war, to read about it, and to brood upon it, and even to long for it, so that they may have that deep experience for themselves. And to many young men war is exceedingly delightful. It gives them adventure, excitement and comradeship. Only the other day a young English soldier said to me: "Do you think this lovely war will ever come to an end?" I said I hoped it would, someday. And he said, "Well, I don't know what I shall do when it comes to an end. It will break my heart. I've had the time of my life." That boy was not quite nineteen. He had been a schoolboy six months before. He had been badly wounded three weeks before. He had been at death's door a fortnight before. He had made an amazing recovery and was panting to get back. There are hundreds of thousands of young men like that, who thoroughly enjoy every minute of it. The older men do not view war with quite such enthusiasm. Their attitude, perhaps, is much like that of the Naval Officer who said the other day: "I do wish to God this war would end, so that I could get the men back to battle practice."

Even if we were able to be rid of all these potential causes of war we should not get rid of evil in this world, and as long as men can be evil, evil men will strike for power, and the only way to resist evil men, when they do evil things, is to use force to them. It often needs a very great deal of force.

Yet when people ask me if I think that wars will cease to be, I always say that I do, because the evil things in this world do get knocked on the head. The dragons and basilisks and cockatrices have become extinct, and most murderers get hanged, and most lunatics get locked up; and men are coming more and more to see that certain evils that afflict life are not inevitable, and are not the will of God, but are simply the result of obsolete and stupid ways of thinking and of governing. It ought to be possible for the mind of man, which made the steam engine, the submarine and the aeroplane, and conquered the Black Death and yellow fever and typhus fever, to devise some means of living, nation with nation, without this periodical slaughter known as war. It won't be easy to devise any such means, men being what they are, with the instincts for war deeply rooted in their hearts, or easily put there by their rulers; yet the mind of man can do most things, if he can only get the will to do them.

Even before this war, when most men were either unoccupied or occupied only in the grim and stupid devilry of plotting and preparing war; men tried to limit and prevent war, the Hague Conferences did sit. They didn't limit or prevent war, because they were not meant to. While they sat, one great power was doubling its army, and a second was doubling its strategic railways, and a third was increasing its navy, and all were afraid, each of the other. How could peace come from men under those conditions?

Then, though they made recommendations, the Hague delegates had no power to enforce them. They knew this when they made them. Their recommendations were therefore not forceful. They seemed to say, that war is inevitable, let us temper its horror. They did not say, war has no business in modern life, henceforth those who make war shall be treated as criminals by an international police.

They could not say that, but the Peace Delegates of the future will have to say it, if there is to be any future. And after this war men will listen to them if they do say it, for after this war men will passionately want to limit and prevent war. They know now, that the devil of war, which they fed with their arrogance, their envy, their strength and their stupidity, is an overwhelming monster which eats them wholesale.

Not long ago, I was talking to an American about this ending of war by internationalism. He said: "If two great peoples would agree to it, it could be done; and if your country and mine would agree to it, it would be done." Don't think me a dreamer, an idealist, a pacifist. I am for the common man and woman, whose tears and blood pay for war. And in that matter of payment, the poor German pays, equally with the poor Belgian. He pays with all he has. On the battlefields of this war I have seen the men who paid. I have seen enemy dead, and Turk dead, and French dead, and English dead, and every dead man meant some woman with a broken heart.

Those men had no quarrel with each other. They lie there in the mud, because man, who has conquered the Black Death and typhus and smallpox, and the yellow fever, has not conquered the war fever. And the war fever takes him in the blood and in the soul and kills him by the hundred thousand.

When the blessed bells ring for peace, this year or next year, in man's time if not in ours, it may be possible to remake the ways of national life more in accordance with man's place in the universe. When that time comes, France, this country, and England, the three countries which have done the most for liberty, will have deciding voices in that remaking. They will be able to declare in what ways of freedom the men and women of the future will walk. I trust that our three great nations may be able to substitute some co-operating system of internationalism for the competing nationalism which led to the present bonfire.

And when that time comes, I hope that one other thing may be possible. I hope that my people, the English, may, as your comrades in this war, do something or be something or become something which will atone in some measure for the wrongs we did to you in the past, and for the misunderstandings which have arisen between us since then. I'm afraid that the memory of those old wrongs may never pass, for nations, like people, do not forget their childhood. Yet I hope for the sake of the world, that it may be set aside, so that your country and mine, which have one great key to understanding, which other nations have not, the same language, may, after this time of war work like friends together, to make wars to cease upon this earth.

[source: *The War and the Future*, New York: Macmillan, 1918]

St. George and the Dragon

*A speech given in New York on
St. George's Day, April 23rd, 1918*

Friends, for a long time I did not know what to say to you in this my second speaking here. I could fill a speech with thanks and praise: thanks for the kindness and welcome which has met me up and down this land wherever I have gone, and praise for the great national effort which I have seen in so many places and felt everywhere. We, who, like you, have had to lay by our pleasant ways, and take up hard ones, and go up a bitter path to an end men cannot see, know how great your sacrifice and your effort are. But I could not thank you or praise you enough, and even if I could, the best praise and thanks are silent. If and when I return to England, I will speak your praise.

So, casting about for a theme, I thought, that today is St. George's Day, the day of the Patron Saint of England, and that today, in the far past, that great knight of God rode out, in the Eastern country, and killed a dragon which had been devouring women, and that Englishmen had thought that deed a holy, and most beautiful and manly thing, and had chosen St. George from among all saints to be their saint, and had taken his banner to be their banner, and called upon him, century after century, when they went into battle. For they felt that such a man lived on after death, and would surely help all holy and beautiful and manly men for ever and for ever.

And I thought, too, that on this day, 354 years ago, the child, William Shakespeare, was born, in that old house in Stratford which so many of you have gone to see. And that on this same day, after he had done his day's work, he passed out of this life, into that Kingdom of England which is in the kindling mind, in all its moments of beauty, and that there he, too, lives for ever, to give peace, even as St. George gives a sword, to all who call upon him.

So, thinking these things, all the more keenly, because I am far from England, in this sweet season of April, when the apple blossom is beginning, I felt that I would talk of England. Not of any England of commerce or of history, nor of any state called England, but of that idea of England for which men are dying, as I speak, along 5,000 miles of war.

I believe that the people of a country build up a spirit of that country, build up a soul, which never dies, but lingers about the land for ever. I believe that every manly and beautiful and generous and kindling act is eternal, and makes that soul still greater and more living, till in the land where manly and kindling souls have lived, there is everywhere about the earth, present like beauty, like inspiration, this living gift of the dead, this soul. And nations are only great when they are true to that soul. Men can only be great when they are true to the best they have imagined. And I believe that in times of stress, in national danger, in calamity, the soul behind a nation kindles and quickens and is alive and enters into men, and the men of the nation get strength and power from it.

I believe that that great soul, made by the courage and beauty and wisdom of the millions of the race, is the god of the race, to protect it and guide it and to lead it into safety. And men turning to it in time of trouble and calamity are helped and guarded by it, and brought out of the land of Egypt by it into their pleasant heritage.

Yet nations, like men, sometimes turn away from their true selves to follow false selves, and to serve false gods. All the old Bible is full of stories of a little nation sometimes true, sometimes false to its soul, and falling into calamity, and then being quickened and helped, and returning to the truth and coming to marvellous things, to the green pastures, where goodness and loving kindness follow men all the days of their life.

Understanding is the only thing worthwhile in this life. Art is nothing but complete understanding of something. All writers long to understand the spirit of their race.

Let me say now, that 25 years ago, it would have been difficult for an Englishman to speak here, about the spirit of England, and to claim that it is something of the spirit of St. George, a manly and beautiful spirit, ready to help someone weaker, and something of the spirit of Shakespeare, a just and tender spirit, fond of fun and kindness and of the rough and busy life of men. That delicate, shy, gentle, humorous and most manly soul is the soul of England. It is in Chaucer, in Shakespeare, in Dickens. It is in the old ballads and tales of Robin Hood, who stood up for the poor, and was merry walking in the green forest. It is in the little villages of the land, in the old homes, in the churches, in countless old carvings, in old bridges, in old tunes, and in the old acts of the English, a shy, gentle, humorous and most manly soul, that stood up for the poor and cared for beauty. No finer thing can be said of men than that, that they stood up for the poor and cared for beauty; that they cared to be just and wise.

Nearly 300 years ago, the life of England suffered a rude change in seven years of civil war. The ways of life which had been settled for five generations were suddenly and completely changed. There followed a turbulent and unsettled century, during which, for reasons of party, a foreign king, and line of kings, with foreign interests, and foreign methods, came into our land.

And at the same time, something else came into our land. Industry and adventure had long been virtues of the English; but now the two together began to create competitive commercialism. And just as competitive commercialism began, a small clique of corrupt politicians, gathered under the foreign king, and by bribery and iniquity of every kind, seized the common lands of the villages of England and enclosed them. Until then, the country folk in England had shared large tracts of land, so that, though they were poor, they still had grazing for cows and sheep and geese, and woodland for firing. Now by various acts of legal robbery these lands were taken from them, and they were reduced to an extreme poverty. They were forced into a position very like slavery. They had no possessions except their right hands. There was no St. George to stand up for them, nor any Robin Hood, except that coarse and bitter truth-teller, William Cobbett. They had the choice to be the slaves of the landowners or of the factory-owners, and the great mass of the populace ceased to have any share of what life offers. The enclosing of the commons robbed them of leisure and independence, the coming of the factories took them from the fields and the old communities, and flung them into new ones, which were allowed to grow up anyhow, without art, without thought, without faith or hope or charity, till the face of the land was blackened, and the soul of the land under a cloud.

If you consider the thought and the voices of that time, you can see that the soul of the land was under a cloud. The thought and the voices of that time are things divorced from the body of the people. The thought is the possession of a few leisured men. It is not the joy of a great body of men. The voices are the voices of a few men crying in the wilderness that things are evil.

The thought of that time was the thought of Dr. Johnson's Club, and of Joshua Reynolds' patrons. The voices are the voices of Wm. Blake crying aloud that he would rebuild the city of God among those black Satanic mills, and of Wm. Wordsworth, who saw that poetry, which should be the delight of all, was become an unknown tongue to the multitude. And later the voices become more passionate and wilder and bitterer. They are the voices of Byron, who saw the foreign king, that royal lunatic, and his drunken but jovial son, and the bought-and-sold politicians who ran the country, for what they were, and mocked them. And the voice of Shelley, who cried to the men of England to shake themselves free, and the voice of Carlyle, who saw no hope anywhere but in the drill sergeant, and the voice of Ruskin, who saw no hope anywhere but in the coming back of St. George.

There was only one question to those men, the-condition-of-England question. Thinking men might justly be proud of certain achievements in those years, many things were invented, many things were thought out, great books were written, and the world was charted and navigated and exploited, but there was no peace in that England for the men with souls to be saved.

The machine worked, it did great things, men could point to its results, but the great men, the seeing men, were unanimous that England was not a merry England for rich or poor. It was still a land where there was kindness and manliness and a love of life and sport and country. But with this, there was an apathy to things which were vital and kindling. The nation was drunken, and that was looked on with apathy, the nation had ceased to care, as it once had cared, with a most noble, intense, and passionate pride, for things of beauty and of style, in life, and art and music and the means of living. And this deadness and apathy and stupidity were become even matters of pride to some. Then the nation, with all its wealth, was an ill-taught, an ill-fed and an ill-clad nation, so that in every city in the land a vast number of souls were ignorant, and a vast number of bodies had not enough to eat nor enough to put on. And the rich, who owned the wealth, had lost the old English sense of splendour of life. They watched the beggary and the drunkenness with apathy. They watched the waste and the degradation of genius without lifting a finger. One of the most delicate silversmiths of our time died of consumption as a seller of cat's meat. One of our most delicate lyric poets died of consumption as a seller of matches in the street. Not all the efforts of all the writers of England could get a theatre for the fit and frequent playing of Shakespeare. Not all the wealth nor all the industry could reduce the paupers of England, the men and women who could not make a living, to less than a million in the year.

So that, early in 1914, England was a troubled and yet an apathetic country, with small minorities breaking their hearts and sometimes people's windows in an effort to bring about a change, and with a vast, powerful, unthinking selfish weight of prejudice and privilege keeping things in the old ruts and the old grooves laid down by the foreign king a century and a half before.

And yet, with it all, there was immense virtue in the land. Work was well done. English goods were well-made. And we were not afraid to let any nation compete with us in the open market. The nations could sell their goods in our markets on equal terms. We had no quarrel with anyone. We wished to show that we had no quarrel with anyone. During the years before the war, we increased our Navy, so that no enemy should attack us with impunity, but we reduced our tiny army by some divisions, and our auxiliary army by an army corps.

People say now that we were wrong. We may have been. At any rate, we did the generous thing, and I don't know that the generous thing is ever wrong. And in any case, we have paid the price.

In the first week of July, 1914, I was in an old house in Berkshire, a house built eight centuries before by the monks, as a place of rest and contemplation and beauty. I had never seen England so beautiful as then, and a little company of lovely friends was there. Rupert Brooke was one of them, and we read poems in that old haunt of beauty, and wandered on the Downs. I remember saying that the Austro-Serbian business might cause a European war, in which we might be involved, but the others did not think this likely; they laughed.

Then came more anxious days, and then a week of terror, and then goodbye to that old life, and my old home in Berkshire was a billet for cavalry, and their chargers drank at the moat. I saw them there. And the next time I saw them they were in Gallipoli, lying in rank in the sand under Chocolate Hill, and Rupert was in his grave in Skyros.

We were at war. We were at war with the greatest military power in the world. We had an army of about 180,000 men, scattered all over the world, to pit against an army of five or six millions of men, already concentrated. We had, suddenly, at a day's notice, with the knife at our throats, to make an army of six or seven millions of men, and we had perhaps trained officers enough for an army of 300,000. We had to enlist, house, tent, train and officer that army. We had to buy its horses and mules, build its cars and wagons and travelling kitchens. We had to make its uniforms and straps, blankets, boots and knapsacks; and, worst of all, we had to make its weapons.

We had the plant for making (I suppose) 50 big guns and 500 machine guns and 50,000 rifles in the year, with proportionate ammunition. Suddenly we wanted 50,000 big guns, and 500,000 machine guns and 10,000,000 rifles with unlimited ammunition, more ammunition than men could dream of, with all sorts of new kinds of ammunition, bombs, hand-grenades, aerial torpedoes, or flying pigs, flying pineapples, egg-bombs, hairbrush-bombs, Mills bombs, trench mortar bombs, such as men had never used. And those things were wanted in a desperate hurry and we had the plant for not one-fiftieth part of them, nor the workmen to use the plant when made, nor the workmen to make the plant.

It is said that it takes one year to make the plant for the making of the modern big gun, and to train the workmen to make the countless delicate machines with which men kill each other in modern war. That was the proposition we were up against, and meanwhile, just across the water, well within earshot of our eastern counties, the enemy, like an armed burglar, was breaking into our neighbour's house, and killing our neighbour's children, taking his goods, abusing his women and burning the house over the victims.

In the first eight days of the war we sent two-thirds of our little army to France (about 120,000 men all told). They marched up to take position, singing, "It's a long, long way to Tipperary." It was not to be a long way to those brave men, for half of them were gone within eight weeks. They were not too well-equipped with guns, nor had they many machine guns, but every man in the army was a very carefully trained rifle-shot. Against them came enemy armies numbering nearly half a million of men.

They came into touch on August 23rd, near Mons, against odds of five or six to one. They were driven back, of course. That little line was turned and almost enveloped. There has been little fighting in this war to equal that first fighting. But one man cannot fight six men: so our army fell back, fighting desperately, in hot weather, for nine days.

Often in that blazing weather, divisions were so footsore that they could go no farther. Then they would take position and lie down and fight. The only rest they had was when they could lie down to fight. And at night, when they got to their bleeding feet again and plodded on in the dark, a sort of refrain passed from rank to rank, "We're the bloody rear-guard, and bloody rearguards don't eat and bloody rearguards don't sleep, but we're up, we're up, we're up the blooming spout."

They fell back for nine days and nights, till the enemy was at the gates of Paris, and the Allied cause seemed lost. You know how the enemy swept into Belgium and into Northern France, with his myriads of picked men, his aeroplanes and overwhelming numbers of guns. They marched singing and they came on like a tide, supping up cities, Liége, Namur,

Mons, Cambrai, as though they were the sea itself. They beat back everything. The French were not ready, the Belgians were only a handful, we were only a handful. And then, when they were at the gates of Paris, the miracle happened. That great army outran its supplies. It advanced so swiftly that the heavy loads of shells could not keep pace with it. Then in September, 1914, that great calm soldier Marshal Joffre wrote those words which will be remembered as long as this war is remembered: "The time has come for going back no further, but to die where you stand if you cannot advance." Then came the battle of the Marne, and people knew that whatever happened there would be no overwhelming victory for the enemy. He was beaten and had to fall back to gather strength for another effort, and all his dreams of sudden conquest collapsed.

But though our armies won at the Marne, it was only by miracle; and the essence of miracles is that they are not repeated. Our side was not ready for war. We were weaker than the enemy in guns, men and equipment. Our task was still to hold the line somehow, without guns, and almost without men, but by bluff and barbed wire, while guns could be forged and men trained. The enemy was ready for a second spring long before we were ready to resist him, and this second spring was not to fail, as the Marne had failed, through want of munitions.

This second spring took place at the end of October, 1914, when we had lost about half our original army and had altogether about 100,000 men in the line, many of them drafts who had not had one month's training. This 100,000 were outgunned and outnumbered. All are agreed that the enemy brought against that 100,000 not less than six times its strength, and the battle that followed (the first battle of Ypres) lasted for twenty-seven days and nights of continuous and bloody fighting. To this day no soldier can understand why the enemy didn't break through. Our line was so thinly held that in many places there were no supports and no reliefs of any kind, and the men stayed in the trenches till they were killed or wounded. That little and weary army underwent a test such as no other army has had to stand. The enemy shelled our line, with a great concentration of guns, and attacked with a great concentration of men, and broke the line at Gheluvelt, near Ypres. It has been thought by some that the enemy had only to advance to crumple the whole army; and destroy the Allied Cause. And then two men (according to the story) saved the issue. Two English soldiers, named Pugh and Black, gathered up small parties of men, regimental cooks and servants, stretcher-bearers, and walking wounded, and held the enemy in check, till what was left of the Worcester Battalion, about four hundred men, could be put in to retake the village. Those four hundred men saved the line and prevented a defeat. Our generals were writing an order for retreat when a staff officer came galloping up to them, in wild excitement, and without a hat, to shout out that the Worcesters had restored the line.

In that most bloody battle of "First Ypres," one English battalion was obliterated, another was remade two and a half times between October and Christmas, a third, which went in 987 strong, came out 70 strong; in a fourth, an officer who returned to duty after two months in hospital, found only one man left who had been in the battalion two months before; all the rest had gone.

After that battle, the mud set in, and stopped all great movements of men and guns. Both sides dug and fortified the lines they were holding, and the war became an affair of siege, until the spring.

Then the enemy launched a third attack against us, which was by much the most dangerous attack of the early months of the war. He began this attack by an intense bombardment of the English and French lines near Ypres. Then, at nightfall, in the April evening, while this bombardment was at its height, he let loose a great green cloud of chlorine gas, which floated across the No Man's Land to our lines. Whenever this gas reached the lines it choked the men dead, by a death which is unspeakably terrible, even for this war.

The men watched the gas coming. They thought that it was a smoke-screen or barrage, designed to hide the advance of enemy infantry. Suddenly they found the green cloud upon them, and their comrades choking and retching their lives away in every kind of agony. For a while there was a panic. The men in the front lines were either killed or put out of action. The communication trenches were filled with choking and gasping men, flying from the terror and dropping as they fled. Night was falling. It was nearly dark, and the whole area was under an intense enemy shellfire. The line was broken on a front of four and a half miles; and for the time it seemed as though the whole front would go.

The gas had come just at the point where the French and the English armies joined each other; at a point, that is, where all words of command had to be given in several languages, and where any confusion was certain to be intensified tenfold; there were many Colonial and native troops there, Turcos, Indians, Senegalese, Moroccans, as well as Canadians, French and English. All the troops there were shaken by this unexpected and terrible death, against which they had no guard.

Then a few officers, whose names, perhaps, we may never know, gathered together the stragglers and the panic-stricken, and called to them to put handkerchiefs and caps and rags of blankets and strips of shirt in front of their faces, and with these as respirators they marched the men back into that cloud of death, and though many were killed in the attempt, enough survived to hold the line, and so we were saved for the third time.

All nations use gas now, but that was the first time it was used. It is a very terrible thing. I have seen many men dying of it. It rots the lungs and the victims gasp away their lives. There is a saying, "If you sell your soul to the Devil, be sure you get a good price." The use of that gas was a selling of the soul, and yet the price gotten in exchange was nothing. They had our line broken with it and for weeks they could have beaten us by it. It was weeks before our men had proper respirators in any number. I do not know why they didn't beat us then; nobody knows. Some think that it was because their General Staff did not trust their chemists.

Just at the time when the gas attack was preparing outside Ypres, a little army of the Allies was landing on the Gallipoli Peninsula, "to assist the passage of the fleets through the Dardanelles."

I have been asked about the Gallipoli campaign. People have complained to me that it was a blunder. I don't agree. It had to be undertaken; to keep Bulgaria quiet, to keep Greece from coming in against us, to protect Egypt and to draw the Turkish Army from the Caucasus, where Russia was hard-pressed. People say, "Well, at least it was a blunder to attack in the way you did." I say that when we did attack, we attacked with the only men and the only weapons we had, and in the only possible places.

In war one has to attempt many things, not because they are wise or likely to succeed, but because they have to be done. In this war, we had to attempt them with insufficient means, because we were unprepared for war.

Consider what that attempt meant.

In the original scheme, the Russians were to co-operate with us, by landing 40,000 men on the shores of the Bosphorus, so as to divert from us a large force of enemy soldiers. We brought our men 3,000 miles across the sea, and we said to them, in effect, "There are the Turks, entrenched, with machine guns and guns and shells. You have only rifles. We have no guns nor shells to give you. Now land on those mined beaches, and take those trenches. The Russians will help to some extent; it will not be so hard." So the men went ashore and took those trenches. Nine days after they were ashore, we learned that the Russians could not land any men on the Bosphorus, and that we were alone in the venture. And then we said to our survivors, "The Russians can't come to help you, after all. We have no guns nor shells to give you. We are so hard-pressed in France that we can't send you any reinforcements. The enemy is entrenched with plenty of guns, and lots of shells, but you've got rifles, so go and take those trenches, too." So the men went and took them. Then we said, in effect, "Men and guns are needed in France, we can't send you any more just yet." So everything was delayed, till the men and guns were ready, and then, when they were ready, the enemy was ready, too, and dysentery was raging and it was very hot, and there was little to drink, and it is a God-forgotten land to fight in, so we did not win the Peninsula, nor anything else, except honour from thinking men.

I know that every man who was in Gallipoli, is and will be prouder of having been there, than of anything in his life, past, present, or to come. Our men kept a flag flying there to which the beaten men of all time will turn in trial.

As you know, in 1915, the war settled down into a struggle between opposing lines of trenches, with daily shelling and sniping and occasional raiding, mining and bombing. The next great attack was the attack on

Verdun, when the enemy launched an army of specially fed, trained and rested soldiers, under a hail of shells, to break through the French lines. That attack lasted with little intermission for four months, and it did not break the line. It very nearly broke it, but not quite. Perhaps nothing can break the line of a free people sworn to hold the gates for freedom. Often in that fight, little bodies of French and German soldiers were shut off for days together by shellfire, men died from hunger and thirst in the wreck of the forts, and those parties of French and Germans would count heads to see which side had won.

And while the attack was at its height, and while Verdun was still in danger, the English and French together counter-attacked in force on a line of 25 miles, further to the north, in the Department of the Somme, and beat the enemy out of his main position there. That put an end to the attack on Verdun. The Battle of the Somme gave another use for the enemy's men and guns. The city was saved. And a great deal more than the city; for the battle of the Somme beat the enemy out of a strip of France 65 miles long by from 12 to 20 deep, where today the great battle of this war is being fought.

This Battle of the Somme was an attack upon some of the most elaborate field fortifications ever made. On the right of the attack, where the French attacked, much of the ground is flat, and without good defensive position, but on the left, where the English attacked, the ground is a succession of rolling chalk downland, rising some hundreds of feet above little valleys. On this rolling downland, the enemy had dug himself in, when he was strong and we were weak. He had made himself so strong there, that he openly boasted that his position was impregnable. He had all the good positions there. His line was so placed, that it was almost always a little above us, and he worked to improve these positions night and day for nearly two years.

Perhaps not many here have seen a first-rate enemy field fortification. I'll try to explain what the Somme position was like.

As you know, the main defence in a modern line is the front line system of trenches.

In front of his front line, the enemy had a very elaborate strong tangle of wire, about 4 feet high and 40 yards across, each wire as thick as a double rope yarn and with 16 barbs to the foot.

Hidden in this wire, under the ground, in converted shell-holes, or in very cunningly contrived little pits, were stations for machine gunners. Some of these stations were connected with the enemy trenches by tunnels, so that the gunners could crawl to them under cover.

In some places, the ground of the wire entanglement was strewn with trip-wire, so near the ground as to be invisible, yet high enough to catch the feet. In the trip-wire were spikes to transfix the men who caught in the trip-wire and fell.

Behind the wire tangle were the enemy first line trenches.

These were immense works, designed as permanent field fortresses.

242

They were always well-made and well-sited. In many important points of the line they were twelve feet deep, and strongly revetted with plank and wicker. At intervals of about 50 yards, in some parts of the line, were little concrete forts for observers and machine guns. These forts were so well-concealed that they could not be seen from without. The slit for the observer or for the machine gun to fire through is very tiny, and well-hidden in the mud of the trench parapet.

These forts were immensely strong, and very small. A man inside one could only be destroyed by the direct hit of a big shell or by the lucky chance of a bullet coming through the narrow slit. You must remember that one cool soldier with a machine gun has in his hands the concentrated destructive power of 40 or 50 rifle men.

In the wall of the trench parapets on this front line, at intervals of 30 to 40 yards, were shafts of stairs leading down 20 or 30 feet into the earth. At the bottom of the shafts were great underground living rooms, each big enough to hold 50 or 100 men. In some places shafts led down another 20 feet below these living rooms to a second level or storey of dugouts.

These places were fairly safe in normal times, though apt to be foul and ill smelling. In bombardments the men kept below in the dugouts, out of danger from the shells, till the instant of the attack, when they could race up the stairs in time to man the fire step, and to get their machine guns into action. During the intense bombardments, the shafts and stairs were blown in, and a good many of the enemy were buried alive in these dugouts. Our men, when they had captured these trenches, usually preferred to sleep in the trenches, not in the dugouts, as they said that they would rather be killed outright than buried alive.

In some parts of the battlefield of the Somme, the ground is channelled with deep, steeped-sided, narrow gullies in the chalk, sometimes 40 feet deep and only 40 feet across, like great natural trenches. Three of these gullies were made into enemy arsenals and barracks of immense strength and capacity. These were, the tunnel at St. Pierre Divion, dug into the chalk, so that some thousands of men could live underground within one-quarter mile of the front line, in perfect safety; the barracks at the Y Ravine, about a mile further north, and the barracks in Quarry Gulley, near the Y Ravine. In all these immense underground works, the enemy had elaborate homes, lit with electricity, hung with cretonne and panelled with wood. Little stairs led from these dwellings to neat machine gun posts overlooking the front line. In one of these elaborate underground dwellings there were cots for children and children's toys, and some lady's clothes. It was thought that the artillery general who lived there had had his family there for the weekend.

Behind all these works, were support and reserve trenches of equal strength, often fully wired in, but with fewer dugouts. Then about a mile or two miles behind the front line, on a great crest or table of high chalk downland, was the second line, stronger than the front line, on even more difficult ground, where you cannot walk a yard without treading on dust of English blood.

Words cannot describe the strength of that old fortified line. It was done with the greatest technical skill. If you went along it, you would notice here and there some little irregularity or strangeness, and then you would look about, till you could see what devilish purpose that little strangeness served. And there was always one. The little irregularity gave some little advantage, which might make all the difference in a battle. The little thing in war alters the destinies of nations. A grain of sand in the body of Napoleon altered the campaign of 1812. I know of one great and tragical battle in this war which was lost mainly through a sprained ankle.

Our old lines faced these great fortresses at a distance of about 200 yards. Our lines are nothing like the enemy lines. There were no deep dugouts. The wire was comparatively slight. The trenches were inferior. It looked as though the work of amateurs was pitted against the work of professionals. Yet the amateurs held the professionals.

When Lord Kitchener went to Gallipoli, he visited Anzac. At that time, life in Gallipoli was becoming anxious, because some 17-inch Skoda guns had been brought down by the Turks and were shelling the position. Our men had dug some dugouts 10 or 15 feet deep to protect them from these shells. They showed them to Kitchener with pride. Kitchener said, "Of course, they may do for Gallipoli, but they aren't nearly deep enough for France. We never go down less than 30 feet in France."

So, when the Peninsular men came to France, they came with the modest feeling that they knew nothing about modern war, nor about digging dugouts, and they went into the trenches expecting to see dugouts like Egyptian catacombs. They found that the only dugouts were pieces of corrugated iron with a few sandbags on the top and some shovelsful of mud over all.

In places where the two lines approached each other at a crest, there had been a two years' struggle for the possession of the crest; for modern war is mainly a struggle for the post from which one can see. In all these places the space between the lines was a vast and ghastly succession of mine pits, fifty or a hundred feet deep, marked with the wrecks of old dugouts, and heads and hands and bodies, and sometimes half full of evil water.

Within the 16 mile limit of the English sector of the Somme field, there were in the enemy front line eight strongholds which the enemy boasted were impregnable.

The Battle of the Somme was the first real measuring of strength between the enemy and the English. In the early battles, the picked men of our race had met their picked men and held them. But the picked men were now dead, and the armies which fought on the Somme were the average mass of the race.

I must describe the Battle of the Somme. On the right, where the ground is flat and there is no real defensive position, the French caught the enemy by surprise, officers shaving in their dugouts, men at breakfast, gun teams going down to water. The French made a royal and victorious advance at once.

Our men attacking the strongholds where the enemy expected us, lost 50,000 men in the first day's fighting and took in that day, the first of the eight impregnable forts.

I don't think you realize what the Battle of the Somme became. It went on for eight and one half months of intense, bloody and bitter battles for small pieces of hill, for the sites of vanished villages, for the stumps of blasted woods and the cellars of obliterated farms.

We got the second of the eight impregnable forts on the fourth day, the third on the seventeenth day, the fourth and fifth on the seventy-sixth day, the sixth and strongest on the one hundred and twenty-eighth day, and the last two at the end.

I cannot tell you how bitter and bloody the fighting in that battle was. The fight for Delville Wood lasted for nearly two months, and in those two months, 400 shells fell every minute on Delville Wood, and not less than 300,000 men were killed and wounded there. That wood during the battle was a scene of death, bloodshed and smash such as cannot be imagined. You walked in the mud on the bones and the flesh of men and on fresh blood dripping out of stretchers. By the side of the track was a poor starved cat eating the brain of a man.

In High Wood they fought till the rags and bones of dead men hung from the wrecks of the trees. In Pozières, men lived for days and nights under a never-ceasing barrage designed to blow them off the ridge which they had won. They were buried and unburied and reburied by shells. There were 20,000 casualties on that ghastly table, and the shell-shock cases leaped and shook and twittered in every clearing station.

Twenty thousand men were killed and wounded in the taking of the nest of machine guns in the subterranean fort of Mouquet Farm. Our men went down into the shafts of that fort and fought in the darkness underground there, till the passages were all seamed with bullets.

We lost half a million men in that great battle, and we had our reward. For in the winter of 1917, in the winter night a great and shattering barrage raged up along the front. It was the barrage which covered the attack on Miraumont and drove the enemy from the Ancre Valley. The next day came the news that Serre had fallen, and we went up and stood in Serre. And Gommecourt fell, and the rain of shells ceased upon Loupart and La Barque, and the news ran along like wildfire, that the enemy was going back.

It was a soaking thaw after frost, and the roads, such roads as remained, were over ankle deep in mud, and our muddy army got up from the mud and went forward through it.

All the roads leading to the front were thronged by our army, battalion

245

on battalion, division on division, guns and transport columns, camp kitchens, and artillery transport, going up in the mud after the enemy.

You could see them bringing the railway forward under fire, under heavy fire, along the Ancre Valley. They made the railway and the road side by side, with shells falling on them and the stink of gas blowing over them. And not a man died there, but died in exultation, knowing that over his death the army was passing to victory.

Today, as you know, the greatest battle of this war is being fought on that ground. And so far, as you know, our men have been hard-pressed and driven back.

It is not easy to stand here, while there, over the sea, those men are standing in the mud, waiting for death to come to them.

It is no light thing to face death in a modern battle, to have been living in the mud, on scanty food, with no rest, in all the terror and filth, among the blood, the rags of flesh, the half buried bodies half eaten with rats, the crashing and screaming of shells, all the confusion of a stunt, and the cries for stretcher-bearers. Only two things are any help in the battlefield, courage and the comrade beside you.

And I know that there is no man in the French and English armies today, standing-to in the mud waiting for death, who does not stand the steadier from the knowledge that this country stands behind him, and that the men of this country are in the line at his side.

We here are not helping in the fight; but we can help in the fight. We can build up behind those men a great wall of love and admiration and courage, so that they can feel it, and rest their backs against it when they are hard-pressed.

It is as well to face the facts of the battle. We have lost a tract of France, and our old graveyards of the Somme, our huts and water-pipes, some guns and dumps of stores and a great many men.

Fortune is like that in war. When Cortes had burnt his ships, and was marching into Mexico, his men growled that they had a hard time, with little food and no rest and bloody fighting. And Cortes told them that they didn't come there to eat cakes of Utrera, but to take their luck as it came and their medicine as it tasted. We came into this war on those terms; so did you.

I've no news to tell you and no comfort to give you. The enemy had more aeroplanes than we had, and hid his preparations from us. He made a big concentration of men and guns, and when the weather favoured him he put them in, with skill and courage, against that part of the line where there are no good natural defensive positions. He took the 5th army by surprise and drove it back. As it fell back, it uncovered the right of the 3rd army, which held the good defensive positions. The 3rd army had to bend back in conformity, till the two armies together reached some sort of a line which could be held. Then the enemy switched his divisions north, and put in his attack on Ypres.

He was able to do this, because his lateral communications, behind his lines, are better than ours. People may ask, in some surprise, "Why are they better?" They are better because the enemy has at his disposal a great body of slave labour which we have not. He has the enslaved populations of Belgium, North France and Poland to work for him.

Then, in all this fighting, our armies have been outnumbered by the enemy. We have had concentrated against us not less than two millions of the enemy. People have asked, in some surprise, "How comes it, that you have been outnumbered?"

We have been outnumbered, presumably because the Allied High Command has judged, that this is not the time for the fighting of the decisive battle of this war, and that the line must be held with comparatively few troops so that the reserves for the decisive battle may be as large as possible.

We must be patient, and wait for the counter, trusting the goodness of our cause.

But in thinking of British manpower you must remember that though all the belligerent countries have to reckon with three big armies, we have to reckon with seven. All belligerent countries have to reckon with their army of the living, their army of the wounded, and their army of the dead. We have to reckon all these, and our armies of the dead and wounded would alone mount up to nearly 2½ millions of men. But we have also to maintain four armies which the other belligerent countries do not have to have.

First, an army of defence, against invasion. This is a small army consisting mainly of elderly men and of lads in training. We have to maintain it; it may be necessary; and "it is better to be sure than sorry."

Then we have armies abroad in distant parts of this war, the army in Italy, the army in Salonika, and the big garrisons in India and Egypt which feed the armies in Mesopotamia and in Palestine. All of these armies and garrisons melt away continually in the fire of war, and everywhere on the roads to those armies, are the reinforcements and the drafts swallowing up more and yet more men.

In Gibraltar, and Malta and Alexandria and Port Said, you will see, every day, some ship filled with our men going out to death in those far fields, and you will see the men standing on the deck and cheering, as the ship draws away and leaves home and sweetness and pleasant life behind, for ever.

Then, besides these, we have the army of the sick. The great epidemical scourges of ancient armies have been nearly eliminated from this war; but we have been forced to maintain armies in distant outposts of this war, in Gallipoli, in Salonika, and in Mesopotamia where the men have suffered much from tropical diseases, dysentery and malarial fever. We have some hundreds of thousands of men who have been weakened by these complaints; not wrecked by them, but so weakened that they cannot stand the life in the trenches.

And besides all those armies, we have a vast army of the very flower of our race, both men and women. It may consist of four or five millions of men and women who work in treble shifts, day and night, as they have worked for the last three years, making the things of war, not only for ourselves but for our Allies. Our Allies are not manufacturing people. Russia made few things, France's coal and steel are in the hands of the enemy, Italy makes few things. We have had to supply these people not only with equipment of all kinds, guns, clothing and shells, but with ships and coal. Not less than half a million men have done nothing in England since the war began but get and ship coal for the Allies. They have sent not less than 60 million tons of coal to the Allies since the war began.

Then a part of that army builds ships, and ever more ships, and yet never enough ships for the needs of this great war and for the supply of our friends.

The enemy spreads abroad lies concerning us. I am not going to answer them. Lies do not last long.

There is no need to lie about a people. Still less is there any need to lay claim to this or that glory. No nation is so bad that it has not something very good in it; and none so glorious that it has not some taint of self.

And I'm not here to sing my country's praises. No one will do that. Patriotism, as I see it, is not a fine drawing of the sword, behind some winged and glittering Victory. It is nothing at all of all that. It is a very sad thing and a very deep thing and a very stern thing.

St. George did not go out against the dragon like that divine calm youth in Carpaccio's picture, nor like that divine calm man in Donatello's statue. He went out, I think, after some taste of defeat, knowing that it was going to be bad, and that the dragon would breathe fire and that very likely his spear would break and that he wouldn't see his children again and people would call him a fool. He went out, I think, as the battalions of our men went out, a little trembling and a little sick and not knowing much about it, except that it had to be done, and then stood up to the dragon in the mud of that far land, and waited for him to come on.

I know what England was, before the war. She was a nation which had outgrown her machine, a nation which had forgotten her soul, a nation which had destroyed Jerusalem among her dark Satanic mills.

And then, at a day's notice, at the blowing of a horn, at the cry from a little people in distress, all that was changed, and she re-made her machine, and she remembered her soul, which was the soul of St. George who fought the dragon, and she cried, "I will rebuild Jerusalem in this green and pleasant land or die in the attempt."

Don't think that this was due to this or that man, to Kitchener, or to another, or to another. It was due to something kindling and alive in the nation's soul.

When I first went to the Somme, it was on the day we took Martinpuich and Flers. And on my way up, I passed a battalion going in. They were being played up by the band, to the tune of "It's a long, long trail awinding to the land of my dreams." It wasn't a long trail, nor a winding trail to most of those men, but only a few miles of a quite straight road to le Sars, where I found their graves afterwards.

That tune is perhaps the favourite tune of the army today. The army knows that it is a long, long trail, and a winding one, to the land of our dreams.

And if in this war it has seemed, that we have done little, if it has seemed, that we retreated at Mons, and only just held at Ypres, and withdrew from Gallipoli, and stood still at Salonika, and were driven back at St. Quentin and are hard-pressed on the Ridge, I think you somehow feel, that with it all, no matter how long the trail is, nor how winding, nor how bitter nor how bloody, we'll stick it, as long as we've a light to go by, even if we're not so clever as some, nor so attractive.

And what is the land of our dreams? We must think of that.

In the Bible there is the story of King David, who was a very generous and very bloody yet very noble man. And David, besieging a city in the summer, was faint from thirst, and he said, "I wish I had some of the water from that pool by the city gate." And three men heard him and they took bottles and broke through the enemy pickets and filled their bottles and brought the water to David. But David would not drink water brought to him at such risk. He said, it would be like drinking blood; so he poured it out to his God.

The men of those armies in the mud are bringing us water at the risk of their lives, the living water of peace, that peace which I think will be the peace that passes all understanding, peace to have our lives again and do our work again and be with our loves again. But if we go back to the world of before the war, that peace won't serve us, it will be a drinking of the blood of all those millions of young men.

I said some time ago, that the only things which matter in war are courage and the love of your comrades. When this war ends, we shall need all our courage and all our comrades, in that re-making of the world, which will follow this destruction. And I hope that when that time comes, you will not think of us again, as cold, or contemptuous, or oppressive, but as a race of men who went down to the death for a friend in trouble, as St. George did, on this day, so many centuries ago.

And in the light of that adventure I hope that we may stand together to remake this broken world, a little nearer to the heart's desire.

[source: *The War and the Future,* New York: Macmillan, 1918]

Introduction to
Edward G.D. Liveing, *Attack*

An Infantry Subaltern's Impressions of July 1st, 1916

The attack on the fortified village of Gommecourt, which Mr. Liveing describes in these pages with such power and colour, was a part of the first great Allied attack on July 1, 1916, which began the Battle of the Somme. That battle, so far as it concerns our own troops, may be divided into two sectors: one, to the south of the Ancre River, a sector of advance, the other, to the north of the Ancre River, a containing sector, in which no advance was possible. Gommecourt itself, which made a slight but important salient in the enemy line in the containing sector, was the most northern point attacked in that first day's fighting.

Though the Gommecourt position is not impressive to look at, most of our soldiers are agreed that it was one of the very strongest points in the enemy's fortified line on the Western Front. French and Russian officers, who have seen it since the enemy left it, have described it as "terrible" and as "the very devil." There can be no doubt that it was all that they say.

The country in that part is high-lying chalk downland, something like the downland of Berkshire and Buckinghamshire, though generally barer of trees, and less bold in its valleys. Before the war it was cultivated, hedgeless land, under corn and sugar-beet. The chalk is usually well-covered, as in Buckinghamshire, with a fat clay. As the French social tendency is all to the community, there are few lonely farms in that countryside as there would be with us. The inhabitants live in many compact villages, each with a church, a market-place, a watering-place for stock, and sometimes a château and park. Most of the villages are built of red brick, and the churches are of stone, not (as in the chalk counties with us) of dressed flint. Nearly all the villages are planted about with orchards; some have copses of timber trees. In general, from any distance, the villages stand out upon the downland as clumps of woodland. Nearly everywhere near the battlefield a clump of orchard, with an occasional dark fir in it, is the mark of some small village. In time of peace the Picardy farming community numbered some two or three hundred souls. Gommecourt and Hébuterne were of the larger kind of village.

A traveller coming towards Gommecourt as Mr. Liveing came to it, from the west, sees nothing of the Gommecourt position till he reaches Hébuterne. It is hidden from him by the tilt of the high-lying chalk plateau, and by the woodland and orchards round Hébuterne village. Passing through this village, which is now deserted, save for a few cats, one comes to a fringe of orchard, now deep in grass, and of exquisite beauty. From the hedge of this fringe of orchard one sees the Gommecourt position straight in front, with the Gommecourt salient curving round on slightly rising ground, so as to enclose the left flank.

At first sight the position is not remarkable. One sees, to the left, a slight rise or swelling in the chalk, covered thickly with the remains and stumps of noble trees, now mostly killed by shellfire. This swelling, which is covered with the remains of Gommecourt Park, is the salient of the enemy position. The enemy trenches here jut out into a narrow pointing finger to enclose and defend this slight rise.

Further to the right, this rise becomes a low, gentle heave in the chalk, which stretches away to the south for some miles, becoming lower and gentler in its slope as it proceeds. The battered woodland which covers its higher end contains the few stumps and heaps of brick that were once Gommecourt village. The lower end is without trees or buildings.

This slight wooded rise and low, gentle heave in the chalk make up the position of Gommecourt. It is nothing but a gentle rise above a gentle valley. From a mile or two to the south of Gommecourt, this valley appearance becomes more marked. If one looks northward from this point the English lines seem to follow a slight rise parallel with the other. The valley between the two heaves of chalk make the No Man's Land or space between the enemy trenches and our own. The salient shuts in the end of the valley and enfilades it.

The position has changed little since the attack of July 1. Then, as now, Gommecourt was in ruins, and the trees of the wood were mostly killed. Then, as now, the position looked terrible, even though its slopes were gentle and its beauty not quite destroyed, even after two years of war.

The position is immensely strong in itself, with a perfect glacis and field of fire. Every invention of modern defensive war helped to make it stronger. In front of it was the usual system of barbed wire, stretched on iron supports, over a width of fifty yards. Behind the wire was the system of the First Enemy Main Line, from which many communication trenches ran to the central fortress of the salient, known as the Kern Redoubt, and to the Support or Guard Line. This First Main Line, even now, after countless bombardments and nine months of neglect, is a great and deep trench of immense strength. It is from twelve to fifteen feet deep, very strongly revetted with timberings and stout wicker-work. At intervals it is strengthened with small forts or sentry-boxes of concrete, built into the parapet. Great and deep dugouts lie below it, and though many of these have now been destroyed, the shafts of most of them can still be seen. At the mouths of some of these shafts one may still see giant-legged periscopes by which men sheltered in the dugout shafts could watch for the coming of an attack. When the attack began and the barrage lifted, these watchers called up the bombers and machine gunners from their underground barracks, and had them in action within a few seconds.

Though the wire was formidable and the trench immense, the real defences of the position were artillery and machine guns. The machine guns were the chief danger. One machine gun with ample ammunition has concentrated in itself the defensive power of a battalion. The enemy had not less than a dozen machine guns in and in front of the Kern Redoubt. Some of these were cunningly hidden in pits, tunnels and shelters in (or even outside) the obstacle of the wire at the salient, so that they could enfilade the No Man's Land, or shoot an attacking party in the back after it had passed. The sites of these machine gun nests were well-hidden from all observation, and were frequently changed. Besides the machine guns outside and in the front line, there were others, mounted in the trees and in the higher ground above the front line, in such position that they, too, could play upon the No Man's Land and the English front line. The artillery concentrated behind Gommecourt was of all calibres. It was a greater concentration than the enemy could then usually afford to defend one sector, but the number of guns in it is not known. On July 1 it developed a more intense artillery fire upon Hébuterne, and the English line outside it, than upon any part of the English attack throughout the battlefield.

In the attack of July 1, Gommecourt was assaulted simultaneously from the north (from the direction of Fonquevillers) and from the south (from the direction of Hébuterne). Mr. Liveing took part in the southern assault, and must have "gone in" near the Hébuterne-Bucquoy Road. The tactical intention of these simultaneous attacks from north and south was to "pinch off" and secure the salient. The attack to the north, though gallantly pushed, was unsuccessful. The attack to the south got across the first-line trench and into the enemy position past Gommecourt Cemetery almost to the Kern Redoubt. What it faced in getting so far may be read in Mr. Liveing's account. Before our men left the trenches outside Hébuterne they were in a heavy barrage, and the open valley of the No Man's Land hissed, as Mr. Liveing says, like an engine, with machine gun bullets. Nevertheless, our men reached the third line of enemy trenches and began to secure the ground which they had captured.

During the afternoon the enemy counter-attacked from the south, and, later in the day, from the north as well. Our men had not enough bombs to hold back the attackers, and were gradually driven back, after very severe hand-to-hand fighting in the trenches, to an evil little bend in the front line directly to the south of Gommecourt Cemetery. At about 11 p.m., after sixteen hours of intense and bitter fighting, they were driven back from this point to their own lines.

Mr. Liveing's story is very well-told. It is a simple and most vivid account of a modern battle. No better account has been written in England since the war began. I hope that so rare a talent for narrative

252

may be recognised. I hope, too, that Mr. Liveing may soon be able to give us more stories as full of life as this.

JOHN MASEFIELD.

[source: Edward G.D. Liveing, *Attack – An Infantry Subaltern's Impressions of July 1st, 1916*, New York: Macmillan, 1918, pp.7–19]

What Britain Has Done

Put Nearly 8,000,000 in Army and Navy – Losses Over 2,500,000

To the Editor of *The New York Times:*

In your issue of today, in the leading article, headed "Changing the Draft Ages," your leader writer uses the following words:

"Great Britain, which has put 7,000,000 men into uniform and into war work at home, and must have lost a good many more than a million men at the front," etc.

Will you allow me to say that your leader writer would have been more accurate had he written, "Great Britain, which has put nearly eight million men into the armies and navy, and hardly less than another eight million men and women into war work at home and abroad, and has actually lost in the field and at sea more than two and a half million men, besides some hundreds of thousands incapacitated through sickness," etc.?

JOHN MASEFIELD.
New York, June 21, 1918.

[source: *The New York Times*, 22 June 1918, p.8]

The Common Task

I thank you all very much for the great honour you have given me today, and for the very kind way in which you have received my name. I can only hope that this University, which has been the first to discover me, will be quite the last.

I must speak a few words to you about literature, which is the only subject I know anything about. You take to literature quite early in life and you look out upon the world. It is a very attractive place for a young man. There are all sorts of glorious and entertaining things there. You put a few of them into a story, or into a song, and you think you have discovered something about life. And then in a year or two you look at those things again, and you see that you know nothing at all about life, but that you have looked into your own heart a little.

Then after a few years you try again. The years seem to have brought you wisdom, and the whole world seems very much more interesting, and you seem to be able to deal with your material with greater power. The colours are intenser, and you think you see behind the working and shifting of men and women in the world some kind of law, some kind of impulse working itself out, and you think you have realized something.

Then after a few years you look at your work again, and you see that you know nothing about life, and that you know nothing about your own heart, but that you have followed a few butterflies somewhere. And then you try again, and you say to yourself, "Surely, those butterflies come up from some spiritual country which lies outside this life of men. They must come from some land where the flowers of thought grow upon the trees."

And you determine that you will follow these butterflies until you come to that land and live there forever.

And then war breaks out.

You give up that search, and you put literature and all connected with it to one side, and you go out upon a difficult – perhaps a dangerous – road which leads to an end that no man can see even after three and a half years.

The War's Effect on Literature

Men have asked me what effect this great war has had upon literature. Well, it has had a great many. It has burned up in its great flame a great deal of nonsense and a great deal of rubbish and a great deal of unreality.

255

But it is useless to expect literature while this world is being torn in pieces. We shall not get the literature of this war until many years after it is over and its passions are all still and its numbers now engrossed have leisure once more. Until that time literature must take a back seat.

I cannot tell you what a pleasure it is to me who was brought up in this great country to realize that it is looking with friendly eyes upon my own country. I think you must realize that there is no man standing in the trenches today in either the English or the French army who is not standing steadier there from the knowledge that this country is behind them and that the men in this country are standing at their side helping to fight this great quarrel. On the day on which I first went to the Battle of the Somme – and it was a great day – on my way up I passed a battalion that was being played up by the band. The band was playing a tune, a song which was made by a Yale man and the music of which was made by a Yale man. It was that song, "It's a Long, Long Trail." Well, that song is by much the most popular song in the British army today, and the British army today knows that it is a long, long trail, possibly a winding trail, to the land of our dreams. But I tell you, all know that no matter how long, nor how winding that trail will be, nor how bitter, nor how bloody, they will stick at your side to the end.

About fourteen months ago I was going through a ruined city in France. There was at one place a ruined factory full of broken sewing-machines at my right, and then at my left was a hospital filled with broken men. And then as I walked in the midst of these ruins I came upon an old French woman sitting at a table selling newspapers to the troops, for hundreds of men came up from the front lines to get the daily papers. As I came out into that square, I heard a soldier shout, "Hurrah, America has declared war on the blackguards!" Another soldier who was older and more thoughtful and more thankful, said, "Thank God! Now perhaps we may have a decent world again." Well, we must think a little about what that land of our dreams is going to be.

I was reading the other day that story of King David, who was a very generous and noble and bloody man, and very fond of war. David was besieging a city one time, and it was intensely hot, and he was faint with thirst. As he was sitting there looking toward the city, he could see the fish pond near the city gate, and he said, "Oh, I wish I had some water from that fish pond." Three soldiers nearby heard him express that wish, and, taking their water bottles, they dashed across the enemy's lines to the fish pond and filled their water bottles and brought them back to David. As they gave it to him, they said, "There is the water. Drink." But David stood up and said, "I am not going to drink that water which you brought to me. That water you brought at the risk of your lives. It would be like drinking blood to drink that water." So he poured it out.

Need for the World's Re-Making

Well, there are those men standing in the trenches today. They are bringing us peace, the water of peace, the peace which passeth all understanding, peace by which we may take up our lives again, and our loves again, and do our work again; but if we use that peace to remake the world on anything like the lines that it was before this war, it will be like drinking blood, the blood of those men in the trenches. We must remake the world a little nearer to the heart's desire.

And I think the only means to do that adequately and conclusively will be for this great country and my own country, the English-speaking peoples, to stand together, determined that the world shall be a better and cleaner and finer place for this war that has broken the world in pieces four long years. Somebody has said that the English-speaking people are a very war-like people but not at all a military people. Well, they are very war-like, and they seem to have a genius for family differences. But I want you to put out of your minds the memory of those family differences. After all, Bernard Shaw was right when he said, "That is not quarrelling; that is English family life." When this war is over I hope you will put out of your minds the memories of our little family misunderstanding of so many years ago, and put out of your memories any quarrels that have come up, or any misunderstandings that we have experienced since that time. Let us work together whole-heartedly to remake the world more in accordance with man's place in the universe. Let us make it a place in which the little peoples of the world will be able to work out their destinies unthralled; let us make it a place in which democracy may come to be a living thing wherever English is spoken.

[source: "from stenographic notes", *Yale Alumni Weekly*, 5 July 1918, pp.1014–1015]

London Street Women

To the Editor of *The Times*

Sir, – I have read with interest Mr. Edward Bok's statement in your issue for today. He does not overstate his case.

I have been in nearly all the big camps, barracks, and naval and flying stations in the United States, and have seen the steps taken by the United States Government to prevent drunkenness and immorality among their soldiers and sailors. They have made it nearly impossible for any man in uniform in the United States to obtain drink or to consort with a prostitute. As a result, their men come here in the condition of trained athletes. There can be no finer body of men in the world.

When they land they find it easy to obtain intoxicants, and almost impossible to avoid solicitation by young women. As a result many, even very many, of their men are infected with contagious diseases before they proceed to France. The matter has caused the liveliest concern among American officers. When known in America there will be, as Mr. Bok says, "an outcry . . . in volume and quality . . . extremely unpleasant to the people of Great Britain."

It frequently happens in war that the standards of life deteriorate under the strain. In this war the strain has been intense for more than four years. Very large numbers of young women, all subject, as we all are, to the strain of the war, have been removed by the events of war from the influences of home; their fathers, brothers and husbands have gone to the front, and they themselves have been left in easy circumstances with every temptation to take what pleasure they can. This condition of things exists in other belligerent countries in Europe, perhaps in all: for in all there are many young people saying, "Let us eat and drink, for tomorrow we die." In this country it is more open and more easy to see than in others.

As it is a condition of things which will most surely harm our prospects (to put the matter on its lowest side first) in this war, by making countless casualties, and make it difficult, after this war to cooperate, as we all hope, in deep and lasting friendship with the United States for the maintenance of the peace of the world, I hope, with Mr. Bok, that "the evil" may "be stamped out."

Yours sincerely,
JOHN MASEFIELD.
Oxford, Sept. 24.

[source: *The Times*, 26 September 1918, p.3]

The Most Heroic Effort

The Dardanelles campaign was the strangest, most difficult, and most heroic effort ever made by the men of our race. It was unlike most of the campaigns in our history in that it was conceived by genius. It was unlike all others in that its failure (redeemed, like all other British failures, by courage and endurance) was relieved by a quality or glamour which lays over all memories of it a glow of beauty. Even now, less than three years after the evacuation, those who were there in the months of exultation, misery, and despair, from April to December, 1915, think of the place and the time as things apart, consecrated for ever by passion, agony, and bloody sweat, but also by another thing, difficult to define yet felt by all as the very heart of romance.

Apart from the beauty which comes with man's courage and sorrow and high resolve, this campaign, above all other campaigns, was set in beauty. Men came to it in ships across a sea glorious with beauty. The light, the mountains and the islands, the plants and flowers, the immense expanse of the Ægean decked the stage for our men as it has never been decked for any campaign in the past. Then, the campaign was not visibly successful, and a man has a tenderness for the fine things which failed. Sir Ian Hamilton may yet see the 25th of April, which some call "Australia's Birthday," a national holiday and day of remembrance.

This book of Mr. Nevinson's* is the first considered and critical history of the campaign. Mr. Nevinson is specially fitted to be the historian of such a venture. He was an eye-witness of the more tragic part of the fighting and the endurance. Beyond all living writers he is qualified by powers of sympathy and of style to understand and to tell of some such struggle as this, where right and wisdom were matched against might and power. The time is ripe for such a book by such a man. In the last three years the official passion for secrecy has been lessened, so that he may say things, and the public lust for the blood of a scapegoat has been sated, so that he may be heard. Mr. Nevinson's book comes when both official terror and public fury permit much of the truth to be known. Not all is yet revealed, nor is full justice yet done. When all the Reports of the Dardanelles Commission are published, if they ever are, the truth

---

* THE DARDANELLES CAMPAIGN. By H.W. Nevinson. London: Nisbet and Co. Pp. xx. 429. With Nine Maps. 18s. net.

will be fully known. Meanwhile Mr. Nevinson's book gives more of the truth of that campaign than any book which has appeared. It is not likely that any other book will supersede it or upset his conclusions.

His story is well-ordered, well-arranged, and well-balanced. His descriptions are just, terse, and full of colour, his descriptions of battle-fields are as precise and as perceiving as good landscape-painting. In the moving passages of that great tragical drama he is both eloquent and austere. In all his criticism he is careful and wise. His book comes not only from a great experience of the peninsula, but from a wide information. Few men, perhaps no single man, saw so much of the peninsula as he. Very few (of those who were there) landed and lived as he did at all three positions – Helles, Anzac, and Suvla, as well as at the advanced bases. Perhaps no man can have talked of the operations with so many of the soldiers and sailors who led them and took part in them. Certainly no single man there had better opportunities for seeing and knowing.

And to what conclusion does this rarely gifted, just, and most eloquent writer come, from the depth of his knowledge and fullness of observation? What caused the failure of the campaign? "The ultimate burden of failure," he writes, "lies on the authorities at home." They, "the authorities at home," not any soldier, flung away the certainty of success long before the troops left England. Napier says somewhere that we are "a very warlike race, but not at all a military one." Somewhere in that very just summary of our people may be found the reason of our failure. "The authorities at home" were warlike but not at all military. They had no knowledge of the strength of our enemy, they showed our enemy what we intended to do, they waited till our enemy was thoroughly prepared, and then launched against them an inadequate force without support. Presently they launched another inadequate force, and then stopped the campaign. Perhaps, finally, it comes down to this, that when this war began we were quite unprepared for war, so that we had neither the men nor the guns for an expedition of the kind.

Some will say: "In that case, 'the authorities at home' ought not to have sent the expedition at all." They ought not to have sent it when and how they did send it, giving full advertisement to the enemy to prepare, and (later on) full time to recover. But the campaign was conceived by genius, and though it had no immediate effect that was not disastrous its real results were profound and beneficial. While I write this the news comes that the Kaiser has abdicated, and that the ships of the Allies are preparing to pass through the Narrows. There is general joy and thanks-giving for these things. And who, in the general joy, thinks for a moment of the part played by the Dardanelles campaign in bringing the war to an end? The campaign was an heroic feat of arms. No thinking man will withhold honour in his heart from Sir Ian Hamilton and those whom he led on that forlorn hope. But how many realise that it was Sir Ian Hamilton and his merry men who broke the power of the Turk for ever? There, in the dust and scrub and stink of Gallipoli, Mesopotamia was freed, the Caucasus relieved, Egypt made safe, and Palestine ours. The Turk was not only broken by us in Gallipoli but he was there sickened of his allies, so that very much of the present happy state of the war is due to this expedition – "equal," as Mr. Nevinson writes, "in splendour of conception, heroism, and tragedy."

This war has shown the world, what the poets have shown to the few, that life, destiny, or the powers which direct man work with irony but with justice. In our seeming failure, which brought in Bulgaria against us, sealed the fate of Kut, and made the collapse of Russia only a matter of time, there was still the seed of victory. Our blow in Gallipoli went home to the Turkish heart, and from that time our enemy's chief ally was a dying man. These things will someday be recognised by the world. Mr. Nevinson's book is worthy of his subject. It is by much the best and most thoughtful history that has appeared about any part of this war.

[source: *Manchester Guardian*, 14 November 1918, p.10]

What First?

Mr. John Masefield – Help Belgium and Serbia.

Belgium and Serbia – these come first in the opinion of one of our finest authors.

You ask me "What first, after the peace?"

First, I hope, a general giving of thanks for our victory and preservation, but after that a great national effort to help Belgium and Serbia, the lands which have suffered most in this war, to support themselves as in the past. After that, I hope that we may turn to upon the tasks of peace with the passionate self-sacrifice and courage with which our nation has faced the tasks of war.

[source: *Answers*, 14 December 1918, p.43]

The Battle of the Somme

TO
MAJOR THE HON. NEVILLE LYTTON

Foreword

I have been asked to write a few words of preface to this little book.

While I was in France, in the late summer and autumn of 1916, it was suggested that I should write a History of the Battle of the Somme, then in its second stage or act. In discussing the plan of the book, it was decided that I should begin with some account of the attacks upon Verdun (which the Battle of the Somme ended), and end with the taking of Bapaume, then hoped for, but not expected to happen at once. In order that I might write with full knowledge, some arrangements were planned, by which I could go again to Verdun, to visit some positions which I had not seen. It was made possible for me to go to the Somme, certain introductions were given to me, and I was formally requested to write the History.

After some delay, I was permitted to go again to the Somme battle-field, and to live on or near it for those months of 1917 when our Armies were advancing in all that area. It was made possible for me to watch the advance of our Armies from point to point and from valley to crest, and to trace those old, much more grim advances, in the area from which the enemy had been beaten in the first months of the attack. During those months I walked over every part of the Somme battlefield in which British troops had been engaged, over every part at least twice, and over many parts, which specially moved me, such as Delville Wood, High Wood, Pozières, Mouquet Farm, Thiepval, and the Hawthorn Ridge, more times than I can remember. I came to know that blasted field as well as I know my own home. I saw much there which I am not likely to forget.

In June, 1917, when I felt that I knew the ground so intimately well, from every point of view, that I could follow any written record or report of the fighting, I returned to England, hoping to be permitted to consult the Brigade and Battalion diaries, as in 1916, when I wrote a history of the campaign in Gallipoli. It was not possible for me to obtain access to these documents, and as only four others, of any worth, existed, my plan for the book had to be abandoned.

Feeling that perhaps some who had lost friends in the battle might care to know something of the landscape in which the battle was fought, I wrote a little study of the position of the lines, as they stood on July 1, 1916. This study, under the title *The Old Front Line*, was published at the end of 1917. I then attempted to write an account of the battle from what I had seen and heard, and had written as much as is here printed, when I was turned to other work, of another kind, many miles from Europe and the war.

Scanty as the books are, they would have been scantier but for him to whom I dedicate them. By his kindness and forethought much which would have been difficult and disappointing was made possible and pleasant. The disappointment of having to forego the task of writing of our Armies in their victory was but a small thing when set beside the memory of so much that was an inspiration and a delight.

JOHN MASEFIELD.

The Battle of The Somme

A moment before the whistles blew, in the morning of July 1, 1916, when the Battle of the Somme began, the No Man's Land, into which our men advanced, was a strip of earth without life, made smoky, dusty, and dim by explosions which came out of the air upon it, and left black, curling, slowly fading, dust and smoke-devils behind them. Into this smoke and dust and dimness, made intenser by the stillness of the blue summer morning, came suddenly the run of many thousands of men at the point of death. Not less than twenty thousand men clambered up the parapet at that instant. They tripped and tore through the wire, already in lanes, and went on to their fronts, into the darkness of death, cheering each other with cries that could be heard above the roaring and the crashing of the battle. On the instant, before all the men were out of the trenches, the roaring lifted up its voice as the fire doubled and the enemy machine guns opened.

Many men among those thousands were hit as they showed above the parapet, many others never cleared the wire; but the rest drew clear and went forward, some walking, some running, most of them in a kind of jog-trot, some aligned in a slow advance or in rushes of platoons, till the green river of the No Man's Land was dotted with their moving bodies throughout the sector. Perhaps not many of all those thousands knew what was happening even quite close at hand, for in those times all souls are shaken, and the air was dim, and the tumult terrible. Watchers in our old lines saw only a multitude of men crossing a dimness which kept glittering. They saw many of the runners falling as they ran, some getting up and going on, others moving a little, others lying still. They saw as it were dead lines, where all the runners fell, even the strongest. They saw promising swarms of men dropping in twos or threes, till the rush was only a few men, who went on until they fell like the others and lay in little heaps in their tracks. There was nothing to show why they fell. Men looked for them to rise and go on with the few little leading figures who were drawing near to the enemy wire. They could see no enemy. They could not even see the jets of smoke, hardly bigger than the puffs blown from a kettle at the instant of boiling, which spurted from enemy machine guns along the whole line.

Within a few minutes, the second and third waves were following on the first, not knowing, in that darkness of dust and tumult, what success had been won, if any.

Our attack was made on a front of sixteen miles. To the south of this, at the same moment, the French attacked on a front of nine miles. Let the reader imagine any narrow strip of twenty-five miles known to him – the course of the Thames, say, from London to Maidenhead, or from Pangbourne to Oxford – suddenly rushed by many thousands of men, many of them falling dead or maimed upon the way. For the look of the charge let him remember some gust of wind on a road in autumn when the leaves are lying. The gust sweeps some array of leaves into the road and flings them forward in a rush strangely like the rush of men as seen from a distance. As in the rush of men, many leaves drop out, crawl again forward, cease, quiver, and lie still; many others lose touch or direction, the impulse may falter, the course swerve, but some are whirled across the road into the gutters at the other side.

To cross the No Man's Land took from a minute to two minutes of time. Perhaps most of those who were in that attack were too dizzy with the confusion and tumult, the effort to keep touch and the straining to find out what was happening to the flanks and in front, to take stock of their own sensations. These things have been said about the attack:

(a) "I heard the man behind me slip on the ladder. 'The damned thing,' he said. 'I'll miss the bloody train.' They were putting over whizz-bangs rather a lot; but I didn't notice any near me. I felt just ordinary.

"Their wire had been nicely cut. I'd been afraid we might be hung up while we cut it. I heard a whut-whut-whut, just like that, just alongside my ears. 'You ———s,' I said, 'that's a bloody machine gun in your bloody wire,' I said. So afterwards, when it was all over, I went back, and they'd got a bloody little machine gun covered over in a shell-hole, shooting through a kind of box in a sort of funnel, along with two Boches; but they'd been caught with a bomb, it looked like."

(b) "I'd had a bet with one of our fellows that there was a sniper's post just where I said it was, 'cos I'd figured it out it must be about there. So when I went over I thought, 'We'll see now who'll get them fags.' The funny part of it was we were both wrong about the sniper. I don't know where he was."

(c) "About an hour before we went over, they got onto our jumping-off trenches and fairly plugged us with a lot of heavy stuff as well; so when we went across I said, 'You ———s, you wait till I get in among you; I'll get some of my own back.'"

(d) "Going across wasn't so bad, but when we started to consolidate our bit of trench we kept running out of bombs. If we could have had a good supply of bombs all day the Fritzes would have had no show at all. Bombs are heavy to carry. One of our bombers must have been hit as he was coming up. He was wearing his bomber's jacket all full of bombs, and they blew him all to pieces. They bombed us out afterwards. They held us up at the end where we were, up against the sandbags, and then they got up like to the side and bombed us clean out. Just before they got us out we found some hairbrush bombs; they don't have them much now, but they had that lot all right."

(e) "What did I think while I was going over? I thought my last hour had come. They'd got a machine gun every five yards, it sounded like. 'By God,' I said, 'give me London every time.'"

(f) "It's my opinion there'll be some queer revelations about this war after it's all over. I often thought of that when we were in it; not about the soldiers so much, but about the financiers."

(g) "After we'd got back into our trenches we saw a big Boche jump up onto the parapet and wave a great big Red Cross flag, and we saw their men go out with stretchers, to bring in our wounded, we thought. Then we saw they were shooting at our wounded. Whenever they stirred they turned machine guns on them; we could see the bullets going phut all round them. So then we looked to see what they were doing with the stretchers. What they were bringing in under the Red Cross flag was our Lewis guns which our poor chaps had been carrying.

"All day long they kept us from bringing in any of our wounded. Whenever our stretcher-bearers went out they turned machine guns onto them at once. But one of our fellows went out and brought in about twenty, one after the other. He carried them in on his back till he was quite worn out. His name was Smiley or some such name."

(h) "The Boche varied from place to place. Just near where we were he was very decent, and sent us in a list of the names of the prisoners he'd taken. Afterwards we found that he'd buried our dead and put up crosses to them: 'To a brave Englander.' 'To brave English soldiers.' This was a fine thing to have done; for it wasn't healthy by any means out in front of his wire. They were Bavarians who did this."

(i) "Before we went over we were in a shallow jumping-off trench. It wasn't a trench, it was really the bank beside a road. We were being shelled with whizz-bangs. We hadn't any real shelter, but were crouched down under the bank. I looked along my men. Some were cursing and mad; I don't think they knew what they were doing, but about every other man was praying."

(j) "I noticed that several men were inclined to take off their clothes before the attack. It may be fear in some cases, but then it was very hot, and there was the feeling that one would advance better free. One wants all one's strength, and the things pressing on the body seem to choke you. During the attack I saw one man who was stark mad and stark naked, both, running round in the No Man's Land, yelling at the top of his voice. They got him into a dressing-station, and they had a bad time with him, for he wouldn't speak, he would

269

only yell, and they couldn't make out whether he was a Boche or one of our own chaps. I don't know what became of him. Probably when they got him down and gave him a bath and cut his hair he remembered himself."

(k) "They call us 'the poor bloody infantry.' We deserve the name, for we get into most of the trouble when there is any, and all of the mud when there isn't. But I say that the airmen have the hardest time, for they're in danger the instant they leave the ground; and they live over the enemy lines, in a cloud of shrapnel, and they come right down to take photographs, or to draw fire when they are spotting batteries, or to scatter infantry. On the 1st of July they were just over our heads, as bold as brass. They spotted for us, and when the Boche counter-attacked they dived right down and took them on with their machine guns. When they come down, I believe they fall asleep at once from nervous strain."

(l) "I made up my mind that I was going to be killed. I was to be in the third wave. While I was waiting, during the last half-hour, I kept saying to myself: 'In half an hour you will be dead. In twenty-five minutes you will be dead. In twenty minutes you will be dead. In a quarter of an hour you will be dead.' I wondered what it would feel like to be dead. I thought of all the people I liked, and the things I wanted to do, and told myself that that was all over, that I had done with that; but I was sick with sorrow all the same. Sorrow isn't the word either: it is an ache and anger and longing to be alive. There was a terrific noise and confusion, but I kept thinking that I heard a lark; I think a lark had been singing there before the shelling increased. A rat dodged down the trench among the men, and the men hit at it, but it got away. I felt very fond of all my men. I hoped that they would all come through it. I had told them some time before to 'fix swords.' I wondered how many of them would unfix swords, and when. Then I thought, 'When I start I must keep a clear head. I must remember this and this and this.' Then I thought again, 'In about five minutes now I shall be dead.' I envied people whom I had seen in billets two nights before. I thought, 'They will be alive at dinner-time today, and tonight they'll be snug in bed; but where shall I be? My body will be out there in No Man's Land; but where shall I be? What is done to people when they die?' The time seemed to drag like hours and at the same to race. The noise became a perfect hell of noise, and the barrage came down on us, and I knew that the first wave had started. After that I had no leisure for thought, for we went over."

(m) "I was in a blue funk lest I should show that I was. We had a sergeant, who was killed afterwards at Le Sars, an Englishman. I really believe he enjoyed it. He was an old soldier who had been in South Africa, an elderly man; quite forty-five or more. He walked up and down in the bay smoking his pipe, with his eyes

270

shining, and every now and then he would say something about South Africa; not about the fighting there, but about some man or other who had got drunk or deserted, or stolen something. He made me feel that, after all, that is what life is: you get together with a lot of other fellows, in a pub or somewhere, and swap a story or two about the blackguards you've known, and then you go out and get knocked on the head by a set of corner-boys."

(n) "I tried to tell myself that I was doing it for this or that reason, to make it sound better; but it didn't make it any better, I didn't believe those grand things. When you are waiting to be killed, those damned newspapers seem damned thin, and so do those damned poets about the Huns. The Fritzes are a dirty lot, but they are damned brave, you may say what you like. And being killed by a lot of damned Fritzes is a damned bad egg, and no amount of tosh will alter it."

North of the Ancre River the fight was to contain the enemy; south of the Ancre we fought to advance. In this volume nothing will be said of the containing fighting to the north of the river, except that it was severe and continuous. It needs, and will receive, a volume to itself. In this volume the story will be that of the advance, during the first stage of the battle, which ended on the 14th of July, and of the great attack on the night of the 14th of July, which ended some three weeks later in the capture of Pozières, and the vital, highest points in the enemy's second line.

In the attack of the 1st of July it happened that our first success in the advance was at the eastern flank of our sector, at the village of Maricourt, where our extreme right joined the extreme left of the French. This account of the battle will begin with this eastern, or right flank of the advance, and will proceed from point to point, westward and northward, to the Leipzig above the Ancre, where the tide of our success was stayed during these first two stages of the battle.

From Maricourt, where the French were fighting beside us, the thrust of the attack was in two directions: towards the east, to the romantic dingle of Favière Wood, and towards the north, to the brickworks of Montauban. These works stood beside a road from Maricourt to Longueval, about half a mile from Montauban village. They consisted of two big blocks of building, one on each side of the road, with outlying offices and furnaces. The enemy had burrowed under them, so as to make an underground fort, to which the ruins of the works, soon nothing more than a heap of bricks, made excellent head-cover. The fort was strengthened with concrete, reinforced with iron girders. It contained living rooms for many men, and emplacements for many machine guns. As it lay on a plateau-top, well back from a contour line, it had a good field of fire in all directions. As at Mouquet Farm, later in the battle, all that could be seen from outside it was a heap of brick. This fort of the brickworks was linked by communication trenches to a strong enemy line which defended Montauban and the two big adjacent woods of Bernafay and Trones. It made an advanced redoubt to these works, just as Mouquet Farm did to the Zollern Trench. Two other outlying forts covered the Montauban-Mametz Road, but, though these were wired, it was thought that they were not likely to be so dangerous as the brickworks. Our preliminary fire upon the brickworks and Montauban was exceedingly heavy, constant, and accurate. It could be well-observed and corrected from observation posts in the trees behind our lines, and the enemy at this part of the line had not, at that stage of the battle, any great concentration of men and guns. It happened that our attack upon the brickworks, Montauban village, and the road down to Mametz, all the extreme right wing of our battle, was swiftly successful, and without great losses. The brickworks had been so rained upon with shells that they gave little trouble, and the Manchesters were established there and in Montauban village before noon. On the left of this successful attack, where our men had to storm the steep little hill on which Mametz stands, the approach was slower; but in the late afternoon Mametz, or what was left of it, was ours, and the cellars and piles of rubble covering machine guns had been bombed quiet.

No attempt was made to storm Fricourt during this first day of the battle. It was thought that the Salient there could be pressed on both sides and so forced to surrender. The capture of Mametz gave us a strong and commanding position on the east flank of the Salient. Its west flank was threatened by a strong attack upon all that side.

This attack, or rather this series of attacks, which had for its objectives the three, four, or five sets of wired lines in the enemy system above a perfect natural glacis, brought our men across the chalk slope, like a slightly tilted table-top, on the west side of the Salient, into position on the west side of Fricourt Wood. With one division entrenched in Mametz and this second division to the west on the line of the Contalmaison Road, the Fricourt Salient was pinched in securely on both sides before nightfall of the first day. It is said that many of the Fricourt garrison, knowing that they were lost, crept out, or rather were withdrawn, from the Salient as soon as it was dark that night.

To the west of this Fricourt fighting, our men got up Chapes Spur, following the spring of the great mine there, and shut in the little village of La Boisselle on that side. The attack upon La Boisselle itself did not carry more than a part of the village. This was not the fault of the attackers, but the result of things which will be described later. While La Boisselle held out, no progress could be made up Mash Valley on its western side. To the west of Mash Valley, the fort or stronghold of Ovillers held out, exactly as La Boisselle did, and for the same reasons, though just beyond Ovillers (on the western slope of Ovillers Hill) our men secured enough ground to flank the place on that side. Still further to the west, on the Leipzig, our men stormed the end of the Salient, beat and bombed the enemy out of the quarry there, and contrived to hold it, though they could not capture the Wonder Work beyond.

To the north of this a very gallant attack was made upon Thiepval. Some of the troops in this attack fought their way up the shallow valley under what was called the Schwaben Redoubt, till they reached a point called the Crucifix, near the enemy's Second-Line System. This point, however, could not be held, so that the end of the Leipzig Salient was the most northern point permanently secured by the first day's fighting.

The evening, like the day, was of a perfect summer beauty, with a slight fine-weather haze. It was good weather for flying, though not perfect for observation. The ground was dry and hard, and the weather promised to be steadily fine. On the whole, the first day of the advance to the south of the Ancre had been very successful. To the south of the Somme, where the ground for many miles together is without those strongly marked tactical features which give good observation and positions easy to defend, the French had made triumphant progress, with little loss, against a surprised and shaken enemy. North of the Somme, we had captured a big bow of land from Montauban Brickworks to Mametz, and another, smaller, but important bow, from Sausage Valley to Fricourt. Fricourt Salient was almost ours; its surrender had been made quite certain by the capture of the flanks of its approaches. La Boiselle and Ovillers were both closely pressed, the Leipzig had been mauled and a part of it taken. Altogether (setting aside the French conquests) we had won some two miles of front for a distance of from half a mile to a mile; that is, we had advanced over about an eighth part of the front attacked. Elsewhere, we had held and shaken the enemy, had captured many prisoners and some guns, and had destroyed many bays of trench and miles of wire.

During all the day, and through a part of the night, many strange things were done and reported. Many small parties of our men attacking in the dust, darkness, and confusion of the battle, over ground pilled of its landmarks and cut into wandering trenches all alike, all ruined, smashed, and full of dead, had gone on in the tumult, far from any planned objective, till they were lost. Even outside the trenches, it is not easy to find one's way over that blasted moor of mud, from which all the landmarks have been blown. Inside the trenches it is almost impossible; one sap looks like another, one communication trench is like another, one blown-in dugout, or corpse, is like another, and all saps and trenches zigzag and run out of the straight, so that one cannot tell direction. These men, wandering forward, perhaps chasing enemies, from one unknown alley to another, in excitement and danger, far from any possibility of direction or guidance, lost themselves, sometimes half a mile behind the enemy front line. The history of these lost parties will never be known; but there were many of them, from a company to two or three men strong, and their achievements, if collected, would make good reading. Some were destroyed or captured; others, building themselves barricades in the enemy trench, fought all day long against whatever enemy came against them, and after fighting all day, till darkness, they fought or picked their way home, often bringing prisoners with them. It is certain that some of these lost men working in parties or alone, coming suddenly upon some hidden machine gun and putting it out of action, were vital to parts of our advance. The coming back of these lost men, with their amazing stories, was one of the wonders of the day.

The night was strange and terrible in other ways. Over all the front of the battle there was a heavy fire from the enemy and a going and coming of men. Captured trenches had to be secured; the new line had to be marked and rounded off, with wire to the front and barricades at the sap-heads. The new positions had to be linked up with the old, so that men and stores might be moved to them rapidly. Much of them had to be repaired; parts of them, for one reason or another, were untenable; from other parts, thrusts had to be made, to clear away the enemy. All this adjustment of the line and the settling of what was to be or could be held had to be done and tested under fire and in the half darkness of a summer night by great numbers of men. All over the battlefield there was a restless movement of multitudes, as the battalions and the carriers moved up and down. Prisoners were being searched, examined, and sent back. The dead were being gathered for burial and the wounded were being picked up from the shell-holes and wrecks of trenches where they still lay. Endless work of preparation went on all over the conquered ground; dumps had to be formed and observation posts to be dug; and signallers with many miles of telephone wire had to link up posts, stations, and positions with the various headquarters. Behind our old lines there was a similar uneasy heaving; for the batteries were moving up.

The night passed in this going and coming of men. A business (as of ants), which seemed confused, yet still had a purpose, covered the field. At the same time the battle raged throughout the sector so hotly that the running fire of flashes never died out of the sky. All over the field the glimmers and bursts of fire lit little places and showed groups of men at work – path-clearers, signallers, carriers – preparing for the morrow. In parts of the field, even at midnight, hand-to-hand fighting went on for trenches and bits of trenches which the fighters could not see. The great owls cruised over the field, crying their cries. Star-shells rose and poised and floated and fell down. The rattle and crash of firing, though muffled in that Silent Land, sometimes rose up to such a pitch that people in Amiens (twenty miles away) got out of bed to listen, and felt their windows trembling like live things to the roll of that great drum.

At dawn on the second day our troops began to put an end to the enemy salient at Fricourt.

Fricourt itself, the little village, is built at the end of a tongue or finger of land which has a narrow gully (with the Contalmaison Road in it) on the west, and a narrow valley (with a stagnant brook in it) on the east. The slope of the tongue, which broadens as it rises, is upwards, towards the north, so that in advancing upon it from the south one has to climb.

Slightly above the village, to the north and north-east of it, is the irregularly shaped, straight-sided wood of Fricourt, which is 1,000 yards long, narrow near the village, but broader higher up, with an average breadth of a quarter of a mile. This wood was now (July 2) outflanked on the east by our troops in Mametz, but it was still a strong enemy fortress, with secure approaches to the salient and secure lines of retreat to the higher fortified ground behind it, further to the north. Like all other parts of the salient, the wood was edged and crossed with deep and strong trenches of the usual enemy pattern, difficult to storm at the best of times. On the 2nd of July this system of enemy trenches was blind with jungle, partly abattis heaped by the enemy as obstruction, partly uncleared scrub, and partly treetops cut off by our shellfire. The trenches at the edges of the wood were strongly manned with rifle-men and machine gunners.

Above the highest, northern part of the wood the ground rises to a high chalk table-land about as big as the wood (1,000 yards long by 4,500 broad) and shaped rather like a boot raised to squash Fricourt flat. On this small boot-shaped plateau were more defences, designed, as a soldier has said, "more as temporary unpleasantnesses than as permanent works." The boot is strangely isolated by gullies and valleys. At the heel is the deep gully of the Contalmaison Road, at the sole is the valley of Mametz, and at the instep is a deep romantic curving valley, with the abrupt, sharply cut sides so often seen in a chalk country. This last valley, from its depth, steepness, and isolation, was known by our men as Shelter Valley.

The defences of the boot-shaped table-land were as follows: a line of trench known as Railway Alley, which ran (N.E.) from Fricourt Wood towards the toe; odds and ends of work about (1) a farm, (2) a copse called the Poodles, and (3), a crucifix along the leg of the boot; a strong field fortress in the biggish copse called Shelter Wood, which hangs like a curtain of shrubs and trees on the steep wall of the valley, at the top of the leg; the trenched copses, called Lozenge Wood and the Dingle, on the heel and back.

Beyond Shelter Valley to the north the ground rises to another hill of about the same height as the boot. Men in important works on this hill could, and did, fire upon our men during all the fighting for the possession of the boot.

At dawn on the 2nd of July our troops advanced to the storm of Fricourt Wood, the Contalmaison Road, Shelter Wood, and as much of the boot-shaped plateau as they could take. As they advanced, the massed machine guns in all the trenches and strongholds opened upon them. They got across the field of this fire into Fricourt Wood to an indescribable day which will never be known about nor imagined. They climbed over fallen trees and were caught in branches, and were shot when caught. It took them all day to clear that jungle; but they did clear it, and by dark they were almost out at the northern end, where Railway Alley lay in front of them on the roll of the hill. Further to the north, on the

275

top of the leg of the boot, our men stormed the Shelter Wood and fought in that 200 yards of copse for four bloody and awful hours, with bomb and bayonet, body to body, till the wood was heaped with corpses, but in our hands.

Long before our men had secured the two woods the Fricourt Salient was wholly ours. The village was shut off from succour and escape by our capture of the end of the wood at about ten o'clock that morning. By noon all the dugouts in Fricourt had been cleared of the enemy, and by tea-time they had become posts and quarters for our own men. They were the first first-rate enemy dugouts captured by us in good condition. They were deep, well-made underground dwellings, electrically lit, with walls panelled with wood and covered with cretonne. They were well-furnished with luxuries, equipment, and supplies. The dugouts, which had once been the headquarters of the hidden battery in the gully, were taken over as dressing-stations. In one dugout there were signs that a lady had been a visitor. In another there was a downward-drooping bulge in the ceiling, where a big English shell had almost come through on some wet day when the ground was soft. The shell had not burst, but no doubt it had "lowered the moral tone some" in those who were sitting in the room at the time.

During the 3rd of July our men stormed Railway Alley and secured the whole of the boot-shaped hill by capturing the other fortresses of the Poodles and the Crucifix.

This Fricourt fighting increased our gains in the centre of our advance. On the right, our men on the top of the ridge of Montauban, though often sharply attacked, and always heavily shelled, were preparing to go down the hill to the attack of the enemy in the valley beneath them.

This valley is a long, narrow valley between big chalk bluffs. The eastern end of it runs into the valley which parts Mametz from Fricourt. Near this eastern end of it, mainly on the steep slopes of the hill, is a long, bent, narrow ribbon of woodland, so planted that each end commands one end of the valley. This strip of woodland is not remarkable in any way. It is a copse hanging on a steep chalk bank, such as one may see in any chalk country. The enemy had made it a strong redoubt to defend the flanks of the valley, and men advancing northward from Montauban had to take it before they could reach the valley and proceed against the hill beyond. From its appearance on the map, which recalls (to the lively fancy) a looping caterpillar, this wood was called Caterpillar Wood, though it is quite as like a boomerang or a sickle. Just to the north of it is a little fortified copsed dingle known as Marlborough Wood. Preparation for the capture of these two strongholds occupied the right of our advance while Fricourt was being taken by our centre.

Meanwhile, on the left of our advance, to the west of Fricourt, our attack had straightened and cleared the line as far as La Boisselle. At this village and at Ovillers, further to the west, our progress was slow and costly.

At both places there was almost no visible enemy work. What trenches remained our men could carry or blow out of trace, but the main strongholds in both villages were not in trenches, but under the wreck of the houses.

It so happened that the lie of the ground made it very difficult for our men to see what was left of either village. Both places lay on the sides of hills in such a way that our best views of them were from distances. Ovillers village lay along a road at right angles with our front line. Rising ground and big enemy parapets hid it from our front line. Ovillers Hill hedged it in on the west side and Ovillers Wood on the north; on the east there was Mash Valley, which still belonged to the enemy. We could see Ovillers from the Usna Hill behind our front line, but all that we could see were a few skeleton sheds of plasterless woodwork still supporting a few tiles, and a number of heaps of broken brick, among which were heaps of earth and the stumps of trees. There was nothing like order or arrangement in the village. The place looked like a deserted brickfield, made blind by the growth of brambles and weeds. There was nothing in the place that looked like a fort or seemed to hold an enemy.

La Boisselle was on a gentle slope above our front line and shut from it by heaps of chalk. It, too, could be seen from the Usna-Tara Hill. It, too, had a few skeleton sheds at that time, and a great many tree stumps, for, though it may seem strange to those who see the place today, when the tree stumps are gone, the village stood in a clump of trees, like so many other Picardy villages.

Those who looked at it through glasses from the Usna-Tara Hill could see little in it that seemed defensible but a collection of mounds of chalk, rubble, and broken brick. Further up the hill on which it stood were enemy lines, with secure communication along the spur from Pozières. The village itself seemed uninhabitable.

It may be that in the archives of the armies engaged there are plans of the enemy defences in both places, as they were before they were attacked and counter-attacked. Both places were as strong as cunning could make them. Underneath both, linking cellar to cellar, and foundation to foundation, were deep, strongly panelled passages, in which, at intervals, were posts for machine guns, so arranged that the muzzle of the gun in its embrasure was only a few inches above the level of the ground outside. From without, one saw nothing, even close at hand, but heaps of rubble and chalk. Within, were these neat narrow galleries, with living rooms beneath them, and secure underground bolt holes to positions in the rear in case of need. They were large scale examples of the Mouquet Farm type of fortress. They were important points; for if they fell they opened the way to the plateau and the whole position south of the Ancre. Orders had been given to the garrisons that they were to hold the places to the death . . . Both places were well-supplied with munitions and food. For water they had underground access to the wells of the villages. For men, they had underground approaches quite unknown to us. They were, in every way, well-prepared, either for siege or assault.

277

It is impossible to take fortresses of this kind swiftly. Even if they are surrounded, as at Mouquet Farm later in the battle, they may still hold out and interrupt an advance. If they are shelled, they are under the ground, unseen and unknown; the shells can only reach them by chance; no man can say that the artillery has destroyed them, even after days of shelling. The area, perhaps a quarter of a mile square, may be whelmed with gas for a week. The defenders have their gas masks and oxygen cylinders. The place may be stormed and covered with troops, who may yet see no enemy, for there is no enemy to be seen, except little spurts of fire from holes a few inches long in the heaps of rubble on the ground. Then if desperate, brave souls among the attackers break into those heaps of rubble with pick and shovel and get down into the galleries and fight there, bombing their way through one black channel to another, till the place is, as they think, clear, there may still come a rush of reinforcements along the tunnels of escape and the conquerors may be driven out.

The attacks upon La Boisselle and Ovillers went on throughout the second day of fighting. The progress made was slight, though many who watched it have said that the fighting round those two points, in these early days of the battle, was some of the hardest, bravest, and bloodiest of the whole war. The enemy knew that we should attack them and how we should have to attack; the ranges were known to an inch, and field batteries were concentrated upon them. Our men had to creep up a glacis, through a barrage, to storm a fort which no man could see. Often, in that groping in the chalk heaps for some sign of the stronghold, the sudden falling of a platoon was the first sign that the objective was reached. Let the reader imagine any quarter mile of hillside known to him, and think to himself that hidden in every ten yards of that space is an infernal machine which will kill him if he touches it or comes near it, but that he has to run to that space, none the less, and destroy every infernal machine, while fire and flying iron rain down upon him out of the air. That was the task at Ovillers and at La Boisselle. The men who went against those two places did not "dodge death," as the phrase goes, they walked and stumbled across a dark lane which was death. There was a sort of belt of darkness, or cloud, in front of those two ruins, and in that cloud death crashed and whirred and glittered and was devilish. Those who stumbled across it unhit had to creep from pit to pit and from ruin to ruin, looking for the holes in the ground through which the enemy was firing. One man, finding an embrasure through which a machine gun was firing, crept to a cover and fired at the embrasure with his rifle, while his mate, with a pick-axe, picked a hole in the rubble above it big enough for them to fling their bombs down. One evil point of both positions was that they stood on spurs of hill which were roughly parallel with each other, and not more than 600 yards apart. Men on the flank of one spur could sit in cover in almost perfect safety, watching our men attacking the other spur on the opposite side of the valley. It was therefore possible for the enemy to put a cross-fire with machine guns

278

upon either attack. Neither attack progressed far during this hot summer Sunday of July 2.

But during the fighting at La Boisselle a party of North Country English soldiers, attacking to the east of the village, met with a success which had not been planned for them. They got into the enemy's line, and (as far as one can tell) progressed eastwards along it, fighting their way, till they were in the village of Contalmaison, nearly a mile from any support. Here they were captured, but as Contalmaison became the central objective, as soon as we held Shelter Wood their captivity did not last long.

Between the 2nd and the 14th of July, our advance was, in the main, a sapping up to the enemy second-line position, which we presently reached and attacked. All of this sapping up was a bitterly hard fight, in which our men and the enemy were hand to hand for many hours together in all the contested points. The men met each other face to face in trenches and shell-holes and blew each other to pieces with bombs point-blank. On the right, fighting on these terms, our men won the Caterpillar Valley; on the left, they attacked La Boisselle, and pushed on at Ovillers so that its capture became certain. But in the centre, the enemy had an intermediate position, where the fighting was more complex, more difficult, and more bloody than on either of the wings. This intermediate position consisted of two parallel spurs of chalk between the enemy's first and second lines. The eastern spur is almost covered with the Wood of Mametz; the western spur is clear of woodland save for two or three tiny copses. It is a bare, swelling chalk hill, on the top of which there stood (at that time) the ruins of the village of Contalmaison.

These spurs lie between those formations in the chalk which lent themselves to the enemy's first and second main positions. Neither would come readily into either big system. The enemy had not taken special pains to fortify them, as the enemy reckons special pains, but both were naturally strong positions, and both had been made stronger by art. These places may now be described.

A boot-shaped chalk hill to the north of Fricourt, and a deep, narrow, lovely, steep-sided gully, known as Shelter Valley, to the north of the boot, have been mentioned. Just beyond Shelter Valley, and bounded by it as by a river, to the west and south, is the big, bold, swelling, rather steep, shovel-headed snout of spur on the top of which Contalmaison stood. Right at the end of this snout, and low down, so as to be almost in the valley, is an oblong copse called Bottom Wood. Just above this, running diagonally across the spur, is a lynchet, once lined with trees. Just above this there is a half-sunken track or lane running parallel with the lynchet. Just above this, on the eastern side of the spur, was a strong enemy work called the Quadrangle, so sited that men approaching it from the south could be seen and fired at from the work itself, from the high ground on both flanks, and from the rear. Well-hidden support-lines linked this work with Contalmaison village (behind it) and with Mametz

Wood (to the east flank). This work defended the spur on the eastern side.

On the west side, the spur was defended (a) by the work in Shelter Wood, which we had won, (b) by two fortified copses to the north of Shelter Wood, and (c) by a field work (to the north of these copses) called the Horseshoe. These western works were not on the spur, but on that side of Shelter Valley which was mainly in our hands.

Contalmaison itself lay on the top of the spur, about 500 yards to the north-east of the Horseshoe. It had a perfect field of fire in all directions. It was trenched about with a wired line, which was strongly held.

In itself, it was a tiny French hamlet at a point where a road from Fricourt to Pozières crosses a road from La Boisselle to Bazentin. It may have contained as many as fifty families in the old days before the war. Most of these were occupied on the land, but there was also a local industry, done by women, children, and old men, of the making of pearl-buttons. There was a church in the heart of the village, and just to the north of it a big three-storied French château, in red brick, with white and yellow facings, and a turret *en poivrière* in the modern style. This château stood slightly above the rest of the village.

The second or eastern spur lies parallel with this Contalmaison spur, and is parted from it by a narrow shelving valley or gully. It is more sharply pointed and shelving than the Contalmaison spur, and (perhaps) a few feet lower. Otherwise, it is of much the same size. The extreme point of this spur is bare chalk hill, but the bulk of it is covered with the big wood of Mametz, which splits (about half-way down the spur) into three projecting tines or prongs of woodland, parted by expanses of fallow. On the map, the wood looks something like a clumsy trident with the points to the south, threatening our advance. The spur rises due northward in a gradual ascent. The highest part of the wood is at its northern limit, and here, at its highest point, the ground suddenly breaks away in what may either be a natural scarp or the remains of an old quarry. The steep banks are wooded over now, and much dug into for shelter. Here the enemy made his main defence, with a redoubt of machine guns and trench mortars.

It seems likely that before the war the wood was without undergrowth; but after the enemy occupation the shrubs were allowed to grow as screens to the defence. The trees were fine, promising timber, but not of great size in any part of the wood. Among them were horn-beams, limes, oaks, and a few beeches. The undergrowth, after two and a half years of neglect, was very wild and thick, especially in the northern part, where there was much bramble as well as hazel-bush. Our bombardment had destroyed many of the trees, and the enemy counter-bombardment destroyed others during the fighting. This made the going below even more blind and difficult, for it had tossed down many boughs and tree-tops, in full leaf, into the undergrowth, so as to make a loose abattis, exceedingly difficult to pierce or see through. In some of the bigger trees

280

the enemy had built little machine gun posts, so well *camouflé* or protectively coloured with green and grey paint that they were almost invisible, even from quite close at hand. Some heavy guns of position were in the wood, and field guns were in battery in the road behind the scarp at the wood's northern end. In the lower part of the wood barbed wire was strung from tree to tree, and machine gun pits were dotted here and there to command the few clearings. Works on the Contalmaison spur, to the west, and on the Bazentin spur, to the east, were so sited that they could rake an attack upon the wood with a cross, flanking, and plunging fire from half-rifle range.

After the taking of the Poodles and Shelter Wood, our men moved to the assault of these two spurs.

On the right they took position on the east flank of Mametz Wood; in the centre they attacked the Quadrangle and the Horseshoe; and on the left, in pouring rain, in the mud of the Somme, they got into the underground pits of La Boisselle, and made the place ours. This pouring rain was a misfortune.

In modern war wet weather favours the defence. It is especially harassing to the attacker when it falls, as it so often has fallen in this war, at the moment of a first success, when so much depends on the roads being hard enough to bear the advancing cannon which secure a conquered strip. Our success between Maricourt and Ovillers had made it necessary to advance our guns along a front of six miles, which means that we had to put suddenly, upon little country roads, only one of which was reasonably good, and none of which had been used for wheeled traffic for the best part of two years, while all had been shelled, trenched across, and mined, at intervals, in all that time, a great traffic of horses, guns, caissons, and mechanical transport. When the weather broke, as it broke on the 4th of July, 1916, the holes and trenches to be filled in became canals and pools, and the surface of the earth a rottenness. The work was multiplied fifty-fold and precious time was lost.

The rain hindered our advance during the next three days, though our attacks on the approaches to Contalmaison and Mametz Wood proceeded. On the west side of the Contalmaison spur our men carried the fortified copses and won the Horseshoe, after three days of most bloody and determined fighting in a little field. On the east side of the Contalmaison spur our men attacked the Quadrangle, got three sides of it, and attacked the fourth. This fourth side, known as the Quadrangle Support, could be reinforced from Contalmaison and from Mametz Wood, and could be observed and fired into from both places, so that though our men got into it and took it in a night attack, they could not hold it.

When the Horseshoe fell, early on July 7, a big attack was put in against the whole of these two spurs. It began with a very heavy bombardment upon the ruins of the village and the wood, and was followed by the storm of the village from the west and south-west, and an advance into the wood. Our men reached the village, took part of it, and found (and released) in one of the dugouts there that party of English Fusiliers who had been captured by the enemy on the 2nd of July. At this point of the attack a very violent, blinding rain began, which went on for twelve hours. This rain made it impossible for our gunners to see where our men were. In order not to kill them, our fire on the ruins slackened, and in the lull, in all the welter of the storm, the enemy contrived a counter-attack, which beat our troops back to the ruins at the south of the village, where they established a line. The attack on the wood brought our line forward through the outer horns of copse up to the body of the wood.

For the next two days our artillery shelled both wood and ruins, while plans were made for the next assault. The only "easy" approach to Contalmaison was from the west, near the Horseshoe, where the slope is gentler than it is to the south or south-west. The eastern approach was still blocked by the Quadrangle Support. The "easy" approach was not without its difficulties. Troops using it had to go down a slope into Shelter Valley (here gentle, open, and without shelter) in full view of the enemy entrenched above him. As soon as they were in the valley, under fire to their front, they were in full view of the enemy round Pozières, who could take them in flank and rear. Worse still, the whole of this part of the valley was commanded by well-contrived machine gun posts on a little spur, sometimes called the Quarry Spur, 500 yards to the north. However, this approach, bad as it was, was easy compared with the others. On the 10th of July the attack on the two spurs began again. In the right and centre our men went into the wood and into Quadrangle Support. On the left, they went across the "easy" approach in four successive waves, behind a "creeping barrage" or wall of shellfire advancing in front of them. They got into the village, without great loss. It was a compact village grouped at a road-knot, with little enclosed gardens. In that narrow space, in the cellars, in the dugouts under the cellars, and in the sunken roads, like deep trenches, close to the village, they fought what many believed to be the hardest body-to-body battle of this war. The village was very strongly held. The garrison outnumbered the attackers; in fact, the enemy dead and prisoners outnumbered the attackers. Contalmaison was won by the manhood of our men. When the enemy broke from the village to escape to the north, some Lewis gunners got on to them and caused them heavy loss.

That night our line was secure in Contalmaison. The Quadrangle to the right of it was ours, and more than half of Mametz Wood was ours. Men can feel what our soldiers faced in the storm of Contalmaison. There they were in the open with the enemy's trenches in front of them up above. But who can tell what they faced in Mametz Wood? The wood was partly on fire and full of smoke. The enemy was in strength and hidden. Our troops in the attack were thrusting through brambles, shrubs, scrub, and hazels, clambering over treetops and broken branches, cutting through wire and stumbling into pits, under what some have described as a rain of bullets, which fell from above and drove in from front and flanks. It is the biggest wood on the field. It is more than 200 acres in extent. There were four of our battalions in it at one time. Our men had to command themselves; for the only orders that could be given to them were to push uphill, driving back the enemy, and to hold what they won. After Contalmaison fell, on the evening of the 10th, the position was easier, on the left flank of the wood. The next day, after heavy losses, our men won the end of the wood, and came out on the other side, facing the Longueval Road, with the enemy main second line straight in front of them not a quarter of a mile away. In the last terrible attack on the end of the wood they took all the machine guns and trench mortars which had delayed the advance.

Meanwhile, away to the right, on the extreme right flank of our advance, there had been much bloody and heroic fighting for elbow room. Our men had tried to widen the gap of their advance by attacks to the eastward. They had captured the big wood of Bernafay, near Montauban, and had attacked the bigger wood of Trones, which lies parallel with it a little to the east. They had captured Trones Wood more than once, but could not hold it, owing to enemy machine guns on the (very slightly) higher ground outside the wood to the north and east. In this fighting, our soldiers came for the first time against the defences of the stronghold of Guillemont.

These assaults on Trones Wood and the capture of Mametz Wood are generally reckoned to be the last events in the first stage of the Somme battle. The wood of Mametz was the last part of the enemy's first-line and intermediate-line defences in the path of our advance. Beyond it was the second main position, which needed a battle to itself. The first main position, in that part of the line, was all our own.

In the twelve days' fighting, on the sixteen-mile front, we had advanced upon a front of about 7½ miles, for distances varying from 1¼ to 2½ miles. It is true that within this captured territory one little patch, the fort of the ruins of Ovillers-la-Boisselle, was still defended, but it was surrounded, it could not be succoured, and had to fall within a few days (it fell on the 17th). The new line ran from Authuille Wood, over Ovillers Hill, so as to shut in Ovillers, across Mash Valley and beyond, so as to shut in La Boisselle, across Shelter Valley and the chalk hill, so as to shut in Contalmaison, and then over the next spur, so as to take in Mametz Wood.

At Mametz Wood, the line turned south, down the gully on the wood's east side for about 1,000 yards, when it turned eastward into the valley of Caterpillar Wood. This valley, mentioned and described some pages earlier, runs roughly eastward for a couple of miles from Mametz Wood. Roughly speaking, it marked our line as it was at the end of this first stage of the battle. Trones Wood, which marked our extreme right, and though not held, either by us or by the enemy, contained a party of our men who could not go on, but would not come back, lies just beyond the eastern end of this valley.

The expanse of ground won by us in these first days of the battle was not large; it made but a tiny mark upon the map of France; but in this act of the war, which was so like a slow siege, victory was not measured by the expanse of territory won so much as by the value of the fortifications reduced. The first-line fortifications which we had taken were as strong as anything in the line and covered Bapaume, with its knot of roads, and the railway junction near it. The first line had been broken without great difficulty, and though the enemy resistance had stiffened and many more guns had been concentrated against us, we were within striking distance of his second line, from near Pozières to Guillemont, and if this fell with reasonable speed, it was thought, by some, that we might be in front of the ridge on which Bapaume stands before the autumn rain made great operations impossible.

The second main enemy line (south of the Ancre) ran from the high ground or plateau top behind Thiepval along all the high part of the desolate, flat, fertile downland which makes the battlefield of the Somme. It runs pretty straight for 3½ miles, from the Ancre to the wood of Bazentin-le-Petit. Here it bends a little, to take in the wood and adapt itself to the ground, which is here thrust into by the two gullies which border Mametz Wood. It then crosses the eastern gully, takes in another wood on a steep hill, called the wood and hill of Bazentin-le-Grand, shuts in the village of that name (which, in spite of its name, was smaller, though more compact, than Bazentin-le-Petit), and continues along the brow of steep, bold, rolling chalk hills for a mile or two. The bold, rolling hills then merge themselves with high plateau land, as dull, but not as desolate, as the high ground above Thiepval. The wood of Trones thrusts a straggling point of woodland into this plateau. To the north of this point is another, larger and broader, wood growing beside what was once a straggling village, built of red brick, and containing a prosperous sugar factory. The village was called Longueval, the wood is the famous wood of Delville. The line took in the wood, turned to the south so as to cover the village of Guillemont, and then ran away downhill, to the broken, steep valleys outside Maurepas and the marshy course of the Somme River.

The line was double throughout. The front line was a deep, strong, well-wired, well-sited trench, containing many dugouts, and one concrete fortlet in the parapet to every fifty yards of front. The line ran at the top of a gentle slope, in some places hardly perceptible, so that the field of fire swept by it was large, without dead ground and without natural cover. The wire in front of the line was formidable, though not so thick and strong as the wire of the first-line system at the beginning of the battle. The second line of this second system lay about one hundred yards behind the front line. It, too, was wired, and the line was a good and well-sited trench, though without dugouts and concrete forts. Parts of this second system became very famous, later in the battle, under many different names. The ominous and bloody names of Zollern Redoubt, O.G. 1 and O.G. 2, were applied to parts of this second main line. They will be mentioned in their proper place.

For two days after Mametz Wood was won there was no main attack, but much work was done in securing the captured ground, repelling enemy raids, and making ready for the assault on the second line. It was decided to attack this second line, wherever our troops fronted it, at a little before dawn on the morning of the 14th of July.

The dangers of the attempt were plain from the lie of the ground. All of this second line was a strong position, even without the hidden defences which nothing but an attack could unmask. To the left, in the centre, and on the right, the ground favoured the defenders. The attackers had to advance uphill, under observation, to positions backed and flanked by great blind woods. The wood on the left (that of Bazentin-le-Petit), though visibly less full of scrub than Mametz Wood, was 1,000 yards broad, sloping gently uphill, like Mametz Wood, and quite likely to be as difficult to take. It was certain to be crossed with many trenches and to contain many hidden machine guns. The formation in the centre, where the wood of Bazentin-le-Grand sticks out on its knoll, offered a problem by itself. If the enemy could hold it, he could make it impossible for us to take the positions on its flanks. If the enemy lost it, yet managed to hold either flank, fire from that flank could make it untenable by us. Setting aside the difficulties of the position to be attacked, we had also to consider the difficulties of our own position, which made a curving, irregular bulge in the enemy front, big if compared with ground won in an ancient battle, but really so small that the centre, about the spur of Bazentin-le-Grand, was within field-gun range from both flanks and received fire from three sides at once.

During the 13th, white leading tapes had been run out to the front as guiding marks to the attackers. At about midnight of the 13th–14th, strong patrols went out to cover the advance. The battalions named for the attack formed up in the open behind these covering squads, and advanced across the open to their positions. There was no moon, and the night, though a summer night and not naturally very dark, was cloudy. All the ground over which the battalions advanced was under fire, and littered and obstructed with the mess of war. In the advance, the men had to cross trenches inclined at all angles to their line of march; they had to pass dugouts, gun emplacements, lines of wire, fallen trees, woodland, brushwood, and copses, and to keep touch, none the less, with the platoons to right and left. It was as difficult as a night march can be, though the distance to go was in all cases less than a mile (uphill). Even for so short a distance, an advance in line of battle by night, over ground so broken, would be a difficult feat in time of peace.

Most soldiers (French and English) who saw the Somme fighting have agreed that this bringing up of the army to attack on the 14th of July was a feat of arms of which any nation might be proud.

The artillery preparation for this attack was fiercer than anything which had gone before it. Longueval, already much battered, ceased to be a village, and Delville Wood took on the appearance of a wood in winter. It was soon to take on the appearance of a wood in hell. At a little after three, in the rather cloudy morning of the 14th, the fire heightened to the roll of an intense and terrible barrage, and at half-past three, in a grey light, "when there was just sufficient light to distinguish friend from foe at short ranges," the artillery lifted and the men went over.

The fight which followed was one of the hardest and most successful in which British troops have been engaged. On the left, our men broke over the line into the wood of Bazentin-le-Petit, which was defended much as the wood of Mametz had been. Our men stormed its trenches, cleared out the machine guns and heavy guns hidden in it, and had won right through it, and come out at the northern end with many prisoners and much material, by seven o'clock. In the centre, our men got into the wood of Bazentin-le-Grand, and into the village of that name beside it. They beat the enemy down the hill beyond, and chased him up the oppo-site slope, where, in a rush, which won the praise of a French General who watched it with admiration, saying that he had never seen such extreme bravery, they got into the village of Bazentin-le-Petit and made it ours.

At this point our men were right up on the high ground of the plateau or plain, with High Wood, like a lonely island of trees, away to their right.

Before the village was secure as a military position the enemy counter-attacked. The attack was beaten off at about noon, but it was repeated a little later with stronger forces and pushed home. This second attack was repulsed after a hard fight. It was followed by a most resolute and extended attack in which the enemy put in his reserves, with orders that the village was to be retaken and the position restored. This attack, falling heavily on our front from the Flers Road in the direction of the cemetery, drove us out of the village as far as the crossroads near the church. Here our supports came in, the village was retaken, and our men beat the enemy back, with heavy losses, to his trench.

At the same time, as the enemy was much shaken from the last of his four defeats, an attempt was made upon High Wood. Cavalry which had been held in readiness, in case a chance should offer during the battle, were now sent forward on the flanks of some infantry to clear the standing corn which covered the field as far as High Wood. The wood itself, which, like all woods within the enemy system, was trenched round, and so netted with lines as to be a very powerful fortress, was shelled heavily. The cavalry (a squadron of lancers) cleared the corn, and the infantry assaulted the southern face of the wood, got into it, went through most of it, and took some prisoners there. The wood is a big plantation, say, 700 yards long by 500 across. The northern side tilts slightly downhill towards the long, bare, gentle slope which made the field of the autumn fighting. The southern side, which was the side attacked by our men on the 14th of July, is nearly flat. The trees are well-grown but not big timber, and the undergrowth at the time of the battle was thick. In the heart of the wood there were at least two permanent concrete emplacements for single heavy guns.

Men who were in this afternoon attack on the wood have spoken of the exultation with which they went in. Firstly, they had beaten the enemy throughout the day, from post to post, and in every one of three big counter-attacks. Secondly, they had won clear from the strip of land poxed with the blastings of two years' fighting. Those who went over that land later in the battle may find it difficult to believe, but on the 14th of July all the field in front of the wood bore harvest, and the wood was green. The coming into that undefiled country was a delight to the men. It is a fact that many of them cheered "for being among green things again." Thirdly, the knowledge that cavalry were fighting side by side with them gave them great joy. They felt that it was a sign that the war of trenches was going to give way to a war of movement, and that perhaps they were on the eve of great events. They took all the wood except the northern point, which was flanked by the switch line to Flers on one side, and by the boundary trench or hedge of the wood on the other. The fighting was very bitter here and very deadly. Long afterwards the bones of an enemy machine gunner, lodged on the spike of a tree, showed what the fight had been.

This taking of High Wood was the high-water mark and limit of the tide of conquest of the 14th of July. It brought us, with a rush, right on to the top of the plateau and (in High Wood) almost to its northern edge, so that our men could see the great, gentle, beautiful valley, coloured with the harvest in all its sweep, and the distant ridge beyond, dark with wood-land, and lined with red brick chimneys above, covering the prize of Bapaume. The left and centre of our attack had endured and achieved more than had been expected. On the right, towards Longueval, our success had been as notable.

On the right our men attacked, roughly speaking, due north, keeping strong flanking parties to the east of their advance to check any attack from the enemy fortress of Guillemont. They rushed the long, straggling northern end of Trones Wood on the slope above them and set free that patrol of two companies of Kentish soldiers who had been fighting there all night surrounded by the enemy. A thrust was then made to the east, towards Guillemont, while the main attack went on, up the slope, to Longueval and the edge of Delville Wood. Our men got into Longueval, cleared the two straggling streets to the road-meet in the heart of the village, and there came against the defence which was to make the place a hot corner for some time to come.

From the heart of the village, where the roads meet near the church, the ground slopes downhill towards Flers. The northern half of the village was built upon this sloping ground, which is a narrow, shallow valley, a quarter of a mile broad, at right angles with the village street. On both sides of the road there were plantations and orchards, not now to be distinguished from the main ruin of Delville Wood, but at the time of the fighting they were separate and fairly trim. The road through these plantations was lined with ruins, which the enemy defended ably. To the north of the shallow valley the ground rose up to the plateau crowned by High Wood. Most of this plateau was still strongly held by the enemy, who could see from it, fairly clearly, through the thinned wood, what was happening in the northern half of the village. The wood and the plantations masked the approach of troops coming to the relief of this part of the village, so that, what with a fairly well-observed artillery fire and a well-hidden line of support, the enemy had an advantage. By midday, the battle of Longueval had become a most bitter hand-to-hand struggle, in which our men gradually got the mastery. Most, or very nearly all, of this northern strip was in our hands by four o'clock, though two points just outside the village – one in the horn of Delville Wood, and one in an orchard on the hill to the west of it – still held out. All this area was soon to become the scene of some of the most terrible of the fighting of this war. Delville Wood was very soon to earn its name of Devil or Devil's Wood. The enemy shelling concentrated on this area and became most terrible.

The fighting here was not without compensation. One who was there remembered the taking of Longueval with pleasure, for in clearing out an enemy dugout he came upon a store of cigars. "Jolly good mild cigars; enough to give every man in the platoon a box, and so many that the Boche must have been giving cigars as an issue, at any rate, to the officers. We thought at first that they may have been poisoned and left behind as a booby trap, but we soon proved that." Another, in the same attack, saw a young private come out of an enemy dugout with a bottle of brandy. He very rashly brandished this bottle, crying out, "See what I've got." An old sergeant saw him, and said: "You're too young to be drinking that poison. You hand that over to me"; so the sergeant had it. But a captain who had seen the matter said to the sergeant: "You're too old to be drinking that poison. You hand that over to me." So the captain took it and kept it. One little action of devotion may be quoted, for even though it deals with eating and drinking, it was yet another of those countless heroisms of the carriers which are so seldom noticed and rewarded, though they happen every day in all weathers and under all fires.

A platoon had been fighting all day in the Longueval district, and had reached a strip of old enemy trench just outside Delville Wood. They tumbled into the trench and prepared to pass the night there. All were dog-tired, much shelling was going on, and all, though hungry, had given up all hope of food. At about ten that night, while they were getting what sleep they could in the devilish racket of the shelling, one of the officers was roused "by a little pale voice asking, 'Is Captain —————— here ?'" It was the battalion mess-servant who had brought up dinner for the officers in a basket. He had picked his way in the dark from Montauban, carrying a heavy basket stuffed with good things, over two miles of road blazing with the enemy barrage. He had brought hot soup in a thermos flask, a tin of salmon, hot bully beef with two vegetables, and some cheese and bread, hot coffee and a bottle of port. When he had served this dinner and collected the dishes and bottles he carried the basket back by the same road, past the same dangers, to Montauban.

This fight of the 14th of July gave us a large stretch of the enemy second line, brought us well on to his fortified plateau, and threatened the great, gently rolling expanse between Delville Wood and Bapaume. Our men had taken many prisoners and much war material. The enemy had lost heavily in killed and wounded, and had been badly shaken in the fighting round Bazentin, on a front of about a mile. When darkness came, our men were at work securing the new positions and linking them up with the line they had left just before dawn.

The new line now ran roughly south to north, parallel with the Albert-Bapaume Road, from Contalmaison to beyond Bazentin-le-Petit. It made a bend at Bazentin, and ran north-easterly to High Wood, which was a salient. From High Wood it bent back, in a south-easterly line, to Longueval and Delville Wood. From Delville Wood it ran southerly, past Trones Wood, towards the Somme River. The attack had been a great success, and had given us more than all that we had aimed for.

There were inconveniences in the new position. All our gains since the beginning of the battle made a salient, liable to be shelled from the front and from both flanks; but at High Wood we held a salient beyond a salient in a position of great importance to the enemy. It was therefore certain that High Wood would be made very difficult to hold. Further to the right, Delville Wood gave observation over so great a tract that the enemy could not afford to lose it; that, too, was certain to be fought for to the last ditch. Our troops attacking or defending Delville had strong enemy positions within half rifle-range on their right flanks and rear, and the only road of supply from Montauban could be shelled from two fronts. Worst of all, the weather was against us: it began to rain hard; the ground became a quagmire; the movement of troops and guns became difficult; and every hardship of war became harder and every difficulty worse. When the cloudy morning came and the fight raged up again, there was bad observation, and our aeroplanes could not detect the new enemy gun positions. With the dawn, attack and counter-attack began: our attacks against the strong points near Longueval, and on the right of our advance towards Ginchy; the counter-attacks against High Wood and against our hold on Delville Wood. During this second day of the fight, High Wood, the narrow salient, became untenable from shelling.

The wounded were carried out of it and the position abandoned, though our line remained not far from it.

At this stage of the battle it became imperative that our extreme right wing, which joined the French extreme left wing in the neighbourhood of Trones Wood, should win room for itself by a thrust to the east. It was necessary that the enemy should be pushed back from his position between Delville Wood and the Somme, so that the dangerous right angle in our line might be straightened out. Already an intense shellfire on the Montauban Road, which was the only line of supply to the troops in that angle, made our position difficult. It was plain that the enemy had now brought up his reserves of men and guns, and that the main agony of the Battle of the Somme, the struggle for the high ground of the chalk plateau, from the little town of Combles, where the dene-holes are, to the Schwaben Redoubt above the Ancre, was about to be fought. The weather, which was in the main against us throughout the battle, was against us now. The third week in July, 1916, when this struggle began, was wet; indeed the latter half of the year, while the fighting raged, was wetter than usual, and the last quarter by far the wettest within the memory of man. The weather did not affect the result of the battle, but it delayed it by many weeks.

The main need was to widen our position by winning more ground to the east. The enemy knew this as well as any soldier whose fate led him along the road by Bernafay Wood in those days. From the moment when our men cleared Trones and entered Delville Wood on the 14th of July, he concentrated a great artillery upon all that angle of the line and poured a continuous rain of shells on our hardly-won positions there. This increased daily for three days and nights, and on the 18th of July, after a very heavy shelling, a powerful enemy counter-attack came down on Delville Wood, and began that series of battles which killed every tree in the wood, and strewed every yard of it with the rags of human bodies. The attack drove us out of most of the wood and out of some of the village of Longueval beyond it, into a line of poor trench which no enemy could ever carry. At the same time, all the right angle of our line was shelled and shelled again, with barrages of all calibres, designed not only to stop our massing for an attack which might give us more room there, but to prepare attacks against us, and to destroy the advantages which had been won.

Though under the fury of this attack the right of our advance was, for the moment, checked, our left (five miles away to the west) was widening the salient thrust by us. On Ovillers Hill, the underground garrison of the Ovillers fortress had surrendered, after a fine defence, and our men had pushed up the Ovillers Spur towards the head of Mash Valley. From the Ovillers Spur, looking eastward, over the broadish, gently shelving Mash Valley-head, they saw the first jutting-out of the parallel spur along which the Albert-Bapaume Road runs. At the jutting-out they saw the cemetery of Pozières, among a clump of cypress trees, and the straggling end of Pozières village, stretching among trees along a lane towards it. This was to be the next prize to be fought for. The attack which won Ovillers, cleared Ovillers Hill, and opened up Mash Valley, secured the western approaches to Pozières. On the same day (the 17th) the troops near the wood of Bazentin-le-Petit bombed out towards Pozières along the lines of trenches known as O.G. 1 and O.G. 2, secured a part of them, and wired them in against any counter-attack. This, though it did not secure the eastern approaches to Pozières, at least secured a part of them. At the same time the shelling from our guns concentrated upon Pozières, and on the long strip of copse or wood beside it.

Towards the end of this third week in July, in hot, clearing, summer weather, some batteries and battalions of fine men were moving along the roads towards the battlefield of the Somme. They had not been "in" in that battle before this, and although they did not know, it seems that they had generally guessed that they were to go in against Pozières. These men and batteries belonged to the Australian and New Zealand Army Corps, and they were coming to the first big battle that had happened since they landed in France. It is said that these troops, as they moved along the roads in the July days between hedges covered with honey-suckle and shadowed by ranks of plane-trees, felt that they were marching in fairyland; for they had seen no such earthly beauty in their own lands over the sea, nor in Egypt and Gallipoli, where they had served. Perhaps no soldiers who have been hotly engaged in a modern battle ever really want to go into another. They go in the knowledge that it is their duty, and that their going may end the war and bring peace. These soldiers went in that spirit, but it is said that they felt satisfaction that they were to take part in a big battle with the enemy against whom they had enlisted to fight. About the 20th and 21st of July they came into camp within sound of the battle, and their officers were able to examine the ground which they were to attack. Their attack was to be the crowning act of that part of the battle. It may be well to describe here the nature of the ground of that little place, which for some weeks was as famous to our nation as the town of Troy.

*   *   *   *   *

Pozières was a little village of no interest and no importance strung along the Bapaume Road near the top of the plateau. It was in the main one street of buildings facing each other across the road. The houses of this street were not all dwellings. Some of them were byres, granaries, and barns, so that the main effect of the street was rude. Most of the houses were built of red brick; the byres and barns were of course plaster or clay daubed upon wooden frames. In the years before the war the village contained about 300 people, most of whom got their livings from the land, for all the plateau was good farm land. It has been said that some of the people (as at Contalmaison) made pearl buttons, but the chief work of the place, as of the Somme battlefield, was farming. The church was the chief building, and next to it in importance was the school. Both seem to have been modern buildings, of no interest. I do not know whether there was any market-place. There was no château. The road ran straight through the village in a north-easterly direction towards Bapaume. It may be said that it cut the village in two, for it divided the one row of houses from the other. In writing of the Battle of Pozières one has to think of this road as a mark or boundary, cutting one part of the battle from the other. Our advance in the battle was towards Bapaume, in the north-easterly direction. It may be better to write of the two halves of the village as lying east and west of the road.

Though the village was poor and without glory it was the home of men who had given its windy perch a beauty. The village was planted with trees. On the eastern side of the road, at the southern end of the village, these trees made a wood of fine timber, 200 yards long by 100 yards across. Orchards and outliers from this wood ran along the outskirts of the village on this side, behind the gardens of the backs of the houses. In the village street there were a few trees. Just beyond the village (at both ends) the fine plane and poplar trees which mark so many French highways made the road a shady avenue. Two hundred yards from the last house, at the north-east end of the village, the road dipped towards Bapaume. Just before the dip down, on the highest ground of the plateau, and a few yards to the west, or left-hand, side of the road, was the village windmill.

The eastern side of the village street had fewer houses in it than the western side. About midway in the village, the *abreuvoir*, or village watering-place for stock, opened from the road on this eastern side. It was an oblong, surface-drainage pond fenced with brick and shaded with elm-trees. On the western side of the road where the main village stood – for on this side the houses had a southern aspect – the ground rose slightly, perhaps as the result of generations of building. The school and the church both stood on this side of the village, though well back from the road. Near the church, a lane or country track ran westward from the high road towards the village of Thiepval, two miles away. A few buildings stood near this lane, well to the west of Pozières proper. Beyond them (to the west) was the head of the Mash Valley, which ran parallel with the high road down to La Boisselle. On the western slope of this valley, perhaps 200 yards from the village, was the village cemetery.

Seen from some little distance, from either side of the road, Pozières was like several other Picardy villages: a church tower and some red-tiled roofs among a big clump of fruit and timber trees, wood, and orchard. Being high up, it was waterless, save for a well or two and the rain. It was also as windy as Troy and as visible. From the north and west it was conspicuous for many miles. Men walking near the windmill could be seen from Serre, Pys, Irles, and Loupart, from three to six miles away.

From the north-east it was screened. From the east, it could be seen within a distance of two miles as a kind of ridge or skyline above the shallow pan which may be called the head of Sausage Valley. On this eastern side a distant view of it was blocked by Bazentin Wood. From the south and south-east, from Contalmaison and from the high road between Mametz and Montauban, it was plainly visible as a clump of trees, and the road to it from Contalmaison was a most conspicuous, whitish, straight line pointing to it. From the south-west, from the high ground of Usna Hill, it appeared as a few buildings, with roofs of red tile in front of a woodland.

The routes by which our troops could attack Pozières were all in full view of the enemy, who had so arranged his trenches and machine guns that to approach from any of the routes was scarcely possible in daylight. The approach by the Mouquet Valley was flanked and enfiladed by fortresses not yet reduced; those by the Ovillers Hill and Mash Valley were commanded throughout their length by the Pozières plateau. The route by the Albert Road over the big central spur led up a natural glacis, strongly wired, trenched, and flanked. The gully or valley between this central spur and the next to the east contained some dead ground, though the greater part of it could be seen from the village. This gully or valley has been mentioned (in the Contalmaison fighting) as the Quarry Gully, from two small chalk quarries on its eastern bank. The small spur to the east of Quarry Gully hid the next valley – which may be called Hospital Valley (because a dressing-station once stood there) – from the village, though all this valley was plainly visible from the enemy trenches at its head, which enfiladed it. Beyond this, to the east, is the big spur on which Contalmaison stood. At the north-eastern side of this spur is the wood of Bazentin-le-Petit, which stands on ground a little higher than that on which Pozières stands. In a way it turns Pozières, for troops stationed there are directly on the village's left flank. Troops advancing from this wood towards Pozières had a better chance of success than from any other point. Near this wood, as has been said, they had secured a part of the enemy main position, and had proceeded along it, westward, bombing from bay to bay in both trenches, to within a third of a mile of Pozières itself.

A road or track runs in Quarry Gully. Another, rather better road, runs in Hospital Gully. Both lead into Pozières.

The Quarry Road starts from the Albert-Contalmaison Road at the top of a rise. Just at the junction it is sunken rather deep between banks. When the enemy held that ground, before the beginning of the Battle of the Somme, he dug into these banks for shelter of various kinds. At the junction of the two roads he had dug a field dressing-station, which was taken over and used by our men when we had won the ground. The junction of the roads was often called Dressing-Station Corner for this reason. But it was always a dangerous place. The enemy shelled it day and night, throughout the Pozières fighting, as a likely piece of road for the passing of men and munitions. Before the end of the Pozières fighting, the junction itself, the strip of road leading downhill from it towards Contalmaison, past the much-blasted copse called Bailiff Wood, and the turn to the left into Quarry Valley, were generally known as Suicide Corner.

The dressing-station was destroyed by a shell during the attack. All the Corner is much battered by shellfire; but the road to Contalmaison, being needed for supply, has been kept in good order. It is now much wider than it was at the time of the fighting. It, too, runs between deep banks at this point. Bailiff Wood may once have cast a shadow on it on summer days, just here, at noon. Since the fight for Pozières, that wood has cast no shadows save from perhaps a dozen spikes of burnt branch, on one of which a magpie has built her nest.

The Corner, towards Pozières, is a rough, steep spur slope, terraced with those regular, steep steps or banks which the French call *remblais*, and our own farmers lynchets. As usual, the enemy had dug down into these lynchets for shelter from our fire. On the level terraces on the tops of the lynchets he had once placed his batteries, and his artillery-men had lived in the dugouts near-by. In one of the officer's rooms there was a library of good books. Early in the Battle of the Somme, our fire made the Corner untenable, the batteries were destroyed or withdrawn, and the dugouts – with their books, furniture, and officer's possessions – were abandoned to us. All these lynchets are much pitted and blasted by shell-fire. There are a few currant bushes on them here and there. The earth is bald, dried reddish mud with a little grass on it. In the winter it looked like the skin of some animal sick of the mange.

From the slopes of the Corner, standing in the wreck of the battery position, one can look up the Quarry Valley and see Pozières at the head of it. From this point, the village seems to stand on a backbone or ridge of earth on the northern skyline. In early July, when our men first saw Pozières from the Corner, it was still fringed with wood on this side, and though the shells had knocked some of the trees away, the place was green and leafy. The trees are on slightly lower ground than the village, for all the fall of the land there is to the south and east. From all this eastern side of the Albert Road, the line of the road along which the village ran makes a kind of ridge or wall. It was a green wall once; early in the battle the dust of the shells had covered it with grey. In the heat haze of July, 1916, that grey wall, with the blue air trembling above it, was the last thing seen by many hundreds of men.

The Quarry Valley is only fifty yards across. On the eastern side of it is the little spur, before mentioned, with its battered copse. The spur, which was once mainly plough land, is fleeced with coarse grass and dandelions. The many shell-holes are reddish all over it, though the red is mixed with dirty fragments of chalk. The spur itself is a small roll or heave of the ground, perhaps forty feet higher than the valley and one hundred yards across at its widest point.

The slope of the spur on its western side facing the Corner is naturally steep, and has been made steeper by man. A little way from the Corner the bank has been cut into for chalk, and the quarry, though hardly more than a recess, gives some sort of shelter. It is about twenty yards long by ten across, and the depth of the cutting, from top to floor, may be twenty feet.

A little further towards Pozières the Quarry Road forks, and near the fork there is a second quarry in which the chalk is much more clearly laid bare. This quarry is twice the size of the other and about half as deep again. It gives better shelter, as it is deeper than the other and equally well-screened, by the lie of the bank, from the view of an enemy artilleryman in Pozières village. From this point the road to Pozières, by either fork, is across the wreck of battle. All the ground has been blasted and gouged by shells. Men have dug shelters there and heaped up sandbags, and the shells have blown all into pits till the earth is all tettered with the pox of war. Here and there, the approach may still be made by trench. The grass and some of the hardier weeds have begun now to grow in some of those furrows; in others even the earth seems to have been killed, like the men buried there. From these gullies of dried, broken, pitted, and blasted mud, torn into holes, often twenty feet long, ten feet across, and seven feet deep, like nothing else on earth, one goes up the slope to that little Troy upon the hill. Presently one passes into an array of ram-pikes and stumps over which the hand of war has passed. It is like some Wood of the Suicides. A few trees in it are still recognizable as trees; some even push a few leaves from their burnt stumps. There are ashes, nuts, limes, and hawthorns. The others are stumps, with bunches of splinters at their ends, or erect hags, or like the posts of some execution corner where men are garotted and shot and hung on the cross. Here the ground is so gouged and blasted that the shell-holes run into each other like sloughing sores. The trenches run for a little, are blasted into the landscape, emerge again for a few yards, and again disappear in some long lake of water or mud. All the ground is littered with the waste of war – tins, equipment, smashed weapons, shells, bombs, bones, rags of uniform, tools, jars, and boxes. In one place, above the wood, in the village itself in what was once the road to Contalmaison, are the traces of an enemy battery position, with broken wheels and many of the wicker panniers used for carrying shells. This road was once hedged, but fire has trimmed the hedge. There are brambles in it still, and dwarf beech, young elm – which will never grow to be old – and the wayfaring-tree. From this point one can enter the village. It was near here that the English-speaking race first entered the village, in the summer night's charge of a year ago.

On both sides of the village street the shells dug confluent pits, then filled them, then dug them again, then dug others, then more, then more, till the ground became a collection of holes with mounds among them. The shells fell thus, on all that ground, for hours and days and weeks and months, till in all the squalor of mud and smash that was once Pozières no sense was left of the home of men. One can see that a village once stood there, for there are broken bricks in the mounds, and old iron farm implements in some of the shell-holes, and the road has been made like a road again. The houses lie in heaps of rubble and small bits of brick, and where the buildings were important these heaps are bigger than else-where.

Three or four landmarks remain on one side of the village and one on the other. On the western side of the road, north of the village, is the mound or hump of the windmill. This is now a heap of earth, cement, and broken concrete stuck about with railway girders. Further south, on the same side, is a part of a single wall of reinforced concrete. This strange grey fragment, which stands on a mound, and was once a part of a very strong enemy fortress built of concrete and iron girders, stands on the site of the school. At a distance it has (to myself) something the look of a loaded camel lying down; but some observers describe it as three flat anvils in a row. It can be plainly seen for many miles in nearly every direction. Further south again, on this side, is the biggish heap of powdered brick, riddled iron, earth, hewn stone, bent metal, and filthy papers that was once Pozières church. At the southern edge of the village on this side, above a lane which straggles round to the cemetery, is another grey concrete fragment, famous in its way. It stands well up on the bank above the lane, overlooking the spur, Mash Valley, and the distance of France, with the trees of the Amiens Road upon it. It is a little observation post, which could, on occasion, be used as a machine gun emplacement. A concrete stair near it leads down to a cellar twelve or fifteen feet below. This little post, barely big enough to hold two men, is less conspicuous from a distance than the school-house fragment, but being in the line of our attack was more of a landmark to our soldiers, who called it Gibraltar. Beside it, almost sunk into the mud, are two old enemy gun emplacements covered with balks of timber.

On the eastern side of the road there is only one landmark. About the centre of the village, close to the road, is a hollowing in the mud, as though there had been more shells all together there than elsewhere. This filthy hollow holds water even when most of the shell-holes are dry. At one side of it, low down, are four or five rows of brick where the foundation of a wall once stood. This place is what remains of the *abreuvoir* or watering-place for stock.

None of these places gives any feeling of the habitation of man. No one, looking at the site of the village, can feel that the place was once the home of 300 human beings, who were born and married there, who lived in that street and got good out of those fields, and heard the bells of the church, and went up and down to market. Looking at the place, one can only feel that it has suffered, and that all round it human beings suffered, in hundreds and thousands, from agony and pain and terror, and that it has won from this a kind of soul.

296

On the western side of the village, beyond the hedges which once closed the gardens at the backs of the houses on that side, the ground slopes into the head of Mash Valley in a slope so mild that it is almost perfect as a field of fire. If you turn your back upon the village, walk for half a mile across the Mash Valley-head, and then look at the village, it appears as a skyline or ridge, with a few tree-stumps upon it, and those other heaps or marks: the windmill, the school, and Gibraltar. Looking round, from that point, one sees only a markless wilderness of shell-holes, full of water or ice in the winter, and of dryish mud at other times, between which, in the summer, a coarse grass full of weeds thrives knee-deep. From the west through the north to the east the land is all this wilderness as far as the skyline. It is a desert of destruction, with no mark to guide upon it. Up those slopes, all looking alike, on to those plateaux all looking alike, our men advanced upon trenches all looking alike. In that desert they had to advance upon objectives which were indeed points on a map, but in the landscape were like every other place in sight. The sea has more natural features than that battlefield. The difficulties of the battle were not wholly those of shells and machine guns, but of keeping touch and direction during an advance.

Now that it is out of cultivation, one can find wild flowers all over that battlefield. In July, when the fighting began, it grew the flowers common in cultivated chalk soils at that time of the year: the purple hardhead, pale purple scabious, pale blue chicory; and the common weeds of cultivation: yellow ragwort, red poppies, and blue cornflowers. In the spring and earlier summer it is thickly set with dandelions. On both sides of the road, but especially near the windmill, there are patches of strongly growing henbit. To the east of the road, on the plateau, and in and near the quarry and middle gullies, there are patches of speedwell, ground-ivy, dead-nettle of two kinds, one with pink, one with yellow flowers (which also grows freely in Mametz Wood). Among the grass one can also find dock, milfoil, starwort, stitchwort, "a white, small, starry, cuppy flower," Venus needle, daisy, field madder, Lamb's lettuce, a cut-leaved wild geranium, a veronica, and the little heart's-ease pansy. Perhaps someday, when Australia makes a Campo Santo of the earth of Pozières, these plants may be set there. In their place at Pozières, they will grow in Australian dust for ever.

The best view of Pozières is from the east of the Roman Road, from the direction of the main Australian attack. From a point 1,200 yards S.E. from the windmill, the appearance is of a valley of sand, with grass in stretches, and Pozières as the wall of an old town on the horizon. The Authuille Wood is just visible over the saddle or dip in the road, and the town is like a long, low dyke of sand sloping gradually up behind the road. Near the windmill, the actual crest, this dyke is more marked. From Contalmaison, one sees the line of the road (the line of the ridge) with some forty stumps of trees beside it. One can see the traffic on the road passing along the ridge, becoming dim against the background of the village, and then standing out again, clear against the sky as it nears the windmill.

The enemy defences at the time of the attack ringed in both village and wood with trenches. The cellars and piles of ruin had been fitted with machine guns, and the mill, the school, and Gibraltar, were all fortresses of the usual strong, defensive type. The external defences seem to have been:

(a) To the north: the two lines, old German lines one and two (O.G. 1 and 2), which were dug so as to enfilade any attack upon the village from the east. At the time of the assault we held these lines to within 600 yards of the village. They lay well to the north of the ruins of the village itself.

(b) To the east: a line shutting in the village and wood, on the line of the old hedge of the wood. This was strongly held.

(c) A sunken light-railway track, which could be held as a trench.

(d) A line or part of a line still further to the east, dug so as to enfilade Hospital Valley, and to link up with the O.G.s.

(e) To the south: a big wired line close to the village, linking it with the intermediate positions at Contalmaison and Mametz Wood. This line ran in front of the lower part of the village, so as to defend the cemetery. From it, minor communication lines ran to the south-west and south-east. All these lines could be, and were, held by the enemy to check our advance. In one of them, last spring, the last surviving hen of Pozières laid some successful eggs.

During the night of Saturday-Sunday, July 22nd–23rd, the troops took up their positions for the attack on the village. The attack was to be made upon the eastern and southern faces of the position by Australian troops and English Territorials. The English were to advance from the direction of Ovillers Hill and Mash Valley upon the cemetery and that straggling end or outlier of the village which stretched out towards Thiepval. Their right was to rest upon the Albert-Bapaume Road, their left on the strong, newly converted enemy lines on Ovillers Hill. The Australian left was to touch the English right at the road, to push up, in the main direction of the road, from Suicide Corner and Contalmaison, by way of the spur, the Quarry Road, and Hospital Road, so as to close in on the village from the south-east. The Australian right, forming up from about Contalmaison Villa, outside Little Bazentin Wood, to O.G. 1, with their faces to the west, were to charge across the plateau, taking whatever trenches there might be in their path, right into the village, through the wood or copse, and across the gardens to the houses. It was known that the garrison of Pozières had been relieved by a fresh division, and that, like other enemy reliefs, this division had brought in plenty of food and drink. The attack had been prepared by some days of shelling over the whole area. Not much of the village was standing, though one observer speaks of some parts of red-tiled roofs near the cemetery. The smash and ruin were general, but the place was not obliterated, nor were all the trees razed. The weather had cleared. It was hot, dry, dusty weather, with much haze and stillness in the air. At midnight on the 22nd–23rd of July the attack was timed to begin. It was the first big fight in which the Australians had been engaged since the Battle of Gallipoli, almost a year before. Then they had fallen in in the night for an attack in the dark, which won only glory and regret. This time the battle was to be one of the hardest of the war, and there was to be glory for all and regret for very many, and the prize was to be the key to the ridge of Bapaume beyond the skyline, with possible victory and peace. At midnight, when the men had reached their starting-places, the attack began, and a great wave of Australian infantry went across the plateau towards the east of the village. A part of this wave attacked the enemy who were still holding out in O.G. 1. The rest crossed the plateau, got into one enemy line, which was lightly held or held only by dead men, took it, got into another (really the sunken track of the light railway) which was held more strongly, took that, and so, by successive rushes, and by countless acts of dash and daring, trying (as it happened) to find objectives which our guns had utterly destroyed, they reached the outskirts of the place, across a wreck of a part of the wood. They made a line from about the southern end of the village to their starting-place near Bazentin Wood.

When the daylight came on that Sunday morning, the Australians were in the village, on the eastern side of the road with the road as their front. Beyond the road they had to their front the tumbled bricks of the main part of the village. To their right, they had a markless wilderness of plateau tilting very slightly upwards to the crest on which the O.G. lines ran. Australians who were there have given accounts of the fighting which won them this position, but, as usually happens in a night attack, those who were there saw little. It seems to be agreed that the second enemy trench was more strongly held than the outer line, and that the right of the attack, which came under direct enfilading fire from the O.Gs., had the hardest task. Some have said that the eastern outskirts of the village were lightly held by the enemy, and that not more than 200 enemy dead were found in that part of the field after the charge, which is very likely, for it was the enemy's custom to hold an advanced post with a few men and many machine guns.

On the left of the attack, on the western side of the road, where the English Territorials were engaged, the objectives were swiftly taken, so that by dawn the village was shut in as firmly from the south as from the east.

When it was light, both sides tried to reconnoitre. Neither side shelled the village for fear of killing its own men, since neither side, as yet, knew how the lines ran. The two sides sniped at each other from the ruins across the road. Early in the forenoon an Australian officer took a small party across the road into the main ruin of the village, and creeping from one heap of bricks to another, surprised, bombed out, and caused the surrender of a section of the enemy, including a regimental surgeon in his dressing-station. The work of linking up the captured positions went on all through the day under a shellfire which increased steadily as the enemy observers came to know what was going on. The sniping sometimes increased into hot rifle fire.

By ten o'clock on that Sunday night, the Australians had plotted out the main stations of the Pozières garrison. They attacked across the road, bombed out some more dugouts, and cleared the scattered groups of enemy out of the trenches, remains of trenches, converted ditches, and old gun emplacements, where they still made a kind of organized resistance. Having won these places, they linked them up into a system, and dug a communication trench by which men could pass across the road from one half of the village to the other. This gave them (and secured to us) nearly the whole village, and though there were snipers and bombers who troubled our men, the enemy made no determined counter-attack in force against the village itself.

When day dawned on Monday, 24th of July, the Australians had secured and were occupying practically the whole of the village, and faced, roughly speaking, to a northern front. In front of them was the gentle depression of the northern end of Mash Valley. To their right the ground was almost flat, though trending very slightly uphill from them to the O.G. 1 and 2, only 200 yards away. A hundred yards behind the enemy lines was the wreck of the famous windmill, marking the highest part of the crest, and the nearest point from which the Australians could hope to see into the valley beyond. The Australians' next task was to attack the O.G. lines on their right flank and front, seize the windmill on the crest, and then to take from the enemy his power of observation and his control of all that system of defence.

Before the attacks began, the enemy bombardment came down. At first it was simply a heavy fire upon the village, but it soon increased to a barrage on the district. Sometimes it would lift, to search Contalmaison and the road past Suicide Corner; then it would play upon the valleys leading up to Pozières and upon those recesses or quarries near them where the little shelter might harbour stores or wounded men. Then it would fall on village and wood in lines and simultaneous dottings of explosion, till a dull red, dirty haze covered the site of the village, and smokes and stinks of all colours and poisons smouldered and rotted in it. In this haze and poison the Australians lived, and dug, and held the line. The first bombardment lasted for four days and nights, and in all that time there was little fighting, by either side, in that district; yet all are agreed that those four days made up some of the hottest battle of this war.

The tactical aim of the Australians was to drive the enemy off the high land. The tactical aim of the enemy was to shell the Australians off it. All are agreed that their shelling was some of the heaviest ever seen. It made a fog all over the high land, and into this fog the Australians disappeared

300

to a feat of endurance which few will know how to praise. So many acts of courage are hot and quick with inspiration, they must be as great a joy to do as to read about. But those swift acts of decision are for individuals, not for masses of men. The holding of the ground of Pozières was done by brigades at a time. Their casualty lists will show the nature of the work. The appearance of the ground and of the graves marks it to the visitor. It was as hard a service as any that has been on this earth.

One who was there has said: "I went in from Sausage Valley way, past Suicide Corner. At first I only noticed that they were shelling Contalmaison like hell, but when I got down by the Quarry and saw what they were serving out on Pozières, by God, I felt, you may call this war, I call it just sending men to be killed. By God, they were sending some stuff over as we went up. The first thing I knew I was completely buried. I was in a trench when it happened, but there was no trench when I got out. That went on all the time that we were in. We would get some kind of trench dug, and then it would be blown in, and the men buried or killed, and all the time there were crumps, whizz-bangs, and tear-shells till you couldn't hear or see. We would get some kind of a line made and try to make a dump, but you might as well have tried to build a dance-hall and give a dance. I looked back one night and saw the dump in the Quarry burning. They had brought up a lot of lights and star-shells and dumped them there, and a shell had got in among them and set them all off together; they lit up the whole sky."

Another who saw the fighting has said: "About the end of July, I had to go to the C.C.S. (Casualty Clearing Station) at ———. The C.C.S. was in the school, at the bottom of a courtyard, and there were benches round the courtyard full of Australians who were all suffering from shell-shock, and they were jumping about and couldn't keep their hands and feet still; I never saw such a sight. One of the doctors said to me: 'I don't know how it is. The Australians must be more highly strung or something. I get more shell-shock cases from among them than from any other units.' 'You silly ———,' I said. 'These poor ——— have been in at Pozières, where they've been shelled to hell for the best part of a week, and nobody else so far has had anything like it.'"

A third has said: "I got a crump on the head the night I first went in, so I don't know much about it, except that that damned trench called Centre Way was a damned unpleasant place to be in."

Centre Way, which is still partly to be traced, ran obliquely from close to the church of Pozières in a north-westerly direction towards the O.G. lines, which it reached about three-quarters of a mile to the west of the windmill. In the markless plain of mud, it was the middle one of three trenches by which the Australians approached the O.G. lines.

A fourth has said: "A damned funny thing happened in the early days of Pozières. The trees in the wood then were not like what they are now, all shot to pieces. Some of them were quite good trees, and we had an O. Pip in one of them (artillery observation post), and had an officer there with a telescope. He was up there with his telescope about the 25th of July. There was a hell of a barrage going on behind him, for they were putting one across the gullies to stop men coming up. He was looking at this barrage one moment, when he saw an Australian coming through the barrage across the open. He was trotting along, almost naked, as we were in the Peninsula, and this officer expected to see him blown to pieces every second, but he came through the barrage all right, and then the officer recognized that it was his own servant coming with a letter. He had to look away for a while, and the next thing he knew the fellow was shouting at him from the foot of the tree. He expected that it would be some urgent thing that might be going to alter the whole campaign, so he put down his telescope, and climbed down and got the letter and read it. It was from the veterinary surgeon, and it said, 'Sir, I have the honour to report that your old mare is suffering from an attack of the strangles.' He acknowledged the letter, and the man went back the way he came, across the open, hopping through the barrage, and got back all right."

Few men can face such a thing as a modern barrage without awe; none the less, these men did face it, and lived in it, for days together. Under the fiercest of its terror, they bombed out towards the mill, got the mill – or the mound on which it once stood – but could not hold it. Coming again they got the mill and made it theirs, and spreading out to the left, they got the O.Gs., and with the English Territorials they moved forward, up the head of Mash Valley, on to the formless, markless, pocky, mud-barren. Up near the windmill, when they got it, they could peer from their lines through the smoke into the Promised Land.

The ground slopes down to the northward from the windmill, at first very slightly. Three hundred yards from the mill, there is a lynchet, some four feet high, running roughly N.W.-S.E. across what was then the Australian front. Beyond this, the ground slopes much more rapidly for some 300 or 400 yards to the village of Courcelette among its trees. When the Australians took the windmill, there was a greenness upon all this slope of hill. The trees of Courcelette were leafy; there were houses in the village; and the great, wide, gently sloping valley beyond was green. It was not long to remain green, but at the Australians' first sight of it it was green and lovely, though in the hands of the enemy. The Australians, looking down from the windmill across the valley, saw that there was no ground for a strong, defensive line nearer than the ridge of Bapaume, three miles away. They knew that the enemy could not hope to make a permanent line nearer than that, for all the nearer ground was under direct observation. They realized that the capture and holding of the Pozières Ridge would lead to the capture of all the valley below it; not immediately – for there is no position which cannot be defended for a time in modern war as long as there are machine guns – but certainly, and before very long. As they looked over the valley, they saw and heard some great explosions not far below them, in and near Courcelette. The enemy was hurrying away his field guns and blowing up his dumps of field gun ammunition.

This capture of Pozières may be said to mark the end of the second stage of the great battle. The first stage ended in the capture of the first line along some miles of front. This second stage ended in the capture of the second line along some miles of front, thus deepening the wound in the enemy defensive system.

The third stage, beginning even then, in the mark-less mud towards Thiepval and on the Guillemont plateau, was to widen the wound.

*   *   *   *   *

Enemies and detractors who hate us have said that, after all, the battle was no great affair; that it took, indeed, a few trenches, at great cost, but did not defeat the enemy nor relieve our Allies, and that we sacrificed our Colonial troops rather than expose our own. Lies are best left to Time, who is the surest confounder of malice; but some must be answered. To these few liars it may be said that the battle was the first real measuring of strength, on equal terms, between the enemy and ourselves, and that, therefore, it was a great affair. In the early years of the war our picked men had fought their picked men, in the proportion one of ours to seven of theirs, and our men had held them and been killed. In the Battle of the Somme, the picked men on both sides being gone, the fighters were the average of each race, and the result proved that superiority of the British which none in our army had ever doubted. It is true, that our men took a few trenches at great cost. It is also true, that they failed to take a few trenches at the first attack. The same is true of all fighting in all wars. But the result of the battle is written plain on the map of France. There on the map, and still more plainly on the sacred soil of France, it is marked, that the battle beat the enemy out of his picked defences, where he was strongest, and drove him back, from ditch to ditch, over a ground where all things were in his favour, in spite of all that he could do, for not less than twelve miles. It is not claimed that this was a decisive defeat of the enemy, to rank with the battles which end wars, but it was a sound beating. He did his best to hold his best fortifications, and he could not hold them: he was beaten out of them. If the battle failed to save Roumania, as some of our enemies (not very wisely) cry, it relieved Verdun. As to the lie, that during the battle we sacrificed our Colonial troops rather than expose our own, the graves of our men, in the mud, by the hundred and the thousand, from Maricourt to Gommecourt, and in every acre of the field, are sufficient answer. For each Colonial lost, not less than nine or ten of our men were lost.

In the area of our advance, between Thiepval and Maricourt, the danger was nearly equal in all places. No part of the enemy line was less than a first-class fortress; all parts were well-contested; and over all parts there was a heavy fire of cannon of all kinds and of machine guns. The

Leipzig, Ovillers, La Boisselle, Fricourt, Mametz, Trones Wood, Bazentin Woods, Mametz Wood, Contalmaison, Pozières, the Village, Mill, and Cemetery, were all as dangerous and as difficult to storm as the objectives of famous sieges: "Number Four Bastion," the Redan, "the Green Ridge," and the rest. At all of them, the attackers moved to the attack knowing that they went to the near certainty of wounds and death. The area of the advance of this first month of the fight is not large. One could walk round the area, visiting all its famous places, in one summer day, for the distance can only be twenty miles all told. Spring and summer have laid their healing hands upon those places since the fighting. The covering of the grass has come to hide the evidence that those slight slopes and tumbles of brick were once terrible both to take and to hold. Men standing in what is left of Delville Wood, or in the wilderness which was once Pozières, will find it hard to believe that for days together fire rained upon those places, and that men by the hundred and the thousand were buried there, and unburied, and killed, and maimed, and blown into little fragments. Our men lie everywhere in that twenty miles circle, sometimes very thickly, in platoons and companies of the recognized and the unknown. They were our men. Men of our race will never walk that field without the thought that the wind blowing there took the last breath of many of our people, and that the dust under foot is our flesh.

Our own men will never want for praisers. But in this great battle, some came as guests, from many thousands of miles away, to fight what they saw to be the battle of free communities. Many years hence, when the facts and passions of this war are dim, English writers may forget, not what these men did, but the measure of their gift to us. Now, while the facts are fresh, one may give their guests first place.

Many battalions did nobly in the difficult places of the battle. The field at Gommecourt is heaped with the bodies of Londoners; the London Scottish lie at the Sixteen Poplars; the Yorkshires are outside Serre, the Warwicks in Serre itself; all the great hill of the Hawthorn Ridge is littered with the Middlesex; the Irish are at Hamel, the Kents on the Schwaben, and the Wilts and Dorsets on the Leipzig. Men of all the counties and towns of England, Wales, and Scotland lie scattered among the slopes from Ovillers to Maricourt. English dead pave the road to La Boisselle; the Welsh and the Scotch are in Mametz. In gullies and sheltered places, where wounded could be brought during the fighting, there are little towns of the dead of all these places: "Jolly young Fusiliers, too good to die."

The places where they lie will be forgotten or changed, green things will grow, or have already grown, over their graves. It may be that all these dead will someday be removed to a National graveyard or Holy Field. There are three places, in that wilderness of the field, which should be marked by us. One is the slope of the Hawthorn Ridge, looking down the Y Ravine, where the Newfoundland men attacked. Another is that slope in Delville Wood where the South Africans attacked. The third is all that great expanse from Sausage Valley to the windmill which the Australians won and held. Our own men lie as it was written for them. But over the graves on these three places it should be graven, that these men came from many thousands of miles away, to help their fellow-men in trouble, and that here they lie in the mud, as they chose.

Not long ago, on that old battlefield, an Australian said: "In the Maori war once, some English surrounded some Maoris and sent to tell them to surrender, since they could not escape. The Maoris answered: "We fight 'Akka, akka, akka' (for ever and for ever and for ever). This makes a good war-cry for us."

When, in future time, the Australian Memorial is placed over the mound of the windmill, to stand sentinel over so many splendid bodies which once went with that cry through the Peninsula and up that plateau, those three words will be sufficient dedication, and sufficient story, for ever and for ever and for ever.

[source: *The Battle of the Somme*, London: William Heinemann, 1919]

1919–1920: Signs of the Times

You ask me to write about "the significance of the past year." I suppose that in many ways, to many people, it has been the happiest year they have known. The losses of the war have been partly atoned for by the joy of peace. That nightmare of horror has been taken from the world. The fever has gone out of the mind. The madness of hatred and suspicion have ceased to rave, and the millions have been given liberty. Whatever troubles the year has brought are as nothing to its mercies, of liberty and peace.

One of the happiest things of this happy year has been the sight (in term times) of thousands of young men set free from the war, released from the shadow of death, to lives of their own. The delight and joy of these glorious young men, made earnest beyond their years by the war's hardships, have made one happy for England's future. Not much can go amiss in a land where such young men are born and bred.

Many of these young men have been but newly released. It is still too early to expect a new message or inspiration, in art or politics, from them. That may come perhaps next year. The great problem of the past year has been to restart the machine of the world in the ways of peace. Most of us wish those ways to be improved ways and the machine to be a better machine. The attempt to restart and to improve the machine at the same time is now proceeding. The life of England has been altered and her conscience shaken by the war. I do not doubt that her great soul will rise to the peace as nobly as she rose to the war, and that in Blake's words,

> Jerusalem will be builded here,
> In England's green and pleasant land.

Now as to the reforms. I suppose that there are in England today –

(a.) A small party of obstructionists opposed to any reforms of the existing system.

(b.) A small party of anarchists, anxious to destroy the existing system at any cost, but with neither the mind nor the power to create anything to take its place.

(c.) A great many earnest men and women of all classes and all creeds giving their minds and lives to reforming the existing system, and succeeding, beyond our dreams and hopes, each month and day.

The first and second parties are without any vision of a human State or of human liberty, but this does not make them less likely either to win adherents or to quarrel.

One of the wonders of this year 1919 has been the triumph of the third party over both the other two. Gradually one sees a finer England shaping and emerging out of the chaos that was. One sees the old system being improved and made human.

Often one sees and hears bitter attacks upon that old system. It is called the commercial system, or the capitalist system, or the industrial system, and it comes in for much abuse. No doubt it deserves some abuse, and has deserved more, but it is a system which keeps the world going and does the work of the world, and under it the Christian populations using it have doubled or trebled. It has had its triumphs as well as its infamies, and, whatever may be said against it, it remains the system by which we millions live, and no other system exists ready to hand to take its place. A system is a thing of slow growth. Men cannot improvise one. It is wiser to patch a leaky ship than to blow her out of the water with all on board, or to try to sail her with her leak.

I claim a right to speak about the system. I have served it as a worker for ten years. Under it I have helped to produce food and goods, to load them and carry them by land and sea to their markets, and to distribute them to their users. I have enjoyed the good and suffered from the bad sides of the system. The main thing to be said for it is that it gets the world's work done.

Nearly all work is pleasant, but much of it is very hard, some, and this perhaps the most necessary, is both hard and unpleasant. Scavenging of certain kinds, the handling of filthy things of certain kinds (coal is one of them) is hard and unpleasant and dangerous.

What our workers are demanding is that the very hard and dangerous and unpleasant work should be well-paid, and not practised for too great a part of a man's day. They claim that the man should not be "subdued to what he works in," but should have the means and the leisure to be a citizen of the world out of working hours.

They claim that men and women should have some security of life; that they should not be subject to "unemployment" which means *enforced starvation or beggary through no fault of their own.*

They claim, but not with one-tenth the necessary force, that all citizens of a State should have the advantages and the opportunities of the very finest education possible, and access to all professions for which they may be able to qualify.

They claim, as a part of this previous claim, that their children should not have to begin to work until they have had leisure and mental training to fit them to choose their work, and to enjoy it when chosen.

Those, roughly, are the claims. Looking back on 1919, one can only think of it as a glorious year in which many of those claims were accepted by our country as the foundation of the England that is to be. I look forward to 1920 with the hope that the regeneration of England may proceed with wisdom and sanity to the ends longed for by her best minds.

[source: *Manchester Guardian*, 5 January 1920, p.6]

Disenchantment

DISENCHANTMENT. By C.E. Montague. London: Chatto and Windus. Pp. 221. 7s. net.

Once, during the war, a well-known statesman was heard describing his recent visit to G.H.Q. His visit had not reassured him as to our immediate prospects in the war, but one thing had impressed him deeply, "They've got an excellent man there," he said. "I don't think they quite realize what an excellent man they've got in Montague."

"They" did not realize it, though a good many others did. Now that the war is over the excellent man has set down what he realized while "they" were still fumbling.

Most of Mr. Montague's book has already appeared in short articles and leaders in the *Manchester Guardian*. There its component parts have attracted much attention, as Mr. Montague's work always will. But now that the many scattered articles are drawn together their effect is increased tenfold. Now one can see that the articles were not written one by one, as memory or the mood prompted, but as parts of an ordered and planned unity which begins and grows and ends like a work of art. The book is of a tense and close and masterly structure.

It is, as an American would say, "Mr. Montague's reaction to the war." It is the summing-up by a most gallant and generous mind of the devotion and martyrdom and disillusion of the four years of struggle. No man is better qualified to write of the war as a whole. Mr. Montague took part in much of the fighting, and must have known more of the British line than almost any living man. He was in the trenches in the beginning of the horror and with the army in Germany at the end. He saw the whole thing from the point of view of a very good athlete with a very good brain. Now here is the result and summary of it.

On the whole, the feeling which the book rouses in the reader is the feeling which G.H.Q. roused in the statesman above-mentioned; that "They," the powers that were, the politicians and War Office, did not know even till the end of the war what excellent men they'd got. That, on the whole, put with scrupulous fairness, is Mr. Montague's subject: the pity of the tragedy of the matter. A fine nation, touched and stirred to the quick, did the most generous act in history. Millions of noble and devoted men, the very pick and flower of the race, in brain and body, gave themselves to the freeing of Belgium. They were handled by what was admittedly the least competent of our public offices, by men who were notoriously not the pick and flower of the race. After some years of bungling and slaughtering, when the spirit was out of the war and the sacrifice had been fouled and the devotion soured, the survivors saw their efforts result in the perpetration of much such a Prussianism as they had fought to prevent.

In describing the progress of a human soul through the purgatory of the war to the disillusion of the peace Mr. Montague has written a very fine book. He has extenuated nothing and set down nothing in malice. I have seen no book about the war so temperate or so human. He was in the war, and being a man of fine intelligence must have suffered more than most from the fools from whom men then had to suffer, but the book is without any littleness or bitterness. Even when describing bits of incompetence, or worse, which are an anguish to read about he has a most generous sense of the incompetent's difficulty and of the sterling quality which often went with the incompetence. But the book is none the less a record that the manhood of the race, after "designing glorious war," became "the sport and prey of racking whirlwinds, unrespited, unpitied, unreprieved, ages of hopeless end."

It is not easy to be wise, even after the event. Perhaps no other race of men on this earth would have done so well as we did, being taken unprepared as we were in 1914. Even if we had scrapped our existing army-machine at the start and begun again from the beginning things might have been no better. The army-machine and the church-machine and the political-machine and the education-machine had been all untested by life for years. Then the war came and probed them and proved them as no machines were ever tested. They were jolly good: they must have been most jolly good: for they didn't break, though, as the Australian said, "they gave a darned big creak."

Perhaps the sufferers from their inadequacy would not agree that they were jolly good. They were not good enough for the fine fellows whom Mr. Montague describes. What human institutions would have been? What comes out from Mr. Montague's pages is that man, the patient, common, courageous man, is so infinitely finer than even the very best of the institutions with which he protects and torments himself. All must have seen the caddis-worm crawling about, a little living soul in a house or shell of rags and patches. So were the men in the armies about which Mr. Montague writes so feelingly. Their house or shell of War Office and Church was a thing of shreds and patches, but they were living souls, put to their trumps, living in the depths of themselves. All earth and heaven would have been less than their deserts. What they got was the War Office and the padre. Perhaps all this Disenchantment had to be in order that the reality might be plain, that man is in himself all earth and heaven, a living soul, dragging about an old museum of torment, without which he could not live. When he realizes this he seeks out some new illusion and feeds it with his hopes and feelings. Then accident makes the illusion an obsession, and the fever of the obsession brings him weak and sick to reality again. It may well be that the war came "because a sheep-boy piped in Thessaly," (or at any rate in the Balkans), but the sheep-boy piping was originally himself an illusion, invented by some *blasé* courtier in a palace of the Ptolemies. When there are too many illusions in the world something violent happens. "A Last Judgment is necessary," so "English Blake" says, "because fools flourish." Perhaps after any Last Judgment the world seems less pleasant than was hoped. The end of a tragedy is not "O Jerusalem, that bringest good tidings, lift up thy voice," but Edgar's lifeless solemnity, "The weight of this sad time we must obey."

But Mr. Montague's book is not a piece of pessimism, as this and the title might suggest. It is wise and hopeful, and it grows, as it goes on, "to something like prophetic strain." Nothing could be better than the chapter "Any Cure?" with the rousing sentence: "Our best friends for a long time to come will . . . find a part of their satisfaction in being nobodies." That, as Sancho Panza says, "is as good as bread."

The book is written in that most apt, happy, witty style which all readers of the *Manchester Guardian* know. It is one of the very best of the books which have been written about the war.

[source: *Manchester Guardian*, 16 February 1922, p.5]

Preface to the Eighth Edition
of *Gallipoli*

I wrote this book during the war, at the request of two of His Majesty's Ministers, in the hope that it might answer certain critics and perhaps change certain feelings then common in the United States of America.

I began to write the book only four months after the end of the adventure of the campaign, when the war had still two and a half years to run. The units and men who had taken part in the campaign were scattered all over three continents, in other campaigns; many of the documents which might have illustrated points in dispute were in Salonika, others were inaccessible, or unsorted (I saw one big store-room filled with bales of them); situation-maps, if any existed, were not to be had; the ground, which might have yielded many secrets, was in the hands of the enemy; the enemy story was not published.

These things made the obtaining of accurate knowledge of the events very difficult. The events of all wars are obscure; history is only roughly right at the best. The events of this last war will be more obscure than those of most, because of the power of silencing opinion and hiding facts possessed by those who waged it.

When I began to write this book, the war had imposed a military censorship upon all the countries engaged.

This censorship was submitted to by the public in every country, in the belief that it would be a sword in the hands of their skilful generals. No doubt in some cases it proved to be so; but far more frequently it served as a shield to hide the incompetence of generals, staffs, War Offices and the politicians who set them moving, or checked them (or set them moving and then checked them), as their ambitions or their cliques dictated. Early in 1916, this censorship was not, in this country, such a power as it afterwards came to be, but, as a matter of course, it barred out the two most important sources of possible information, the Admiralty and the War Office.

Besides this suppression of fact, the censorship suppressed comment, on the ground that criticism of certain measures or men "gave comfort to the enemy," even if the men and measures criticized were giving the utmost comfort to the enemy by their results. The campaign in Gallipoli was brilliant and bold in idea, and generous in intention. It was designed as a way out of the mud of Flanders, and as a help to Russia, who had saved us and France at the Masurian Lakes, and was now herself hard-pressed. It was opposed from its inception by many people with power, who believed that our share in the war should be fought on the Western Front. These many people with power were overruled in council, but never controlled outside it. They were against the campaign throughout; they were able to decry, thwart, starve and wreck it. The campaign was lost by their decrying, thwarting and starving the brilliant, bold and generous. These things were vital to the story of the campaign, yet the censorship forbade them to be printed: they would have given "comfort to the enemy." These were some of the drawbacks to writing history under a censorship.

Besides all these drawbacks there was another, that the book was needed in a hurry. It was necessary that our enemies and critics in Russia and America should be answered soon. Though their statements were clumsy and false, they were accepted, because they were the only statements offered. Great events have made that time most distant and dim, but it must be remembered that the sympathy of the United States was vital to the Allied Cause throughout the war. Generally speaking, the sympathy of the United States was with the Allied Cause throughout the war. But within the United States, at all times, there is what is called a "body of opinion" hostile to this country for religious, political, historical or pseudo-historical reasons. The members of this hatred are seldom American by birth, and perhaps never American by nature. They control newspapers, pulpits and other means of making public their prejudice, which they do from policy, sometimes in the name of religion, at all times. During the war events caused by the war gave them opportunities of making their prejudice not only popular but dangerous. This campaign of Gallipoli gave them one such opportunity. In the very days on which I began to write this book other opportunities occurred; nor had I written far beyond the Landings before another opportunity, perhaps more pleasing to them, came to make them rejoice.

Though in any time of calm the mind of America estimates this body of hatred truly, in a time of passion, when the mind is not calm, it may be misled by it. The time of passion was then with us, and the events of that time were giving to that body of hatred a power of damaging our cause not easily understood by statesmen three thousand miles away. To myself, who know America well (for an Englishman), it seemed a dangerous power, made the more dangerous from the want of contra-diction. The statements of our haters were made loudly, from the malice of their invention; no statement of our case was made in reply. When I began to write this book the thought of that organized hatred ever at work against us, and of that criticism, weighty in nothing save the hate behind it, was a prompting to be swift to answer.

But with all this prompting to be swift, it was not easy to decide what could be done. A history was plainly impossible: the information was not there; and even if it had been, the passions raised by the campaign were running too high, among those concerned, for calm statement. Plainly, something of the nature of a history was needed. And yet, how could I decide, on the spur of the moment, how much of a history would be possible, when I did not know what information could be had or would be permitted to be used?

After a day or two, I decided that I could write a rough short sketch, description, or summary, of the events, from personal knowledge, and from the books, newspaper articles and memoirs which had appeared since the Landings, and from the published despatches (these last exceedingly full, clear and vivid). At this point in my troubles I received a great encouragement. Through the kindness of some officials of the Foreign Office, and the helpful courtesy of Major (now Colonel) Daniel, and of Captain Atkinson and his assistants, I was given (beyond my hopes) access to some roughly sorted brigade and battalion diaries. These were, of course, nearly always least perfect for the weeks when the fighting was fiercest, but some (especially the Australian diaries) were full of most vivid, accurate and interesting descriptions of critical hours and days. Without such diaries the book would have been difficult to write; but having them, I felt that I could make a tale of the campaign which would perhaps be a help to those who failed, and give the lie to our enemies. I knew, as I wrote, that the book would be a sketch, faulty, full of little errors, from the difficulties in the obtaining of knowledge or criticism, but that the main lines of it would be true, as they are.

It has often happened, in the course of my life, that in moments of difficulty an unexpected help has come, exactly suited to that difficulty. This "charity of unseen guards" was helpful to me several times as I wrote this book, by bringing me in moments of difficulty face to face with men who, having been present at obscure points in the fighting, could tell me exactly what I wished to know.

The book was begun in April, finished in July, and published in September, 1916. I write this Preface exactly seven years after the book was brought to an end.

Since that time this campaign in Gallipoli has been fittingly and finely chronicled by Sir Ian Hamilton himself, by Mr. H.W. Nevinson, and (lately) by Mr. C.E.W. Bean. Future histories will probably be combinations and annotations of the works of these three writers, who write from a fulness of knowledge which I had not, and with a freedom from the censorship which checked myself. Those three histories are the standard works on the campaign.

It is to those three standards, not to this little sketch, that the reader must go for knowledge of the campaign.

I shall be very glad if my little imperfect sketch may serve as a primer, to induce men to read them.

As I have said, my book was written to answer certain critics. It answered them; but answering does not silence critics, it makes them change their ground and howl abuse. The kind of criticism to which my book replied was the common kind, of misunderstanding founded on antipathy. A narrow mind is a little cup easily filled with an antipathy. To such cups the antipathy is very dear, since it fills the mind. Men will give up house and home and go out and do absurd and heroic things for their antipathies. Hatred will drive wherever Love does not lead. Let men be careful, therefore, of those who stir up hatred. A wise man once said that "all nations pay sooner or later for the sins of their Press." The payment, unfortunately, is not made by the sinners, but by poor men out in the mud somewhere, far enough from the evening edition which chronicles the receipt.

But besides answering critics, I hoped "to change certain feelings then common in the United States of America." That hope, like all worthy hopes, had life in it, and, therefore, prospered. The nations of men exist by what is best in man, and are destroyed by what is devilish in him; everybody knows that, yet destruction continues, because little narrow minds, full of evil, in palace, pulpit, school, or newspaper, "fast for strife and debate, and to smite with the fist of wickedness" under some damnable pretext of false knowledge or falser faith or falsest history.

America is a great country, twenty years ahead of Europe in all mechanical contrivance, seven centuries behind her (luckily) in tradition and racial memory. During the next twenty years America will have her first great flowering time in all the arts; her marvellous energy will pass into beauty of every kind not yet attained by man. It should be the hope of every Englishman that that great country, so soon to be the greatest country in all that wisdom values, should think well of this country, whose tongue she speaks and whose sense of liberty she shares.

This seems to be a wandering from the dead in Gallipoli, in their graves among the tamarisks; but it is not so. Wherever they lie, they call, in their mute way, to all the world to think well of this country; for they were free men who gave their lives for an idea. They lie quiet, and are done with trouble. "It is very lonely there," a man writes to me; "hardly even a goatherd goes there." There are thirty-eight thousand of them: the manhood of a city. Eight years ago they were the pick of a race that cares for freedom, coming as the freight of fifty ships, to fight things stronger than themselves. As the ships moved out to take them to their graves, even in the months when victory was no longer thought of, those soldiers cheered.

They came from safety of their own free will
To lay their young men's beauty, strong men's powers,
Under the hard roots of the foreign flowers,
Having beheld the Narrows from the Hill.

JOHN MASEFIELD.

[source: *Gallipoli*, [new edition], London: William Heinemann, 1923]

Any Dead to Any Living

Boast not about our score.
Think this:– There was no need
For such a Sack of Youth
As burned our lives.
We, and the millions more,
Were Waste, from want of heed,
From world-wide hate of truth,
And souls in gyves.

Let the dead bury the dead.
Let the great graveyard be.
Life had not health to climb,
It loved no strength that saves.
Furbish our million graves
As records of a crime;
But give our brothers bread,
Unfetter heart and head,
Set prisoned angels free.

[source: *Any Dead to Any Living*, New Haven: The Yale Review, 1928]

Foreword to E.J Rule,
Jacka's Mob

During the war the English suddenly became aware of a new kind of man, unlike any usually seen here. These strangers were not Europeans; they were not Americans. They seemed to be of one race, for all of them had something the same bearing, and something the same look of humorous, swift decision. On the whole, they were taller, broader, better looking, and more graceful in their movements than other races. Yet, in spite of so much power and beauty, they were very friendly people, easy to get on with, most helpful, kindly, and hospitable. Though they were all in uniform, like the rest of Europe, they were remarkable, in that their uniform was based upon sense, not upon nonsense. Instead of an idiotic cap, that provided no shade to the eyes, nor screen for the back of the neck, that would not stay on in a wind, nor help to disguise the wearer from air observation, these men wore comfortable soft felt slouch hats, that protected in all weathers and at all times looked well. Instead of idiotic clothes designed for appearance on a parade ground, these men wore clothes in which they could do the hardest of hard work and then fight for their lives. Instead of bright buttons and badges, "without which," as a general once said to me, "no discipline could be maintained," these men carried in their equipment nothing that added to the worries of war. When people asked, who are those fellows, nobody, at first, knew.

The strangers became conspicuous in England after about a year of the war. They were preceded by the legend that they had been "difficult" in Egypt, and had had to be camped in the desert to keep them from throwing Cairo down the Nile. Then came stories of their extraordinary prowess in war. Not even the vigilance of all the censors could keep down the accounts of their glory in battle. For themselves, they were a very modest company, whom sometimes one could hear singing (to the tune of "The Church's One Foundation"):

> We are the Anzac Army,
> The A.N.Z.A.C.,
> We cannot shoot, we don't salute,
> What ——— good are we?
> And when we get to *Ber*-lin

The Kaiser he will say,
"Hoch, Hoch! Mein Gott, what a —— odd lot
To get six bob a day!"

Since that time, the Australian Army has become famous all over the world as the finest army engaged in the Great War. They did not always salute; they did not see the use of it: they did from time to time fling parts of Cairo down the Nile, and some of them kept the military police alert in most of the back areas. But in battle they were superb. When the Australians were put in, a desperate feat was expected and then done. Every great battle in the West was an honour the more upon their banners.

As it chanced, I was often in company with members of this army. It is a pleasure to me to write these lines as a preface to the story of some of their doings here set down by Mr. Rule. The admiration that one had for them becomes deeper and more full of gratitude as time goes on and the truth of the war becomes known. No such body of free men has given so heroically since our history began.

John Masefield
Boars Hill,
Oxford.

[source: E.J. Rule, *Jacka's Mob*, Sydney: Angus and Robertson, 1933, pp.[vii]-viii]

Red Cross

I remember a moonless night in a blasted town,
And the cellar-steps with their army-blanket-screen,
And the stretcher-bearers, groping and stumbling down
To the Red Cross struggle with Death in the ill-lit scene.

There, entering-in, I saw, at a table near,
A surgeon tense by a man who struggled for breath.
A shell, that shattered above us, rattled the gear,
The dying one looked at me, as if I were Death.

He died, and was borne away, and the surgeon wept;
An elderly man, well-used, as one would have thought
To western war and the revels that Death then kept:
Why weep for one when a million ranked as naught?

He said, 'We have buried heaps since the push began.
From now to the Peace we'll bury a thousand more.
It's silly to cry, but I could have saved that man
Had they only carried him in an hour before.'

[source: *The Queen's Book of the Red Cross*, London: Hodder and Stoughton, 1939, p.29]